LANGUAGE, MAN and SOCIETY
Foundations of the Behavioral Sciences

PRINCIPLES OF MORAL AND POLITICAL SCIENCE

by

ADAM FERGUSON

With a New Preface by

Lawrence Castiglione

VOL. II

AMS PRESS, INC.
NEW YORK
1973

LANGUAGE, MAN and SOCIETY
Foundations of the Behavioral Sciences

This reprint series makes available some of the most important works upon which the modern behavioral sciences were founded. Each book has been chosen for its relevance to the general theme of communication and, more specifically, to the various relationships between language, the individual, and society. The areas of discipline covered include psychology, anthropology, sociology, linguistics, and communication disorders.

Each book in the series contains an introduction or preface written by an expert in the field, thus supplying the reader with the orientation needed to place the data in its historic context. It is our hope that the reprinting of these works, with their added critical apparatus, will encourage further research into the history of the behavioral sciences.

We would like to express our thanks to the members of our editorial advisory board for their valuable assistance in preparing this series.

R. W. Rieber
John Jay College, City University of New York
General Editor

PRINCIPLES

OF

MORAL

AND

POLITICAL SCIENCE;

BEING CHIEFLY A

RETROSPECT of LECTURES delivered in the College
of Edinburgh.

BY *ADAM FERGUSON, L.L.D & F.R.S.E.*
LATE PROFESSOR OF MORAL PHILOSOPHY.

IN TWO VOLUMES.

Huc enim pertinet, animal hoc providum, fagax, multiplex, acutum, memor, plenum rationis et confilii,
quem vocamus hominem, præclara quadam conditione generatum effe a
fummo Deo.   Cic. de Legg. Cap. VII.

VOL. II.

EDINBURGH:
PRINTED FOR A. STRAHAN AND T. CADELL, LONDON;
AND W. CREECH, EDINBURGH.

M DCC XCII.

Library of Congress Cataloging in Publication Data

Ferguson, Adam, 1723-1816.
    Principles of moral and political science.

    (Language, man, and society: foundations of the
behavioral science)
    Reprint of the 1792 ed. printed in Edinburgh for
A. Strahan, T. Cadell, and W. Creech.
    1. Ethics. 2. Political science. I. Title.
B1413.P74 1973   170   71-147970
ISBN 0-404-08222-X

Original pagination maintained

Original Trim size: 8 1/4 X 10 1/2
Trim size of AMS edition: 6 X 9
Text size reduced 10%

Reprinted from an original copy in the collections of
the University of Pennsylvania Library

Language, Man and Society. General Editor, R.W. Rieber,
John Jay College, New York, N.Y.

Copyright (c) 1973 by AMS Press, Inc.

International Standard Book Number
Complete Set: 0-404-08222-X
Volume Two: 0-404-08224-6

C O N T E N T S

OF THE

SECOND VOLUME.

PART II.

Of Moral Law, &c.

CHAP. I.

Of the Specific Good incident to Human Nature.

CHAP. II.

Of the Fundamental Law of Morality, its immediate Applications and Sanctions.

Sect·

C H A P. III.

Of Jurifprudence, or Compulfory Law.   Part I.

C H A P. IV.

Of Jurifprudence.   Part II.

Refpecting the Defences of Men.

CHAP.

CHAP. IV.

Of Moral Action and the Characteristics of a Virtuous and Happy Life.

CHAP. VI.

Of Politics.

ERRATA.——VOL. II.

Page 89. l. 12. *for* ftates *read* ftakes.
   Ibid. Note, *for* ferva *read* feria ; *for* defecerant
     r. defecerunt ; *for* contendant r. contendunt.
   92. l. 27. *for* fake *read* the fake.
   168. Note, *for* aftringimus *read* aftringimur.
   199. l. penult. *for* relation *read* relations.
   224. l. 24. *for* fentiment *read* fentiments.
   269. l. penult. *for* that *read* like that.
   294. l. 20. *for* their *read* there.
   301. l. antipenult. *for* effect *read* affect.

Page 319. Note, at bottom, *dele* Rex vixit male.
   364. l. 15. *for* principle *read* principal.
   387. l. 12. *for* will *read* well.
   414. l. 6. *for* I *read* It.
   442. l. 26. *dele* being.
   448. l. 21. *dele* 2d, Or.
   468. l. 10. *dele* not. *for* as to *read* not to.
   469. l. 15. *dele* is.
   493. l. 12. *for* ties *read* duties.
   509. l. 25. *for* man *read* human.

PRINCIPLES

OF

MORAL AND POLITICAL SCIENCE.

PART II.

Of Moral Law, or the Diſtinction of Good and Evil, and its Syſtematic Applications.

CHAP. I.

OF THE SPECIFIC GOOD INCIDENT TO HUMAN NATURE.

SECTION I.

Introduction.

THE diſtinction of phyſical and moral ſcience has been ſtated in the former part of this work; the one being occupied in ſolving queſtions of theory or fact, the other in ſolving queſtions of right: But, notwithſtanding the propoſed method required that queſtions of fact, or mere explanation, ſhould be conſidered a-

A part

part from queftions of eftimation and choice; yet the good of which man is fufceptible, and the evil to which he is expofed, having frequently occurred, as facts of the greateft importance relating to him ; and the advancement of moral fcience itfelf having made a confiderable article in the hiftory of his purfuits and attainments; it was impoffible not to touch upon thefe fubjects, in laying the foundation of this more particular difcuffion, in which we are now to proceed.

Having, however, in the former part, chiefly attended to the facts conftituent of man's actual ftate, and ferving to form his capacity and give intimation of his future profpects; we are now, in the continuation of our method, come to a point at which the diftinction of good and evil, and its applications, are the direct and immediate objects of our inquiry. But as in the paft, where the ftatement of fact was the principal object, we could not always with-hold fome view to its confequence; fo now, although our principal object is to purfue the inference to be drawn from facts already ftated; yet, as we may, by referring to former obfervations, fometimes incur the charge of repetition; it is hoped that the favour, due to a fubject fo important, may plead in excufe of the neceffary references, even if they fhould be repeated.

Science, in every application of the term, implies the knowledge of fome one or more general principles with their applications. whether in directing the will, or in explaining appearances, and connecting together our conceptions of things.

The fpecific principle of moral fcience is fome general expreffion of what is good, and fit to determine the choice of moral agents in the detail of their conduct.

3

To

To inveftigate fuch a principle relating to man, it will be neceffary to recollect what is known of himfelf; and of the fituation in which he is placed. Our information is to be collected from his experience of what is agreeable or difagreeable to him, and the refult will amount to a choice of that, on which he is chiefly to rely for his happinefs, and to a caution againft that, of which he is chiefly to beware as leading to mifery.

Thefe firft and principal points of choice or rejection being fixed, the lines of moral wifdom and precept will flow from them in every direction, whether leading to the difcernment of perfonal qualities, the foundations of law, manners, or political eftablifhments.

The diftinction of good and evil originates in the capacity of enjoyment and fuffering. Infomuch that, without the intervention of mind, or fome feeling nature, all the varieties of matter and form befides, would be indifferent. Good may be defined, that which being enjoyed conftitutes happinefs; and evil, that which being incurred conftitutes mifery.

Philofophers of old employed themfelves chiefly in fearch of a fupreme good; and the term was familiar in the language of their times. We are told of two principal opinions which were entertained on this fubject. One, that pleafure, another, that virtue was the chief good. But as the patrons of the firft could not propofe to affert, that all pleafures were equal, no more could the other mean, that virtue was not a pleafure. They were agreed indeed in the general affertion, that what they termed virtue was the only fecure and true fource of enjoyment; but they defcrib-

ed.

ed their virtues differently. Though to both it was a ftate of tranquility and exemption from fear and forrow, this exemption was fuppofed by the one to be obtained by a feclufion from care, and by indifference to all the concerns of mankind, whether private or public. By the other, virtue was fuppofed to confift in the affectionate performance of every good office towards their fellow creatures, and in full refignation to providence for every thing independent of their own choice. Their different fchemes of divinity clearly pointed out their oppofite plans of morality alfo. Both admitted the exiftence of God. But to one the deity was a retired effence enjoying itfelf, and far removed from any work of creation or providence *.

The other confidered deity as the intelligent principle of exiftence and of order in the univerfe, from whom all intelligence proceeds, and to whom all intelligence will return; whofe power is the irrefiftible energy of goodnefs and wifdom, ever prefent and ever active; beftowing on man the faculty of intelligence, and the freedom of choice, that he may learn, in acting for the general good, to imitate the divine nature; and that, in refpect to events independent of his will, he may acquiefce in the determinations of providence. " How great is the privilege of man," fays Antoninus, " to have it in his power to do what God will approve, and " to receive with complacency whatever God fhall ordain."

In conformity with thefe principles, one fect recommended feclufion

---

* Omnis enim, per fe, divum natura, necefse 'ft
Immortali ævo fumma cum pace fruatur,
Semota ab noftris rebus, fejunctaque longe ;
Nam privata dolore omni, privata periclis,
Ipfa fuis pollens opibus, nihil indiga noftri,
Nec bene promeritis capitur nec tangitur ira.

clufion from all the cares of family or ftate. The other recommended an active part in all the concerns of our fellow-creatures, and the fteady exertion of a mind, benevolent, courageous, and temperate. Here the fects effentially differed, not in words, as is fometimes alledged, but in the views which they entertained of a plan for the conduct of human life and the choice of their actions. The Epicurean was a deferter from the caufe of his fellow-creatures, and might juftly be reckoned a traitor to the community of nature, of mankind, and even of his country, to which he owed his protection.

The Stoic enlifted himfelf, as a willing inftrument in the hand of God, for the good of his fellow-creatures. For himfelf, the cares and attentions which this object required, were his pleafures ; and the continued exertion of a beneficent affection, his welfare and his profperity.

It is by no means indifferent what opinions we fhall entertain on thefe fubjects. Good and evil are known or apprehended by us under a variety of denominations. And happinefs or mifery are fuppofed to be conftituted by the diftribution of thefe in our lot. If the things we term good be inconfiftent one with another, it is furely of confequence to the moft unthinking mind to afcertain where the preference is due; and, when this point is determined, to avoid the diftraction of a doubtful choice on any particular occafion. If, on the contrary, the objects ftated under the denomination of good, when well underftood, coincide in their effects, it is reafonable that we trace them to this point of coincidence, and reft the project of happinefs or fafety, not on any partial and exclufive felection ; but on the proper ufe and conduct of the whole.

The

The terms in common ufe under which we diftinguifh the fubjects of defire and averfion, are chiefly *Pleafure* and *Pain, Beauty* and *Deformity, Excellence* and *Defect, Virtue* and *Vice, Profperity* and *Adverfity* ; or, in a form more comprehenfive, and arifing from the diftribution of thefe, *Happinefs* and *Mifery.* Under one or other of thefe titles we fhall probably find every conftituent of good or of evil; and, in following the track of ordinary experience or reafon, arrive at a final decifion of what is beft for mankind, and eftablifh a principle of eftimation and choice, upon which to determine every queftion of right or propriety relating to the affairs of men.

SECTION

SECTION II.

Of Pleafure and Pain, or Things agreeable and difagreeable in general.

UNDER this title will occur to be mentioned pleafures and pains of mere fenfe, of affection and paffion, of active exertion and conduct.

Pleafure and pain, for the moft part, are co-relative terms: Where any circumftance is pleafant, the privation of it is painful; and, converfely, where any circumftance is painful, exemption from it is pleafant. Upon this account, when we have fpecified the one, it will not always be neceffary to mention the other.

In the actual arrangements of nature, throughout the animal kingdom, things falutary are pleafant, and things pernicious are painful. Pleafure is made an inducement to the performance of thofe functions, which are required to prefervation or well being; and pain is employed as a warning to avoid the occafions of deftruction or harm.

When

When a certain end is obtained in the ufe of a pleafure, it is obferved that the inducement to any farther exertion in that particular inftance is withdrawn; and attempts to prolong or continue the gratification, as they might be pernicious, fo they are attended not only with fatiety, but even with difguft and pain.

As in this wife and beneficent inftitution of nature, to preferve her works, there are pleafures attending all the ordinary and falutary functions of animal life, there are pains, alfo, which attend whatever is pernicious to the animal frame; and the final caufe or purpofe is evidently the fame in both; that is, by inviting to what is falutary, by deterring from what is pernicious, to excite the languid animal to what is ufeful; and to roufe the fuffering animal to fuch efforts as may be effectual to remove the occafion of harm; and, in either way, to confult his fafety.

For this purpofe, although the occafions of pain, like the occafions of pleafure, may be temporary, yet, as it is neceffary that the pain fhould continue until the caufe of harm be removed, or even that the pain fhould increafe while the caufe of harm is increafing, or the danger to animal life is augmented; there appears to be a fufficient reafon why fufferings, incident to the animal frame, fhould in many inftances be of longer duration, and greater intenfity, than the correfponding enjoyments or pleafures which are deftined to recommend the ordinary functions of life.

It appears, therefore, with refpect to animals in general, that the purpofe of nature in the diftribution of fenfation, is to provide for the fafety of the individual, and the fucceffion of the fpecies, at the fame time that an eftablifhment is made for enjoy-

3

ment

ment, fo far as is confiftent with thefe ends. In this diftribution, there is a prefent reftraint from what would be painful in
the future ; and a prefent direction to what may contribute to
future enjoyment, as well as fafety : And there is a fufficient
reward for the performance of functions which enter into the
courfe of a regular and well ordered life. The individual, in
general, is kindly amufed and gratified in the act of preferving
himfelf and continuing his fpecies, and the gratification or amufement, in the cafe of moft animals, is fitted to occupy a confiderable part in the duration of life.

Man is fufceptible of animal pleafure and pain, in a manner
which argues the purpofe of nature refpecting him, to be nearly
the fame as with refpect to other beings endowed with life. He
alfo is deftined to do what is neceffary for his prefervation : but
the mere gratifications of appetite which ferve to obtain this purpofe, are not fitted to occupy an equal portion of his time; and
more is left, in his cafe, to the operation of principles in which
he ftands diftinguifhed from other parts of the animal kingdom.
When his prefervation is fecured, the life he preferves ftill requires to be otherwife occupied. Like the other animals, he enjoys his food, the fupply of his wants, and the gratification of
various appetites. But no one ever thought of prolonging the
gratifications of hunger, for inftance, fo as to pafs a life of enjoyment at table, as fome animals appear to do in the ufe of food,
at their ftall or their pafture.

If man were not too proud for fuch a choice, nature has
not qualified him to perfift in it. The pleafures of fenfe are
merely occafional and temporary. They are, in their nature
alfo, mixed and alloyed with pain. Animals are to be deterred

Vol. II.   B   from

from what is hurtful, as well as allured to what is falutary; and man himfelf, with all his knowledge of the end in view, muft be prompted, in the detail of his actions, by the admonitions of pain as well as pleafure.

The feeling, which prepares the animal fenfe to be gratified in the fupply of a want, is more or lefs a feeling of pain; and enjoyment is a mere relief from this feeling. Attempts to prolong the gratification beyond its natural period, bring a new fpecies of pain, in the effect of fatiety. Still more, excefs of any kind is productive of fuffering and harm: So that this fource of enjoyment is ever impure, either in refpect to the pain that precedes it, or in refpect to the difguft and harm that may follow from the unguarded purfuit of enjoyment.

Whilft men, therefore, may admire the order of nature in this particular, and comply with it as an article of good fenfe and propriety, few, who are engaged in the fpecific purfuits of human life, look upon the pleafures of mere fenfe as matters of principal regard. Moft men become comparatively indifferent to their perfonal accommodations, in proportion as they are engaged in bufinefs, either private or public; or in the view of objects that ftrongly affect them, in behalf of their own honour and intereft, or in the caufe of their family, their friend, or their country.

To the other animals, as well as to man, mere exercife is grateful; and the efforts they are led to make for the prefervation of life are, on this account, in part, conftituent of their ordinary pleafures. The ends, to which their active purfuits are directed, are fubjects of hope; and give joy in the profpect, as well as in the attainment or ufe. And, although the correfponding apprehenfions,

3

henfions of ills to be feared, may anticipate the fufferings of for- PART II.
row, yet the fyftem of animal life, in general, is fo arranged, CHAP. I.
that, in the exertions required to felf-prefervation, the pleafur- SECT. II.
able prevail over the painful ; and the general afpect of living nature is expreffive of alacrity and joy.

The powers of reflection in the mind of man, that enable him
to anticipate the future, as well as to recal the paft, qualify him
to enjoy, or expofe him to fuffer, from this quarter, in a much
higher degree than any of the other animals. Hence arife the variety of his paffions, hope and fear, joy and grief. The foundation of hope is the expectation of fome good that is future, and
therefore probably in fome degree an occafion of fear alfo. Grief
has reference to fome evil endured ; fear, to an evil apprehended.
Either is a painful ftate of the mind, in actual diftrefs, or in anxiety and folicitude, difqualified for any prefent enjoyment beyond
what mere hope can fupply : But, with refpect to the objects,
whether of hope or of fear, the moft agreeable ftate of the mind
is alacrity in the reafonable exertions they fuggeft, and in the ufe
of means to obtain or avoid them, which providence has put in
our power.

Security is, of all circumftances, the moft conducive to pleafure. Hence the value which *poffeffion* acquires in paffing into
property, that is, in being fecured: and the moft agreeable
ftate of the mind, in this refpect, is the confcioufnefs of a bleffing
of which neither chance nor caprice can deprive us. A bleffing
which confifts alone in the chearful performance of what we are
entrufted to do, and in contentment with the fcene of action in
which we are placed.

B 2   Man,

Man has much of his employment, as well as the gratifications of fenfe furnifhed to him by the concerns of of his animal life. In thefe confift that complicated object which he terms his intereft; and from thence arife many of the occafions on which he is employed for himfelf, for his country, and his friend.

The materials, which he ftrives to amafs for his own ufe, ferve him alfo as the means of beneficence to his fellow creatures. In his intelligent or diftinctive character, his occupations multiply and vary indefinitely; and the mere fupplies of animal life are to him of lefs confequence, than the exertions of mind in which they engage him. In thefe his ingenuity and his affections are agreeably engaged in forming his defigns, in recollecting his experience of the paft, in conducting the prefent, and in preparing for the future.

It has been well obferved, that every exercife of the human faculties, into which malice or fear do not enter as motives, and every exercife which is not carried to fome pernicious extreme of fatigue, is in its own nature agreeable *.

" The neceffity of action," fays the Rambler, "is not only " demonftrable from the fabric of the body, but evident from " obfervation of the univerfal practice of mankind †, who, for " the prefervation of health," (he fhould have faid for pleafure,) " in thofe whofe rank and wealth exempts them from the necef- " fity of lucrative labour, have invented fports and diverfions, " though not of equal ufe to the world with manual trades, yet
of

* V. Theorie des Sentimens Agreeable.
† See Rambler No. 36.

" of equal fatigue to thofe who practife them ; and differing on-
" ly from the drudgery of the hufbandman or manufacturer,
" as they are acts of choice, and therefore performed without the
" painful fenfe of compulfion. The huntfman rifes early, pur-
" fues his game through all the dangers and obftructions of the
" chace, fwims rivers, and fcales precipices, till he returns home
" no lefs harraffed than the foldier, and has perhaps incurred
" fometimes as great hazard of wounds or death ; yet he has no
" motive to incite his ardour ; he is neither fubject to the com-
" mands of a general, nor dreads any penalties for neglect and
" difobedience ; he has neither profit nor honour to expect from
" his perils and his conquefts ; but toils without the hope of mu-
" ral or civic garlands, and muft content himfelf with the praife
" of his tenants or companions."

" But, fuch is the conftitution of man," continues the fame
author, " that labour may be ftiled its own reward ; nor will any
" external incitements be requifite, if it be confidered how much
" happinefs is gained, and how much mifery is efcaped by fre-
" quent and violent agitation of the body."

This author, in other parts of his work, or throughout the general ftrain of the whole, reprefents human life as a ftring of il-
lufions, a tranfition from hope to hope, never from enjoyment to
enjoyment : It is pleafant, therefore, to find him acknowledge a
fource of prefent enjoyment, even amidft drudgery, toil, and danger, fo frequently ftated by himfelf as conftituents of mifery :
It is pleafant to find him acknowledge, that, even labour is its
own reward ; and, in this ftep at leaft, lead the way to an opinion, that all the exercifes of a manly, and beneficent mind, though
a fpecies of labour, may alfo be their own reward, and not the
lefs

lefs a reward to him who labours in them, that he may be acting under the influence of an affection, alfo, in its own nature complacent and agreeable.

Even the vulgar are aware that to be happy, they muft be employed, or have fomething to do ; and it is obvious to the moft fuperficial obferver; that life is agreeable chiefly to thofe, who, being engaged in fome juft and honourable purfuit, in any laudable profeffion, public truft, or employment, do not embarrafs themfelves with any thing beyond the difcharge of their duty. In contraft with thefe, we may place the examples of others who are ever fo intent on the future as to neglect the prefent. Who fhrink from the duties of their ftation, under the notion of trouble, who decline any concern in the welfare of others, as an avocation from the care of their own. They would have fomething to do: But feem to think that their occupations fhould approach the neareft that is poffible to idlenefs. They fly from bufinefs ; for it feems to be a tafk. They do not confider how they may benefit others ; for, that were to neglect themfelves: but they fwim rivers and fcale precipices, becaufe they are at liberty to do fo, and becaufe they can afford the expence of horfes and dogs.

Living natures in general are diftinguifhed by the exertions they are qualified and difpofed to make. Man, as we obferved, ftands foremoft in this diftinction. His exiftence confifts in a feries of active exertions, and he enjoys the exercife of his faculties in the conduct of affairs, and in bufinefs, no lefs than in what he is pleafed to term amufement and paftime.

Benevolence is an active principle, and an agreeable ftate of the mind, rendering the prefence and welfare of other men an
occafion

occafion of pleafure, and fitting the individual to his relation in fraternity of natures like his own. The pleafures of fociety are the exercifes of a focial nature. They mix with the functions of animal life, and are, in reality, the principal caufe of many enjoyments which are fuppofed to refult from the gratifications of fenfe. The pleafures of the table, for inftance, are more thofe of fociety than of gratified appetite. Whence it is elfe that the meal, when taken alone is a mere fupply of neceffity ; but in company, and in the gaiety of fociable intercourfe, is of fo much confideration among the enjoyments of life ?

To be employed is agreeable ; but employments differ no lefs than fenfations. The employments of a mild and benevolent affection are placid and happy. Thofe of a rancorous and malicious temper are convulfive and wretched.

Many of the objects which we endeavour to obtain in human life, like the game that is purfued by the hunter, are chiefly to be valued for the chace they occafion. But it is not, therefore, indifferent on what object we beftow our labour. As things vifionary or impracticable lead to certain mortification and difappointment, fo things depending on chance, or the will of other men, if conceived to be neceffary, expofe to like difappointment ; or, under the apprehenfion of adverfe events, are the occafions of continual anxiety, dependence, and fear.

Things that are not of themfelves of any abfolute value, but exift merely in being compared with what is poffeffed by other men, as *dominion*, *precedence*, and *rank*, *renown*, and *celebrity* ; even *riches* and *fortune*, beyond what is neceffary to fubfiftence and well-being, engage us in purfuits that are not only precarious in the event, but in their nature fubjects of competition,

jealoufy

jealoufy, envy and malice. The operation of parties in thefe pur- fuits are mutual impediment and mutual offence; and the efforts of one to better himfelf is confidered as an act of hoftili- ty, or carries the afpect and the infection of malice to others.

Malice is known to be a ftate of extreme fuffering or pain ; it operates abroad in pernicious effects, and appears on the counte- nance in peculiar features of deformity and horror. It has per- haps no other fource in the human mind, than this unhappy choice of an object, in which the profperity and fuccefs of one is difappointment and detriment to another. Or if this unhappy choice be fufficient to account for malice, we are forbidden by reafon to look for any other caufe. It is a maxim in reafon, that no more caufes are to be affigned, than exift in nature, and are fufficient to account for the phenomena *.

We may therefore venture to affume, that malice is no where inftinctive, but muft have proceeded originally upon fome pre- conceived notion of competition, of harm to one from the wel- fare of another, of provocation or fear; and is therefore, for the moft part, entertained in the form either of *Envy*, *Revenge*, or *Jealoufy*.

Thefe are the great fources of mifery to mankind. *Envy* is pain inflicted by another's good. *Revenge* is pain to be remov- ed or alleviated, only by another's fuffering. And *Jealoufy* is pain fuffered under the apprehenfion of what another may do or may have done: All of them fufceptible of unequal degrees ; but in the flighteft degree unhappy, and in the higheft degree conftitu-

2

ent

---

* Vide Newtoni Principia, lib. 3. ab initio.

ent of extreme virulence and of anguiſh, to which the preſence and welfare of a fellow creature alone, may give occaſion ; and, from which a being, who is doomed to ſociety, has no means of eſcape, but by removing the evil of his own diſpoſition.

Beſides the propenſity of man to join the herd of his ſpecies, a diſpoſition, which operates even with the malevolent, and is common to all the gregarious animals ; the candid have, in their minds, a principle of affection, and love ; a capacity of goodneſs by which they are diſpoſed or qualified, in different forms, to make a common cauſe with their fellow-creatures. The diſtreſs of another is to them an occaſion of commiſeration or pity ; his welfare an occaſion of complacency and joy. To the ſociable nature of man, the joint exertions or ſtruggles of numbers in the ſame cauſe together, bring into actual exertion, the higheſt powers of enjoyment as well as of action.

Commiſeration or pity, being a participation of diſtreſs, implies ſuffering, and yet is known to be agreeable ; inſomuch, that the humane do not wiſh to be relieved of their pain otherwiſe than by the relief they can give to thoſe they commiſerate or pity. They regret the ſuffering of others ; but enjoy their own ſympathetic emotions ; willingly ſhed the tears of compaſſion, and in this feel, with the poet, that,

The broadeſt mirth unfeeling folly wears,
Is not ſo ſweet as virtue's very tears.

Pity is prevented, in particular circumſtances, by the prevalence of other paſſions, whether *indignation, reſentment,* or *fear.* *Indignation* hardens the heart againſt thoſe who ſuffer for any

VOL. II.   C   flagrant

flagrant crime.; *refentment* againſt thoſe who have given provocation; and *fear*, though not a diſpoſition to act offenſively, yet
hardens the heart againſt the feelings of candour or pity, more
perhaps than any other paſſion: Hence, among the evils of cowardice we may juſtly reckon cruelty to the vanquiſhed, no leſs
than inability to contend with thoſe that reſiſt, or who alarm our
fears.

Commiſeration or pity, in the candid mind, is beſtowed indiſ-
criminately and univerſally on the innocent who ſuffers: But
benevolence, in its other forms, is particular in its choice, and
implies predilection for an object; whether the companion with
whom we are familiar, the friend we love, or the country to the
ſervice of which we are devoted.

An agreeable intercourſe may have place, even with perſons
unknown; or is eaſily formed, amidſt the firſt or moſt general appearances of intelligence and fairneſs of diſpoſition. The
manners of the candid, even among ſtrangers, conſtitute a mutual
exchange of good offices, and in human life are an ordinary and
continual ſource of agreeable ſentiments.

In friendſhip, benevolence is the engagement of choice, and
renders every intereſt mutual to the parties concerned. The affection in which it conſiſts, and the confidence it inſpires, conſtitute a principal ſource of ſecurity and pleaſure.

Over and above theſe operations of a benevolent affection, man
is qualified to entertain the ſame diſpoſition, in a form yet more
comprehenſive. The collective body of men in a country or nation is, to its own members, an object of the moſt ardent affection.
While

While the citizen reveres the institutions and the laws of his country, while he rejoices in its prosperity, and laments the calamity or
distress which befals it, he is often made to forget himself, and to
sacrifice his own interest or safety as an individual, to that of the
community in which he is included. Interest is frequently supposed
to be the ruling passion of mankind; yet this sacrifice of interest
and of life, to the objects of public affection, is frequently made;
and, under national establishments that are happily constituted,
is not above the reach of ordinary men.

The general tendency of benevolence, like that of the animal
propensities, is to preserve the human race, and to render man
useful to his fellow creatures; but, while the selfish principles o-
perate to the preservation of the whole, by preserving or consulting the safety of individuals apart, benevolence forms a general
band of connection, and is at once a common source of enjoyment
and pleasure to many. It renders the participation of other men,
in the favours of providence, an occasion of satisfaction and joy.
While it seems to render the humane a servant to the distressed;
the affectionate devoted to the interest of his friend and his country; it renders this service, and this devotion also, a principal source
of enjoyment to himself: differing from the gratifications to which
any mere animal propensity is competent, in being exempt from
satiety, and in being fitted, by occupying indefinite portions of
time, to fill up the duration of human life, and to become not only
the spring of particular and occasional action, but the source and
constituent of felicity to those who act. So much that, in the
course of a sociable and beneficent life, and in the offices of private
friendship, or of public station, a person may occupy with satisfaction every moment that can be spared from the necessities of
his own condition.

C 2

But,

But, over and above the pleafurable or painful ftate of our feelings, which arife from the proper or improper difcharge of our
animal functions ; from the purpofe to which we employ our faculties, and the manner in which we are affected towards
our fellow-creatures ; thefe very circumftances become, by
reflection, the fource of additional enjoyment or fuffering. Confcioufnefs of propriety, in the conduct of our natural propenfities;
attainments of knowledge, or intellectual ability; integrity, candour, and good-will to our fellow-creatures, are fources of the
pureft fatisfaction and pleafure. The confcioufnefs of brutality,
folly, cowardice, malice, or guilt, on the contrary, is conftituent
of extreme fuffering, in the feelings of fhame, and remorfe.

It is fupremely agreeable to perceive, in the works of nature,
the marks or expreffions of wifdom and goodnefs, on which we
may rely for the happy difpofal of all things : And we may conclude, from the whole of thefe particulars, that the preferable
pleafures of human life confift in fobriety, benignity of temper,
or good will to mankind, and beneficent actions, with a perfect
confidence in the wifdom and goodnefs of Providence.

The contemplation of beauty and excellence, in whatever fubject, is matter of delight, and forms an agreeable ftate of the mind.
The obtrufion of uglinefs or defect is of a contrary nature : And
thefe are fources of enjoyment and fuffering peculiar to man. He
alone, among the living natures known to us, appears fenfible to
the diftinctions of beauty and deformity, of excellence or defect ;
and he alone, for ought we know, apprehends any gradation of
worth in the fcale of being. He alone applies the canons of excellence and defect, of merit and demerit, to himfelf, and to his
fellow-creatures ; finding a moft agreeable ftate of his mind in
the

the confcioufnefs of integrity and juftice, or the moft painful and diftreffing reflections in the confcioufnefs of wickednefs, debafement, and folly. Complacency and peace of confcience are expreffions of the one; fhame, remorfe, and defpair, are expreffions of the other.

The fool may enjoy his folly, and the madman may enjoy his frenzy; but no one will congratulate the perfons who are fo affected with pleafure. The enjoyments of human nature require the warrants of reafon and truth; and no perfon, in his fenfes, can be reconciled to a ftate, in which he knows his own character to be marked with deformity, meannefs, or vice, nor think that he can be truly happy, in the abfence of every good quality which can be required to adorn or perfect his nature.

The foundations of a pleafure, fo effential to happinefs, merit a feparate confideration in the following fections.

SECTION

S E C T I O N   III.

Of Beauty and Deformity, Excellence and Defect.

IN the rational nature of man, there are principles which do not terminate merely in fensibility to pleasure and pain, or in mere active exertions; but confift in a kind of cenforial infpection, over the general tenor of enjoyments and actions; ferving to diftinguifh, among pleafures, the elegant and beautiful from the inelegant and deformed ; and, among fpecimens of exiftence, the perfect or excellent, from the defective or imperfect. Such is the difcriminating power of intelligence, by which the qualities of things are eftimated; by which unequal meafures of worth are conceived, and the gradations of excellence affigned in the fcale of being.

In the exercife of thefe reflex and cenforial powers, there is great enjoyment and fuffering, according as the objects of them are happily or miferably diftributed to ourfelves or others. *Difguft*, *indignation*, *remorfe*, and *fhame*, are among the pains of
1   which

which they render us fufceptible; *delight, efteem, approbation,*
confidence, love, and *peace of mind* and *of confcience,* are among their
gratifications, or happy effects.

In the difcernment of external objects, there arifes a fentiment,
which may be expreffed in terms of praife or blame, of eftimation or contempt; and which frequently conftitutes, or fenfibly
modifies, the general affection of the mind, in refpect to the diftinction of good and evil; for, as good is pleafant, fo, alfo in
many inftances, is it eftimable: As evil is painful, fo alfo is it,
in many inftances, vile and contemptible.

Of thefe fentiments, the fpecific occafions or objects are termed
beauty and deformity, excellence and defect.

To perceive beauty or excellence, is to admire or efteem: And,
leaft thefe expreffions, which are applicable to fubjects of the
higheft nature, fhould appear too ftrong, when applied to matters
of inferior confideration, in which fome degree of beauty neverthelefs may be admitted; let it be remembered, that it is the fpecies of fentiment, not any meafure of the emotion, or degree of
merit in its object, which we are now about to confider.

Admiration and efteem, like benevolence and love, are agreeable fentiments; fo much, that, to admire or efteem and to be
pleafed with an object, are expreffions often mutually fubftituted one for the other.

We are pleafed with beauty and excellence; we are difpleafed
with deformity and defect: But all that pleafes is not beautiful
or excellent; nor all that difpleafes, deformed or defective. We
know

know not, however, frequently, how otherwife to exprefs the
pleafure we take in any fubject, than by pronouncing it excellent
or beautiful ; nor how to exprefs the difpleafure we feel, otherwife
than by pronouncing the caufe of it, ugly or defective. The
wonderful organ of human language does not always ferve the
purpofe of difcrimination, even where it is of the moft real importance to ftate the fubjects of confideration apart.

We may, neverthelefs, endeavour, in this place, to confider
beauty and excellence, as diftinguifhable from other caufes of
pleafure, by the fpecific accompanyment of efteem or preference,
to which, even if no one fhould admire, we conceive the object
entitled ; and to confider deformity and defect as diftinguifhable
from other caufes of pain by a peculiar fentiment of difapprobation
or contempt; of which we conceive them to be proper objects,
even if the world fhould not perceive the defect or the deformity.

Thefe fpecific fentiments, differing either in refpect to the occafion on which they arife, or the degrees of intenfity with which
they are felt, have, in every language, a variety of appellations or
names. In our language, *approbation* and *difapprobation*, *efteem*
or *admiration*, oppofed to *indifference*, *difguft*, or *contempt*, make
a part of the terms by which we exprefs them.

The ingenious author of fome Effays on the Nature and Principles of Tafte, has obferved, that material fubjects give fenfation and perception of reality ; but no emotion or fentiment of
beauty or deformity, except fo far as they are affociated with fome
object of affection, whether character or difpofition of mind ;
chearfulnefs or melancholy, wifdom, goodnefs, or power.

2   If

* Mr Alifon.

If a fubject pleafe, in confequence of its being affociated with
fome object of efteem, the delight it affords is properly enough claffed with the fpecies of fentiment which we are now confider-ing; but if it be affociated only with utility, fafety, or joy, it may pleafe in confequence of this affociation : But the compound fo made up is not any more a fubject of admiration or efteem, than is the pleafurable circumftance by which it is recommend-ed.

Attempts have been made to refolve this principle of efteem or admiration into fome of the other principles or forms of proceed-ing, equally familiar in the operations of the human mind; and confequently, to account for the ufe of thefe terms, without the neceffity of fuppofing that there is in nature any diftinction of excellence, or in us any diftinctive faculty by which it is known. And it fhould follow, from any theory of this fort, that, in reality, we miftake for efteem fome other operation or affection of mind: but, in fuch fubftitutions of one fpecies of affection for another, it does not appear that any advantage is gained. We neither can refolve the fentiment of admiration or efteem into any thing better known than itfelf, nor the good qualities of mind, into any thing that, being more in our power, may fhew us a readier way to the improvement of our nature.

We fhall, therefore, be contented with giving to the fentiments which beauty or excellence occafions, fome one of their ordinary names of preference, whether delight, approbation, or efteem. The fubjects of beauty and excellence themfelves, in the mean

Vol. II.   D   time,

time, though thus agreeing in the clafs of fentiments to which they give occafion, feem to be disjoined in nature ; or by us, at leaft, to be conceived apart. Beauty is fometimes faid to cover defects ; and excellent qualities are faid to be concealed under apparent deformities. Beauty frequently ftrikes, from the firft and more obvious afpect of things ; excellence is to be collected by obfervation of their effential qualities. Every perfon, that enters a room, prefents at once the beauty of which he is poffeffed. His excellence, in the mean time, or effential good qualities, are to be known only upon farther acquaintance. Thefe epithets, however, in proportion as the fubjects of them come to be underftood, gradually approach in their applications, and feem at laft to unite in the fame thing. When apparent beauty is found to conceal defects, it ceafes to be admired, or even incurs contempt. When apparent deformities are found to conceal effential good qualities, we not only ceafe to contemn, but, from a principle of retributive juftice, are the more inclined in the fequel to admire that we at firft overlooked the value of our object, whether perfon or thing : So that the progrefs of intelligence in the difcernment of excellence and beauty feems to terminate in a point, which unites thefe epithets into one general ground of preference; and which, in that cafe, we fhall perhaps be more inclined to exprefs in the terms of perfection and excellence, than in that of elegance or beauty, which ftill carry a reference to firft and external appearances.

In the fyftem of nature, there is a beauty that belongs to the mechanical, to the vegetable, the animal, and intellectual kingdoms.

In the mechanical kingdom, the principal, if not the fole conftituent

ftituent of beauty, as the *Pere Buffier* has well obferved, *is order;* or, as the fame author farther explains this term, the *apt combination of parts, whether fimultaneous or fucceffive, for the attainment of a beneficent purpofe.*

Mere matter, though perceivable by fenfe, is in itfelf indifferent to any affection of the mind, except fo far as fome object of afection is affociated with it. With an apt combination of parts for a beneficent purpofe, are affociated the fupreme objects of admiration, love, and refpect; viz. *wifdom, goodnefs,* and *power.* The affociation is not cafual, or derived from mere analogy or likenefs, but from the effential and infeparable relation of caufe and effect.

The fyftem of nature is fublime in refpect to the might of its Author. It is beautiful, with refpect to the regular fitnefs of parts for the attainment of their ends, and in refpect to the beneficent purpofe which they are fitted to ferve. The latter circumftance, above all, is effential to their beauty.

The fruits of continual exertion, without the regularity that proceeds from a well-concerted defign, as in the meaninglefs activity of children and reftlefs animals, overturning and difplacing whatever comes in their way, produces diforder, confufion, and extreme deformity: The regular tradefman fhudders at their being admitted into his work-fhop.

A defign at the fame time may be perceptible; but, if directed by folly or malice, it is an object of difguft or of reprobation, not of admiration or efteem. The figures of birds, beafts, cones, or pyramids, cut out of an evergreen, in the antiquated garden, have

D 2

marks

marks of defign; but frivolous, and contemptible. The piece of ftatuary, of which we are told, in the bull of Phalaris, or in the Apiga or fpoufe of Nubis, may have been exquifite in the workman-fhip; but the defign was hideous or cruel: And, as the mere indication of mind is ambiguous, the indication of perfidy and malice is horrid; beneficence alone, directed by wifdom, is fupremely beautiful.

In the material fyftem of nature, the beneficent purpofe of its Author is manifeft in the accommodations provided for beings diftinguifhed by their organization, or beings endowed with life. Thefe, in our terreftrial world, are plants, animals, and men. The elements are difpofed to promote the vegetation of plants; and thefe to furnifh their fubfiftence and place of abode to animals; and the whole to furnifh the materials of fupply, and the fubjects of thought and contemplation to the living and intelligent nature of man.

In the living kingdom of animals, the fame beneficent purpofe, while it extends to the general fyftem, partly terminates alfo in the animal himfelf. He is made that he may be gratified, as well as that he may gratify others; and both are effential to the excellence and beauty of his frame: For this his organization is admired, and the profperous ftate of that organization is fo much valued, under the denomination of health.

With refpect to man, alfo, the beneficent purpofe of nature, fo far as we are yet qualified to difcern it, terminates in himfelf; not in the individual confidered apart, but in the fubferviency of many to the common caufe of the whole. The individual is made that he may be gratified; but his chief gratification is made

to

to confift in beneficence, or a participation in the welfare of mankind. He is an active power in nature, which cannot fufpend
its exertions, without incurring a ftate of wearinefs, fuffering,
and difguft. He is a beneficent power in nature, to whom benevolence is pleafure, malevolence is pain ; and who cannot willingly forfake the paths of beneficence, without incurring the
chaftifement of remorfe. His beauty and excellence is a participation, however faintly obtained, of that wifdom and goodnefs
which conftitute the fplendor and majefty of the works of God.

To perceive beauty, in any material fubject, is to perceive in-
dications of wifdom and goodnefs; and, if we are afked, why
wifdom and goodnefs fhould be admired ? we may anfwer, For
a reafon like to that for which pleafure is coveted; becaufe in itfelf defireable and good. While other things are defired or efteemed on account of the pleafure they give, or the excellence they
conftitute, pleafure and excellence are themfelves defired or e-
fteemed, on their own account.

In the fcale of natures fufceptible of excellence or perfection
intelligence is fupreme, and wifdom and goodnefs are the fupreme perfections of intelligent being. Their prefence, when
fuggefted by the order of nature, awakening the fentiments of admiration, are termed beautiful ; but, in the mind itfelf to which
they belong, are more properly termed its excellence, perfection,
or merit. Folly and malice, on the other hand, may, in a figurative ftile, be termed the deformities of mind ; but are more
properly referred to the predicaments of defect, guilt, and demerit.

From the whole, there is reafon to believe, that beauty when
real

real may be refolved into excellence and, that deformity may be refolved into defect; the one an effential diftinction of good, and the other of evil: That both, or either, can have exiftence in mind alone; fo that, in this queftion, man is doubly interefted: He is concerned in the exiftence of excellence or beauty, as prefenting him with an agreeable object of contemplation and love; but more efpecially as conftituting an admirable ftate or condition of nature, attainable by himfelf.

In the human figure, there is one beauty of form in the ftructure of its organs, or in the found ftate or configuration of the whole perfon, indicating exquifite defign, wifdom, and goodnefs, of the Maker.

There is another beauty, confifting in the afpect and expreffion of the mind, that occupies and actuates this created frame, indicating good fenfe, equanimity, and benevolence of temper.

In both, it is the beauty of mind that ftrikes through the form of a work, or the afpect of a perfon: The wifdom and goodnefs of the Creator, in the one; or the good meaning and temper of his creature, in the other.

Where one of thefe beauties exifts, in any degree, the other may be fenfibly wanting. Thus, we are familiar with inftances, in which perfonal defects are compenfated with a favourable expreffion and benevolence of afpect; or inftances in which natural advantages are deformed by an afpect of vanity, malice, or folly.

The antient artifts, in the features of Medufa, though a Fury,

2   feigned

feigned to themfelves the moft perfect form ; or fuppofed her countenance to be caft in the moft exquifite mold of natural beauty ; but of an afpect, derived from the temper within, fo terrific and hideous, as to appal the moft daring, and even to turn thofe on whom fhe looked into ftone.

Mind, we have reafon to believe, predominates in nature ; fo that, in a comparative furvey of all that exifts, whatever is not mind would be as nothing.

It is *heat*, we are told, that gives fpring and agitation to the mechanical world. Remove this ingredient, and all matter would freeze into one folid mafs, and become the formlefs repofitory of inertia, darknefs, and death.

In the fame manner, and with ftill greater confidence, may we not fay, it is mind that ftrikes out from the forms of body, in the lovely afpects of excellence and beauty ? And it is the diverfity of operating minds, in fuch forms of matter, that gives the diftinction of beauty and deformity to fubjects otherwife, in their own nature, indifferent.

What were millions, and myriads of millions, of corpufcular particles affembled in the body of the fun, without the benignant power that renders him the fource of heat and of light to furrounding worlds ? What were thefe worlds without the beneficent impulfe that gives them motion, and retains them in their orbits, at a proper diftance from the fource of light and of heat ? And what could avail their motions, without this combination of elements on their globes, that fit them for the refidence of living natures ?

The

The same thing, multiplied through innumerable systems, owes its magnificence to the greatness of might and of thought, that acts in the formation and conduct of such boundless scenes of existence.

The distinction of excellence and defect, so obvious to man in the contemplation of his own nature, and so easily transferred by association to any of his works or external circumstances, is the radical principle of elevation or progression in the human mind, to which there is ever presented, as an object of desire, something higher and better than is possessed at present. This principle, in all its forms, proceeds upon some pre-conceived notion of absolute or comparative excellence, in respect to which the mind is never disposed to acquiesce in its present attainment. Birth, fortune, power, and other constituents of rank, are the circumstances in which the vulgar of every condition strive to excel one another. The dwelling, the furniture, the equipage, and the table of the rich, flatter his vanity more than his sense of pleasure; and stir the emulation more than the appetite of those who admire his condition.

Whoever would govern mankind, if he can command their conception of what is excellent, or lead them to associate honour with the task he would have them to perform, will find no farther difficulty, in procuring from them every sacrifice of pleasure, interest, or safety. This, as we have formerly observed, is the honest man's integrity, and the gentleman's honour, which neither will forego to preserve his fortune or his life. It is the soldier's glory, which renders danger and hardship agreeable; it is the martyr's crown, which renders extreme suffering, and the prospect of death, an occasion of triumph and joy.

On

On a fubject of fo great importance, and of fuch powerful effects in human life, it behoves us to examine our opinions, and to be well founded in the conceptions, to which we thus furrender and deliver up all the other powers of our nature. If there be an excellence or beauty, fpecific to man, we may prefume that, in the contemplation and poffeffion of it, his fupreme good, the moft agreeable ftate of his nature, and the happieft courfe of his life is likely to confift.

PART II.
CHAP. I.
SECT. III.

SECTION

S E C T   IV.

Of Virtue and Vice.

WHen, in the manner of laſt ſection, we have reſolved the excellence and beauty of this created frame into the wiſdom and
goodneſs of God ; and return from this contemplation of nature
to conſider, what is the ſpecific excellence of man ; we muſt recognize in him at once a conſtitution or form received from his
Maker, and together with the gifts of intelligence and free will,
a perſonage and character to be aſcribed to himſelf. In reſpect
to either, he is diſtinguiſhed in nothing ſo much as in this power
and diſpoſition to perceive, with delight, an intelligent and beneficent Author in the ſyſtem of things around him. Were he
thus to judge of any human production, his perception of
beauty in the work would argue ſome participation in the genius
of its Author.   May we not therefore, conceive, that his admiration of what appears in the univerſe of God, implies ſome qualification to participate in the godlike principles of beneficence and
wiſdom.   In this ſyſtem, of which he is a part, the meaſures of
providence are taken, and the deſign is carried into execution ;
he too is deſtined to act : But when we conſider the magnitude of

I   this

this fyftem, and in how many ways, of which he cannot trace
any tendency to the purpofe of univerfal good, he himfelf may be
affected, his concurrence in the defign is likely to be merely paffive, or
fo far only as to make him bear with complacency what the general
order requires, rather than to call upon him for any active exertion directed to a purpofe fo far extended beyond his comprehenfion.

Even when we confider the world of men and animals, how
far extended beyond the reach of any active interpofition of the
individual for its general good, we muft fuppofe that the character of goodnefs, applicable to man, in refpect to this object alfo,
confifts in pious refignation to the will of God; or, at moft in
perfect good will to mankind, in every inftance in which the active power of an individual can apply. Fortunately for him,
when he acts in particular inftances, for his friend, his neighbour,
his country, or for any of the human race, there occurs, an occafion to practife and to promote that mutual affection, fidelity, juftice, and humanity, which in fact are a common blefling
to mankind; infomuch, that for him to adopt and to commu-
nicate the effect of thefe characters, is to act for the good of
his fellow-creatures; and, fo far he becomes an able and a will-
ingn iftrument in the hand of God for the beneficent ends of his
providence.

The merit of this character, however, is more a fubject of confcioufnefs, or intuitive judgement, than of difcuffion or reafoning; and
they who are, in common life, moft decided in their choice of good
actions, proceed upon the ground of their affections and fentiments, more than upon any information derived by inveftigation
or refearch. In attempts at fcience, however, we muft defcend
to particulars, and endeavour to collect, by induction from the

E 2   phenomena

phenomena of that nature we are confidering, what may be its deftination, and what the ftandard by which its worth is to be eftimated.

Among fubjects organized, we have already obferved that man is diftinguifhed as living and active; among the living and active, he is diftinguifhed as intelligent; or endowed with powers of difcernment, apprifed of the diftinction of good and evil, and invefted with freedom of choice. Among the gregarious animals, he is diftinguifhed as affociating and political, and confcious of his ftation as a member in the community of his fellow creatures. The order of nature itfelf is in a certain degree manifeft to him; he is fitted to hold communication with its Author, to apprehend his will, and to become a willing inftrument in promoting the ends of his government.

In ftriving to conceive the deftination of fuch a being, we may with great confidence reject the idea of its being limited to the prefervation of mere animal life, or even, as Epicurus affumed, to the poffeffion of mere pleafing thoughts or fenfations of any fort. There is an active character to be fuftained, and a part to be filled up; firft, in the community of men, who are partners in the joint caufe of humanity and juftice. There is a world of ftill and living nature, in the midft of which this active being muft acquit himfelf, with fenfibility in refpect to fome, and with circumfpection and care refpecting the whole. There is a commanding order of things, to which he muft accommodate himfelf, which he is required to ftudy, and concerned to know; and to which, even where it exceeds his comprehenfion, he muft with fubmiffion furrender his will.

To fill up fuch a part are required *fkill*, *difcernment*, or knowledge, *fit difpofition*, *application*, and *force*: Hence the four- cardinal

dinal virtues, celebrated in the fchools of philofophy, *Wifdom*, *Juftice*, *Temperance*, and *Fortitude*.

Wifdom is the virtue of intelligence, or a juft difcernment of the confiderations on which we are to rely for happinefs, and the undifturbed poffeffion of the faculties which are given for the government of life. Man, in his character of intelligent being, is active in a form, and to an extent, greatly fuperior to any of the other animals. Every quality of his nature is an energy, not a quiefcent mode of exiftence ; and, whatever be the limits within which he is deftined to exert his faculties, within the fame limits, and in the fame form of active exertion, are to be found his excellencies and defects, his enjoyments and fufferings.

The lot of man is not, like that of the other animals, at once completely furnifhed by nature ; he is invefted with powers, and left to employ them for his own advantage, or that of his fellow-creatures. He merits the praife of wifdom, or he incurs the imputation of folly, according to the ufe which he makes of his intelligent faculties ; and in this, perhaps, gives the firft and moft ftriking fpecimen of the excellence or defect, of which he is fufceptible. His powers of conception, when well employed, lay the foundations of wifdom ; when mifapplied or neglected, lay the foundations of folly ; and fo far prefent him to his fellow-creatures, as an object either of efteem and refpect, or of contempt and derifion.

With the exception of a few determinate inftincts, fuch as direct him on particular occafions to the means of felf prefervation, or fuch as connect the individual with his kind, man, we have obferved, is left to follow the dictates of his own obfervation, difcernment and experience.

experience. In nonage or infancy, indeed, he is committed to the difcretion of his parent; but, in the more advanced periods of life, he is committed to his own. His inftinds and appetites are feldom to him, as they are to the other animals, determinate guides in the application of means to the attainment of his end, or feldom fecure him in the proper choice and meafure of his gratifications. When urged by hunger, though in the midft of plenty, if the fruit or fpecies of food prefented to him be new or untried, he muft proceed with caution in the ufe of it, and examine well, before he ventures to tafte; much more before he ventures to feed on viands unknown, though of the faireft appearance.

Although his gratifications, like thofe of the other animals, when the purpofe of nature is ferved, frequently determine or pall on the fenfe; and fatiety, even in his cafe, might be fuffici-ent to guard him againft excefs; yet he is, by an error of his imagination, frequently led to exceed even thefe limits, and to feek for pleafure, where it is not any longer to be found, in the objed of a fatiated appetite. In him, therefore, the defects of inftind muft be fupplied by refledion; and, he is to be taught, by experience and obfervation alone, to diftinguifh the real fources of perma-nent happinefs.

As to man, therefore, the errors of his own imagination, as well as the defects of his inftind, are occafions of evil, they are to be fup-plied or correded by the proper ufe of his intelligent powers. And it may be afked, Are we to confider the intelligence of man as a mere fub-ftitute for the corredtnefs of choice to which the other animals are formed by nature, and to eftimate its value, by its apparent deftination to do for him what inftind, and the want of imagination, have done for the brutes? This were to fuppofe him deftined to attain,

tain, by a tedious and uncertain procefs, that of which other animals are at once poffeffed by the fuggeftion of a fpecific propenfity The bee, without any other direction than this, conftructs his cell upon a model which the moft perfect fcience of mechanifm cannot improve ; and poffeffes that fkill, from the firft, which in the human fpecies, many ages and fucceffive trials are required to obtain.

Animals, in general, whatever be their diftination, are enabled to fulfil it at once. They acquiefce in their ftate, or enjoy its advantages, without any fenfe of its wants or defects. Man, at his outfet, being worfe provided than any other animal, is accordingly not difpofed to acquiefce in his primary ftate. The wants or defects of his firft condition feem, in the exercife of his faculties, to prefs him with all the force of neceffity ; but, after his firft wants or defects are fupplied, fancy fucceeds to neceffity ; and, whatever fupply he may have gained, or accommodation provided for himfelf, he is ftill urged with a defire of fomewhat beyond the prefent attainment, and is as little difpofed to acquiefce in the higheft, as in the loweft ftate of his animal accommodation. The fpur of impatience to better himfelf, which, in his rudeft condition appears neceffary to his prefervation, continued on to his ftate of higheft attainment, feems to form in him a principle of progreffion, of indefinite or endlefs extent. He is made intelligent, not merely that he may be able to procure a fupply to his animal wants, but his animal wants appear to be multiplied, and his fancy rendered infatiable, that he may find an early fcope for the exercife of his intellectual powers, and, by the indefinite purfuit of their ends, make that progrefs in knowledge, which conftitutes fo effential a part in the excellence or perfection, of which his mind is fufceptible.

We

We may thus collect the fpecific excellence of any nature, from its capacity, and from the direction of its progrefs ; and that of man, in particular, from his capacity of receiving information, of improving in difcernment and penetration, and from the progrefs he is qualified to make in thefe particulars. In him, the mere continuance of life is a courfe of obfervation, and repeated occafion, on which to exercife thofe faculties of the mind, which improve in being employed.

Man becomes powerful in the fyftem of nature, in proportion as he becomes knowing or wife : And the fpecies, in this particular, feems well apprifed of the ftandard by which to afcertain its own merits or defects. Signal ability and underftanding are admired, comparative incapacity, and dulnefs are defpifed. And there is, therefore, in refpect to him no difficulty in collecting the grounds of efteem or contempt, whether we confider *a priori* what is fuited to his deftination, or attend to the reception which his qualities meet with in the eftimation of his kind.

Philofophers have thought, that every fubject of commendation, to which human nature is competent ; every virtue and every conftituent of happinefs, might be comprifed under the title of *wifdom*, or the excellence of intelligent being ; that, on the contrary every fubject of difpraife or contempt, every vice and every character of mifery, might be comprifed under the title of *folly* : But, it is not neceffary, nor perhaps even expedient, thus to force the attributes of human nature, under fingle appellations, however comprehenfive or general. Although it is both wife and profitable to love our fellow creatures, we can no more become affectionate to our friend, in the mere fearch of wifdom, than we can in fearch of our intereft. Our conftitution

3　　　　　　　　　　　　　　　muft

muſt have the ingredient of benevolence, in order that a mind well informed may improve upon this principle of nature, and learn to direct it aright.

" There are good qualities," ſays the Duke de la Rochefou- cault, " which degenerate into faults when they are natural, and " others which are never perfect when they are acquired. It is " neceſſary, for inſtance, that we ſhould become by reflection " ſparing of our money and of our confidence ; on the contrary, " we ſhould by nature be furniſhed with benevolence and va- " lour." The underſtanding at the outſet has its perfection to acquire ; the heart is good by the inſpiration of nature.

But, in whatever terms we propoſe to expreſs the ſtandard of eſtimation relative to man whether *wiſdom*, *virtue*, or *goodneſs of heart*, there are various conditions required to the perform- ance of his part, and which muſt occur in every ſtatement of qualities, that conſtitute the ſpecific excellence or perfection of his nature. He is formed for ſociety, and is excellent in the de- gree in which he poſſeſſes the qualifications of an aſſociate and a friend. He is excellent, in the degree in which he loves his fel- low creatures ; he is defective, in the degree in which he hates them, or is indifferent to their welfare. Benevolence, therefore, is a principal excellence of human nature ; and malice an article of extreme vileneſs or defect. Theſe are the great ſources of merit and demerit ; of juſtice and beneficence, on the one hand ; of wrong, iniquity, and cruelty, on the other ; a diſtinction, to the reality of which mankind in all ages have borne the ſtrongeſt teſtimony : To which, on the one hand, they have paid the higheſt tribute of eſteem and of love ; and, on which, on the other, they have pour- ed forth the higheſt meaſures of contempt and deteſtation.

With refpect to *Temperance*, it is a beautiful part, we may again obferve, in the œconomy of animal life, that things pernicious are painful, and things falutary are pleafant; that even things faluta-ry and pleafant, in the proper ufe of them become painful, in the abufe, or when carried to excefs. Under this conftitution of na-ture, the mere animals are fafely directed through life; but man's animal frame is either originally lefs perfect in this refpect, or is difturbed by the operations of a fancy, which lead him to look for enjoyments beyond the foundations which nature has laid.

By nature, the gratifications of appetite are occafional, and do not occupy any improper portion of time; but the voluptuary conceives them as a fource of continued enjoyment: And fenfua-lity is a diftemper of the imagination, not a diforder in the bal-lance which nature has eftablifhed between the animal and the rational part of man's conftitution. The voluptuary does not en-joy more than the abftemious; but he employs more of his time in vain attempts to reftore a fatiated appetite, and to render that continual, which nature has ordained to be occafional and tem-porary.

As great inequalities of character and eftimation refult from the different degrees in which men avoid the habits of debauchery on the one hand, or gain the habits of a juft application to the better purfuits of a rational nature, on the other; there is, in this particular, much room for wifdom, and much danger from folly. In this, as in many other inftances, man is deftined by nature to govern himfelf, or to make the beft of materials which become pernicious, if he abufe or neglect them; and which, to fecure the proper ufe of them, require his utmoft attention and care.

This

This virtue, among the active qualifications of man, may be referred to the title of application; for the pursuit, which the temperate withholds from the mere objects of animal gratification may be applied to the better and more worthy objects of human life. Sensuality, indeed, for the most part, is selfish and more solicitous about the gratifications of appetite, than about the concerns of other men; and temperance being an exemption, at least from this principle of selfishness, lays open the mind of man to those incitements of benevolence and candour, from which the disinterested are prepared to act. Temperance, therefore, in this point of view also, may be reckoned among the primary excellencies of human nature; intemperance or sensuality may be reckoned among its most real defects.

With respect to *Fortitude*, the fourth in the enumeration of cardinal virtues, we may observe that, in every active nature, besides the disposition, the application, and the measure of skill, in respect to which such natures may be unequally estimated, there is a measure of force also required to support their active exertions, and a measure of weakness sufficient to frustrate the purpose of nature, or to betray the confidence that may be placed in the highest measures of skill and of good disposition.

Force of mind has a peculiar reference to the state of man, to the difficulties, hardships, and dangers, in the midst of which he is destined to act. In the support of what is honourable and just, he has sometimes occasion to suffer what is inconvenient or painful to his animal frame. In espousing the cause of the just, he may incur the animosity and opposition of the wicked.

In

In performing the offices of beneficence to others, he may encounter with hardſhip or danger to himſelf.

But this circumſtance, which ſeems to reſtrain or limit his activity, ſerves rather to whet his ſpirit, and increaſe his ardour in 'the performance of worthy actions. The difficulty he ſurmounts becomes an evidence of the diſpoſition which he approves, and actually endears the object for whoſe ſake he expoſes himſelf. Hence it is, that ingenuous minds are confirmed in the love of virtue, in proportion as it becomes a principle of elevation, of heroiſm, or magnanimity. Theſe, it is ſcarcely neceſſary to obſerve, are primary topics of praiſe, and principal excellencies of human nature, while puſilanimity and cowardice are amongſt the loweſt ſubjects of contempt.

From theſe particulars, then, we may collect that the excellence of a man includes the following particulars: *Wiſdom,* or ſkill to chuſe, and to accompliſh what he ought to attempt; a *benevolent affection,* which wiſdom is fitted to direct; an *application of mind,* which inferior conſiderations cannot divert from its purpoſe; and a *force,* which oppoſition, difficulty, or danger, cannot diſmay. And, as the excellent man is wiſe, beneficent, courageous, and temperate; the defective, on the contrary, is fooliſh, malicious, cowardly, and ſenſual. The wiſe chuſe, among their ends, what is beſt; among the means they employ, what is moſt effectual. The benevolent are committed to their beſt affections; the courageous are exempted from the ſuffering and the weakneſs of fear; the temperate reſerve their faculties, and their time, for the beſt and worthieſt occupations of their nature; and, if from this ſtatement of the excellence to which human nature is competent, we look back to what has been already obſerved on the ſubject of pleaſure

and

and pain, we fhall have reafon to conclude, that the Author of nature has not only made that moft agreeable which is moft fa- lutary ; but that more efpecially conftituent of happinefs, which, in the eftimate of human qualities, is alfo moft excellent, or moft highly efteemed.

To be confcious of excellence, from the very nature of appro- bation and efteem, is a ftate of enjoyment ; and, to be confcious of vilenefs or defect, a ftate of fuffering : Or, if thefe fentiments could be fuppreffed, ftill, the conftituents of man's fpecific excel- lence, *Wifdom, Juftice, Temperance,* and *Fortitude,* apart from any reflections they may bring, are in themfelves, either an exempti- on from pain, or an acceffion of pleafure. And providence feems to intend, that this diftinction, which is the fource of elevation, integrity, and goodnefs, in the mind of man, fhould be the guide, by which he is moft fecurely led to the higheft enjoyments, to which his nature is competent. The excellence and beauty he ad- mires may become an attribute of his own mind ; and, whether in reflection or action, conftitute the moft agreeable ftate of his nature.

If we thus figure to ourfelves an active intelligent being in the beft ftate of which he is fufceptible ; this, in refpect to him is to be virtuous. Or, if we fhould be difpofed to confider even the excellent mind, in refpect to its external relations and effects ra- ther than in refpect to its own conftitution, we may obferve, that the wife, the courageous, the temperate, and the benevolent, are of all others moft likely to ftand well-affected to their fellow crea- tures, to the univerfe, and to the Creator of the world ; that none are fo likely to recognize the providence and moral government of God, or to fettle religion itfelf on its beft foundations of inte- grity

PART II.
CHAP. I
SECT. IV.

grity and goodnefs. But before we proceed to ftate the conclufion of this argument, in any general expreffion of the fupreme good to which human nature is competent, it is proper to take into our account alfo, what may occur on the fubject of profperity, or of thofe external advantages in which the gifts of fortune confift.

SECTION

SECTION V.

Of Prosperity and Adversity, or the Gifts and Privations of Fortune.

To this title may be referred *health, strength, birth, riches,* and whatever else may be supposed to constitute the difference of situation or rank in society. The possession of them is coveted, and the privation is shunned, for reasons peculiar to each.

PART. II.
CHAP. I.
SECT. V.

Health is to the animal frame, what wisdom and goodness are to the intellectual nature of man, its sound and perfect state. *Strength* is also the measure of animal power, in surmounting difficulties, and performing the labours that require it. *Birth* constitutes rank, apart from any consideration of fortune or personal qualities. *Riches* consist in the store which is provided for the supply of animal wants, accommodation, or ornament.

The reasons for which these advantages are severally coveted are extremely obvious. Health is an exemption from the sufferings incident to disease; and it is a fitness of the living frame

for

for all its active exertions. It enhances the value of life, as implying all the principles of life in their state of greatest advantage. This blessing, however positive as it may appear to be,
is most sensibly felt in the privation of it. Ill health and disease greatly increase the difficulties which patience and fortitude
have to encounter, and tend to weaken or disqualify the mind
for the practice of these virtues.

Strength of body is in some measure an appurtenance of health.
It is unequal in the make of different persons; but is most entire
in any given constitution, in the most prosperous state of the animal functions. So far as the constituents of wealth are necessary
to the preservation of animal life, their value is evidently commensurate to that of life itself: But it is difficult to draw the line
of separation betwixt convenience and absolute necessity, or between articles of convenience and those of mere decorum and
fancy. There is a gratification proposed in the use of all or any
of them separately, which gives rise to a hasty presumption that
men are happy in proportion as they have accummulated the
means of such gratifications. The rich can purchase the services
of the poor, obtain their attendance and respect; and by these
circumstances seem to rank in a superior station. Birth is attended with similar advantages; and, although it may have originated
in the riches, as well as some heroic distinction of ancestors, at
some distant period, is neverthelefs by a wonderful caprice in the
imaginations of men, reckoned the more illustrious the farther
back that its source, or the original merit from which it is derived
is retired from the fight.

The possession or privation of these advantages depend upon
circumstances which mankind cannot command, nor even enu-

I   merate:

merate : They are therefore, independent of the human will. They form the occasions on which a person may adopt a proper or improper conduct ; and for this he is accountable, although he is no ways accountable for the event that may follow from his best endeavours. Happily for mankind, in this distribution of their trust, it is observed, even to a proverb, that they are happy or miserable, not in proportion to the measure in which they possess or are deprived of external advantages, but in proportion to the temper of their own minds, the conduct which they themselves have adopted, and the use which they make of the means with which they are furnished by providence.

To the person who abuses his *health*, it is no advantage ; because he has taken occasion from it to give scope to his folly or his vice. And if it has encouraged or supported him in the practice of either, although to another it might be the occasion of good, to him it is at least the occasion of evil. To preserve, under the disadvantage of ill health, equanimity and a temper undisturbed ; to submit with chearfulness to the restraints which disease may impose, serves to disarm this enemy, or render his presence an occasion of good to the person who can thus acquit himself properly.

The effects of disease in different persons are no doubt unequal ; and in some instances, whether owing to comparative weakness of mind, or intensity of suffering, it is no doubt sufficient to deprive animal life of its value : But this is rarely the lot or condition of man ; nor is it that, against which a person, who would avoid the evils of human life, is most concerned to be on his guard. " You " are afraid of sickness, poverty, and death," says Epictetus ; " but, " if you had been afraid of fear itself, you would have shewn " yourself better apprised of your real enemy." Disease of the

VOL. II. G mind

mind is more to be dreaded than that of the body: For one that is afflicted with a gangrene of the flesh, thousands incur the gangrene of envy and malice, or are bloated with vanity and folly.

Bodily *strength*, as well as health may be abused ; and, to those who consider it as an article of vanity, is for the most part an occasion of brutality and extreme folly. Joined to strength of mind, it may qualify the hero to act his part in the field, or in scenes of violence: But strength of mind without it can find many substitutes ; and the heroic part may be acted as well on the sick man's litter as on the warrior's horse.

Riches, it cannot be doubted, derive their value from the use to which they may be employed, in preserving, accommodating, or adorning the state of man, in profit to ourselves or beneficence to others.   With riches, as well as birth, there is an association of personal excellence, tending to constitute a superiority of estimation or rank ; and, with poverty, there is an association of comparative defect or meanness.   The first accordingly is from a desire of preferment ardently coveted ; the other, under a notion of degradation, is carefully shunned.

Among rude nations, although property be acknowledged and unequally distributed, its principal use being to secure the necessaries of life, and this use being obtained, without being rich, it is difficult to perceive in what consists the advantage of wealth. " A Hottentot," says Sparman, "is rich, in proportion to the number " of his cattle: But the richest is cloathed, fed, and attended, no bet- " ter than the poor; more trinkets of brass, of shells, or beads; more fat " in dressing his victuals, or in anointing his body: The honour
" or

" or advantage of being able to maintain more fervants and cow-
" herds. And the divine pleafure of doing good to his fellow
" creatures, is that which conftitutes the diftinction of rank
" in this fimple race of men."

In the competitions of vanity, riches are more an object of oftentation than of enjoyment or ufe; but, in the breaft of the mifer,
they are affociated with fafety more than with either of the former
confiderations. Perfons of this defcription, we are told, even in
the midft of plenty, are haunted with the fear of want, whilft they
hoard up riches, they refrain from the ufe of them; and, inftead
of affecting the rank which their wealth might beftow, ftill cling
to their fuppofed pledge of fecurity, under the afpect of meannefs and
poverty. Enjoyment, however, is the charm with which riches
are fuppofed to attract the wifhes of ordinary men. It is the fpur,
under which mankind have ftriven to improve and to extend all
the arts which tend to the accumulation of wealth. It is that
which caufeth the poor to look up to the rich with fentiments of
admiration or envy, and caufeth the rich to look down on the poor
with contempt or pity.

But with refpect to *enjoyment*, there is good reafon to believe, that habit reconciles mankind, or renders them indifferent nearly alike to their refpective fortunes. It is not doubted,
that the meal of the peafant is equally relifhed with that of his
lord; that fleep on a ftraw matrafs is no lefs undifturbed than
on a bed of down, or under a canopy of ftate: Infomuch
that contentment, or the want of it, in different conditions
of life, are even to a proverb obferved to be equal. If the poor be
haunted with wifhes for fomewhat beyond his prefent condition,
fo alfo is the rich; and it is probable that the comforts of either

would

would be more felt in the privation than in the actual use. The ordinary course of life appears indifferent: They are pleased chiefly with accessions that seem to exceed, or displeased with privations that impair the advantages to which they are accustomed.

Occasional privations, at the same time, even of what are thought the essential comforts of life, are endured with alacrity and cheerfulness in the midst of any ardent pursuit, whether of business or sport. The soldier is chearful in the midst of hardship or toil, or in the face of danger, encountered in discharging the honourable duties of his station. The huntsman incurs almost equal danger with equal alacrity; and, whatever his hardships may be, has not any pretence for complaint, because they are voluntary. Compared to either, the ordinary life of a beggar, which is ever looked on with contempt or pity, is easy, affluent, and secure.

The enjoyments or sufferings, which we commonly ascribe to riches or poverty, are in reality, in a great measure, derived from the unequal degrees of consideration or esteem with which they are attended. The soldier and the gentleman hunter either gain, or do not lose in point of rank, by the hardships or privations of ease to which they submit. The one is actually raised in his own, and in the esteem of others, by the danger he braves. The other too is no way degraded, or rather maintains his station by his contempt of repose, and by his parade of horses and dogs, which makes a part of the distinction he enjoys among his neighbours.

Nothing is better established in reason, than that the value of external circumstances depends on the degree in which they are

2   felt.

felt. Profperity is of no value, to thofe who feel it not; or to whom it only minifters an occafion of peevifhnefs and dif- content. Adverfity is no evil to thofe, who fuffer nothing from it ; or who are contented and chearful, in the midft of fuppofed diftrefs. And, if there were no other reafon to deny the certain- ty of any effect from external circumftances, the unfettled opini- ons of men, refpecting the happinefs of different fituations, are fufficient to fhew that experience does not warrant our fuppofi- tion of happinefs or mifery, attached to any particular mea- fures of fortune. Some conceive happinefs to be the lot of thofe, who are placed in the higher ranks of life ; others believe it to be the portion of thofe who remain in the lower ranks ; and many believe, that both are miftaken,—that it belongs to the middle ftation, equally remote from the exceffes of luxury, or the preffure of want. In the mean time, wherever folly, malice, cowardice, and debauchery are found, there is fuffering and mi- fery to be found alfo. Thefe are not the neceffary appurtenances of any fituation, whether middling, high, or low ; nor is any fi- tuation fecurely exempt from them. The oppofite virtues of wif- dom, goodnefs, temperance, and fortitude, are equally a bleffing in every fituation, wherever they are found ; whether on the throne of Aurelius, in the fervitude of Epictetus, or any interme- diate ftation : And, as there is fcarcely a fituation to be found, in which the four and malignant do not complain; no more is there a fituation in which the good humoured and chearful are not content.

From thefe and other appearances, it fhould feem, that al- though providence has deftined human life to pafs away in the practice of arts ; in tranfactions and purfuits, which relate to the gifts of fortune, as to their immediate object ; that neverthelefs there is not any precife meafure of thefe gifts required, to enable the

the poffeffor to pafs his time agreeably. To be reafonably and properly occupied about them is enough : but this occupation may take place in any ftate of their diftribution ; and, although it feems to be the inftitution of nature, relating to mankind, that their active exertions fhould originate from the want of a fupply to their animal neceffities ; yet is it provided, alfo, that their felicity fhould be a quality of their own affections and actions, not of the fupply they have obtained ; that it fhould not depend on e-vents, or on circumftances in which the conditions of men are fo unequal, and fo little at their own command.

In confidering man's place and diftinction in the fyftem of nature, we have had occafion to obferve ; that, being difpofed to enjoy his own active exertions, and to improve by the exercife of his faculties, many apparent comparative defects of his animal frame, and the wants to which he is fubjected, have a fignal pro-priety in his lot. To him, difficulty, delay, and danger, are the occafions of ingenuity, perfeverance, and courage. He is mafter of his own actions ; but the circumftances, in which he is to act, are wifely withheld from his difpofal. For it being the nature of an active difpofition to prefs towards every advantage ; and to haften the removal of every obftruction, and of every inconveni-ence ; if this could be done by a wifh, there would not any long-er be an occafion for active exertions : And if, on the contrary, the laws of nature were infcrutable, and events no way affected by any means in the power of man to employ, there would be no-thing for him to ftudy and nothing to be done.

The fcene of nature, indeed, is in both thefe refpects well fuit-ed to man. The powers that operate connot be controuled by his will ; but the laws, according to which they proceed, may be known, and meafures taken to influence the refult of their opera-

3   tions,

tions. He is encouraged to ply his induſtry and his ſkill ; and his work is not accompliſhed in ſingle efforts. Upon a diſappointment, he muſt renew his endeavours ; and, even when moſt ſuccefsful, repeat or follow them up with ſomewhat farther in the line of his purſuits. The mixed ſcene of diſappointment and ſuccefs ever preſents him with a ſpur to his exertion, with admonitions to care, and incitements to induſtry, with encouragements to hope or apprehenſions of failure ; and, furniſhes him with occaſions, and with the materials of beneficence to others, as well as of profit to himſelf.

It is particularly happy, in reſpect to this inſtitution of his nature, that the conduct, tranſaction, and intercourſe, in which the materials of art engage mankind, are agreeable to their active diſpoſition, while the meaſure in which theſe materials accrue to any one, is in ſome meaſure indifferent. All the beſt or the worſt affections or paſſions of the human mind, are to be found indifferently wherever mankind are placed. As the active ſcenes of life may be ſupported by the healthful and vigorous, the virtues of equanimity, patience, and fortitude, may be practiſed by thoſe who labour under all the infirmities of diſeaſe or a ſickly conſtitution. As candour and humanity may be practiſed by the powerful, towards thoſe who depend on them ; ſo may the correſponding virtues of reſpect and good will be practiſed by the dependent towards their ſuperiors. Although the gifts of fortune are to thoſe who poſſeſs them materials of beneficence, yet they are not the ſole materials, nor is this uſe of them limited to any meaſure or degree of the poſſeſſion. The poor man who kindly ſhews the benighted traveller on his way, may have done an office of more real moment, than fortune may have given the rich occaſion to perform in any circumſtance of his life. The

greateſt

greateſt benefaᴄtors to mankind have been poor; and the greateſt benefits have been done by with-holding, not by laviſhing
the communications of wealth. Socrates and Epaminondas,
even in times when poverty was frequent, were diſtinguiſhed a-
mong their fellow citizens, by this diſadvantage: But the one, by
his ſuperior abilities, not only ſaved his country from a foreign
yoke, but raiſed it to a pitch of glory, which filled the mind of
its citizens with ſentiments of elevation and of honour. From
the other originate the purſuits of moral wiſdom, in which all
the nations who ſpoke the language of his country became ſo e-
minent; and to him, perhaps, we owe that we are now employed,
not in gratifying a mere curioſity, in matters over which we have
not any controul; but in ſtudying the powers of our own nature,
the province in which they ought to be exerted.

It was by with-holding, not by an eaſy payment of a trifling
tax, that Hampden laid the foundations of that political freedom which his country now enjoys: And we may conclude, from
the whole of theſe obſervations on the gifts of fortune, that they
are valuable only in the uſe which is made of them; and that
the proper uſe is equally valuable in whatever meaſure thoſe gifts
are beſtowed or with-held. Providence, in our apprehenſion has
indefinitely varied the ſituations of men: But to an obſerver,
who can penetrate through the firſt appearance of things, there is
a condition common to all mankind; that is, a fit ſcene in which
they are to aᴄt, and a felicity to be obtained by proper aᴄtion.

SECTION

S E C T VI.

Of Happiness and Misery,

IN the variety of denominations which we have been confidering, whether *pleasure*, *virtue*, or *prosperity*, the object of those who employ these terms, is to mark, in particular instances, the object of choice ; or, in the greatest possible measure of all these particulars united together, to express what they conceive to be happiness.

If we have understood the terms aright, and fairly estimated what is best, in the different denominations of good, and what is worst, or most to be dreaded, under the different denominations of evil, the conclusion of reason, as formed in the confideration of any article apart, will be the same throughout: That the preferable pleasure, as well as the highest merit, is found in the course of a virtuous life; and the pain most to be dreaded, or the specific defect or debafement of human nature, confifts in folly, malice, or cowardice. The gifts of fortune have their use in

PART. II.
CHAP. I.
SECT. VI.

being

being the means of life and the inftruments of virtue, or in furnifhing a fcene for the exercife of good fenfe and beneficence ; but
they are fo far from being an occafion of good to thofe who abufe
them, that this abufe contaminates every other fource of enjoyment, difappoints the mind of its better and higher qualifications,
impairs its faculties, and multiplies its fufferings and its defects.

The only queftion that remains therefore is, under what title
we are to felect this fupreme or principal good, which is the genuine ftandard of eftimation to mankind, whether under the title
of *pleafure*, the *proper ufes of fortune*, or *virtue*.

The general term, *Pleafure*, includes many particulars of unequal value, and in common language is employed frequently to
fignify fenfuality and diffipation, in contradiftinction to bufinefs
or any ferious application of the mind. It behoves us, therefore,
to fpecify our pleafure, before we refer to it as the object of choice.
And when we have done fo, the particular we have felected, not
pleafure at large, is the proper ftandard of eftimation.

Happinefs has its feat in the temper, or is an agreeable ftate of
the mind ; and cannot always be confidered as a proper ufe of external advantages ; for it does not always proceed to the production of any external effect. As virtue is the preferable pleafure, fo is it alfo the proper ufe of the fortune or fituation in which
we are placed. It is beft, then, that we fix our attention immediately on the real good qualities of our own nature, and the
virtuous life they fupport, as the conftituents of happinefs ; and
that we confider the debafements of folly, malice, cowardice,
intemperance, and a vicious life, as the conftituents of mifery.

3

Whether

Whether thefe be the fole conftituents of happinefs or mifery, we need not be anxious to enquire ; for the choice on every occafion will be the fame, whether we confider them as the fole or the principal fpecies of good and of evil.

It is of little moment to be told of a good, which we cannot command, or of an evil which we cannot avoid. Our object in every cafe, is to make fuch a choice of the things which are in our power, that is, of our own conduct and actions, as to do the beft which the cafe can admit for ourfelves or our fellow creatures.

Every circumftance, in the lot of man, evinces the cafe of a being deftined to bear an active part in the living fyftem, to which he belongs. His very fubfiftence requires fuch a part. To obtain it, he muft ftudy the laws of nature, invent and practife a variety of arts. He is born in the fociety of his parents ; and, for a confiderable period of his life, owes, not only his well-being, but his prefervation alfo, to their unwearied and anxious care. So foon as he is fit to act for himfelf, he is urged, by the moft ardent and irrefiftible paffions, to become the parent of a family in his turn ; a condition in which affections are experienced, more powerful than intereft or felf-prefervation. The company of his fellow creatures is ever required to his fatisfaction or paftime. He may be unfociable, but is not folitary ; even to behave ill, he muft be in fociety ; and if he do not act from benevolence, he will act from intereft to over-reach, or from ambition to command his fellow creatures, or from vanity to be admired, even by thofe whom he neither efteems nor loves. To fuch a being, it were vain to prefcribe retirement from the cares

of

of human life. If he is not engaged as a friend, he will be baited as an enemy; and, if his mind have not the confiderations of juftice, humanity, and public good, to occupy him, it will fink into a degree of brutality or languor, the reverfe of that tranquillity of mind, and of thofe agreeable thoughts, and emotions which Epicurus propofed to cultivate, in a ftate of feclufion from the concerns of fociety, whether private or public.

Nature has made the fubfiftence, the fafety, and accommodation, of human life to depend upon certain external circumftances and poffeffions, to which men, accordingly, with good reafon, direct their attention. They are the objects of art and induftry, and furnifh the occafion of invention, and other trials of genius to the mind of man, which is ever bufy, and which is at once gratified and improved, by its active exertions.

Many of its efforts are employed in guarding or in accumulating external poffeffions. The event, or the meafure of fuccefs, we have obferved, is precarious; and, on the whole, independent of this circumftance, mankind exhibit very unequal degrees of happinefs or mifery. They are happy in applying to their object with proper meafures of wifdom, diligence, benignity and fortitude. They are miferable in folly, flothfulnefs, malice, intemperance, or cowardice; but in the different meafures in which they attain to the gifts of fortune have equal opportunities for either. It is by the part which he acts, or has acted, that a perfon is happy or miferable, not by the event of his purfuit, or by the meafure of external advantage he has gained: for we muft forever repeat, that, under very great inequalities in refpect to thefe advantages, there are equal examples of enjoyment or of fuffering.

3   It

It is happy therefore to fullfil the deſtination of nature; to ply the induſtry, the invention, the ſtudy which ſhe has made neceſſary to our wellbeing; to embrace the objects of that ſocial affection with which ſhe has inſpired our minds; and to conſider, that as our ſtate of greateſt proſperity, in which we are moſt effectually employed with benignity towards our fellow creatures, and ſubmiſſion to the will of God, in whatever he has aſſigned for our lot.

The happy, under every event, whether of ſucceſs or diſappointment, proceed with alacrity in the diſcharge of ſuch offices, and in the purſuit of ſuch objects as the occaſion ſuggeſts. The miſerable, in proſperity, ſwell into inſolence; or, upon a reverſe of fortune, ſink into deſpair, and neglect the good which is in their power, becauſe there is another ſuppoſed good which they cannot command.

What is the leſſon of reaſon then to the poor man, who complains of his lot, or rather who enquires what, in the ſituation which providence has aſſigned to him, is required to be happy? He may be told, " Providence has given to you, and to all other " men, a ſet of wants; and it is the will of providence that you " proceed to ſupply them: Be diligent, induſtrious, and frugal: " Do whatever the preſent moment requires with benignity and " fortitude. Theſe are the conſtituents of happineſs, and not " leſs in your power than they are in the power of your richeſt " neighbour."

This temper of mind, however, under the ſhocks of adverſity to which men are ſubject in the ordinary puſuits of life, may be ſuppoſed to be of difficult attainment. It is, nevertheleſs, attained ed by numbers, who, in their ordinary condition, poſſeſs the gifts of fortune in lower meaſures, than that to which many who ſink under ſtrokes of adverſity are actually reduced. At any rate, the perſon who does not poſſeſs the virtues which conſtitute happineſs, muſt not complain of their inefficacy ; for they cannot be ſuppoſed to have effect, where they do not exiſt.

It may not perhaps be aſked, what will make the rich man happy ? for he is ſuppoſed to be ſufficiently happy in being rich. He muſt not be diſmiſſed, however, under this apprehenſion, untill his own ſenſe of the matter is taken. It is probable, that he will deny he is rich ; that he will be found to have wants no leſs numerous than thoſe of his poorer neighbour. Under this aſpect of his ſtate, the leſſon of wiſdom to him is preciſely the ſame as to the former. Be diligent, induſtrious, and frugal, reſpecting the management of your own affairs : be candid, ingenuous and humane in your tranſactions with others. Fear not that the event will be ſuch as to deprive you of theſe bleſſings: They are the greateſt of which human nature is ſuſceptible ; and providence has given a place for the enjoyment of them in the ſituation of the rich as well as in that of the poor.

If the rich man ſhould acknowledge that he has not any wants ; but in this very circumſtance ſhould find a ſource of diſtreſs, which is not uncommon in the caſe of thoſe who, as they are pleaſed to expreſs it, have nothing to do : the miſery of ſuch perſons, they may be told, is not an exceſs of riches, but a defect of underſtanding, and a corruption of heart. The firſt attempts to correct ſuch folly are made in recourſe to multiplied amuſements and paſtimes ; and we muſt, indeed, prefer any ſpecies of harmleſs diverſion to the devouring tooth of liſtleſs pride, peeviſhneſs, or melancholy. But it ſhould ſeem, that, to a perſon in this ſituation

ation, it might foon be made evident, that offices of benefit to mankind fhould be a more effectual amufement to himfelf, than any mere trifling paftime, which is not attended with any effect whatever beyond the amufement of the prefent hour.

If the fick man fhould complain of his lot, or defire to know by what means he may efcape from his fufferings, he may be told to get well as foon as he can; and if this fhould appear to be mockery; becaufe his grievance actually confifts in his not being able to get well; on this fuppofition, the beft thing he can do, is manfully to bear what cannot be helped. Fortitude may not eradicate pain; but is furely the beft and happieft expedient to which the fufferer can have recourfe in his ftate; and may, in fact, to the ftrenuous mind, conftitute a greater bleffing, than even that of being exempted from pain. In ftriving to find an expreffion or rule by which to diftinguifh the happy, we may venture to affume two general propofitions.

I. The firft is, That happinefs, whatever be its caufe, is itfelf an attribute of the mind.

II. The fecond is, That a perfon, when faid to be happy, can juftify this affertion only in proportion as his enjoyments are habitual, lafting, and conceived to be fecure.

The firft of thefe propofitions is too evident to need much illuftration; and it is only by a figure of fpeech, which in rhetoric is termed the abufe of words that we ever feem to exprefs a contrary opinion. Happinefs is peculiar to fentient beings; or is

proper

proper to mind, the great receptacle of enjoyment and suffering, as well as perfection and defect. When we say of an external situation, that it is a happy one, we mean to affirm only. that it is fit to produce happiness in the mind that enjoys it; and thus, by a well known figure, put the supposed cause for the effect.

But in what concerns the mind of man, external causes have not any necessary effect. The most fortunate circumstances which imagination can suggest do not produce any agreeable affection in the mind of the peevish or melancholy; and many circumstances of apparent distress do not fret or discompose the contented and chearful.

Reason, then, seems to require, that we correct this abuse of language; and reserve the appellation of happiness for mind, to which alone it is applicable, and in which it forms the distinction of goodness and worth.

In the mean time, it is not disputed, that external circumstances have their value, although they are not sufficient to secure the happiness of those who are placed in them. They include the ordinary means of subsistence and self-preservation, and have therefore a value commensurate to the value of life itself, which cannot be preserved without them. But this value, great as it may seem, is still undetermined, until the nature of that life which is preserved shall be specified. It may be happy, and it may be miserable; and, although nature has wisely given an instinctive desire to preserve it upon either supposition, and the object of instinct is life; yet the sole object of reason is happiness; and mere life, or the means that preserve it, apart from this object is of a value yet ambiguous or uncertain.

So

So far. there will not probably be any difference of opinion; but. if merely to live be no more than a capacity either of happiness or of mifery, we fhall be ready to enquire what are the additions which life may receive, that will render it happy on the one hand, or miferable on the other?

To this queftion, anfwers will be given as various as the conceptions or ruling paffions of men. It is a maxim, that *Taftes* are not to be contefted; and, on the fubject of happinefs, it is fcarcely permitted for one man to prefcribe for another. To the vulgar, happinefs appears to be the portion of the young, the gay, and the profperous. It fhrinks from the touch of the laborious, the fevere, and the thoughtful. It is the ftate of a moment. The fame perfon may be happy or unhappy, and pafs from one ftate to the other as quick as the fucceffions of thought. The boy feeks it at play, and the man of bufinefs in fome event, on which his hopes are fufpended.

To fuch minds the event, while in expectation, gives a profpect of happinefs; but, upon its arrival, generally difappoints the hopes which it gave: And they are the happieft amongft ordinary men, who do not dwell upon fuch difappointments, but at the clofe of any one purfuit, adopt fome new one with equal alacrity.

Is man, therefore, doomed to reft the happinefs of every prefent moment, on the profpect of fome future event, which upon trial is found to be illufive? This, in fact, is the cafe with many of thofe who have devoted themfelves to what they are pleafed to call the ferious concerns of human life, profit, preferments, or

VOL. II.   I   fame;

fame ; and yet there are perfons who have no fuch ferious objects
in view, who, without regard to the future, enjoy the exercifes
and occupations of the prefent hour.　Such are the huntfman in
his chace ; companions in their converfation or play : in all of
which the end or the ftake is a trifle. But exercifes of the mind
or the body are highly agreeable, and " labour itfelf," in the
words of the Rambler, " is its own reward."

To a mind confcious of this law of its nature, the object, it
may be thought, fhould be to exert itfelf properly upon all occafions ; to propofe reafonable ends, but never to fink under any
event, nor even to incur any grievous difappointment, fo long as
the mind finds occafion to employ itfelf properly.

The exercifes of good fenfe and of wifdom are, in their own
nature, agreeable. They proceed upon a juft difcernment of
objects, and do not give way to illufive hopes or unmanly fears.
As it is the excellence of a focial being to be the friend of thofe
with whom he affociates ; fo the love of mankind is to man, as
fuch, the principal fource of enjoyment alfo.

Courage and fortitude, being the excellencies of an active nature deftined to ply in the midft of difficulties, dangers, and
hardfhips, are, to the perfon who is endowed with them, not
lefs a fecurity for the poffeffion of all the faculties which nature
has furnifhed for fuch occafions, than an exemption from fear ;
and an alleviation of the fuffering which hardfhip or danger produces, in the timorous or defponding mind.

It may be thought, perhaps, that exemption from difficulty
or danger is preferable to refolution or force of mind ; and it

may

may be thought wifer to feek for places of fafety from which the
caufes of fear being removed, there is not any occafion to exercife the virtues of intrepidity or courage.

The wife, no doubt, will avoid unneceffary occafions of fuffering or of danger ; but thefe, notwithftanding, are, by the appointment of providence, fometimes a part of his lot : And if the
fearful could remove every real caufe of alarm from human life,
where is the place of fecurity in which the coward will not figure
to himfelf objects of fear and diftruft ? Where is the bed of rofes
on which the Sybarite will not find the doubled leaf ? Or where
are the circumftances of affluence and eafe to which the difcon-
tented and the peevifh may not impute the fufferings of his own
fretful temper ?

The virtuous are not deceived, when they avoid the excefs of
an animal gratification, or reject fenfuality as their guide to enjoyment. It is well known, that temperance is eligible, as the
proper œconomy even of animal pleafure ; and, the more that
fuch pleafure is valued, the more we fhould value thofe habits
of life, which preferve the animal organs in a proper ftate of enjoyment. But temperance is the œconomy of pleafure, ftill, in
a higher fenfe than this : It is the œconomy of the wife ; who,
knowing the higher purpofe of his nature, will not fubmit to beftow an improper part of his time or attention on objects of inferior confideration or value.

To the fecond propofition, then, we may fubjoin, as its application and its comment, That happinefs is conftituted in the
mind, by the continued habits of wifdom, benevolence, fortitude,
and temperance : And the reader may be addreffed, nearly in the

I 2   fame

fame terms which the emperor Antoninus addreffed to himfelf;
" If you difcharge your prefent duty with diligence, refolution,
" and benignity, without any bye views ; if you adhere to this,
" without any farther defires or averfions ; completely fatisfied
" in difcharging your prefent offices, according to nature, and
" in the heroic fincerity of all your profeffions, you will live hap-
" pily. Now, your doing this none can hinder."

This account of happinefs does not preclude any reafonable attention to the ordinary concerns of human life. Nay, requires fuch
attention, as part of the offices of a man, and in the performance
of which his happinefs confifts. It precludes only fo much dependance of mind on the events of fortune, as difable it for the
proper difcharge or continuance of its office, with refpect to thefe
or any other object of reafonable care.

It were unhappy to neglect any means that might tend to obtain the proper end you propofe : but it is more unhappy to
be fo affected with any event whether adverfe or profperous, as to
become unfit to continue or repeat the exertions of a diligent and
beneficent mind. Such exertions are the foundation on which you
are to reft for happinefs. Events you may endeavour to obtain
or provide ; but they may alfo happen contrary to your wifhes ;
and your happinefs cannot confift in events which you cannot
bring about, although it may, and actually does, confift in the
temper you command and the part you act, through all the variety
of events to which you are expofed.

On this fubject, *good fenfe* need not charge itfelf with the paradox, which, we are told, was mantained by oftentatious zealots,
whether of the Epicurean or the Stoic fchool, that all external

fituations

fituations are equal ; and, that the perfect man would be equally
happy in the bull of Phalaris, as on a bed of rofes.

Fortitude, of a very inferior meafure to this, is furely a valuable quality ; but, in whatever meafure or degree a wife man poffefs it, he will not, without neceffity, or fome adequate inducement, run himfelf into fufferings of any fort. Such pain or inconvenience, as he has actually incurred, he will be happy to endure, without repining at providence, or intermitting the exercife of his mind and his faculties. If he be in profperity, he will think the happy part committed to his choice is moderation, equanimity, and beneficence ; if, in adverfity, the fame virtues ftill remain to be exercifed in the manner which the occafion prefcribes.

SECTION

S E C T I O N   VII.

Of the actual Measures and Sources of Good and Evil in human Life.

THE value of virtue, as we have endeavoured to define it, will not be queſtioned : For who can doubt the value of a wiſdom, which cannot err ; of a temper, which is ever joyful and ſerene, in its exertions for the good of mankind ; of a temperance, which no allurement of falſe pleaſure can miſlead ; or, of a fortitude, which no difficulty or danger can embarraſs or appal ? This, we may be told, is firſt to imagine perfect happineſs, and then to give it the name of virtue ; whilſt the whole is ideal, and never realized in the caſe of any human creature.

Such, indeed, is the nature of abſtract ſcience, we ſyſtematize our own thoughts, leaving the application to be ſeparately made. On the ſubject of morals, more eſpecially, we propoſe to inquire, not what men actually are ; but what they ought to be, or what are the ideas, upon which they may, and ought to determine their choice in particular inſtances.   But, although this be a ſuf- ficient anſwer to the objection which is ſometimes made to moral
ſcience,

fcience, as a fcheme of vifionary and unattainable perfection. It may not be improper to confider what are termed virtues and vices in the minds of ordinary men ; with their various degrees and occafions, in order to fhew that there is not any intention to obtrude definitions and divifions for hiftorical facts; and even, that the impracticability of perfect virtue is no reafon why we fhould abate our endeavours to do well. *Perfection* is ever to be aimed at, even by thofe who incur *defects* ; and *defects* always to be fhunned, even by thofe who come the fartheft fhort of *perfection*. If the moralift is not to enjoin *perfection*, he muft do, what of all things is moft contrary to reafon, recommend *defects*. The conditions of men are extremely unequal ; yet, no one is fo high in the fcale of being, as that he may not move a ftep higher, and no one fo low, as that he may not get into the way of advancement. Although he may not attain to all the perfections of the wife as defcribed in any of the antient fects of philofophy ; yet he may not incur all the miftakes of the foolifh, and the fewer the better. Happinefs, it fhould feem from the obfervations of the laft and fome of the preceding fections, is a term of praife equivalent to merit, and confifting in the uniform tenor of a virtuous life : But, as *honefty confifts in meaning well* *, it fhould alfo feem that happinefs is within the competence of every human creature : Whence is it, then, in any inftance fo imperfectly obtained ? And whence is it, that fo many complain it is placed beyond their reach ? They furely do not confider it as an attribute of their own will and affections.

Men of fpeculation have rifked a conjecture, that all the difference of genius or character, which have appeared in the world

3

may

---

* *Laudandaque* velle fit fatis.

PART II.
CHAP. I.
SECT. VII.

may be traced to fome cafual fuggeftion of fentiment or thought; or to fome fpecific occafion, that ftirred the peculiar paffion, and roufed the original effort, which, continued into habit, gave the individual his bias to a diftinguifhing caft of genius or character through life †. But, without pretending, in this manner, to level the original diftinctions of nature we may venture to affume, that men are much affected by early impreffions; and continue to take much of their characters from the notions they entertain, and the habits of thinking they have acquired.

As we may know what a perfon thinks from his actions, fo we may guefs how a perfon will act. from our knowledge of his habitual ways of thinking, let it be conceived that to live virtuoufly is to be happy, that to have an evil or malicious thought is mifery; and let thefe ideas be ever prefent to the mind, as the idea of his treafure is ever prefent to the mifer, or the importance of his own perfon is ever prefent to the coxcomb; and the apprehenfion of a happinefs fo conftituted, will amount to a fteady principle of integrity and beneficence; as their refpective habits of thinking are, to the mifer, and the coxcomb, the effence of avarice, impertinence, and folly.

Self-conceit muft appear in oftentation, or in a continual obtrufion on the notice of other men. The admiration of birth and fortune, in one clafs of men, may betray itfelf in pride and contemptuoufnefs, in another clafs, may appear equally in envy and malice, or in fervility or meannefs. The temper alfo re-acts upon the judgement. The chearful are inclined to think of gay fubjects; the melancholy, to entertain gloomy apprehenfions of things; as

the

† Helvetius de L' Efprit.

the courageous are inclined to confide in their fellow creatures, and the cowardly are inclined to diftruft them.

We are difpofed towards the objects around us, either as the other animals are difpofed towards the objects of fenfe, by an original inftinct, or blind propenfity of nature, or by a relation, peculiar to intelligent being, that of the conception we have formed, or the habit of thinking we have acquired.

Such is the foil, in which the moralift is deftined to fow, to plant, and to make his trial of what can be reaped; without being difcouraged, becaufe the full bloom of terreftrial paradife is not every where, or perhaps not any where, to be feen on the earth; and the faireft fruits come, mixed with the noifome productions of the wildernefs.

Moral fcience operates for our good, only by mending our conceptions of things, and correcting or preventing the errors from which moral depravity or mifery proceeds. The very appellation of good, though no more than a name habitually beftowed upon its fubject, has great effect, on particular occafions, in warping the judgement, and in directing the choice. It was for this reafon, probably, that philofophers of old appeared fo anxious to fix the application of terms, as well as to ftore the mind, with juft conceptions. They propofed, that the firft principle of morality fhould eradicate every falfe apprehenfion on the fubject of good and evil; and fo become fufficient to give a juft direction to the will and affections, wherever they proceed on the pre-conceived notion of things.

Epictetus feems to reft the foundations of virtue and happinefs on the proper difcernment and choice of objects, which are in our own power, in contradiftinction to things which are not in our power. Among the things in our own power, he reckons " our opinions, our purfuits, our defires, and averfions ; and, in " a word, whatever are our own actions." Among the things not in our own power, he reckons " body, property, reputation, " command, and, in a word, whatever are not our own actions *." Attachment to the firft, and indifference to the fecond, are, according to him, the effence of wifdom and happinefs.

It is furely happy for any one to be confcious that the beft things are in his own power : But, in this, the vulgar are frequently deceived ; and recur to fortune, as more in their power, than the attainments of a happy mind. They feek for happinefs in external accommodations, rather than in any quality or condition of their own nature : and feem to think external circumftances more in their power, than their own actions ; or, what is worfe, think their own actions of value, only fo far as they affect their fortune.

To this ground of diftinction, which is laid by Epictetus, we may fubjoin another, relating to the fame fubjects ; but taken from a different confideration of them, that is, from the confideration of their value, whether real or fuppofed, which is in fome inftances *abfolute*, in other inftances merely *comparative*. Among things of abfolute value, are to be reckoned chiefly the habits of a *virtuous* life, *intelligence*, *benevolence*, *temperance*, and *fortitude* ; or, in fhort, the *good qualities* which form the beft condition of human nature ; and which they, who poffefs them, enjoy the more that others partake of the fame bleffings. Among advantages

tages

* Epiclet. Enchiridion, cap. I. Mrs. Carter's tranflation.

tages merely *comparative*, on the contrary, we may reckon *pre-*
cedence, and *fuperiority*, whether of *riches* or *power*; and, in a
word, all the circumftances, in refpect to which the *elevation* of
one is *depreffion* to another.

In a former fection, there was an attempt to account for the o-
rigin of malice, from an error or defect of underftanding, in admitting advantages or difadvantages which are merely *comparative,* as principal conftituents of happinefs or mifery. Under this
apprehenfion, although a perfon were by nature difpofed to benevolence, he is, by the interference of interefts, checked in the
effect of this difpofition. And, among parties fo ftated, the celebrity of one being obfcurity to another, or the precedence and preferment of one being degradation to the other, they are, in the
midft of fuch purfuits, naturally rivals and competitors, and
have more frequent occafions of hatred and diftruft than of confidence or good will *. " The king †," fays Baffompierre, "after
" he had given the command of his army in Italy to his brother,
" bethought him how much the glory to be won in that fervice
" would obfcure his own; and, fo powerful is jealoufy, even a-
" mong relations, that he took this fo ftrongly into his head, or
" rather into his heart, as to deprive him of reft." In this rage
for comparative advantages, the fuccefs of one is difappointment
to another; and the induftry of one to better himfelf a fcheme
of hoftility to thofe who muft fink under his elevation.

From this fource are derived, jealoufy, envy, and malice, thofe
K 2
waters

* See Sect. of the Origin of Evil.

† Lewis XIII. and XV.

waters of bitternefs, which flow fo plentifully in human life. The wretch, whofe principal aim is to furpafs other men, joins to fufpence, hinderance, difappointment, mortification, and all the the evils of a precarious fortune, the impoffibility of extricating himfelf, without a total reverfe of all his imaginations and thoughts. To become candid and humane, he muft change ob- jects of his hatred and diftruft into objects of good will and be- nevolence; and confider his fellow creatures in fociety, as the procurers of much convenience and benefit to himfelf, not merely as rivals and competitors, under whofe profperity or elevation of rank he is doomed to fink, or incur degradation.

Purify the mind of this taint, and moft of the evils in human fociety are done away. Defire would be placed chiefly on thofe things which are of abfolute value; which any one may poffefs in the higheft degree, without detriment to another; or rather, which, being in the poffeffion of one, prove an aid to others in the attain- ment of like bleffings.

The reputation of virtue, like celebrity in any other way, may engage men in competition and rivalfhip; but virtue itfelf is pro- moted by the prevalence of virtue in the world. The lamp of wifdom is lighted by communication with the wife; and bene- volence is infpired in the fociety of the benevolent. Fortitude and temperance gain ftrength by example. Whoever can reft upon thefe qualities of fupreme value, as the conftituents of hap- pinefs, finds no occafion on which to feel the unhappy paffions which terminate in malice. He is gratified in the welfare of other men; and wifhes for their elevation in goodnefs and virtue, as he wifhes for the rifing of the fun upon the world, as a common be- nefit to all who partake in his influence.

                                                        Antoninus

Antoninus was happy, not in wearing the purple, nor in pof-
fefling the throne of Cæfar; but in the attainments of a fteady
and beneficent mind. In thefe he was no man's rival, and was
ready to fhare every blefling, even with thofe who attempted
to fupplant him in the empire *.

We err, in deriving the corruptions, which are imputed to
great cities and courts, from the love of pleafure, and from the
profufion of wealth, with which the love of pleafure is gratified.
The mere voluptuary is innocent, compared to thofe who are
deeply infected with malice, envy, and pride ; a generation of
evils begot upon emulation, competition, or the apprehenfion
of comparative advantages, whether precedence, titles, or wealth.
Wherever the roots of fuch evil are planted, the concourfe
and affemblage of men, from which we fhould otherwife expect the practice and improvement of every focial difpofition,
but renders the growth of malevolence more copious and
rank. Competitors for the luftre of equipage and drefs, might
have flept in quiet, or enjoyed tranquillity, at their return from a
brilliant affembly, if the luftre of fome other perfon had not proved an eclipfe to theirs ; or, if his equipage and liveries had not
appeared to furpafs their own, and to carry away from them the
attention of the world.

We may therefore admit, that fuch errors of the imagination
are conftituent of moral weaknefs, and fcarcely feparable from actual depravity of the heart. If no external confequence fhould
follow, we may thank the adminiftration of regular goverment,
which

* See his Recommendations to the Senate in behalf of Caffius.

which checks the tendency of unhappy paffions ; and applaud the eftablifhed decency of manners, which require certain meafures or appearances of candour to be preferved, even between parties at variance with one another ; and which not only conceal the torment of unhappy paffions, but tend, in fome degree alfo, to conciliate good will, by infpiring forbearance, where the tendency of competition is to awaken jealoufy, or hatred, and give occafion to offenfive behaviour.

The great weight of corruption, proceeding from the jealoufy of competitors for riches, power, and court favour, without the counterpoife of external reftraints, from decency and good manners, funk the capital of the Roman empire, and the palace of Cæfar, into fcenes of the moft atrocious brutality, perfidy and cruelty : And, it muft be confeffed, that the confideration of fuch confequences would be fufficient to warn us againft like notions of good and evil: or, if men were to form their opinions, not on the evidence of fact, but on the grounds of expedience ; nothing can be more evident, than that a conception of happinefs, in things out of our own power, or in things of which others are in hafte to prevent our enjoyment, by ftepping before us, muft be attended with fruitlefs longings, heart burnings, jealoufy and malice. But, if fuch be the nature of good, relating to us, philofophers, it will be faid, may difpofe of names as they may think proper, and call any gift of fortune indifferent ;· but they themfelves will not be the lefs defirous to poffefs it. Nor can men be required to have any other conception of good and evil, than what the real afpect of things in nature ferves to fuggeft.

So much is admitted ; and the queftion relating to *what is good*,
whatever

whatever notion of things it be moſt expedient for us to entertain, muſt recur for ſolution to the tribunal of faᴄt and experience.

Let the faᴄt therefore decide! Are men happy or miſerable, in the preciſe degree of their good or ill fortune ; or of their precedence to others ? If ſo, fortune and precedence are the ſole good. But, if men are found equally happy, or equally miſerable, under great varieties of rank and fortune, it is evident that the meaſure of happineſs or miſery is not to be taken from thence ; and that a wiſe man will not adopt an opinion, nor countenance a form of expreſſion, at once inexpedient and contrary to faᴄt.

In fixing the notions of good, it is not wiſe to rely for happineſs, on things which are not in our own power ; on things which are not of any abſolute value ; but, which pleaſe only by compariſon with what other men poſſeſs, and which therefore engage us in a competition and ſtrife, adverſe to the beſt and happieſt qualities of our nature.

Neither is it wiſe to rely for happineſs on the mere poſſeſſion of things, which may be well or ill uſed, and which, in being abuſed, are no leſs the occaſion of miſery, than in being properly uſed they are the occaſion of happineſs.

As happineſs is a condition of the affeᴄtions and temper, mere external ſituation is not to be conſidered as any part of it, farther than the external circumſtance is able to produce that internal condition, or happy ſtate of the mind.

The Stoics, proceeding upon one or other of theſe maxims, limited the appellation of good to virtue, that of evil to vice alone.

3

Under

Under this limitation, their famous paradox, *that pain is no evil*, and the gifts *of fortune indifferent*, meant no more, than that there was not any moral turpitude in pain; and that the gifts of fortune neither exclude, nor fecure, the poffeffion of virtue. This, indeed, they confidered as fufficient confolation to thofe who labour under any external inconvenience, whether of adverfity or pain.

As a material on which virtue may operate; as an inftrument of beneficence; as a ftake, for which men are to play, and become gainers or lofers for themfelves or others in the game of human life, they allowed that external poffeffions have their ufe, and that they merit the attention of the wife: but to rely on them in any determinate meafure for happinefs they mantained to be extreme folly. In purfuance of this doctrine, they would not proftitute the denomination of good to any thing that was not virtue; nor permit any thing to be called evil that was not vice; and would not have a man fet his heart, or rely for happinefs, upon any thing beyond his own province of refponfibility or conduct. In this manner they ftrove to cultivate an elevation of mind which would not owe its good to any contingent circumftance, nor to any will but its own. They would fet at defiance the events of fortune or the caprice of other men. They would not be in fear of any adverfity which could not hinder their acting a virtuous part; nor be flattered with a profperity which could add nothing to the merit of a virtuous life.

The Peripatetics were content to remain on a ftep below thefe high pretenfions. They too held virtue to be the fupreme good, and had juft maxims of integrity and honour, but comparatively
enfeebled

enfeebled, as the Stoics alledged, with a notion that even thefe de-
pended on fortune for part of their effects. While they affumed
virtue, or a laudable part to be acted in the community of mankind as the fupreme good; and reprobated the reclufe tranquility, or felfifh enjoyments of the Epicurean, as poifon to the foul
of man, and death to his beft and happieft affections; whilft
they allowed, that the higheft meafure of fortune never could be
brought into competition with any confideration of juftice or
duty; they ftill required profperity, to compleat the felicity even
of a virtuous life.

In this argument, the Stoics, though charged with paradox,
and themfelves the more ordinary butts of ridicule, yet turned this
weapon againft their antagonifts : " You allow," they faid, " that
" virtue is the conftituent of happinefs, and even that fortitude
" is a virtue; and yet to complete that happinefs, you require a
" fortune, which virtue defpifes, and an eafe in which fortitude
" is not required. You tell us of a good which the thief may
" fteal from his neighbour; which the mifer may lock up in his
" coffers from all the world; which the glutton may devour at
" a meal; which may be denied to the worthy, and lavifhed on
" the vile. You preach up moderation, and even abftinence,
" with refpect to this good. You own it is mean to be folicitous
" about it; and noble to defpife it. You call that a good, therefore,
" of which the contempt is wifdom and honour; of which the
" privation did not marr the happinefs of Epaminondas and
" Socrates; nor fecure the condition of Darius or Crœfus. The
" wife man, they faid, will acquit himfelf properly with refpect
" to the gifts of fortune; but, for his happinefs, will rely upon
" what he himfelf does; not upon what he poffeffes; upon the

" general refolution, integrity and goodnefs which are his own;
" not upon the caprice of other men, nor upon the meafure or
" degree in which the materials on which he is to work falls to
" his fhare."

This may well be confidered as a degree of perfection, far raifed above the ordinary ftate of human nature : It is, neverthelefs,
that, for which it was given, a noble idea, upon which the ingenuous mind cannot too nearly form itfelf.

Men very commonly fuffer themfelves to depend, for prefent
comfort, upon fome diftant object, or the hopes which they entertain of the future.   This is no more than a habit of thinking ;
yet it may produce frivolity and weaknefs, if not depravity of
mind, or neglect of duty.   The future feldom comes up to the
expectations that were formed of it : But it is the nature or
character of feeble minds, notwithftanding the fallacy of paft expectations, to apprehend a future, on which, to the neglect of
prefent objects or duties, they ftill continue to rely.

Material fubjects, or external circumftances of any kind, except fo far as they affect the organs of fenfe with pleafure or pain,
are in their own nature indifferent; and, if beyond this they excite defire or averfion in the mind, it is by means of fome quality, whether of good or evil, honour or difhonour, which are not
inherent to the fubject itfelf ; but affociated with it, in the conception which the mind entertains.   The mifer has affociated
happinefs with money, in his conception of riches ; and is infatiable of wealth.   The ufurper has affociated honour with power
or dominion ; and fticks at no means, whether of infinuation or
force to obtain his end.

I

Whatever

Whatever be the habitual conception, and the habitual purfuit, thefe form the ruling affection or paffion of the human mind : If the object, in itfelf, were fitted by nature to excite fuch affection or paffion, as the juice of an orange produces the fenfation of fweet, the affections or paffions of all men, like the fenfation pro- duced on their palate, would be the fame. But, while fenfations are uniform, conceptions are various ; one perfon hopes for what, to another, is an object of fear : Infomuch, that many have thought themfelves juftified in concluding, from thefe appear- ances, that there is not in reality any ftandard, by which to rec- tify or to fix the apprehenfions of men. But, as we have found the diftinction of good and evil fufficiently eftablifhed in the nature of things, we have only to apply this diftinction, in order to correct any miftake or falfe apprehenfion, refpecting the fub- jects of eftimation or choice ; and, in our endeavour fo to profit by the exercife of reafon, confifts the fruit of that information on the fubject of good and evil, which it is the object of moral fcience to obtain or convey.

SECTION

S E C T I O N   VIII.

The fame Subject continued.

'Α τ8ς μεν ειδοτας καλ8ς και αγαθ8ς ηγειτο ειναι; Τ8ς δε αγνο8ντας
ανδραποδωδεις αν δικαιως κεκλησθαι.

PART II.
CHAP. I.
SECT. VIII.

IF, to avoid the imputation of vifionary fchemes, it be required
to keep in view the actual ftate of men's minds, as well as the abftract idea of what they ought to be, we may continue to offer a
fpecimen of the opinions, or habits of thinking, in which the characters of men commonly originate; trufting that a few examples may be fufficient to lead every perfon in purfuing the fame
tract of obfervation for himfelf.

There are perfons, we know, who do not fo much reprobate
the vices to which mankind are fubject, as depreciate human nature

ture itfelf. This is an unhappy turn of thought, tending to ftifle the fentiments of humanity or good will towards others, and to check the efforts of any ingenuous endeavour in the perfon who would improve himfelf. Man is formed to take part in the common caufe of his fellow creatures; and he fuffers in thinking meanly of their nature: He is formed for progreffion; and is fruftrated in having his pretenfions ftated fo low as to check his exertions. Men will not attempt what they think is altogether vifionary and beyond their reach: But, in the gradation of human character, there are every where faults to be corrected, and improvements to be made, of which the fmalleft poffible effect is ever preferable to none. Socrates believed that men might be difpofed to mutual beneficence, and that numbers were fo difpofed. Ariftippus conceived that all pretenfions to the love of others were falfe; and that every one propofed to be of ufe only to himfelf. The one was inclined, by his conception, to benevolence and magnanimity; the other to felfifhnefs and diftruft.

There is an error feemingly oppofite to this depreciation of human nature; but, in its defects, alfo productive of mifery. Such is an overweaning conception or imagination of what men actually are, producing an ill founded confidence in the fuppofed prevalence of generofity, magnanimity, truth, and fincerity, of which the undiftinguifhing affumption not only expofes the mind to folly, difappointment. and other effects of miftake ; but leads, in the fequel, to the very oppofite extreme of diftruft of mankind, and defpair of virtue.

To the well-informed and the well-difpofed, virtue is not the lefs real that vice is frequently oppofed to it. The mixed fcenes of human life are its proper ftation. Here, it is equally fignaliz-

I ed

ed in withstanding the evil, as in co-operating with the good; and its happiness depends, not upon the consent or participation of others, but on the degree in which it exerts itself.

It is unhappy to rest our choice of good qualities on the supposition that we are to meet with corresponding qualities in other men; to apprehend that candour and humanity are due only to the candid and the humane; or, that want of merit in others will dispense with that justice or liberality of conduct, which it is our happiness to maintain for ourselves.

In consequence of such conceptions, we sometimes repent of the good we have done, when, (as we suppose), the parties concerned appear unworthy of kindness: And, in such instances, the rule of our conduct is taken from what others deserve, not from what is becoming in ourselves. Want of merit in the world is alledged, as an excuse for indifference to mankind; and what is perhaps in us a desire to shift our own duty, is mistaken for the severity of virtue. Instead of ingenuous actors, we become squeamish observers of other men; and, taking offence at their behaviour, indulge animosities little short of malice.

It is unhappy to consider perfection, more as the standard by which we may censure others, than as the rule by which we are to conduct ourselves.

We are by nature enabled to conceive a measure of excellence beyond what we are able to attain. This, when the standard is applied to ourselves, may become a source of indefinite progression; but, when applied only to other men, is a pretence for invidious

dious cenfure; infomuch that, a principle, which ought to incite in us the choice of good qualities, and a difpofition to correct our own faults, is employed only as an occafion of contempt or malice towards our fellow creatures. Every ill difpofition is unhappy; but the mifery is then the moft complete, when ill difpofitions fet up for cenfure, and affume the pretence of holy zeal, or concern for what is right.

It is a wretched opinion, that happinefs confifts in exemption from labour, or in having nothing to do.

This opinion is taken up, perhaps, from the abufe of words, when we contraft the enjoyment of fome fuppofed good with the expectation and purfuit of it. In this contraft, we fancy that enjoyment begins only when labour has ceafed; and, in this apprehenfion, the world is full of expectants, who think, that their happinefs is deferred by the labours and toils they undergo in finifhing the tafk which Providence has prefcribed to them. They figh for relief from trouble, and fometimes obtain it; when, fortunately for the inftruction of mankind, they fhow, by their example, that the languors of in-occupation are more grievous than toil.

The wifh to have nothing to do, is moft excufeable in perfons who, having labours prefcribed by neceffity, are frequently urged on to fatigue. The powers of human nature are limited, and require alternate periods of repofe as well as exertion; but, as the too long continuance of labour is grievous, fo the continuance of inaction, beyond the time that is required for repofe, is attended with a wearinefs and languour, no lefs diftrefsful than fatigue.

The

The notion, that happiness confifts in relief from any active engagements, is eafily accounted for, alfo, in the cafe of thofe who, having a tafk to perform, never engage in it willingly. The tafk poffibly confines them, and prevents their application to any thing elfe, while it does not fupply thofe real exertions of mind, which never fail to make the time that is well employed pafs away with delight. The perfon who is thus confined, without being occupied, miftakes his averfion to confinement for an averfion to bufinefs; and his longing for a change of occupation he miftakes for a diflike to exertion. Thus, while the fchool-boy is confined on his form, his heart and his mind are in the play-field. As he does not apply to his leffon, nor even attend to it, while he reads it, he is only confined, not occupied. What we term his averfion to application, and his longing for the hour of difmiffion, is an ardor for employment; and, in fact, when free to chufe for himfelf, he betakes him to a labour, in which every mufcle of the body, and every faculty of the mind, is ftrained or exerted to obtain the object of fome hazardous or toilfome conteft.

It is thus common, through life, to be reluctant in bufinefs, and fond of amufement: But, while in declining bufinefs men feem to reckon any kind of employment a grievance, they, by recourfe to hazardous fports and diverfions, make ample confeffion that fome kind of active and even ferious engagement is indifpenfably neceffary.

The diftinction between bufinefs and amufement is perhaps not eafily fettled, or confifts intirely in this, that bufinefs is prefcribed by fome confideration of intereft or duty; and amufement is taken up, in the beginning at leaft, without any fuch ferious concern.

But

But if bufinefs be diftinguifhed by the importance of the objeƈ, on which it proceeds, amufement foon becomes infipid, unlefs means are found fufficiently to intereft the mind, and exercife its faculties. This end, indeed, is obtained by the votaries of play, in creating to themfelves a rifk, which far exceeds that of the merchant in the adventures of his trade, or thofe of the politician in his profpeƈts of elevation or power. The hazards incurred by either are infipid, compared to the chances of lofs or gain, in which the finifhed gamefter is known to involve himfelf. Nor is this a refinement only of polifhed ages. The mere favage, after he is ftript of all his other poffeffions at the gaming table, clofes the fcene with a throw, on which he ftates the freedom of his perfon *.

Bufinefs, to thofe who are really occupied, may have all the qualities of an agreeable paftime. If it be a diligent performance of the offices incumbent on a man of integrity and virtue, it will join the fatisfaƈion of a mind confcious of duty, to that of a mind employed in the exercife of its faculties, and exempt from fear, malice or remorfe. So that, to thofe who decline bufinefs for the fake of amufement, it may be faid, that they rejeƈt what is fitted to employ them agreeably ; and in order to quicken the feelings of a mind which is become languid for want of employment, betake themfelves to purfuits in which they become a prey to evil paffions. Such is the effeƈt of diffipation, a weaknefs of the mind which loaths its beft occupations, as the fickly ftomach is found to loath the moft wholefome food.

We may conclude, therefore, that the love of amufement is

Vol. II.   M   unhappy,

---

* Aleam (quod mirere) fobrii inter ferva exercent, tanta lucrandi perdendive temeritate, ut cum omnia defecerant, extremo ac noviffimo jaƈtu, de libertate et de corpore contendant.   TACIT. de Moribus German. c. 24.

unhappy, if it proceed from a notion, that any thing can amuſe us better than the duties of our ſtation, or that any employment is more to be wiſhed for than that preciſely which in the preſent moment has fallen to our ſhare. If any one have formed ſuch a notion, he may be told to beware of it. It will diſqualify him for his beſt enjoyments and embitter his life with peeviſhneſs and melancholy.

It is unhappy to conceive beneficence as an effort of ſelf-denial; or to conceive that we lay our fellow creatures under great obligations, by the kindneſs we do them.

This notion refers chiefly to acts of charity or liberality; in which the beneficent gives to another what might be of uſe to himſelf. It were vile to be inſenſible of ſuch merit; but the perſon, who gives ſuch proofs of goodneſs, is himſelf the laſt to over-rate its value. " If I have done a kindneſs to my fellow crea-
" tures", ſays Antoninus; " is not this itſelf my benefit? let me
" not forget it, nor ever ceaſe to do ſuch things".

To the ſame effect, alſo, we may tranſcribe the following paſſage:
" There are ſome who, when they have done you a good office,
" are apt to remind you of it. Others do not mention what they
" have done; but have it uppermoſt in their thoughts, and con-
" ſider you as their debtor. A third ſort do not ſeem to know
" what they have done; but are like the vine which produces its
" grapes, and *has done*, when it hath yielded its proper fruit.

" As the horſe when he has finiſhed his courſe; the hound,
" when he has ended his chace; the bee, when it has made its
" honey; ſo he, who is truly a man, performs a good office,
" without

3

" without any noife ; and proceeds to the next that occurs to be
" done, as the vine, in its proper feafon, renews its foliage and
" its fruit. We ought to be of the number of thofe, who do
" not feem to know the good they have done : Nay but ought
" we not to be confcious of beneficent intentions ? Is it not the
" property of a focial being, to wifh well to his fellow creatures.
" Yea, fo help me God, to defire, too, that his fellow creatures
" fhould be fenfible of his beneficence? What you fay is true,
" yet, if you mifapprehend what I faid above, you will belong
" to one of the former claffes, and be among thofe who are led
" afide from perfection by fpecious reafons. But, if you are
" willing to obferve the diftinction, that is made between thofe
" firft claffes and the others, do not be afraid that it will caufe
" you to fail in any focial action *".

If virtue, whatever be its external mode of exertion, be itfelf
the excellence or good of human nature, (and we do wrong if we
admit of any thing elfe as virtue) or, if it be, in the intellectual
world, what health, and ftrength, and beauty, are in the animal
kingdom ; there is no reafon to apprehend, that a fellow creature
is obliged to us for being virtuous, any more than he would be
obliged to us for being in health.

The offices of a found mind are as natural to the virtuous, as
thofe of a found body are to the healthy. The humane and the
candid can never ceafe to perform the offices of humanity, and
candour, although they do not confider, in what degree others
may be obliged to them for fo doing.

M 2 It

* Anton. lib. v. c. 6.

It were unhappy to confider virtue as a tafk, confifting of external performances, enjoined under the fanction of rewards and punifhments. We can no more become benevolent, from the hope of reward, or the fear of punifhment, than we can poffefs ourfelves of fortitude from the love of eafe or averfion to trouble. The ingenuous and high minded believes the reality of future rewards and punifhments ; but, if they are any thing different from the poffeffion or privation of that goodnefs, to which he afpires, they are mere acceffaries to the confiderations from which he acts; they may be ufeful, in reftraining a criminal difpofition, but are not neceffary, in directing or forming the virtuous to his duty ; much lefs, is a regard to them an effential conftituent of his character.

If the future lot of the righteous be happy, his prefent condition in the practice of virtue is fo alfo ; and it were abfurd, furely, to conceive that a perfon muft not prefer the good which he may now enjoy, but for fake of a good which he is to enjoy hereafter.

It is unhappy to admit of any confideration in competition with our real good. " There is hardly a man to be found," fays an ingenious obferver*, " who would not rather be in pain, to appear " happy, than be really happy, to appear miferable." So familiar are the examples of paradox, even in the conceptions of the vulgar. As they examine their own afpect by reflection from a mirror, they judge of their own condition by reflection from other men's thoughts ; confult the opinion of others, rather than their own feelings; prefer confideration, or the reputation of worth, to worthinefs itfelf; and do not fo much confider how far they deferve praife, as how far they poffefs it.

This

* The Tatler.

This is beginning the work of felicity at the wrong end; labouring for a fuperftructure before they have laid a foundation; and ftriving to produce a fhadow without any fubftance.

All men would be happy. The moft erroneous paffions miflead from this object only by miftake; and, it is to miftake their own aim, when they would produce abroad the appearance of happinefs, before they have poffeffed it in the qualities of their own minds. The reality will not fail to carry its external appearances; or, if it fhould be unobferved or miftaken, the difadvantage is comparatively of fmall account.

It is fufficient refpect to the opinions of other men, that we are pleafed with their teftimony, without facrificing the confcioufnefs of an ingenuous mind to what the world may think, or without preferring the appearances of merit to the real though filent poffeffion of it.

In this, the miftake is doubly to be regretted, as it implies the fubftitution of a falfe object for the true one, and the fubftitution alfo of what is precarious, and depending on the caprice of others, what is matter of anxiety and difappointment, for an attainable and fecure poffeffion. Such is the choice which the vain-glorious has made, in preferring the opinions of other men to the poffeffion of real good qualities in himfelf, which he might cultivate fecurely, and on which he might rely without any hazard of a difappointment.

It is unhappy to depend for enjoyment on what we cannot command, or to fix our defires on what is beyond our reach.

Thus,

Thus, it were unhappy for the labouring man, to long for exemption from labour.   It were unhappy, in the poor, to aim at
appearing like the rich ; to long for an equipage, a retinue, a palace, a table ; and think himſelf excluded from happineſs, in being deprived of theſe things.

Ambition, or the unwearied deſire of ſomething higher than
we poſſeſs at preſent, is a principle well ſuited to the nature of
man ; and it is, in ſome one or other of its applications univerſal
to mankind.   If it apply to invigorate the practice of virtue, and
the exerciſes of a mind, ingenuous, candid, and humane, this every one has in his power.   If it apply to the conduct of ordinary
buſineſs, whether private or public, ſtill the perſon ſo engaged
may be well employed for the preſent ; and, if he complain of
miſery in the abſence of his object, we may venture to queſtion
the wiſdom or the temper of his mind.

The ingenuous, the ſtrenuous, and ardent, though we ſhould
ſuppoſe them not to reflect on the merit of the part which they
are acting, are happy in the very exerciſe of their diſpoſitions and
powers ; and this is ſo far from being inconſiſtent with the purſuit of an object, that it requires, or pre-ſuppoſes ſome object to
engage the mind, and give occaſion to the exerciſe of its faculties.

   " That the mind of man," ſays the Rambler, " is never ſa-
" tisfied with the objects immediately before it, but is always
" breaking away from the preſent moment, and loſing itſelf in
" ſchemes of future felicity, and that we forget the proper uſe of
" the time now in our power, to provide for the enjoyment of
                                             " that

" that which perhaps may never be granted us, has frequent-
" ly been remarked; and, as this practice is a commodious sub-
" ject of raillery to the gay, and of declamation to the serious, it
" has been ridiculed with all the pleasantry of wit, and exagge-
" rated with all the amplifications of rhetoric. Every instance,
" by which its absurdity might appear most flagrant, has been
" studiously collected; it has been marked with every epithet of
" contempt, and all the tropes and figures have been called forth
" against it.

" Censure is willingly indulged, because it always implies
" some superiority: Men please themselves with imagining that
" they have made a deeper search, or wider survey, than others,
" and detected faults and follies, which escape vulgar observa-
" tion," &c.

" This quality of looking forward into futurity," continues
the same author, " seems the unavoidable condition of a being,
" whose motions are gradual, and whose life is progressive: As
" his powers are limited, he must use means for the attainment of
" his end, and intend first what he performs last; as, by conti-
" nual advances from his first stage of existence, he is perpetually
" varying the horizon of his prospects, he must always discover
" new motives of action, new excitements of fear, and allure-
" ments of desire.

" The end, therefore, which at present calls forth our efforts
" will be found, when it is once gained, to be only one of the
" means to some remoter end. The natural flights of the human
" mind are not from pleasure to pleasure, but from hope to
" hope.

" He

" He that directs his steps to a certain point must frequently
" turn his eyes to that place which he strives to reach.   He that
" undergoes the fatigue of labour must solace his weariness with
" the contemplation of its reward."

So far this author seems to contend for a reliance on the future,
as the principal constituent of present happiness; and it may
be difficult to combat any folly, if this Hercules with his club
stands in the way to defend it.   He may, however, be quoted
against himself.   " Labour," as he has stated in another place,
" is its own reward;" and, in the sequel of the passage now quoted, he owns, " that some caution against keeping our view
" too intent upon remote advantages, is not without its useful-
" ness"

It is the object of reason, in this matter, to distinguish the
objects to which our views may be safely directed, from those
which mislead our desires, and furnish nothing to gratify the
mind for the present, besides a vain expectation of the future.

Of the latter kind, are all those objects, which are so far out
of our power, that we cannot form any reasonable plan of exertion or application in the pursuit of them.   To indulge in the
hope or desire of such things, is that cause of misery, which we
are now considering.   Under its effects, the misguided mind is
urged by a sense of its wants, but is precluded from any agreeable exercise of faculties, or of power to obtain their supply.

With a better choice of an object, the case may be different.
A person may *direct his steps* to a certain point, and frequently

3   *turn*

turn his eyes to that place which he strives to reach, while his walk is pleasant, and the exercise it gives him is eligible, upon its own account.

Nor is this any great effort of philosophy, or aim at perfection: It is common in human life, in all its innocent or rational pursuits: It is the course in which men have enjoyed the exercise of their faculties, and by that exercise improved their powers; in which they have been led to observe the system of nature around them, to extend their knowledge, and to multiply arts, whether lucrative or agreeable. It is in the present occupation of their nature they find occasion, whether for opposition or concert, and have their abilities or their disposition to beneficence brought to the test. So that, in numbering the blessings of human life, we may venture to reckon the act of pursuing its object, as of more value than the object pursued; and may rely much more, for happiness, upon the means which are employed for the attainment of our end; than we are to rely upon the end itself, even when obtained: Insomuch that, if any person looking forward to the future is unhappy for the present, we may venture to affirm, either that he has mistaken his object, and fixed his desires on that which does not admit of his taking any reasonable measures for the attainment of it; or, that if his object be reasonable, and such as he may pursue with advantage, he has certainly failed in the proper exercise of his faculties, in that course of industry and diligence, which his object prescribes: Insomuch, that *raillery and censure* too are very properly applied to those, who, *ever intent on the future, are unable to enjoy the present.*

Whatever be the end, which persons of this description propose to themselves, their present sufferings imply sloth, ill temper, and

VOL. II.   N   pusillanimity, pufillanimity; either a want of proper exertion for the attainment of their end, or the wrong choice of an end which does not admit of any reafonable exertion.

Wherever the faculties are reafonably exerted, if to this we join the exercife of good affections, the fenfe of innocence and beneficence, magnanimity, courage and temperance, the one an exemption from unreafonable fear, the other an exemption from brutal exceffes, the caufe of happinefs is prefent, and does not depend upon any thing future.

Perfons bleffed with alacrity and goodnefs of difpofition, are thus happy in the courfe of their ordinary purfuits ; and, even while their object is diftant. So the boy is gratified at his play,, the gentleman at his fport, the plowman at his labour, the tradef-man in his workfhop, the foldier on his march, the ftatefman in his office; and each, proportioned to his alacrity, and to the application he gives to his bufinefs. So that, in cenfuring thofe who, from their attention to the future, are unhappy at prefent, it is not the ordinary ftate of a man, or of a progreffive being, that we cenfure ; it is the vice, and the folly of thofe, who, from floth or the defects of temper, are difqualified to employ them-felves well for the prefent.

It were unhappy to think ourfelves unable to ftruggle with difficulties, under which others appear to be much at their eafe.

In refpect to what nature will bear, one perfon may ferve as a model to another ; and teach him what he may endure or per-form. The peevifh may be apprized of his own ftrength, by the

example

example of numbers who are chearful under hardſhips, no way leſs grievous than thoſe which cauſe him to repine.

Man is not formed to acquieſce in any preciſe ſituation. In the beſt, he finds ſomething to do; and, in the worſt, is then only unhappy, when he ſuffers his courage and powers of exertion to be overwhelmed. While he exerts himſelf to remove an inconvenience, he ought to be ſo far patient under it, as, in his endeavours to procure relief, fully to poſſeſs himſelf and his faculties.

In the variety of conditions incident to mankind, reſpecting the meaſure of their external ſupplies and accommodations, we may accordingly obſerve a wonderful latitude, in the meaſure of hardſhip or inconvenience to which they can ſubmit, joined with a continual deſire of improving their condition, even when at the beſt. Here is contentment joined to impatience, of that with which they are content. Both are neceſſary qualifications of man's progreſſive nature: The diſadvantages, under which he labours in any one ſtate of his fortunes, do not diſqualify him from proceeding with alacrity, diligence, and ability, in mending his condition; nor does any advantage he ever has gained ſo far content him, as to terminate any farther exertion of his faculties.

This happy mixture of fortitude under preſent inconvenience, with a vigorous effort of mind, for the removal of it; although the juſt balance of temper be frequently overſet in the minds of particular men, is, nevertheleſs, a general characteriſtic of the human ſpecies.

The weak are querulous and peeviſh in their preſent ſituation,

N 2

yet

yet do not exert themſelves to remove the cauſe of their ſuffering.   They ſee numbers, on every ſide, who bear ſuch a lot as
theirs with indifference, and yet are pleaſed to think themſelves
ſingularly wretched.   They are ſo, no doubt ; but it is a wretch-
edneſs of temper and opinion, not of external condition.

In ſuch inſtances, frequently, the mind is wounded, rather in
its conception of dignity, than in its ſenſation of harm, from the
actual effect of external circumſtances.   Certain privations are
conceived to effect a diminution of rank ; and the very pride,
which is offended in this diminution, diſables the ſufferer from
endeavouring to procure his relief.   Pride is ſupine, ſullen, and
liſtleſs ; in many other reſpects, a principle of miſery or ſuffering ; and, in this, a diſqualification for any of the efforts, which
are required to reform either the character of the man, or to remove any cauſe of complaint from abroad.

There are ways of thinking, which miſlead and tend to corrupt
whole nations at once.   Falſe notions of religion, which interpoſe
the authority of God in behalf of any frivolous or cruel practice ; ſyſtems of bigotry and intollerance, which ſet mankind at
variance, and lead to perſecution and mutual deſtruction, on the
ſcore of difference in matters of faith or worſhip ; falſe notions of
honour, which promote quarrels, diſtruſt, and mutual wrongs ;
falſe notions of liberty, that indiſpoſe men to ſubordination, or
public order ; falſe notions of government, that ſubſtitute force
and diſcretionary power, for law and juſtice ; falſe notions of
rank that attach elevation to mere birth and fortune, excluſive of
merit ; or that proceed on a notion of eminence, which no
public ſervice or luſtre of character can ſupply.   Under ſuch apprehenſions, a diſtinction or ſuppoſed elevation of rank, which
                                                              ought

ought to incite the mind to noble actions, ferves to difcourage thofe who would afpire to real greatnefs ; and flatter thofe who think themfelves great, with the notion of an exemption from the neceffity of merit, or of any good quality whatever.

From the example of mankind, in numberlefs inftances, the importance of opinion or habitual conception is obvious. The perfon who habitually conceives that the church yard is haunted, or that goblins ply in the dark, trembles with fear, where another having no fuch conception is calm and undifturbed ; and the mind, in either cafe, may be faid to be the author of its own good, or its harm. The one may fuffer himfelf to be infected with that weaknefs, or the other may be corrected of it, according as they neglect or employ their reafon to its proper ufe.

The opinions which tend to happinefs are the reverfe of thofe which tend to mifery. In treating of the one, we naturally refer to the other. In oppofition to that corrupt ftate of apprehenfion, in which the diftinctions of fortune are fubftituted for thofe of merit and demerit, we may obferve it is happy to be guided in our eftimation of perfons not by fortune and fafhion, but by the merit of intelligence, probity, equanimity, and candour.

In matters of mere inclination or will, it is natural to become in ourfelves what we admire in other men. And perfons, to whom the ftandard of eftimation is perfonal worth, have already received the bias of an ingenuous mind to integrity and honour; fo much, that to efteem and to love thofe virtues in others, amounts nearly to a poffeffion of them in ourfelves.

To be ready, on all occafions, with difcernment and truth, in

matters

matters of duty, to ftate to ourfelves,—This is what I have to do, and this is the part for which I am refponfible; with a habit of limiting our own defires to a full and perfect difcharge of the office fo affigned us, is rather indeed the effence of happinefs than a mere conception tending to obtain it.

All men partake in the concerns of ordinary life, and cannot without abfurdity neglect their own fubfiftence and accommodation, the œconomy of their fortune, the fettlement of their families, the defence and welfare of their country; but happy are they who, in fuch matters, can diftinguifh the part affigned to themfelves from the part which Providence has referved to itfelf. To man it is given to exert his natural powers with diligence, benignity, and courage; but the event, in every tranfaction is at the difpofal of Providence; and the happieft conception or habit of thinking, of which man is fufceptible, is, that the part affigned to him may be equally fupported under every change of events, and that events do but form a change of the fituation in which he is to act. Let him fincerely lament the misfortune of his friend or his country; but let him be ready, alfo, with all his ability, to retrieve fuch misfortunes.

Life itfelf, with all its fupports, is precarious and temporary. The longeft liver muft die, and the fhorteft liver can do no more. For us, it is happy to know, that our concern is to conduct ourfelves well through life, whether it be fhort or long. Benevolence and courage are fufficient to happinefs; malice and cowardice conftitute mifery, whether the life in which they are incurred be of long or fhort duration.

It is happy to conceive the integrity, diligence, and fidelity, which

which are in our own power, though unobferved by others, as the completion of good to ourfelves. It is happy to conceive the debafements of a malicious and cowardly nature, not as matters of degradation merely in the opinion of other men, but as in themfelves the completion and effence of all the evil to which we are expofed.

In the relations of mankind, the brother cannot rightly act the part of a ftranger, the citizen the part of an alien, nor the individual, confidered apart from every particular relation, rightly forget that he is a man, and has a common caufe with mankind. On this fubject, every juft conception is productive of happinefs, and leads the individual to confider himfelf as furrounded with objects of affection, and the affection he bears in his mind as the principal excellence of his own nature.

It is happy to know, that the caufe of juftice and goodnefs is fecured by infinite wifdom and power; to conceive ourfelves as inftruments in the hand of God, to be employed for the good of his creatures, and our happinefs as confifting in the willing confent of our minds to be fo employed.

The adorable perfections of God infpire a confidence, a veneration, and love; which amount, at the fame time, to a conviction, that goodnefs and wifdom, even in fuch meafures of them as are communicable to created beings, are of the higheft value; and the affection they infpire is in itfelf a difpofition to receive the communication of them.

It is happy, in every place, to carry in our thoughts, that we are in the fituation in which it is the will of God that we fhould act;

3

act; and that to act, in such situations, with diligence, integrity, and good will to mankind, is the part he requires of us.

Whoever thus habitually thinks or conceives of himself, is possessed of religion, virtue, and happiness. This no one can procure for another. It is left by the Almighty for every one only to procure it for himself. Aurelius accordingly procured it for himself, but could not for his son. With this unhappy person, notions imbibed among the meaner domestics of the palace precluded the instructions of the father and of the friend.

If happiness were an attainment of the mind, to be acquired as a science or an art is learnt from a master, the teacher might justly be considered as the vicegerent of God; and no place could contain the numbers that would flock to his school. But, in this the Almighty has delegated his power to every person only respecting himself: But he has provided a discipline, in the result of which, perhaps, even the most depraved may, in the end, become willing to avail themselves of the trust which the Author of their nature has reposed in them. When error, and folly, and profligacy, drained to the bottom of the cup, shall have led the mind to nauseate the draught, better thoughts may arise, and man, thoroughly apprised of what is evil, may become willing to remove it, and intentionally work himself into habits of what he conceives to be good.

Such may be, respecting the most refractory subjects, the effect of a moral government, which actually operates in the nature of things, and in a manner of which we have formerly endeavoured to remark some particulars. Reason and knowledge may hasten its effects; and for this purpose our feeble endeavours

to

to erect the fabric of fcience, that they who refort to it may proceed on a juft knowledge of their place and deftination in the
fyftem of nature.

The happy, without incurring either dejection or pride, from
events whether profperous or adverfe, rely chiefly on what is of abfolute value, health of body and foundnefs of mind; and may
reckon, as their higheft privilege, the power to preferve, in all the
varieties of fortune, a difpofition, candid, fearlefs, temperate, and
juft. Even among the gifts of fortune, they can obferve and enjoy
matters of abfolute value, in refpect to which there is no poffible
ground of interference or competition: Such are the bleffings
which nature has equally provided for all men: The water of
the fountain, or of the running ftream; the light of the fun; and
the vital air of the atmofphere; exiftence itfelf, in fhort, or admiffion to behold this magnificent fcene of the univerfe;—compared to which, any or all the comparative fuperiorities of one
man to another difappear, and are as nothing. Society itfelf is felt,
by the happy, as a common bleffing to all its members; and, like
the air they breathe, equally neceffary to the rich, who would avail
themfelves of the labour and fkill of others, as it is to the poor,
who would obtain the reward of their labour.

C H A P. II.

OF THE FUNDAMENTAL LAW OF MORALITY, ITS IMMEDIATE APPLICATIONS AND SANCTIONS.

S E C T I O N I.

Of the Law, or first Principle of Estimation in the Character of Man.

BY feparately examining the nature of *good* and *evil*, under the titles of *pleasure* and *pain*, of *beauty* and *deformity*, of *excellence* and *defect*, *virtue* and *vice*, of *happiness* and *misery*; we have endeavoured to arrive at some general conception of what is best for mankind.

PART II.
CHAP. II.
SECT. I.

Thefe

These articles we have found to differ chiefly in words, but in matter and substance to be nearly the same. The same qualities of *wisdom, goodness, temperance,* and *fortitude,* which constitute the excellence of human nature, are constituents also of its beauty and its happiness. The opposite qualities of *folly, malice, debauchery,* and *cowardice,* which constitute its defect, constitute also its *deformity,* or *turpitude,* and its *misery.*

The different appellations in question have a reference to different aspects, under which the subject may be considered. Beauty and deformity have a reference to the qualities of good and evil, in respect to their first appearances or aspect. Excellence and defect, virtue and vice, have a reference to their reality in the character. Happiness and misery have a reference to the state of enjoyment or suffering, which they constitute in the mind.

If we should endeavour to concentrate this description, or reduce this enumeration of qualities, to some one general principle the most likely to unite the whole, we should be limited in our choice, probably, to one or other of the qualities first mentioned, in the estimate of characters; that is, either to *wisdom,* or *goodness.*

The other two qualities, whether of *temperance* or *fortitude,* considered apart, are less likely to secure the whole. *Temperance,* considered as mere abstinence from improper gratifications, without any positive direction of the mind to a better purpose; or considered as restraint from evil, without the formation of a disposition positively good, would constitute a very imperfect model of excellence or felicity.

3   *Fortitude,*

Fortitude, confidered as a mere force of mind, without any fpecification of a choice or direction, in which that force fhould be employed, might be exerted equally for a wrong as for a right purpofe ; and courage, prompted by folly might be employed for the deftruction of its owner, like the brutal ftrength of that wreftler * ; who could tear open the cleft of a tree, but who could fuffer himfelf at the fame time, to be caught in it.

The term equivalent to *wifdom*, among the antients, was employed by them to comprehend every article of praife, and enabled them alfo to comprife the laws of morality in the fingle recommendation of this quality. In our tranflation of that term, however, the fenfe is more limited ; and, were we to ftate wifdom as the fundamental principle of morality, we fhould be thought to fubftitute a prudential choice of our interefts for what ought to be matter of affection, and the effufion of a benevolent heart. Mere prudence is an excellence of the underftanding only ; but virtue includes, as a preferable confideration, the energy and direction of an amiable and happy difpofition.

It is well known that, to fecure a proper choice of conduct, on all occafions, good affection or difpofition is not lefs neceffary, than able judgement : Nay, we may be convinced, from experience, that perfons of common underftanding, with fit difpofitions, are lefs apt to err on trying occafions, than the ableft underftanding unfupported by any goodnefs of heart; or than mere underftanding, warped as we may fuppofe it to be in the defect of good difpofitions, by motives of a different tendency.

If

* Milo of Crotona.

If we are, therefore, to contract our defcription of happinefs, or reduce it to a point, around which the moft valuable qualities of human nature are likely to be collected, we may venture to felect that of goodnefs, or benevolence, as the moft likely to ferve our purpofe; and, by way of principal or fundamental law of moral wifdom, may affume, that the greateft good incident to human nature is the love of mankind.

The different forms or afpects of this difpofition, as it may be exercifed in pity to the diftreffed, or in candour and humanity indifcriminately towards all men; as it may be exercifed in the mutual confidence of friends, or in the love of a citizen to his country, have been already ftated; and although, in this place, its defignation in the mind of a man be taken from his relation to mankind, a title under which are comprehended objects the moft intimate to him, and the leaft likely to be miftaken by him; yet, the difpofition fo characterifed is in reality a fufceptibility of juft affection towards every object, whether of pity, refpect, or veneration; whether the loweft or the higheft that can enter the thoughts of a well difpofed and a happy mind.

The love of mankind, on every arduous occafion is an aid to the judgement, in directing the conduct which a wife man is deftined to hold: In difficult fituations, it is a noble fupport of courage. Even the timorous become bold under the inftigation of a warm or generous affection; the humane, by habits of benevolence, are fecured againft the effect of difpofitions comparatively inferior or mean; and ordinary men, when roufed to feelings of generofity or pity, remain infenfible to the allurements of inferior pleafure, or the fufferings of pain.

I   The

Benevolence, therefore, may in fome degree be confidered as a principle of wifdom, of fortitude, and temperance ; and, as it either infpires or requires for its fupport every other good quality of human nature, we cannot greatly err, in affuming it as the fundamental or primary objeſt of moral law. Its external effeſts, expreffions, or appearances, are the fupreme objeſts of efteem and complacency ; and its reverfe, cruel infenfibility, and malice, recolleſted in ourfelves, or obferved in others, are the fupreme objeſts of remorfe, of indignation and hatred.

Hence it is, that the murderer is the common objeſt of deteftation to himfelf and all men ; and without waiting for the conviſtion of external evidence, is fo often betrayed by the horrors of remorfe which affeſt his own mind.

SECTION

SECTION II.

Of the firſt and more general Applications of Moral Law.

THE applications of a phyſical principle are made, either to the formation of theories, and the explanation of phenomena; or to the production of effects, and the practice of arts.

Phyſical ſcience is fruitful of arts, or enables the perſon who is acquainted with the operative laws of nature, to direct its operations to his own purpoſe. Moral principle being a juſt conception or adequate expreſſion of what is good, is fruitful of wiſdom and proper conduct. Its firſt application is to form the temper, to correct falſe apprehenſions of things, to confirm the truth, to cultivate juſt affection, and to direct the energy of a ſtrenuous mind in external actions, and to induce and confirm all the habits of a virtuous life.

There is one point of view in which the ſciences, whether phyſical or moral, unite their effects. That point to which they ſeverally

verally tend, when phyfical fcience becomes comprehenfive of
the order of nature, or lays open the view to infinite goodnefs and
wifdom ; and moral fcience, abftracting from local forms and obfervances, becomes in the mind a principle of extenfive benevolence,
by which the individual ftates himfelf as a part in the order of
nature, and entirely devoted to the will of its Author.

In thefe points of view, fcience may be confidered as the higheft attainment of created intelligence, and its neareft approach
to a communication with the fupreme Creator ; an approach, in
which, through the medium of knowledge, it receives an im-
preffion, and contemplates a form of beauty, the moft likely to
command its affections.

The diftinctions, which we have been confidering, of *enjoy-
ment* and *fuffering*, of *excellence* and *defect*, of *happinefs* and *mifery*,
fubfift in the mind, and may be conceived as properties of mind,
abftracted from any external effect or appearance whatever.

At the fame time, as every property of the human mind is a
modification of an active animal, as well as of an intelligent being,
as it is a meafure of power, or a direction of will, forming the e-
nergy of a nature fo mixed, and of which the effects muft appear
wherever the living nature is deftined to range or to ply its exertions, we cannot fuppofe the mind to poffefs any quality, whether
of excellence or defect, that is not attended with a fuitable confequence in the tranfactions of life.

Hence it is, that the animal and phyfical actions of men prefent an object of moral difcernment, and furnifh fubjects of commendation and cenfure, more obvious to moft men than even the

VOL. II. P qualities

qualities of mind itſelf, when they attempt to conceive ſuch qualities apart from external expreſſions or effects : And, as men, in ſome inſtances, do not appear to be aſſured even of their own thoughts, until they have put them in words ; ſo they are, with much better reaſon, doubtful of what may be the qualifications of any other perſon, until he has given to his thoughts and diſpoſitions their effect in his conduct.

Virtue, therefore, in the mixed nature of man, is at once a condition of his mind, an aſpect and carriage of his perſon, and an ordinary ſeries of action, fitted to his ſituation, as the member of a community, in which the conduct of every particular perſon contributes its ſhare to the good or the evil incident to the whole.

So far the ſubject admits of a general ſtatement, in which there is no difficulty. In the more particular treatment of it, however, ſome difficulties have ariſen, which it may be proper to ſtate, before we enter on the detail of moral obligations and duties.

Theſe difficulties relate to the phenomenon of *moral approbation*, conſidered as a ſubject of theory ; or to the different opinions of men, on the ſubject of moral actions and duties, conſidered as a ſtandard of eſtimation for mankind.

Relating to theſe ſubjects, we may enquire, firſt of all, upon what principle men proceed, in eſtimating the morality of actions ? Next, Whence the difference of opinion, on the ſubject of moral duties ? Whence the real gradations of *merit* and *demerit ?* And, from the obſervations that may occur, endeavour to col-

I   lect

lect fome fundamental rule or canon of eftimation, refpecting the morality of external actions, and the propriety of manners, before we proceed to confider the variety of fanctions, under which fuch actions are required; or before we enter on the feparate departments of fcience, to which the ftudy of morality refers, under the titles of *jurifprudence*, *cafuiftry*, and *politics*.

SECTION

S E C T I O N   III.

*Of the Difficulty which has arisen in accounting for Moral Ap-
probation.*

IF, according to the refult of our enquiries on the fubject of
good and evil, what is required as the excellence or virtue of human nature, alfo conftitute happinefs ; and if vice, on the contrary, is to be dreaded as the conftituent of mifery; there cannot be any doubt of the choice to be made.

But virtue, even to thofe who are far from confidering it as
happinefs, is ftill matter of efteem and refpect; and vice, even
where the vicious are conceived to poffefs the good things of this
life, is reprobated and condemned : Infomuch, that virtue is approved even by thofe who depart from it; and vice is difapproved
even where it is embraced.

This fentiment, therefore, is of a peculiar nature, not a fpecimen
of mere defire and averfion, directed to a particular object ; but a
cenforial act in the mind of man, having cognizance of a *right* or

a

a *wrong* in the meafure or tendency of his own defires or averfions, even when they have moft entirely determined his will.

Doctor Clarke, and fome others, confidering virtue as the fitnefs of man's character and practice to his own frame, and to his
place in the fyftem of nature ; and, confidering reafon or underftanding itfelf as competent to obferve the fitnefs of things, have
affumed human reafon as the principle of moral difcernment.

This fyftem is nearly the fame with that which, making virtue to confift in the conformity of will to truth, makes reafon alfo the arbiter of right and wrong, as of truth and error.

But thefe fyftems have been rejected, as unfit to explain the
phenomenon of moral approbation; which, being itfelf an affection or fentiment of the mind, muft be derived from a principle
to be fought for among the confiderations that influence the will,
not among the perceptions of mere intelligence, which go no farther than to remark the exiftence of things.

Upon this ground, men of fpeculation have had recourfe to various confiderations of *utility*, private or public ; of *fympathy*, and
of *moral fenfe*; to account for the approbation or difapprobation
of actions which they themfelves or others perform.

The inveftigation and application of any one of thefe principles, joined to the refutation of others, has amounted to treatifes,
and led to difcuffions of great length. But the utmoft that can
be done in this place and in a mere fummary ftate of fo much argument, is to enumerate a few of the principal theories ; and endeavour

deavour to extricate the mind from the perplexity, which so many discordant accounts of the same subject may occasion.

In the mean time, the *Regulæ Philosophandi*, or canons of reason, as they are prescribed in other examples of physical investigation, must be sustained in this *.

I. *We are not to assign, as the cause of any appearance, what is not itself known as a fact in nature.*

Upon this principle, we reject *hypothesis*, or the mere *supposition* of a cause, of whose existence we have not any previous knowledge; as the vortex of Des Cartes is rejected in accounting for the planetary revolutions.

On this rule, it is probable that none of our theorists will trespass; for, although some have proposed to account for intelligence itself on the supposition of some occult configuration or motion of material atoms, constituting reflection and thought; yet, as the mind, when so constituted, ever acts upon some consideration known to itself, it is impossible to think of explaining an act of the mind, in any particular instance, without recurring to some one or other of the considerations, on which the mind is generally known to proceed.

II *We are not to deduce effects from causes, which, though real, are unfit to produce the effect.*

In the *connection of cause and effect*, in contradistinction to a mere fortuitous contiguity of circumstances, there is supposed a
continual

---

* Vide Newtoni Principia, lib. iii. ab initio.

continual or infeparable accompanyment of one with the o-
ther. Wherever the caufe exifts, there muft the effect exift alfo.
And the converfe. They are ever to be found together, and in
the fame proportions.

Upon thefe principles, actual *utility*, whether private or public, will not account for the phenomenon of moral approbation.

For, apart at leaft from any *private utility*, it muft be acknowledged that men approve of virtue, as it was exhibited in fcenes
long fince paft, and on occafions in which they could not poffibly
have any private or interefted concern.

The fentiment of approbation, therefore, is certainly not proportioned to the private benefit actually received from the action
approved, by the perfon who approves.

Utility, as it concerns mankind indifcriminately, and without
any limitation of perfons and times, is certainly more likely to
account for this phenomenon.

Virtue is no doubt of a nature to be ufeful to mankind; but if,
under the title of *utility*, as is probable, we refer to the external
effects of virtue, we fhall not find moral approbation keep pace
with the actual meafure of benefit mankind received from this or
any other caufe.

There are many examples of great utility, in which no fubject
of moral approbation is conceived. Land is fertile; a tree is
fruitful; a fteer performs much ufeful labour; yet, in thefe
there is no fubject of moral efteem. The fuppofed caufe, contrary

trary to rule, is found to exift in many fuch inftances, without producing the effect it is brought to explain.

In anfwer to this objection, it ufed to be admitted, by the author of this fyftem, " that moral approbation does not extend to " matters of mere phyfical utility ; or is limited to mind, and its " active exertions." This limitation, accordingly, may be admitted : But actual utility, even in affections of mind, does not always amount to a fubject of moral approbation. What more ufeful in nature, than the difpofition of every man to preferve himfelf ; for, on this the fafety of the whole depends: Yet its moft reafonable effects are merely tolerated, feldom applauded as virtue, and often reprobated as felfifhnefs and vice.

This effect, alfo, of moral approbation is fometimes found without the actual utility which is fuppofed to be its caufe.

The mere attempts of a virtuous man to ferve his friend, or his country, is an object of moral efteem ; not only where he may have failed in his purpofe, but even where the event may have been calamitous to himfelf, or to others. The perfon, who dies with his friend, in attempting to fave him ; the perfon who finks under the ruins of his country, in ftriving to preferve it ; is no lefs an object of moral approbation, than the moft fuccefsful adventurer in either caufe. And, if fuccefs, for the moft part, give luftre to enterprize, the tender melancholy that arifes from a tragic event, is well known alfo to enforce the love of virtue, without regard to utility, of which the idea is excluded by the want of fuccefs.

It appears plain from thefe inftances, that moral approbation,

3   though

though limited to the exertions of mind, yet does not accompany every useful exertion; nor even where it applies, does it require any actually useful effect. The will alone is sufficient to procure it: This, in other words, is to admit that benevolence, not actual utility, is the object of moral approbation: And, concerning this, most parties may be agreed. Even Mr Hutchison, who affumed a moral fenfe, as being a fpecific faculty, required to diftinguifh between moral good and evil, confidered *benevolence*, neverthelefs, as the effence of moral good, or that quality which mankind, by their fenfe of right and wrong, are enabled to diftinguifh as good.

The benevolent will concur, one with another, in every thing that is for the benefit of mankind ; but, in accounting for moral approbation, we muft ftill return to the confideration of that peculiar fentiment of eftimation, of which virtue is the object. And the whole muft end in a confeffion, that virtue, of which a principal part is benevolence, is eftimable in itfelf, not merely as the means of obtaining any other end.

If, in the term *utility*, we include whatever is beneficial, or tends to the benefit of mankind, then is virtue itfelf, or its conftituents of *wifdom, goodnefs, temperance,* and *fortitude,* the greateft good of which human nature is fufceptible: And we only rifk mifleading the mind from its principal object, by fubftituting utility for the more proper expreffion of a bleffing important to the perfon whofe character it is, more than even to thofe on whom any of its external effects are beftowed.

It were prepofterous to exprefs the value of happinefs, by calling

VOL. II.   Q   ling

ling it ufeful. Or, if a perfon who is happy in himfelf be thereby difpofed to be ufeful to others, it were prepofterous to fay, that the happinefs of one perfon is valuable only fo far as it is ufeful to another.

Virtue is, no doubt, fupremely ufeful, even in the ordinary fenfe of this term. Juftice, liberality, and charity, appear in acts of beneficence; and render thofe who are inclined to prac- tife them, the guardians and friends of their fellow creatures. Even what we term acts of prudence, fortitude, or temperance, though feeming to terminate in the welfare of the perfon acting, are in fact prefervatives of good order, and contribute to the wel- fare of mankind. The benevolent man is the more ferviceable to his fellow creatures, that he is in himfelf prudent, fober, and in- trepid. The oppofite vices are deftructive, pernicious, or un- ferviceable.

This tendency of virtue has been fet forth in colours of glow- ing and fuperior eloquence *.

The external effects of virtue are acknowledged; but we can- not fuppofe that the fentiment of love, or refpect, of which virtue is the object, is refolveable into a mere confideration of conveni- ence or profit; nor can we overlook its value in conftituting the worth and felicity of thofe by whom it is poffeffed, for the fake of a convenience it may procure to others, who, without any merit of their own, may wifh to derive benefit from the external effects of merit in other men.

Upon

* See Hume's Moral Effays.

Upon this principle of utility, the diftinction of right and wrong appears to be refolved into a mere difference of tendency, or external effect in the actions of men. In another ingenious attempt to explain the fame phenomenon, the approbation of virtue is refolved into *fympathy*, or what may, for ought we know, be a kind of accidental humour in thofe who approve or condemn a fuppofed virtuous or vicious action.

Sympathy, in common language, is limited to *commiferation* or *pity*; but, has of late, by men of fpeculation, been extended to fentiments of *congratulation* alfo. It may be fuppofed either merely inftinctive, and a contagion of fentiment, as when without any knowledge of a caufe, we laugh with thofe who laugh; become gay with the joyful; or fad with the melancholy: Or it may be fuppofed to proceed from a conception of the occafion or caufe, whether joyful, provoking, or melancholy, that is the motive of action, or object of paffion. And it appears to be in this laft fenfe, that *fympathy is* affumed as the principle of moral approbation.

When the obferver feels, in a certain degree, the paffion or motive by which another is actuated, upon a fuppofition that the fame thing had happened to himfelf; this participation of fentiment is fuppofed to conftitute approbation. Thus, when a perfon complains or exults, if the obferver, upon a ftate of the cafe, partake in his forrow or his joy, it is faid, that *he cannot but approve of it.*

If the joy or grief exceed what the obferver *can go along with*, it is condemned as weaknefs or levity: if it fall fhort of what the obferver is difpofed to feel, it is condemned as infenfibility: if

nearly

nearly what he himself would feel in a fimilar cafe, it is efteemed or refpected as proper ; and fo on of every other paffion or fentiment appearing in the conduct of human life.

It may be difficult, in this account of the matter, to fix where the moral quality refides ; whether in the perfon obferved, in the obferver, or in neither feparately, but in the mere concurrence of one with another.

This laft, indeed, or a mutual fympathy, may imply that the parties are fatisfied with one another ; but, in the fenfe of all mankind befides, their agreement may be wrong : And, if the action of one perfon need the fympathy of another to juftify it, we are ftill to enquire in what manner is that fympathy itfelf evinced to be right.

This theory proceeds upon an affumption, that to partake in any paffion or fentiment, or to be confcious that we ourfelves fhould, in like circumftances, be fo affected, is to approve of the motive to action, and to approve of its effects : But it is acknowledged, on all hands, that approbation or difapprobation is a fpecific fentiment, not a fpecies or degree of any other fentiment : That it concerns the right or wrong of other paffions, whether original or fympathetic, and therefore enabling the mind, on occafion, to pronounce of fympathy itfelf, whether it be proper or improper.

If, in judging of this theory, we recur to the maxims of reafon already cited *, we fhall find them violated in this, no lefs than

in

* Regulæ Philofophandi Newtoni.

in the affumption of utility, for a principle of moral approbation.
That is, the effect will be found without the fuppofed caufe, and the
caufe will be found without its fuppofed effect. In refpect to acts of
uncommon bravery, we admire the more for being confcious that
we ourfelves could not have done fo much. Although we are
confcious that, in extreme indigence, we ourfelves muft have afked for relief, yet we do not admire a beggar. Although we are
confcious that with money we ourfelves fhould have bought an
eftate, yet we do not admire the purchafer. Although we fym-
pathize very feelingly with the admirer of a fine woman, we do
not miftake his paffion for virtue, any more than we miftake for
generofity the choice made by him who bought an eftate. There
is fympathy, as well as utility, without approbation ; and there is
approbation without either ; for we fometimes have an idea of
what we ought to have done, or to have felt, as very different
from the part which we actually take in the feelings of other
men. And it is remarkable that fympathy fhould be then only
equivalent to approbation, when we fympathife with the benevolent, the difinterefted, the courageous, and the juft.

But, if it fhould be acknowledged, that, to partake in the fentiment of another is to approve, and not to partake is to difapprove
of his conduct, it remains, upon this fyftem, to be ftated, by what
fympathy it is that we judge of ourfelves.—

If, by the actual participation of others in our fentiments and
actions ;—it fhould follow, that, in actions concealed from the
world, there fhould be no confcience of right or wrong ; or that,
in actions fubmitted to vulgar judgement, we fhould be in great
danger of error ; the multitude is often ill informed, and otherwife ill qualified to judge of merit. And this indeed is fo far
acknowledged,

acknowledged, in forming the theory in queſtion, that virtue is not referred to the teſt of actual ſympathy, but to the teſt of a ſympathy, imagined and ſelected in the caſe of a well informed and impartial obſerver.

Here too there is a maſterly tone of expreſſion * ; and, if eloquence were the teſt of truth, no want of evidence to obtain belief: But, in this reference to a ſuppoſed well informed and impartial obſerver, there is an implied confeſſion, that there is ſome previous ſtandard of eſtimation, by which to ſelect the judge of our actions ; and this ſtandard, by which we are enabled to ſelect an impartial and well informed ſpectator, to whoſe judgement we refer, or by which we are enabled to judge of ſympathy itſelf, as well as of every other action or paſſion, is that principle of moral approbation, of which we are now in ſearch.

This is not merely a queſtion of fact, as in other examples of phyſical theory: For we do not enquire what men actually do in any number of inſtances ; but what they ought to do in every inſtance? what is the principle of moral diſcernment on which they may ſafely proceed, whether in judging of others, or in chuſing for themſelves ?

Sympathy is no doubt a part in the ſocial nature of man. Individuals mutually beſtow, and delight to receive it; but, like every other natural diſpoſition, it is ſuſceptible of abuſe, and by no means a ſafe or an adequate principle of eſtimation. As the preſumptuous appreciate others by their own ſtandard, the weak and dependent riſe or fall in their own eſteem, according to the value that is put upon them by others ; but neither one nor the other, ſurely, ſhould be ſet up as the models of perfection to mankind.

It

* Vide Smith's Theory of Moral Sentiments.

It is difficult to name the power by which man is enabled to
diftinguifh between right and wrong, without recurring to the ge-
neric appellation of fome of his other faculties, as *fenfe, perception,*
or *judgement*. This power has accordingly been termed a moral
fenfe, or a fenfe of moral good and evil ; and the name has led to an
hypothefis or fuppofition, that as nature, in the cafe of different a-
nimals, has fuperadded to the other principles of fenfitive life, fome
peculiar faculty of *feeing, fmell,* or *feeling,* as in the lynx's eye, the
hound's noftril, or the fpider's touch; as to other qualities of the
loadftone, are joined the magnetic polarity and the affinity to iron :
So, to the mind of man, over and above the powers cognitive and
active, the Maker has given a power judicative, refpecting the merit or demerit of character, and approving or difapproving even
the difpofitions, from which the moral conduct proceeds.

Lord Shaftefbury fometimes ufes the term moral fenfe, as expreffive of a confcious difcernment of moral good and evil, but
feems to refer to the fact merely without any thought of an hypothefis to account for the phenomenon of moral approbation.
It was enough, in his apprehenfion, that the diftinction of moral excellence is real, and that we are by our nature well qualified to perceive it. In this, alfo, the fects of antient philofophy
feem to have acquiefced, without requiring any other account of
the matter.

If it be underftood, therefore, that difficulties arifing on the
queftion of theory, relating to the explanation of the phenomenon of moral approbation, do not amount to any degree of un-
certainty in the fact ; and, if it be admitted that moral right
and wrong are of the moft ferious confequence to mankind ; the
faculty, by which we perceive the oppofite conditions of men in

3   this

this particular, may be known by any name that does not tend to confound the fubject with others of a different nature.

If *moral fenfe*, therefore, be no more than a figurative expreffion, by which to diftinguifh the difcernment of right and wrong, admitting this to be an ultimate fact in the conftitution of our nature; it may appear nugatory to difpute about words, or to require any other form of expreffion than is fit to point out the fact in queftion. And if this fact, though no way fufceptible of explanation or proof, being uniform to a great extent in the operations or nature, is itfelf a law, not a phenomenon; it may no doubt ferve as a principle of fcience, to account for appearances that refult from itfelf, and to direct the practice of arts throughout the departments in which it prevails.

Thus the laws of *motion, gravitation, cohefion, magnetifm, electricity, fluidity, elafticity*, and fo forth, which are not explicable upon any principle previoufly known in nature, are neverthelefs received as unqueftionable facts, and with great advantage purfued to their confequences in the order of things. In this purfuit they furnifh at once a fecure direction to the practice of arts, and the moft fatisfactory account of appearances in the terreftrial and folar fyftems.

Men of fpeculation were fometimes amufed with conjectures, refpecting the caufe of *gravitation*, and the intimate nature of other *phyfical laws*; but fcience made little progrefs, while thefe were confidered as phenomena to be explained, and not as principles of fcience applicable to explain their diverfified effects throughout the phyfical fyftem.

3   Such

Such, alfo, we may fuppofe to be the fate of theory, when employed to explain the law of eftimation in the mind of man. The exiftence of this law is known, as the exiftence of mind itfelf is known, without any thing previoufly underftood, from which to infer or explain it, or on which to reft our belief of its truth. Its applications, in our judgement of manners, are no lefs proper than the application of any phyfical law in accounting for its own fpecific appearances. They enable the moralift, in particular inftances, to afcertain what is good for mankind; and to form a regular fyftem of moral eftimation and precept, throughout all the fubdivifions of *law*, of *manners*, or political *inftitutions*.

We may, or may not, conceive the power of difcerning between excellence and defect, as a faculty inherent to intelligent being. To fuch being, indeed, it appears effential to be confcious of himfelf; and in his attainments, whether actually varied, or only conceived to be variable, it may be effential that he confider unequal degrees of *excellence* and *defect*, as meafures of the *good* or the *evil* of which he himfelf is fufceptible. Created intelligence may advance in the ufe of this difcerning faculty, and have a continued approach to the model of divine wifdom; a termination from which its diftance may diminifh, but at which it never can arrive.

The effence of almighty God we muft conceive to be moft *fimple ;* being that which neceffarily exifts from eternity. Of his fupreme intelligence, we have full evidence in the fyftem of nature ; and of his diftinguifhing the oppofite conditions of moral good and evil, there is equally irrefiftible proof.

The diftinction of excellence and defect originates in the unequal conditions of mind, and the difcernment of fuch condition is not only peculiar, but neceffary alfo to the courfe which created beings of this order are deftined to run. Hunger and thirft, or any other incitement to felf prefervation, is not more effential to the animal frame, than the preference of what is perfect, to what is defective, is to the conftitution of mind : It is a prefervative of reafon, a main fpring of exertion, and a princple of advancement, in the track of intelligent nature.

Hence it is that numbers of men, who are far from conceiving virtue as the conftituent of happinefs, neverthelefs confider it as the conftituent of excellence and perfection, which they behold with refpect and efteem.

Man alone in this animal kingdom, for ought we know, apprehends the gradation of excellence in the fcale of being; and, though all men are agreed upon the reality of a comparative eminence, in the afcending fteps of this fcale, it may be difficult to affign the principle of eftimation, fo as to juftify the preference which is given to one order of being above another. Mr Buffon afcribes this preference to the greater number of relations, which certain orders of being bear to the fyftem of nature around them *. " In the multitude of things
" prefented

---

* Dans la foule d' objets que nous prefente ce vafte globe dont nous venons de faire la defcription, dans le nombre infini des differentes productions, dont fa furface eft couverte et peuplie, les animaux tiennent le premier rang, tant par la conformité qu' ils ont avec nous, que par la fuperiorité que nous leur connoiffons fur les etres vegitans ou inanimes. Les animaux ont par leurs fens, par leur forme, par leur movement, beaucoup plus de rapports avec les chofes que les environnent, que n' en ont les vegetaux ; ceux-ci par leur developpement et par leur differentes parties, ont auffi une plus grand nombre de rapports avec les objets exterieurs, que n' en ont les mineraux ou les pierres, que n' ont aucune forte de vie ou de movement, et c'eft par ce plus grand nombre de rapports que l' animal eft reellement au deffus du vegetal, et le
vegetal

" prefented on this globe ; in the infinite number of different
" productions, with which its furface is covered or peopled, the
" animals," he obferves, " occupy the firft or the higheft rank,
" whether by their refemblance to us, or by the fuperiority
" which we perceive in them, to the vegetable or inanimate na-
" tures. The animals, by their make and by their fenfitive and
" moving powers, have many more relations to the fubjects a-
" round. than the vegetables have. Thefe, in their turn, by the
" unfolding of their parts ; by their figure, their organization,
" and growth, have many more relations than the minerals, or
" any mere lifelefs mafs of matter. And it is by virtue of this
" greater number of relations, that the animal is fuperior to the
" vegetable ; and the vegetable is fuperior the mineral. Even we
" ourfelves, confidered in refpect to the material part of our
" frame, are not otherwife fuperior to the animals, than by a
" few relations more, fuch as accrue to us from the ufe of the
" hand and the tongue ; and, though all the works of God are
" in themfelves equally perfect, yet, in our way of conceiving
" them, the animal is moft compleat ; and man the mafter-piece
" of all."

This is, perhaps, the firft attempt that ever was made to give
a reafon why animals are reckoned of a higher order than plants,
and thefe of a higher order than minerals or unorganized matter
of any fort. And though no one difputes this order of things, yet
this attempt to explain it will fcarcely appear fatisfactory. Many
will

vegetal au deffus du mineral. Nous meme, a ne confiderer que la partie materielle
de notre etre, nous ne fommes audeffus des animaux que par quelques rapports de plus,
tels que ceux que nous donnent la langue et la main ; et quoique les ouvrages du
Createur font en eux-memes tous egalement parfaits, l' animal eft, felon notre façon d'
apercevoir, l'ouvrage le plus complet de la nature, e l'homme en eft le chef d' ouvre.

will be ready to afk, why eftimation fhould keep pace with the number of relations, which a fubject bears to other parts of the world around. One relation, compleatly and beneficently adjuft-ed, may be preferable to many. And, if a beneficent purpofe can be obtained by one relation, however fimple, the multipli-cation muft appear rather a defect than a beauty. It appears, indeed, that where a number and variety of expedients or rela-tions are wanting to obtain a purpofe, the difpofition and ability to combine fuch a variety to one common beneficent end, is a great perfection in the power by whom fuch arrangement is made. When man has formed to himfelf any number of relations to the fubjects around him, fuch as he bears to the field he has cultiva-ted, the city he has built, the work of any kind he has performed, the law or inftitution he has adopted; in fuch relations, indeed, the fuperiority of his own nature appears : But, in what his Maker has done for him, or for the other animals ; in what is done for plants and minerals, it is the majefty of God that we revere ; and the relations of things merely inanimate ferve only as the fteps, by which we are led to contemplate the wifdom and goodnefs of the firft caufe,

In this fenfe, we already obferved, beauty and excellence are afcribed to material fubjects. And the inequality of rank which appears fo real in the fyftem of things, is a mere gradation of the luftre or effect, with which intelligence, or its principal features of goodnefs and wifdom, are made to appear in the different orders of being. The eloquent naturalift, cited above, feems to drop his arithmetic of relations, when he confiders the pre-eminence of intelligent forms : in the fyftem of na-ture. For he applies it only to the material part of man ; and, in reality, mere number of relations could ill account for the fu-periority of any nature whatever ; as the relation between any

3   two

two fpecies of being muft be mutual, and in point of number at leaft the fame ; for fo many relations as man has to the fyftem of nature around him fo many precifely muft the fyftem of nature have to him. But no one ever queftioned the pre-eminence of intelligent being; ever required an account to be given of it ; or defired to know by what faculty it is perceived. Dimenfions are meafured by fome ftandard quantity of the fame dimenfion ; length, by fome ftandard meafure of length ; and folid content, by fome ftandard meafure of folid dimenfion ; and why not intelligence, alfo, by fome ftandard conception of intelligent nature. The degrees to be eftimated confift in variable meafures of wifdom and goodnefs ; and whoever has an idea of thefe, will judge accordingly of the fpecimens that approach to the ftandard, or of the defects that come fhort of it.

Some who have carried the analogy of animal fenfe and perception into this fubject, have ftarted a queftion, whether moral excellence be not a fecondary quality; that is, like the perception of fmell, found, or tafte, if it may not proceed from a caufe in nature very different from that we conceive * ? But in the efteem of wifdom and goodnefs, there is not any danger that the quality we conceive is different from the quality that exifts, as our conception of found is different from a tremor in the particles of air: for it is the very exifting thing itfelf of which we have a conception, taken indeed from feeble, occafional, and paffing fpecimens, but eafily abftracted by us from their defects and imperfections, to ferve as a ftandard of eftimation for what we propofe as the model of excellence, wherever our judgement applies or wherever a choice is to be made.

If

* Vide Lord Kames' Moral Effays.

If we are afked, therefore, what is the principle of moral approbation in the human mind, we may anfwer, It is the *Idea* of *perfection* or excellence, which the intelligent and affociated being forms to himfelf; and to which he refers in every fentiment of efteem or contempt, and in every expreffion of commendation or cenfure.

Nay, but mankind are not agreed on this fubject; they differ no lefs in what they admire, than in what they enjoy. The idea of pefection no doubt may be affociated with fubjects divefted of merit : But notwithftanding the effect of fuch affociation in warping the judgement, virtue is approved as the fpecific perfection or excellence of man's nature ; and as no one ever inquired why perfection fhould be efteemed ; it is difficult to conceive why they fhould look for any other account of moral approbation than this.

From the predilections of birth and fortune, few, if any, are altogether blind to the diftinctions of wifdom and folly, of benevolence and malice, of fobriety and debauchery, of courage and cowardice. And if thefe characters of mind could be perceived without the intervention of external figns; the difference of judgement on the fubjects of moral good and evil would, in a great meafure difappear ; or there would not be fo much diverfity of opinion as we obferve amongft men, concerning the forms or defcription of virtue. But the external actions which may refult from any given difpofition of mind being different in different inftances, may occafion a difference of judgement, or a variety of cuftom and manners ; and fuggeft the neceffity of a principle or ftandard of eftimation, on which their rate of merit or demerit may be fafely eftablifhed. We accordingly proceed to the confideration of thefe particulars.

3   SECTION

SECTION IV.

*Of the Difficulty of reconciling the different Judgements of Men relat-
ing to the Morality of External Actions.*

WHEN the reality of any moral diftinction is queftioned, we naturally refer to the general fenfe of mankind on the fubject. To give this evidence, however, its full effect, in fupporting the reality in queftion, it is fuppofed, that mankind ought to be una-nimous in their verdict, and agree, not only in admitting, that there is a diftinction, but agree alfo in the defcription of fubjects, or in the choice of particulars, to be ranged under the oppofite predicaments of moral good and moral evil.

PART II.
CHAP. I.
SECT.IV.

If men, it may be alleged, have a difpofition to felect objects of commmendation and cenfure, and yet are not agreed in their choice, we muft fuppofe their difference of judgement to arife, not from a want of difpofition in them to find out the truth, but from the want of a fufficient difference in the nature of things to lead or to eftablifh their judgement.

Sceptics

Sceptics, accordingly, in order to repel the evidence of reality in matters of moral diſtinction, refer to the contradictory notions of mankind, on the ſubject of manners.

" Mankind," they obſerve, " blame in one perſon, and in one
" caſe, what they applaud in another. Thus, to deceive or to
" kill is in one inſtance condemned, in another is applauded or
" permitted. What is held forth as a ſubject of praiſe in one age
" or country, is overlooked or neglected in another. What, in
" one age or nation, is permitted as allowable or innocent, in an-
" other is reprobated and abhorred, under ſome denomination
" of impiety, inceſt, or blaſphemy *.

" Certain forms of behaviour, forms of expreſſion or geſture,
" are in one country, or amongſt one ſet of men, required to
" good manners, or received with complacency ; whilſt they are
" conſidered as an unpardonable injury or inſult in other na-
" tions, or in other companies.

" In one nation, we are told, it is reckoned an act of filial piety
" for a ſon to kill his ſuperannuated parent ; in other countries,
" this, though we ſhould ſuppoſe it to be done with conſent of the
" perſon ſuffering, would be detected as a moſt horrid inſtance
" of murder and parricide.

" The definitions of crimes vary in the laws of different coun-
" tries : Inſomuch, that what is deſtined to ſevere puniſhment in
                                                    " one

* Profana illic omnia, quæ apud nos ſacra ; rurſum conceſſa apud illos, quæ nobis inceſta.

Tacitus de Judæis, Hiſt. lib. v. c. 4.

" one country, is fuffered, in another, to efcape with impunity, even
" without cenfure. Thus, theft, which was punifhed at Athens,
" was encouraged in Sparta.

" All men are loud in commendations of virtue; but obferve
" their applications of this term, how different in the detail of
" particulars? Among the antient Romans it meant valour a-
" lone. Among the Jews it meant zeal for their own inftitutions,
" and animofity to the reft of mankind. Among houfewives it
" means œconomy and notable induftry In Italy it means a
" tafte for antiquities, and curiofities of nature or art."

From the whole of thefe inftances it is propofed to infer, that
there is not any certain rule of approbation or difapprobation refpecting the manners or behaviour of men. And notwithftanding the effential felicity and merit of wifdom and goodnefs as
qualities of intelligent being, it muft be allowed to follow from
fuch varieties of apprehenfion, refpecting the morality of external
action, that the diftinction of right and wrong cannot be taken
from the mere phyfical action itfelf, or that mere external movements of the body have not the fame power to command our
moral feelings, as they have to command our perception of their
form and phyfical effect.

When the fhutters of a window are opened, and the light is
admitted, every object in the room is illuminated; vifion is diftinct to all who have organs of fight, and the perceptions of magnitude, figure, and colour are the fame to every one prefent.
When certain tremors are produced in the air, every ear is ftruck
with the fenfation of found; and however one perfon may differ
from another in his conjectures refpecting its caufe, or even re-

Vol. II. S fpecting

specting the musical effect, the tone produced is the same to every one by whom it is heard.

The same thing may be said with relation to the form and consequence of any action or movement of the body. All who are present perceive the same physical operation, and the same continuance or change of condition in the subject affected by such operation. A life may be taken away or preserved in their sight, and there is no difference of perception respecting the physical cause or the physical consequence. May we not presume, therefore, that if moral right and wrong were equally apart in the form of an action, as is the physical description of it, the perceptions of men in this respect also would be equally uniform.

The contrary, however, is observed to be true. The same physical action in one instance is applauded as a virtue, in another instance is reprobated as a crime; or rather, to speak with more propriety, where the physical action is the same, the moral action is altogether different; and is an object of approbation or disapprobation, corresponding to that difference of the moral quality.

For an example, in which the physical action may, in repeated instances, continue the same, while the moral action is extremely different; we may suppose the death of a man, effected with a sword, in the manner in which executions in some countries are performed; in which assassinations are committed; and battles are fought. In all these instances the physical action may be precisely the same, and every spectator have the same perception of it; but the moral action may be, and frequently is, extremely different.

To

To devife the death of a man is criminal in the *robber*, who, to ftrip the traveller of his property, attacks him on the high way. It is criminal in the *affaffin*, who, from jealoufy, revenge or malice prepenfe in any other form, lays a fnare for the life of his neighbour. But in a perfon who *defends* himfelf, in a *judge* who has condemned a criminal, or in the officer who conducts the execution of a *juft fentence*, the fame phyfical action may be *innocent* ; may be the difcharge of a *duty*, or an act of *public juftice*. In a foldier, who, at the hazard of his own life, kills the enemy of his country, the material effect produced is precifely the fame, with that which is criminal in the affaffin or in the robber. But the moral action in thefe inftances is extremely different: In the firft it is efteemed as of the *higheft merit*, in the others it is condemned as of the moft *atrocious guilt*.

Under this feeming difference of judgement refpecting the fame action, there is actually no more difference refpecting the moral apprehenfion than there is refpecting the phyfical effect. While every one perceives that a man is killed, every one perceives alfo that the affaffin or the robber did wrong in killing him ; that the foldier acting in defence of his country, or the officer of juftice in execution of a legal fentence, did right. In the affaffin or robber this phyfical act was an act of malice or rapacity ; in the judge, magiftrate, or foldier, it was an act of public juftice or heroic valour : And mankind, we may repeat, are as little at variance with refpect to the moral quality of the action in either cafe, as they are with refpect to the mere form or defcription of the phyfical operation.

We are familiar with this diftinction between the phyfical and

the

the moral action, under a variation of circumstances which diverfify the cafe : And though the difference of judgement is more ftriking in fuch inftances than it is in any other ; yet no one thinks himfelf authorifed from thence to queftion the reality of moral diftinctions. There are indeed no fpecimens of moral good and evil more ftriking than thofe which are prefented by the fame phyfical action, performed by different perfons and in different circumftances; from the motives of benevolence and duty, on the one hand, or of malice and depravity on the other.

Every one is aware of the different judgements to be given where the cafes are different; and to give the variety of judgement an appearance of contradiction in the eftimate of moral good and evil, we muft have recourfe to examples lefs familiar and in which we are lefs qualified to diftinguifh the moral from the phyfical qualities of an action. We are at a lofs, for inftance, when we are told, that what is punifhed as a crime in one country is rewarded or commended as a duty in another ; becaufe we are not qualified to perceive in what manner the moral action, under a different fet of manners from our own, fhould be differently *underftood*, or in what manner the fame moral action fhould refult from phyfical performances extremely different.

This defect, however, may be eafily fupplied, if we confider, firft of all, that men have different opinions refpecting external objects, and in one country value that as an honour or a benefit, which in another is rejected as pernicious, or as an infult : Farther, that many of the actions of men are confidered more as *expreffions* of what they mean or intend, than as operations materially beneficial or hurtful. In the firft inftance, men proceed up-

I

on

on different notions of what is beneficial or hurtful. In the o-
ther they exprefs or interpret their intentions differently.

In fome countries honour is affociated with fuffering, and it is
reckoned a favour to kill, rather with circumftances of torture
than otherwife. This is confirmed in our account of the manners
of fome American nations; and in the fortitude with which an In-
dian matron fubmits to extreme fuffering by fire on the funeral
pile of her deceafed hufband. She courts the flames, with a zeal
and enthufiafm more ardent than that with which fhe reforts to
the bridal bed, or fhould mount the throne of ftate in a terreftrial kingdom. Whatever conceptions mankind may have formed of external objects and circumftances, as matters of defire or
averfion, it is natural for the benevolent to do what he himfelf
and the world around him conceive as a benefit, and to avoid
doing to others what they, or he himfelf, conceives as harm or
an infult: And as it is a maxim in law " Volenti non fit injuria";
fo it is naturally apprehended, under a variety of opinions refpecting external objects, that it is beneficent to treat every perfon in the manner which he himfelf conceives to be beneficial or
kind.

The fafety and the juftice of this maxim, refpecting matters of
a certain confequence to the welfare of mankind, may no doubt
be queftioned; and errors of choice, where they do not proceed
from malice may be imputed to folly; but the rule that every one is
to be ferved or obliged in his own way, ought not to be queftioned refpecting matters of indifference, or of fmall moment. Thefe are varioufly employed by nations, as the figns or expreffions of good
or ill difpofition; in the fame manner as, in the ufe of language,
words,

words, or articulate founds, are adopted as the figns or expreffions of meaning, intention, or will.

Of this fort, no doubt, is much of the form and ceremonial of common life. It is the form of refpect in Europe to uncover the head: In Japan, we are told, the correfponding form is to drop the flipper, or to uncover the foot. The phyfical action in thefe inftances is different, but the moral action is the fame. It is an act of attention and refpect; difpofitions equally acceptable, whether expreffed in words, geftures, or figns of any other fort.

Perfons, unacquainted with any language but their own, are apt to think the words they ufe. natural and fixt expreffions of things; while the words of a different language they confider as mere jargon, or the refult of caprice. In the fame manner, forms of behaviour, different from their own, appear offenfive and irrational, or a perverfe fubftitution of abfurd for reafonable manners.

To the ignorant or to the proud, who confider their own cuftoms as a ftandard for mankind, every deviation from that ftandard is confidered, not as the ufe of a different language and form of expreffion, but as a defect of reafon, and a deviation from propriety and correctnefs of manners.

Among the varieties of this fort we find actions, geftures, and forms of expreffion, in their own nature indifferent, entered into the code of civil or religious duties, and enforced under the ftrongeft fanctions of public cenfure or efteem, or under the ftrongeft denunciations of divine indignation or favour.

I   Numberlefs

Numberlefs ceremonies and obfervances are adopted in the ritual of different fects, for the fame reafon that words are adopted in the vocabulary of different languages, though with a different effect on the minds of ordinary men.

In religion, the rite is fuppofed to be prefcribed by the fame authority to which the forms of devotion are addreffed. The neglect of it is fuppofed to conftitute offence before that tribunal whofe condemnation is fatal. The fubftitution of any other rite is fuppofed to be profane, or an unpardonable infult to the object of worfhip. Under thefe apprehenfions, arbitrary figns of devotion are fuppofed effential to religion ; and deviations from the eftablifhed practice, or any variation in the ufe of fuch figns, is purfued with that vengeance which the zealot thinks neceffary to recommend him to God.

In many examples of this fort ; as in the ufe of different languages, the people have not a different meaning, but merely a difference of the founds in which their meaning is expreffed ; fo in the rites of devotion or worfhip, they admit a variety, not of the fentiment but of the external performance, which they employ as a fign or expreffion. And if in the different forms and ceremonies, which they practife, in their own nature indifferent or innocent, they equally mean to acknowledge and to adore the intelligent power and moral government of God ; the zeal with which they condemn and perfecute one another, on account of fuch difference of forms and ceremonies, is no way more rational, than it would be to fofter national animofity on the fcore of a different language or accent of fpeech.

This

This ufe of external action, as a fign for the purpofe of mere expreffion, is not confined to obfervances in their own nature altogether indifferent : Men freely incur phyfical inconvenience for the fake of fuppofed moral good ; and actions, in their phyfical tendency actually pernicious or ufeful, are often more confidered in refpect to the meaning and intention of thofe who perform them, than in refpect to the actual benefit or harm, which they are fuppofed to produce. A kind intention, made known in any trivial matter, operates more powerfully on the affections, than gifts of the greateft moment, beftowed in a manner lefs gracious, or lefs expreffive of kindnefs.

Injuries are not always meafured by the actual harm which is done, nor malicious intention inferred in the higheft degree, from the nature of the weapon with which a perfon is affaulted. A gentleman in modern Europe, as we have formerly obferved, is more offended with the ftroke or threat of a ftick, than with the wound of a fword.

Thefe are no more than inftances of the power of opinion, and habits of thinking, by which things, in their own nature agreeable or difagreeable, are affociated in the fame conception with feelings and qualities of the mind with which they have not any neceffary or original connection.

From the whole of thefe obfervations, then, we may conclude, that, without any variation in the ideas of *excellence* and defect, men may vary in their judgement of external actions. A different perfon, or the fame perfon in different circumftances, may act differently, and in this there is nothing to unfettle the judgement

ment of moral *right* and *wrong*. Different opinions relating to external effects, whether fuppofed beneficial or hurtful, may lead men, with the fame candid or malicious intention, to act and to judge very differently. Any action, that is confidered merely or chiefly as an expreffion of will or meaning, may be differently underftood in the form of different countries; and in none of thefe inftances is there implied any difference of apprehenfion relating to the intimate nature of moral *good* and *evil*. The firft may be termed a difference of the *cafe*; the fecond a difference of *opinion*; and the third a *difference* of *interpretation*.

What is obferved of a difference in the laws of different countries, or in the terms of a different language, will be equally found not to affect the original or the effential diftinction of moral right and wrong.

We are not to expect, that the laws of any country are to be framed as fo many leffons of morality, to inftruct the citizen how he may act the part of a virtuous man. Laws, whether civil or political, are expedients of policy to adjuft the pretenfions of parties, and to fecure the peace of fociety. The expedient is accommodated to fpecial circumftances, and calculated to reprefs the fpecific diforders peculiarly incident to particular fituations.

The higher duties of morality, beneficence, and fortitude can feldom if ever be made the fubject of law. The vileft of moral depravities, envy, and malice, can only be reftrained from a few of their overt or moft flagrant effects. The law muft be contented to reftrain fuch open and flagrant diforders; and, where the people are prone to any particular fpecies of irregularity, the law may be

VOL. II.   T   fpecially

fpecially directed to reform it, or even with greater feverity punifh, the firft approach to fuch irregularities, and treat fuch approaches as a greater crime than even the perpetration of greater
evils, to which the people are lefs difpofed, and from which the
public therefore has lefs to apprehend.

In fome of the fmaller ftates of Italy, where family feuds and
quarrels fo often prevailed, it was made capital, we are told, to
fhed a fingle drop of blood in the ftreets. Where frauds committed on the revenue are more frequent, and more to be apprehended than private robberies, the law naturally directs its
feverity to the quarter from which the public intereft is moft
deeply annoyed. And its enactments are to be confidered, not
as inftructions of morality, but as the convention of parties particularly fituated, and mutually engaged to fupport the caufe of
a community, depending on circumftances peculiar to their own
fituation.

If the law, in this manner is to be confidered as a local expedient provided for the welfare and peace of communities ; the
language of the people, we may believe, is not always calculated
to exprefs the mere abftract diftinctions of right and wrong ; but
to difcriminate virtue and vice under fuch diverfities of external
form, as they moft frequently take in particular circumftances,
and under fpecific fyftems of manners. Fortitude is made to exprefs not mere ftrength of mind in the abftract ; but has a reference, at the fame time, to the particular and more ordinary form
in which there is occafion to exercife this virtue ; whether in heroic patience or military valour. Goodnefs is not employed to
exprefs benevolence in the abftract, but has a reference to the form
in which there is the moft frequent occafion to practife beneficence,

3   whether

whether in charity to the poor, and in relieving the diftreffed; or in acts of public fervice, and private humanity or candour.

In every language there is a multiplicity of terms in which general praife and blame are expreffed ; but of fuch terms it is obferved, that no two are fynonymous. There is implied in every term of praife a complication of circumftances. In fome principal parts of the combination the terms agree, but in fome other part, perhaps, in fome minute circumftance of the occafion on which the good qualities are difplayed, or of the effect they produce, the meaning of the term is, in fome degree, diverfified, fo that any one of the terms fo diftinguifhed cannot, with propriety, be fubftituted one for another. Honefty cannot be fubftituted for probity, however nearly approaching in their meaning ; nor is goodnefs with propriety fubftituted for either.

In the general appellation of a good man, befide the more important conditions of humanity, faithfulnefs, and beneficence, which recommend one man to another, there is, in particular fituations, fome reference to particular circumftances, to which perfons in thofe fituations have peculiar occafion to attend ; as, among merchants, the qualities of punctuality and regard to credit, which mutually recommend the parties in their dealings with one another ; in literary focieties, learning and genius ; in national councils, and public affemblies, mafterly judgement, and powerful expreffion ; in warlike nations, manhood and military valour ; and men, in all thefe different inftances, beftow the general term of praife, with a particular implication of the circumftance peculiarly required in their own condition.

Words derived from the fame ftock, and paffing into different

T 2   rent

rent languages, thus affume, in fome particular refpects, a diffe-rent meaning in the application made of them by different na-tions. As from the *honeftum* of the Romans, is derived the *honefty* of the Englifh, and the *honetteté* of the French ; but who-ever fhould tranflate the one into the other, would lofe the mean-ing of his original, and fubftitute different circumftances of com-mendation, in paffing from one language to another ; not be-caufe thefe nations have different ideas of what is commendable ; but becaufe they have come to exprefs different articles of com-mendation in a term of the fame origin.

What is commended by one nation in any given term of praife, is commended by another in a different one ; and they difagree in the ufe of words, not in conceiving the diftinctions of right and wrong ; for each is ready to acknowledge the value of what the other commends, as foon as he underftands the mean-ing of the word in which it is commended.

SECTION V.

Of the Fundamental Rules of Morality relating to External Actions.

THE firft law of morality, relating to the mind and its affec- PART II.
tions, requires the love of mankind as the greateft good to which CHAP. II.
human nature is competent: If it fhould appear that mankind SECT. V.
are not agreed in the defcription of external actions that flow
from this principle, nor in the choice of favours to be expected
from the beneficent, it may be afked, by what rule is the friend
of mankind to conduct himfelf? What is the harm from which
he is to abftain, and what the good office which he is to perform
to his fellow creature?

To this queftion we may anfwer, in general. that, notwithftanding the varieties of manners, in different ages and nations,
and the different interpretation of favours or offences, which, in
the ftile of declamation, may be made to appear fo formidable
and fo perplexing, in the choice of virtuous actions; yet, that
mankind in reality do not fo far miftake the pernicious for the
ufeful,

useful, nor the deſtructive for what tends to their preſervation, as that the beneficent needs to be at a loſs, in determininig what is in him a natural effect of benevolence or of good will to his fellow creatures. In every particular ſociety, theſe points are ſettled ; and few have occaſion to transfer their beneficence from one ſcene to another, in which the conſtituents of a benefit are differently conceived or differently underſtood.

Notwithſtanding the diverſity of opinions which men may be ſuppoſed to entertain, with reſpect to the morality of particular actions, yet, in every age and nation, in every rank and condition of men, there is a rule of propriety, which, though it may be different in different inſtances, is to each the canon of eſtimation, and the principle from which they are to judge. Admitting ſuch differences, then, as they affect particular articles of propriety, this may be laid down as a law of external action for mankind ;—That, in matters phyſically indifferent or of ſmall moment, men are to obſerve the rules eſtabliſhed in their own country or in their own condition ; as they ſpeak its language and wear its dreſs : That, in judging of behaviour, in other countries, or in other ſituations, they are not to eſtimate proprieties of conduct by the ſtandard of their own manners or cuſtoms ; but, to allow every nation the free and diſtinctive uſe of its own.

This rule applies chiefly, if not wholly, to matters of propriety, decency, and common civility ; with reſpect to which, it is obvious, that as the object is to do what is inoffenſive, what is agreeable or obliging, it is proper that the perſon, acting in matters phyſically indifferent or of ſmall moment, ſhould conſult the opinions of thoſe he would oblige rather than his own.

Even,

Even, in matters not altogether phyfically indifferent, and in refpect to which unequal degrees of conveniency or inconvenien-cy may be apprehended in the practice of different nations; it would be an error in point of propriety if any one fhould deviate from the manners of his own country, under pretence that he meant to fubftitute what he thought an improvement. He might, in the fame manner, apprehend, that the language of his own country were inferior to that of a neighbour, or the fa-fhion of its drefs lefs convenient ; but, any extreme or fingular affectation of thus deviating from what is common in fuch mat-ters, under the notion of exhibiting fomewhat fuperior is ever ftigmatized, or is confidered as the mark of a fool or a cox-comb.

Where nations, or different ranks and conditions of men, vary from one another in fuch immaterial forms and obfervances, they are faid to differ in point of manners ; and, as they are feveral-ly to be judged of by the ftandard of their own cuftom or prac-tice, none has a right to apply that ftandard, in eftimating the manners of others. This rule may be applied, not only to mat-ters purely arbitrary, like the forms of falute, or the titles of ad-drefs, but even to all thofe matters, to which men though not originally indifferent, are in effect by cuftom or habit, reconcile-able, or attached. Though to others from an oppofite cuftom and habit, fuch examples may appear awkward or abfurd, it is not to be expected of perfons in any particular age, nation or rank, that they fhould have any apprehenfion in fuch matters different from that of their own nation, condition, or age.

Men of all ages and nations however have been generally difpofed

pofed to trefpafs on this rule, and to judge of other men by the ftandard of their own manners and cuftoms. This error is equally the concomitant of ignorance and of national pride, and few are qualified to diftinguifh what is effential in the character of nations from what is an article of variable inftitution or cuftom, and though fuppofed erroneous, yet confiftent with the nobleft qualities of the mind. Homer fung of great men, who performed for themfelves the functions of butcher and cook, and who ferved up the mefs on which their guefts and themfelves were to feed : He is therefore faid by a late celebrated wit, to have fung of coarfe or inelegant heroes *: But the manners of men are variable in different ages ; and the fame virtues and vices, the fame elevation or meannefs, may be exhibited under this or any other variety of manners. The moral of Homer has accordingly been equally admired by thofe who could hire butlers and cooks to ferve them, as by others who themfelves dreffed and ferved up their own provifions. In this matter the Roman critic appears to have differed from the French one.

Trojani belli fcriptorem, maxime Lolli,
Dum tu declamas Romæ, Prænefte relegi ;
Qui quid fit pulchrum, quid turpe, quid utile, quid non,
Plenius ac melius Chryfippo et Crantore dicit.

This latitude of judgement, however, relating to the variety of manners, which may be admitted, as confiftent with equal or fuperior degrees of merit in different nations, hath limits beyond which it cannot be fafely carried. Should we fuppofe a nation to reject what is evidently falutary, and to prefer a cuftom

3   which

---

* " D' avoir chanté des heros groffiers." This expreffion is to be found fomewhere in Voltaire's Works.

which is pernicious ; this, no doubt, would come under the denomination of abfurdity and folly, rather than a mere variety of manners : It would furnifh other nations with a fubject of juft ridicule or cenfure, and juftify the individual, when better informed, in counteracting the practice of his own age or country. The virtuous citizen in fuch inftances ftrives to preferve his country, although the practice in fafhion fhould tend to its ruin.

Virtue is fo far from being valuable, merely on account of its external effects, that the greateft and moft beneficial effect it can produce is the communication and propagation of virtue itfelf; " You will ferve your country more," fays Epictetus, " by raifing " the fouls, than by enlarging the habitations of your fellow citi- " zens." And this is the greateft benefit which any man can receive from his virtuous neighbour, that he become, like him, wife, courageous, temperate, beneficent, and juft.

Fafhion fometimes leads to effeminacy, fervility, prodigality, and debauchery. Where nations differ from one another in thefe refpects, they are juftly faid to exhibit, not a difference of manners merely, but certain degrees of corruption and depravity. If they fhould be ignorant or infenfible of the pernicious tendency of what they do, even this ignorance or infenfibility is a heavy article in the charge of corruption or vice to which they are expofed, and it muft be admitted, that the fingularity of an individual, which in any inftance of mere arbitrary manners were an error and a blemifh, would in fuch inftances as thefe be a merit and a juft topic of praife. *Among the faithlefs faithful only he*, is made the diftinction of an angel of light *.

It muft no doubt therefore be eftablifhed as a rule of action,

VOL. II.   U   that

* See Paradife Loft.

that wherever the manners of our country are dangerous to its safety or have a tendency to enfeeble or to corrupt the minds of men; to deprive the citizen of his rights; or the innocent of his security; it is our duty to do what is for the good of our fellow creatures, even in oppofition to the fafhion and cuftom of the times in which we live.

Some rites in religion, as well as obfervances in the ceremonial of life, are of a nature phyfically indifferent, and fit to be retained as mere arbitrary figns or expreffions of the affection, which religion or good manners require. But, as there is a merit in refifting practices extremely inconvenient, though required under the notion of good manners; fo there is wifdom in abftaining from acts of cruelty, though required under the notion of devotion or fanctity.

The human facrifice performed, or the cruel perfecutions that have been practiced under this notion, did not proceed, like the voluntary fufferings of the enthufiaft, upon an idea, that it was good for himfelf to fuffer; but upon an idea, that the Deity who requires fuch victims is jealous, vindictive, and cruel; or is to be gratified with the infliction of human mifery: And fuch practices, therefore, are to be counteracted, not merely as a miftake of what is beneficial or falutary, but as a corruption of religion itfelf; and as a fubftitution of malice or cruelty, where the mind fhould be taught only to form to itfelf models of perfection and goodnefs, as incitements to veneration and love.

SECTION

S E C T I O N VI.

Of the same Subject, continued.

IT is obfervable that, in many things, whether ufeful or neceffary there is a certain meafure to be kept preferably to any other whether greater or lefs. The lefs is defective, and inadequate to the occafion, the greater is exceffive and erroneous. The juft *mean* is learnt by experience; and, when known, is the proper object of choice.

It is not uncommon to confider *virtue* itfelf as a *mean* between two extremes towards either of which any deviation from the middle path is vice. Thus *liberality* is confidered as a *mean* betwixt *prodigality* and *avarice*; *bravery* as a *mean* betwixt *temerity* and *cowardice*; *temperance* as a *mean* betwixt hurtful *abftinence* and *pernicious excefs.*

U 2

Eft

Eſt modus in rebus, ſunt certi denique fines,
  Quos ultra citraque nequit conſiſtere rectum *.

This method is adopted in one of the moſt elegant and maſterly productions of antiquity, on the ſubject of ethics or manners † ; and there is no doubt, that propriety of conduct may be rendered perceptible and evident, not only when ſingle actions are ſeparately deſcribed, but alſo when placed in contraſt with any deviation from what is right, whether on the ſide of *defect* or *exceſs.*

Such illuſtrations, however, if uſeful in treating of the external effects of virtue, may rather ſerve to miſlead, in conſidering the excellency or depravity of mind, from which thoſe effects proceed.

Wiſdom and *goodneſs* are abſolute, not relative, ſubjects of eſteem. There may be a *defect* of either, but no *exceſs.* In the defects of intelligence, there is folly ; but, in the higheſt meaſure of which it is ſuſceptible, there is no blameable extreme of wiſdom. There is no extreme of juſtice ; nor in the mind, be the quality of whatever denomination, is there any extreme of what is right.

In practice, indeed, beneficent intention may produce too much or too little effect. The proper medium or mean, betwixt the extremes, to be found by obſervation or experience, is
                                                            itſelf

* Horace.

† Ariſtotle's Ethics.

itfelf derived from a previous knowledge of what is right; and
is not by any means to be confidered as an original ftandard of choice, even in matters of external convenience.

Mediocrity is certainly, not always upon its own account, an object of eftimation. In matters, rather ornamental than neceffary to human life, it is the reverfe of a commendation. In matters of genius, for inftance, whether *poetry, eloquence, politics,* or *war*, it is better not to have any pretenfions, than to have a mediocrity, which is likely to engage the perfon poffeffed of it in a courfe, of which he is not likely to attain the end. It is better to follow tamely in the track of others, than to affect the command, or the difplay of abilities, which miflead or difguft the more, that they fubftitute a mediocrity of effect, where an exertion of the higheft degree is required.

Wherever the *mean* betwixt two *extremes* is the preferable object of choice, it feems to be fixed by its comparative utility, not by any original perception of merit, in *mediocrity* itfelf, confidered apart from its ufe. In the extreme of too little, there is a defect of utility; in the extreme of too much the excefs is pernicious: And the falutary, or moft ufeful meafure, is that which determines the middle way to be chofen between the extremes: So that we are to look for the rule, by which this *mean* is to be diftinguifhed, and the very confideration which recommends it in the circumftance of its abfolute utility, or fitnefs to ferve the purpofe of nature.

If the ill effect of extremes fuggeft the expedience of recurring to the proper mean in every inftance of human conduct, fome apprehenfion of the proper meafure or end of action is neceffary

to

to point out the evil of extremes, which confift in a deviation from the middle path towards either fide, of excefs, or of defect. And, if the confideration of *extremes* ferves to illuftrate the *mean* betwixt them, it is evident that the knowledge of that *mean* is required to point out the boundaries beyond which all that exceeds, or falls fhort, is in *extreme*, and pernicious.

SECTION

S E C T I O N   VII.

Of the unequal Degrees of Merit and Demerit in External Actions.

MERIT is the prefence of that quality which, whatever it be, PART II. is the object of moral approbation ; *demerit*, on the contrary, CHAP. II. is the abfence of fuch quality ; or the prefence of any quality SECT. VII. which is the object of difapprobation.

From the obfervations, that have occurred under a few of the preceding titles, it fhould appear, that neither mediocrity of ef-fect, fympathy of feelings, nor actual utility, is the fpecific ob-ject of moral approbation ; that moral good and evil are peculiar to mind ; and that the *merit* of an action, or the object of moral approbation in any action, is the prefence of qualities which con-ftitute the fpecific excellence of mind : Such are *wifdom, goodnefs, temperance,* and *fortitude.* That efforts of *benevolence,* or good will to mankind, properly fupported with intellectual ability, ap-plication, and refolution, conftitute actions morally good. That

2

malice,

malice, however directed or fupported, conftitutes an action morally evil.

This diftinction is, to us, not only matter of perception and difcernment, but awakens a fentiment or paffion, by which we are difpofed to accumulate *good* on the *good,* and *evil* on the *evil.* While we perceive that beneficence is a bleffing, we would willingly confer additional bleffings. Perceiving that malice is a curfe, we would willingly inflict additional fuffering. This fentiment is partly implied or expreffed in the terms of *merit* and *demerit.*

That the good deferves to be rewarded, and the evil to be punifhed, is an apprehenfion which we are born to entertain, and is juftly confidered as a fymptom or earneft of the moral government of God, under which men being infpired with a difpofition to diftributive juftice, become inftruments of Providence for its actual effect. This difpofition operates moft powerfully, perhaps, in its animofity to what is *wrong.* The right is firm upon its own foundation, and needs not the prop of extraneous reward; while the wrong feems to call for interpofition, to prevent, repel, or repair its effects.

Hence it is that *wrongs* are diftinguifhed under their refpective denominations of *guilt* or *demerit,* more precifely, perhaps, than the oppofite degrees of merit. The *right,* however, alfo has its gradations, and the actions of men their unequal meafures of approbation or efteem. Actions, which indicate good will to mankind in the higheft degree, are thofe commonly which we conceive to be of the higheft *merit ;* as the effects of malice prepenfe are, on the contrary of the higheft *demerit ;* and thus the prefence of good or ill difpofition is not only attended with mo-

2   ral

ral approbation or difapprobation ; but the meafure of the effect, in fuch inftances, is alfo ever found in juft proportion to that of the caufe.

Perfeverance in the exercife of any good difpofition, is admitted as an evidence of its power ; or is the indication of a mind exempt from thofe paffions or views which occafionally miflead the will, or interrupt the tenour of a virtuous conduct.

Hence it is, that a beneficent courfe of life, uniformly purfued ; that duties performed in the midft of *difficulty, danger*, or unmerited *obloquy*, in the midft of *allurements*, that would *feduce*, in the midft of *pain* or *fuffering*, that would deprefs the mind, or daunt the refolution, as they carry evidence of a difpofition proportionally vigorous and unfhaken, are juftly eftimated of the higheft *merit*.

Hence it is alfo, that fuperftitious Afceticks having a view to the circumftances that would prove the force of a virtuous affection, if any fuch actually exifted, while they withdraw from the world, and fhun every occafion on which good difpofitions towards mankind are exerted, miftake fafting, abftinence, and corporal penances, for articles of merit towards God. They attach the efteem that is due to *merit* to the circumftances of difficulty or fuffering, in which merit if real might fhine out with advantage ; but which voluntarily incurred, and without any rational object, only give evidence of mifapprehenfion and folly.

Befides the immediate effects of wifdom and benevolence, which form the higeft order in the fcale of *merit*, there are articles of inferior confideration, fuch as propriety, decency, civility and

politenefs,

politenefs, which may proceed from a difpofition or habit of doing that which is agreeable, or of avoiding that which is offenfive to others ; a difpofition in its own nature exquifitely amiable, and whofe effects are efteemed proportionally to the evidence they bear of its reality ; although, from the mere occafions on which it is exerted, the higheft meafure of virtue could not be inferred.

In comparing fuch examples together, we find, though without any precife diftinction of name, a gradation in the fcale of *merit.* by which men in the courfe of life are unequally the objects of approbation or efteem.

At the fame time, there is a correfponding gradation in the fcale of *demerit,* which is not perhaps more obvious ; but is thought to require a more pointed difcrimination of names, fuch as thofe of *crimes, offences,* and *faults.*

Crimes, or actions of the higheft demerit, are fuch as proceed from malice, under any of its ordinary forms, whether of *envy, emulation, jealoufy* or *revenge* ; or fuch as proceed from any habit or paffion, as from *covetoufnefs, fenfuality,* or *ambition,* in gratifying of which the criminal has occafion deliberately to trefpafs on the rights, or to difturb the peace of his fellow creatures.

When the crime proceeding from one or other of thefe motives is committed under circumftances of peculiar truft, or againft perfons peculiarly entitled to refpect and affection, the atrocity of guilt or degree of demerit is rated accordingly ; and pernicious actions, performed deliberately, intentionally or knowingly, though not originally fuggefted by malice, yet as they imply great
                                                                    defect

defect of the oppofite good difpofitions of humanity or candour, PART II. and thereby give evidence of great depravity, have a correfpond- CHAP. II. ing degree of *demerit*. SECT. VII.

The perfon who without having entertained any malice, neverthelefs deliberately kills that he may rob, is juftly reckoned guilty of murder ; and he who knowingly performs an action pernicious to his neighbour, though only from a motive of intereft or conveniency to himfelf otherwife allowable, is neverthelefs in fuch inftances, juftly reckoned guilty of a heinous crime.

As perfons thus deliberately offending are not likely, from mere recollection, to repent of the actions, which, under a recollected perception of their pernicious nature, they already performed; the peace of fociety, and the fafety of innocence, require, that fuch perfons fhould be reftrained by the fear of punifhment ; and, if not reclaimable, that they fhould be removed by exile or death from the fociety they difturb or moleft.

What in the fcale of reprobation is qualified with the more venial name of *offence*, may, in refpect to the external effect, be equally hurtful with what is denominated a *crime*.

Under this title of an *offence*, the peace of fociety may be difturbed, or a citizen may fuffer in his perfon or effects ; but when this proceeds not from malice, nor from an ordinary habit of indifference to the rights of others, but from a fudden and occafional emotion or paffion, which may hurry a mind, otherwife difpofed to innocence and good will, into an action pernicious or hurtful to thofe whom it may concern, the demerit is proportionally alleviated.

X 2   Such

Such offenders, on the returns of reflection, are capable of sincere repentance, and they may be reclaimed by such measures of punishment or animadversion as awaken their remorse, and put them on their guard against like slips of temper or effects of provocation.

Under the latter denomination of a fault, we may conceive, and often have occasion to admit, a lower degree of demerit than is implied in either of the former titles. Of this a person may be guilty, if, from ignorance or inadvertency, he shall be the cause of harm to his fellow creatures, although he have not either the deliberate intention of the *criminal*, nor the unruly passion of the *offender*.

Faults of inadvertency, or of ignorance may have unequal degrees of demerit. Where the case by its general importance, or by any peculiar circumstances of personal concern calls up the attention in a special degree, *inadvertency* is proportionally inexcuseable, and may justly incur high measures of punishment.

Ignorance of what, by the general condition of our nature, by our profession, or by any peculiar opportunities of instruction, we ought specially to know, becomes faulty in proportion as these circumstances accumulate.

On this account it is a just maxim in the cognizance of *crimes*, that ignorance of the *fact* may be admitted as a plea of innocence, but that ignorance of the *law* never can be admitted to justify what is illegal. Thus a person, who, in shooting his arrow to a distance, shall wound his fellow creature, may plead
his

his ignorance of the *fact*, or his ignorance that there was any PART. II.
perfon in the way of being fo wounded ; but he cannot plead CHAP. II.
ignorance of the law, or that he did not know it was a crime to SECT. VII.
injure or wound his fellow creature.

The law of nature, fuggefted by the regard which a man naturally has for mankind, cannot be fuppofed unknown, without
an implication of the greateft depravity ; and if any one, accufed
of an action pernicious to his neighbour, fhould plead that he did
not know it was wrong to do harm, he would, in that very plea,
eftablifh a heavier charge of depravity againft himfelf, than any
occafional or tranfient action could imply.

The fum of this argument is, that although external actions
confidered apart from will, intention, or difpofition of mind, like
mechanical caufes of any other fort, may be productive of benefit or harm ; yet they do not appear to be vefted with any moral
quality, until the movement performed is traced to its connection with the difpofition of mind from which it proceeds. This
is admitted not only with refpect to involuntary or convulfive
motions, in which the arm of one man, in a fit, may be fo
thrown about as to wound another: It is admitted, alfo, with
refpect to voluntary actions, in which a perfon may cafually, or
without any blameable inadvertency be the phyfical caufe of
harm to another.

The diftinction of moral good and evil cannot be afcertained
in the defcription of mere external action ; nor can the merit or
demerit of a man be known until he has acted. Infomuch, that
although in abftraction we may take afunder, and ftate apart,
qualities of the mind and movements of the body, yet thefe in
3   reality

reality are combined together in the conception which men mutually form of their moral diftinctions.

Wifdom and goodnefs are the conftituents of merit; proper and beneficent actions are the evidence of wifdom and goodnefs. A feries of beneficent actions implies benevolence; a feries of pernicious actions implies malice; proper conduct implies wifdom; improper conduct implies folly: And, wherever wifdom and goodnefs exift, proper and beneficent conduct will follow, as the tree produces its fruit, or the caufe in any other inftance is followed by its effect.

External action, confidered as a feature of the human character, or as an emanation of good or ill difpofition, is a proper fubject of moral approbation or cenfure, or comes properly within the direction of moral government or law.

The fame law, that recommends the love of mankind as an excellence and a blefling to the mind of man, muft likewife recommend beneficent actions under the predicament of moral duty; and the law which reprobates malice muft reprobate pernicious actions alfo.

When we have thus traced the approbation of external actions to that wifdom and goodnefs, which is the fource of fuch actions, we may fuppofe a queftion to be put on the fubject of moral action, the fame as that we fuppofed on the fubject of natural beauty; If external actions be approved on account of the wifdom and goodnefs from which they proceed, on what account are wifdom and goodnefs themfelves approved? And we may repeat, That wifdom and goodnefs are approved on their own account: Or, if this anfwer fhould not be fatisfactory, we may change the terms, and fay, That wifdom and goodnefs are

approved

approved as conftituents of perfection and happinefs, and in this terminate our feries of reafons, which, however continued through any number of fteps, muft lead at laft to fomething that is efti- mable on its own account.

The hufbandman values a manure becaufe it promotes the fer- tility of his land. He values fertility on account of its produce ; the produce on account of its application to the purpofes of fub- fiftence and accommodation ; and thefe on account of their ef- fect in preferving life ; and if he values life, on account of the happinefs of which it is fuceptible, ftill in the end there muft be fome confideration that is valued on its own account. No feries in human affairs is infinite, and every choice which is made of one thing on account of another, implies, that there is fomewhere, and however remote from the prefent ground of our choice, an object that is actually valuable upon its own account.

In the fcale of created beings the intelligent is fupreme, and approaches neareft to the eternal fource of exiftence and excel- lence. If intelligent beings themfelves may be unequal, and rife above one another in their unequal approaches to Supreme wif- dom and goodnefs, fuch gradations acknowledged amount to an acknowledgement alfo, that in perfect intelligence there is an ex- cellence or a good which is in itfelf the Supreme object of venera- tion and love.

SECTION

SECTION   VIII.

Of the Obligation and Sanctions of Moral Law.

PART II.
CHAP. II.
SECT.VIII.

MORAL law in the moſt general form, as has been already ſtated, is an expreſſion of what is good, and therefore an object of choice.

To every rational choice there is an *obligation* and a *ſanction.* Theſe terms are not ſynonymous: and yet their diſtinction is more eaſily underſtood than expreſſed in any other form of words.

Obligation, in the original ſenſe of the term, ſeems to imply ſome tie or bond, * which is incurred by the perſon obliged; while *ſanction* implies the conſideration by which he is induced
to

* *Obligatio* eſt juris vinculum, quo, neceſſitate aſtringimus alicujus rei ſolvendæ ſecundum noſtræ civitatis jura.

Inſt. Juſt. lib. III. titulo decimo quarto.

to fulfil that bond. So that, in making a free choice, the reality of a good forms the obligation, and the confequence to be apprehended forms the fanction. Or, if a perfon fhould fay, that he is not obliged to chufe what is good, and may, if it fo pleafe him, prefer mifery to happinefs, he may be told, that this is not the language of intelligence ; nor can it be ferioufly held by any one who takes the words in their ordinary meaning.

To the queftion, therefore, that may arife in this place, Why any one fhould chufe to be virtuous rather than vicious ? It may be anfwered ; Becaufe virtue is happinefs, vice is mifery ; and in this contraft is implied at once all the good of which human nature is fufceptible, and all the evil to which it is expofed. In what, therefore, we may be afked, does integrity differ from what is fo loudly complained of under the notion of felfifhnefs ? In nothing but in that which is of all others the moft effential diftinction,—the wifdom of a choice which is made by the one, and the folly of the other. Thofe we call felfifh endeavour to fupprefs the beft and happieft fentiments of their nature, and become difaffected or indifferent to their fellow-creatures ; while the virtuous have a common caufe with mankind ; and, being fecure in the enjoyments of an affectionate temper, partake in the good which providence has difpenfed to the whole ; and are ever happy in promoting the fame end to the utmoft of their power.

Some writers on the fubject of morality, and lawyers for the moft part, confider obligation as refulting from the command of a fuperior, and the fanction, or caufe of compliance, as refulting from the power of that fuperior to enforce his commands. They are ufed to confider laws that may be enforced ; and in their notion of moral obligation, would recur to an authority that is fit to enforce the obfervance of moral duties.

But power employed to determine the will of a free agent muft operate in prefenting motives of choice ; in prefenting happinefs as the reward of fidelity, and mifery as the punifhment of neglect : And whether this be done by fo ordering the nature of things, that virtue fhall be its own reward, and vice its own punifhment ; or whether it be done by a fubfequent act of will and difcretion, in rewarding the good and punifhing the wicked, in a way not previoufly connected with the part they have acted, the reality of the obligation, and the fanction is the fame : For if, in the nature of things, moral good be conftituent of happinefs, and moral evil of mifery, what can Almighty power do more to determine the choice of the one and the rejection of the other ? If we conceive any fanction of moral law as different from this, it muft however terminate in the fame effect.   For what are the honours and rewards which men beftow upon virtue, or the chains and imprifonment which they award to the wicked ?   What is the heaven which religion decrees to the one, or the hell which is provided for the others ? but happinefs and mifery in other terms, or terms, if you will, in which every one is left to conceive what will operate moft on his own apprehenfions and feelings.

In the cafe of man, furely, it requires no great effort of underftanding to perceive that wifdom, benevolence, temperance, and fortitude are happy qualities ; that malice, folly, and cowardice are wretched.

And if it fhould be thought neceffary to confider moral law as the command of a fuperior, this may be done without departing
                                                                              from

from that original doctrine of nature we have ftated,—that *moral* PART II.
good is the fpecific excellence and felicity of human nature, and moral CHAP. II.
depravity its fpecific defect and wretchednefs. SECT VIII.

The Sovereign of the univerfe, by having made things as they
are, has given his command, and promulgated his law in behalf
of morality ; and in every inftance of conformity to his law, and
in every infraction of it, continues to apply the fanction of happinefs and mifery. Wifdom, benevolence, fortitude, and temperance, he has faid fhall be the conftituents of happinefs ; folly,
malice, cowardice, and debauchery fhall be the conftituents of
debafement and mifery. We may therefore chufe to treat of
moral obligation as the tie of reafon, to prefer what is highly valuable in itfelf and eligible upon its own account; or we may
treat of this obligation as the tie of reafon, binding the creature
to obey his Creator, in making a choice, in fupport of which the
Creator has exerted, and will continue to exert, his fovereign
power.

In chufing what is morally good, it is happy to know that we
obey our Creator ; and in obeying our Creator, it is happy to
know, that what he commands is the fpecific good, and felicity
of our nature.

To feparate thefe confiderations were doubtlefs of ill effect ;
and the fanctions of morality would be lefs powerful upon either
principle apart, than they are upon the foundations of both u-
nited. Merely to obey, without a fenfe of goodnefs and rectitude
in the command, would be greatly fhort of that duty which we
owe to our beneficent Maker ; and the love of virtue is no doubt
greatly encouraged by the confideration, that Almighty power,
in the eftablifhed order of things, is exerted in its favour.

Y 2 In

In the genuine alliance of religion and morality, the wisdom and goodness, which we perceive to be the constituents of happiness, are likewise enjoined by the sovereign command of God. They are presented to our thoughts, as attributes of the Supreme Being himself, and as forming in him the objects of reverence and of love; and our own capacity of attaining, in any degree, to a participation of these qualities is considered as the highest perfection or prerogative of our nature.

To the ingenuous mind this constitutes the obligation, and the sanction, whether of religion itself, or of moral duty. If we should be disposed farther to enquire; by what sanction the profligate may be reclaimed from their profligacy, or by what means those who are disposed to the commission of crimes may be actually restrained from disturbing the peace of society? the answer may be difficult.

Mankind from age to age have laboured upon this subject; have urged the reasons of morality; have denounced the vengeance of God against iniquity; have held up the sword of justice, and threatened to exterminate the wicked; and all this, though no doubt with great effect, still without being able to reclaim the depraved from their vices, or to prevent the commission of crimes.

Happiness is misunderstood; religion is slighted, the movements of justice are slow, and defer the infliction of punishment, till after the wrong is committed.

Men have the concerns of animal life, as well as those of intelligent

3

telligent being, to care for; and, however evident the co-incidence of happinefs and of duty, neither the degree of this evidence, nor that of any other fact, is at all times fufficient to guard the imagination againft the admiffion of falfe apprehenfions.

In the conceptions of ordinary men, there are advantages, whether of wealth or pleafure, which it is their intereft or paffion to obtain : But there are means feemingly effectual to obtain thefe advantages, from which they conceive it their duty to refrain. They are tempted by the end ; they are reftrained by the law of morality, which forbids the means. While they continue to think in this manner, the obligation and the fanction of the moral law may, in their apprehenfion, be either the confcioufnefs of what is right and wrong ; the general efteem or contempt of mankind ; the awe in which they ftand of the fupreme Being ; or the arm of the magiftrate, which is lifted up to protect the innocent againft the wrongs which they are difpofed to commit : So that, in this view of the matter, and as conceived by ordinary men, the fanctions of morality may be enumerated under the titles of *confcience, public repute, compulfory law,* and *religion.*

With refpect to the firft, it may be obferved, that perfons who diftinguifh between their intereft, on the one hand, and their duty on the other, frequently conceive thefe objects to be in oppofition, and fit to diftract their choice. They frequently feel the confideration of their intereft more cogent than that of their duty, but ftill do not confound thefe confiderations together, nor lofe the fenfe of moral obligation while they trefpafs on the maxims of moral law. In departing from their duty, they are ftill confcious of its reality, and affected with remorfe and fhame : So that the fanction of confcience is entire, even when it is neglected.

It

It were irrational in a man to hurt himself; and the neglect of this rule is marked with a confcioufnefs of folly. But it has pleafed the Almighty, that we fhould hold every perfon under a different form of obligation required to confult the welfare, or to abftain from the offer of harm to his neighbour. This form of obligation perceived carries with it the fanction of innocence, amounting to a high meafure of fatisfaction in the confcioufnefs of integrity, and a high meafure of remorfe, of diffatisfaction, and fuffering, in the confcioufnefs of any criminal trefpafs on the rights of a fellow creature.

With this, in fome degree, is connected the fanction of public repute alfo, in which every perfon apprehends that he is an object of efteem or reprobation to other men.

As man is formed for fociety, he is juftly made to enjoy or to fuffer under the approbation or difapprobation of other men, as well as under his own. The complacency, therefore, of his fellow creatures, who efteem and who confide in him, or the averfion with which they reprobate or fhun him, are powerful acceffaries to confcience in urging its dictates.

Many articles of decency, or even propriety of manners, are derived from cuftom, or the arbitrary conceptions of men, relating to fuch matters. For the obfervance of thefe articles, public repute is the peculiar fanction. The obfervance of fome determinate forms is of great confequence to public order; and individuals, even in matters of indifference, muft not think themfelves at liberty to flight the authority of their age and country, in the forms of behaviour, which they are required to obferve.

States

States or regular communities alſo have their rights, which they are prepared to maintain by force. They have their laws to which the magiſtrate is empowered to compel obedience. For theſe purpoſes the community is armed, fortreſſes are built, and military forms eſtabliſhed. Tribunals are erected for the trial of crimes; officers are entruſted with public force; *chains, fetters,* and *public priſons,* and the other apparatus of coercion, are provided for the guilty. In theſe inſtitutions, there is a ſanction of force to ſupport the obligation to innocence, to preſerve the public peace, and to ſecure the harmleſs in the poſſeſſion of his rights. Such may be termed the ſanction of compulſory law, which, though not in every inſtance proper to obtain acts of beneficence, yet in every inſtance is applicable to reſtrain the commiſſion of crimes.

In aid of the magiſtracy, alſo, in every well ordered community, inſtitutions of religion are wiſely adopted, and the authority of religion is impreſſed on the minds of men, by ſolemn rites ſignificant of the preſence of God and the homage which is due to him.

We may avoid for the preſent entering into any queſtion relating to the abuſe of ſuch inſtitutions, whether to the purpoſes of public tyranny or private gain. We conſider them only with a view to their proper uſe in confirming the obligations to innocence and duty.

Man, we have had occaſion to obſerve, is formed for religion as well as ſociety. He is capable of perceiving univerſal intelligence in the fabric of the univerſe. He perceives in the predi-

3

lection

lection for juftice and innocence, in the horrors at guilt which
are impreffed on his own mind, the will of that fovereign authority which reigns in the fyftem of nature.   To him the confcioufnefs of integrity and goodnefs is peace and amity with God:
The confcioufnefs of depravity and wickednefs is rebellion and
enmity ; the one rendering exiftence itfelf a bleffing, in the confidence of prefent and future protection ; the other rendering life
itfelf a curfe, under the horrors of prefent remorfe, and the fear
or apprehenfion of future and impending evils.

Such is religion in the form of mere reflexion as it operates in
the mind ; in the form of a public eftablifhment it operates in the
manner of compulfory law, with the denunciations of future punifhment and the hopes of future reward.   But the government
of God, more comprehenfive than the government of man, extends
to the mind as well as to external actions, and carries the application of compulfory law to reftrain not only the overt acts of iniquity, but even the thoughts, wifhes or purpofes which may lead
to fuch external effects ; requiring fuch a guard upon the mind
itfelf as may fupprefs the firft approaches to evil, and induce habits of innocence and of virtue.

Juft religion, befides its effects as a reftraining principle is in
itfelf a fource of elevation and of goodnefs in the mind of man. In
what is the love of God different from the love of goodnefs itfelf ?
Or in what is the defire to act a part agreeable to the Supreme
Being different from that elevation of mind with which the worthy afpire to perfection ?

In this enumeration of fanctions, or motives to determine the
virtuous choice, included in the general and comprehenfive diftinction

tinction of good and evil. We have mentioned thofe of *confci-*
ence, of *public repute*, of *religion*, and *compulfory law*.

Such then we may conceive to be the practical obligations of men, and fuch to be the fanctions to which they either do, or ought to, recur in fettling the tenor of their affections and of their conduct *.

In the farther arrangement of our fubject, we may avail our-felves of a divifion that naturally arifes from the confideration of thefe different fanctions, and may confider the requifitions of compulfory law; or rights to be fupported by force, apart from the maxims of beneficence and duty, which are urged by the other confiderations now mentioned. The firft will extend to every cafe in which force or compulfion may be properly employed. The fecond, to thofe cafes in which the obligation of moral duty, however ftrong, cannot properly be enforced, and muft be left to the free will of the agent.

The firft may be termed *jurifprudence*; the fecond *cafuiftry*, or that part of moral fcience which relates to action and the charac-teriftics of a happy life. And to thefe may be fubjoined, under the title of *politics*, the difcuffion of material queftions, relating not merely to men as members of fociety, but to the fociety itfelf, in refpect to its inftitutions and forms. And under one or other of thefe titles may be comprifed all that yet remains to be done in obfervance of the method which has been propofed for this work.

VOL. II.   Z   CHAP.

---

* Juris precepta funt hæc: Honefte vivere, alterum non lædere, fuum cuique tribuere.

Inft. Juft. lib. i. par. 3.

C H A P. III.

OF JURISPRUDENCE OR COMPULSORY LAW.

PART FIRST.

SECTION I.

Of the Principle of Compulsory Law.

IT is a well known fact, that mankind fometimes employ force to obtain the obfervance of moral laws, and that the right to compel the performance of a duty, though not univerfal in every cafe, is, at leaft, in fome inftances fully acknowledged.

We are now to inveftigate and to ftate the principle from which this right in any cafe can be derived.

Z 2

It

It may be obferved, that in all the inftances in which the right of one man to compel another is acknowledged, compulfion, either in its immediate operation, or in its final effect, is an act of defence.

The fovereign employs force to defend his country againft foreign enemies, or to make reprifals for a wrong that is done to his fubjects. The magiftrate employs force to reprefs crimes; the citizen to defend his dwelling or his perfon. And even in exacting the payment of a debt; or in requiring the performance of a contract, there is no more than an exaction of what is juftly due; or, as we fhall have occafion to evince, no more than an act of defence on the part of the exactor, maintaining a right of which he is already in poffeffion.

The great principle of morality extends to beneficence, as well as innocence; but from this account of the circumftances in which compulfion is applicable, the principle of compulfory law is limited to the repulfion of wrongs, and to that part in the object of the moral precept above cited, which forbids one perfon to be the author of harm to another *.

In fearch of this or any other principle in nature, by whatever fteps we proceed, we muft arrive at laft at fomething that is felf-evident. And fuch we may fay is the maxim, *That every innocent perfon may defend himfelf*; to which we may join what is equally evident, that *every one having power, may employ it in defence of any other innocent perfon.*

To the purpofe of defence a fufficient meafure of *force* is required.

* Alterum non lædere.

quired, and in many inftances is the only means that can be
fuccefsfully employed. A perfon difpofed to commit an injury
may not be perfuaded to defift from his purpofe ; nor can he be
eluded perhaps by any artifice or ftratagem ; it remains therefore
that a *force* fuperior to his may be the only means fufficient to
reftrain him.

In every cafe of defence, force is employed to fecure the innocent, rather than to obtain, from thofe who would injure him, the
difcharge of a duty. And the fpecific end of compulfory law being to repel a wrong, the means are adequate and juft.

But if any one, inftead of difputing the legality of *force* in a
cafe of defence, fhould contend, that it is not peculiar merely to
fuch cafes, but may be employed, not only in defending a right, but
in obtaining any other end beneficial to mankind ; that as religion and virtue are confeffedly of the higheft value, every effectual means, and force no lefs than any other, may be employed to obtain them, whether by propagating faith towards God or
charity towards men.

Thefe no doubt are bleffings, in obtaining of which no effectual
means are to be fpared ; but if we wifh to promote the caufe of
religion and virtue, means are to be employed which inform the
mind, conciliate the affections, and gain the will. To thefe purpofes *force* is inadequate. Its effects, on the contrary, are to render
the understanding lefs docile, and to alienate the mind. And it
muft be rejected as an inftrument of inftruction or moral improvement ; becaufe it would be irrational to employ means which
have a tendency adverfe to the purpofe for which they are employed.

Nay, but force is competent to obtain, even from thofe againft
whom.

whom it is employed, the external fruits of faith and charity ! To this it may be anfwered, That if thefe fruits be required as a moral good in thofe who are made to yield them, the reality of any fuch good may be queftioned ; or rather it is evident, that a forced performance of fuppofed good works does not conftitute any good in him who is compelled to perform them. Virtue cannot be forced. It is voluntary, or it does not exift. Faith is fincere; or its profeffion is a mere hypocrify.

If the fruit of good works be required in one man for the benefit of another ; it is evident that force cannot be juftly employed for this purpofe. Benefits extorted by *force* are robberies, not acts of beneficence.

We may conclude, therefore, that the ufe of force, which is admiffible in the cafe of defence, whether immediate or remote, is alfo limited to fuch cafes ; and that although men are bound, under every other fanction of duty, to avoid being authors of harm, yet, that they are, in this duty of abftaining from harm, peculiarly repreffible by force alfo : And from this we may fafely affume, that the *right of defence is the fpecific principle of compulfory law.*

In treating of this fubject, accordingly, we are not fo much to confider the obligation under which every perfon lies to be innocent, as to confider the right which every perfon has to defend himfelf, and his fellow creature, by every effectual means in his power.

This right amounts to a permiffion of whatever may be neceffary to fafety, but does not contain any pofitive injunction to do all that may be wanted for this purpofe. A perfon attacked

3   in

in his perfon may kill the aggreffor ; but is not required to do fo much.

In the application of our principle, therefore, we endeavour to point out how far the right of defence extends, but do not, in any cafe whatever, pretend to lay the perfon who defends himfelf or his neighbour, under any tie of neceffity to go to the utmoft extent. The citizen, it is admitted, may kill the houfe-breaker who alarms his dwelling in the night, but is not required to proceed fo far : Nay, on the fuppofition that he may defend himfelf and his dwelling, without having recourfe to this extremity, he is by the law of nature actually reftrained from it.

In conceiving a juft and compleat act of defence, we muft fuppofe fome thing that is to be defended or maintained ; and fpecify the means that may be lawfully employed for this purpofe.

That which a perfon may lawfully defend or maintain is termed his *right*. The circumftances under which a right is expofed or invaded may point out the means which are adequate and neceffary to its prefervation ; and the fubject of jurifprudence or compulfory law, fo conceived, admits of being divided into two principal parts, of which one relates to the *rights* of men, the other to the *means of defence*.

SECTION

S E C T I O N II.

Of the Term Right in its moſt General Acceptation.

THIS term is ſometimes an adjective, employed to diſtinguiſh the quality of an action that is proper or morally good; and, in this ſenſe, to aſcertain what is *right*, is to apply the principle of moral law to the particular ſubject in queſtion.

In our preſent inquiry, the term *right* has a different meaning: It is a ſubſtantive, the name of a thing, or relation of a perſon to a thing, and not the mere quality of an action. It may be reckoned among the ſubjects which are not ſuſceptible of a formal definition. But, we may recur to the caſes in which it is ſuppoſed to exiſt, and leave the mind to collect its meaning from a conſideration of the point, to which it refers in all the caſes enumerated.

Thus, a perſon has a *right* to the uſe of his faculties and powers; he has a *right* to enjoy the light of the ſun, and the air

3   of

of the atmofphere ; he has a *right* to the ufe of his property, and PART II.
the fruits of his labour. Thefe, are felf-evident propofitions, and CHAP. III.
the meaning of the term *right*, which occurs in all of them, may SECT. II.
be collected from its uniform fignification in each. Agreeably to
this rule, *right* is the relation of a perfon to a thing in which no
alteration ought to be made, without his own confent.

In this circumlocution, the names of *perfon* and *thing* imply, that
a *right* is the appurtenance of a perfon, or of a being vefted with
choice and volition, and has reference to the will of fuch perfon
refpecting the object of his choice. This object may fubfift in
the perfon himfelf, in his lot or poffeffion, or in any conftituent
of his being or ftate whatever.

It is a part in the focial nature of man, that *rights* are to different men mutually objects of confideration and acknowledgement.

The concern of a perfon in his own right, is implied in the
principle of felf-prefervation ; his concern in the rights of others
is implied in the principle of fociety, or in the fympathy of man
with his fellow creatures.

Wrong is the violation of *right* ; and, the fame concern
which interefts the mind in the prefervation of the one, is a
caufe of refentment on occafion of the other.

There may be a *claim* or *pretenfion* without a *right* ; but a right,
whatever be the fubject to which it refers, is exclufive, and fufficient to fet afide every fuppofeable claim or pretenfion to the
fame fubject.

VOL. II.   A a   Although

Although numbers at once may lay claim to a right, there can be no more than one to whom it is due ; and the object of difcuffion, under oppofite claims, is to determine with whom the right fhall be found to exift : So that, although the right of any two or more perfons may be queftioned, or their pretenfions remain undecided, yet every queftion of right implies, that a juft title, wherever it be found, is exclufive of every other claim or pretenfion whatever.

Although, therefore, in the loofe application of words, or in common language, we fometimes ufe the terms right, claim, or pretenfion promifcuoufly ; yet, in propriety of expreffion, it is well known, that there may be a pretenfion or a claim where there is no right, and that a right may remain unclaimed and undecided.

From inattention to the propriety of language, or from a wifh to make way for a favourite tenet, by the help of fome ambiguity, it has been faid, that in the ftate of nature, or prior to convention, all men had equal rights to all things ; the meaning muft be, that prior to convention, no right was afcertained ; and that as no perfon had any right, fo all men were equal in this refpect. How far the pofition is true even in this fenfe we fhall have occafion to confider.

In the mean time, we affume, that the right of one perfon precludes a fuppofeable right in any other perfon to the fame fubject : And fo far it is proper that the term be underftood, before we proceed to confider the different denominations under which rights may be known. As they differ in refpect to the fubjects

jects in which they are conftituted, fo they differ alfo in refpect Part II.
Chap. III.
Sect. II.
to the origin or fource from which they are derived.

Among the fources of right we fhall find, that the law of defence itfelf may be numbered ; and, upon this account, before
we proceed to confider the diftinction of rights, efpecially in refpect to their origin, it may be proper to ftate the law of defence
in its moft general terms, as a fource to which among others we
may have occafion to recur in treating this part of our fubject.

SECTION

SECTION .III.

Of the Law of Defence in General.

PART II.
CHAP. III.
SECT. III.

ACCORDING to the law of defence a *right* may be maintained by any means which are *effectual* and *neceffary* for this purpofe.

It were irrational to employ means ineffectual, and it might be cruel in fome inftances to employ feverities that might have been fpared.

If means are fuppofed to be neceffary, it is implied that the end cannot be obtained without them ; and to fuppofe that a defence is allowed, and yet that the neceffary means are prohibited would be to fuppofe, that the law of nature is inconfiftent with itfelf; propofes the end, and yet forbids the purfuit.

It is true, that in fome cafes the neceffary means may be fo fevere, and even fo deftructive to the party againft whom they are

are employed, that humanity revolts againſt the uſe of them ; and perſons of a certain mild diſpoſition may ſubmit to harm, rather than employ, for defence, meaſures of any cruel effect to which the aggreſſor may have expoſed himſelf.

In the conteſt of parties even the aggreſſor does not immediately forfeit every right ; and there are accordingly limits to the very means of defence that may be employed againſt him ; but the forbearance of any neceſſary means of defence however ſevere, is a voluntary effort of goodneſs in the perſon wronged, not ſuch a conceſſion as the aggreſſor may claim as a right due to himſelf.

As the law of defence, therefore, permits the uſe of any means which are neceſſary, ſo it allows to the perſon againſt whom they are employed, an exception in the want of neceſſity, when means deſtructive or harmful are unneceſſarily employed againſt him.

The object of law being to maintain a right, every exceſs of harm beyond what is neceſſary for this purpoſe is itſelf an injury, and gives to the party, ſuffering under it, a right of defence. So much is implied in the terms *effectual* and *neceſſary*, by which the means of defence are characterized.

Under the general notion of ſafety are included not only the *repulſion* of a wrong that is offered, but likewiſe the *prevention* of a wrong that is apprehended, and the *reparation* of a damage that has been done ; ſo that the law of defence conſiſts of three clauſes.

1ſt, That a wrong apprehended may be *prevented.*

I

2d,

2*d*, That a wrong offered may be *repelled*.

3*d*, That *reparation* may be exacted of a damage received.

According to the firft claufe, every party may provide himfelf with the neceffary precautions againft the harm to which he may think himfelf expofed.

According to the fecond, he may repel an affault, or turn away from himfelf an evil that is intended or dreaded.

According to the third, he may compel the injurious to make reparation: And in this laft claufe particularly are found certain claims of right which we are not qualified to difcufs, except fo far as the claufe itfelf is ftated and underftood.

It is to be remembered alfo, that in every queftion of right men are permitted to act as *auxiliaries* as well as *principals*, and that where a third party interpofes, the law of nature, in all its limitations and claufes, and in every cafe of defence, applies e-qually to the one as to the other.

SECTION

SECTION IV.

Of the general Titles under which the Rights of Men may be classed.

IN a subject familiar and obvious to every person there is more danger that we overlook what is evident, than what may require investigation and research.

After having assumed as a self evident maxim, that a person may defend himself, it appears unnecessary to subjoin, or it is rather a repetition of the same thing in other words, to say, that he may defend his person, the limbs and organs of his body, and exercise the faculties of his mind.—Yet these, in pursuing our subject methodically, we shall have occasion to cite; and much depends on their being kept in view, when we would discuss certain questions relating to the origin as well as progress of justice in the affairs of men.

These are original appurtenances of human nature or inseparable from it, and the maxims of justice relating to these subjects

jects

jects muft have been coeval with the fubjects, and infeparable from human nature alfo.

There cannot therefore have been a time in which man had yet to acquire his right of defence in refpect to the particulars mentioned, nor a time in which it was not juft to refpect the perfon of a man, as much or more than to refpect his poffeffion or his eftate.

In this view of the matter, juftice cannot be faid to be an artificial virtue, any more than the perfon of a man to which it refers is artifical.   And no time can be affigned for the commencement of a perfon's right to defend himfelf different from the time at which he began to exift.   In every ftate of his exiftence, by whatever name we call it, whether the ftate of nature, the ftate of fociety or convention, as every one had a right to defend himfelf, fo in every one it would have been wrong to invade that right.

It is abfurd therefore to allege, that in any ftate of mankind all men had equal rights to all things, or that the right of any one to defend his own perfon took its rife from convention.   It is indeed probable, that fuch a doctrine never would have been advanced, nor would juftice in the moft general and comprehenfive terms have been fuppofed to be an artificial or adventitious virtue; if reafoners had not overlooked the felf-evident rights of the perfon, and carried their view at once to matters of property in which the right is confeffedly artificial or adventitious.

With refpect to fubjects of poffeffion or property, it is admitted, that until they were poffeffed by fome one, they were open

to

to any one, and became matter of juſt poſſeſſion to the firſt occupier.

To theſe only Mr Hobbes ſeems to have adverted, when he
ſays, that in the ſtate of nature " all men had equal rights to all
" things ;" and the meaning muſt be, that no one had any right
to any thing until he had occupied it : That occupancy was e-
qually open to all men ; but he ought to have ſubjoined, that after
a ſubject was fairly poſſeſſed, no one had a right to diſturb the
firſt occupier in his uſe of the ſubject.

The undeniable evidence of obvious and uncontrovertable
truths makes it abſurd or impertinent to ſtate them for information, or in the form of diſcovery ; but to aſſume principles, or to
adopt concluſions in direct contradiction to ſuch obvious truths
may indeed have the merit of novelty, or ſeem to proceed from
profound obſervation, but is certainly in a much higher degree
abſurd than the repetition of any truth, however obvious and
previouſly known.

To guard againſt the firſt of theſe errors we may be obliged
to incur the ſecond, and attempt the enumeration of rights even
under titles to which the attention of all mankind might be taken for granted, without any mention of them.

On this account, then, we begin with obſerving, that the rights
of men may be conſidered, either in reſpect to their ſubject, or
in reſpect to their origin.

Conſidered in reſpect to their ſubject, they are by lawyers ſometimes termed *perſonal* and *real* *.

Vol. II.　　　　　B b　　　　　　　　Conſidered

* See Blackſtone's Commentaries on the Laws of England.

Confidered in refpect to their origin, they may be termed *na-tural* and *artificial*; or, in terms perhaps lefs apt to be miftaken, *original* and *adventitious*.

Perfonal rights fubfift in the perfon, and relate to the con-ftituents of his nature and frame. Such are the limbs and organs of the body, and the faculties of the mind, with the ufes of both. Such is life itfelf, freedom of innocent action, and enjoyment of what, without injury to another, is fairly occupied.

Perfons are diftingifhed in the terms of law under the names of perfons *natural* and perfons *artificial*. The individual is a per-fon natural; corporations, ftates, or any plurality of men acting collectively, or under any common direction, are perfons artifi-cial.

In perfons of the latter defcription, political forms, and the conftituent members of the body politic, analogous to the frame and organic parts of the natural body, may be confidered as matter of perfonal right to the community.

Rights *real* fubfift in things feparate from the perfon, provid-ed they may become fubjects of exclufive or incompatible ufe. Such is the right which a perfon obtains to the clothes with which he is covered, or to the ground or other fubject which he has fairly poffeffed.

Real rights, or the right to things, may be referred to three principal heads: *Poffeffion,—Property,—*and *Command*.

3   The

The right of *poſſeſſion* ſubſiſts only ſo long as the thing is in actual uſe, and may therefore be tranſient or ſubject to intermiſſion.

The right of *property* is excluſive, and continues even during the intermiſſions of actual uſe ; it continues therefore until it has ceaſed with conſent of the proprietor.

The right to *command* reſpects the ſervices or the obedience ſuppoſed due from one perſon to another.

Rights conſidered in reſpect to their ſource, being *original* or *adventitious*, it is of moment with reſpect to the firſt to ſpecify their ſubject ; and with reſpect to the ſecond, to aſcertain the titles on which they are founded.

SECTION

S E C T I O N   V.

Of Rights Original.

THE fubjects of original right, being coeval with man, muft be limited to the conftituents of his nature, or the common appurtenances of his kind.

Original rights are therefore perfonal, and exprefs what every one from his birth is entitled to defend in himfelf, and what no one has a right to invade in another.

Thefe rights may be modified by alienation or confent ; but, prior to convention of any fort, remain entire, and in one perfon exactly correfpond to thofe of another.

The exiftence of every fuch right is felf-evident : It may be overlooked from inadvertency or defign, but being once ftated cannot be controverted.

Mr Hobbes in laying the foundation of his fyftem appears to have overlooked the original rights of the perfon : But if they had been ftated to him, or if he had been afked, whether every perfon in his fuppofed ftate of nature had not a right to preferve himfelf? or whether any perfon had a right to deftroy his innocent neighbour? it is difficult to conceive, that a perfon, who acknowledges the obligation of one man to keep faith with another, fhould not acknowledge alfo his obligation to abftain from any harm to his perfon.

SECTION

SECTION VI.

Of Rights Adventitious.

PART II.
CHAP. III.
SECT. VI.

IN the term *adventitious* is implied a preceding period of existence, however short, in which the thing adventitious was yet
future; a time in which it began to be, and a subsequent period
of its continuance.

In the first period of man's existence, he had his original rights;
in a second period those rights may be modified by his own consent, or new rights accrue to him from some act of his own, or
the voluntary deed of some other person concerned.

Original rights are recognised upon being merely stated; adventitious rights require to be supported by evidence, in which
the manner of their acquisition is to be cited and considered.

When a person lays claim to the exclusive use of any subject,
or requires the service and obedience of other men, he may be
asked,

afked, whence his right is derived? or by what evidence he is enabled to fupport his claim? Such right, however fairly conftituted, is ftill matter of difcuffion, and the object of fcience, in every fuch difcuffion, is to afcertain by what means a fubject, not originally matter of right to any one, may become fo to fome one; or, in other words, if a claim fhould be laid to any fuch right, it is material to know by what evidence it may be evinced or fupported.

As rights perfonal, agreeably to the definition which hath been given of them, for the moft part are original, or coeval with the exiftence of the perfon. fo the rights real, fuch as *poffeffion*, *property*, or *command*, are, for the moft part adventitious, and may begin to exift at any period fubfequent to the exiftence of the perfon and the thing to which they relate; and, as both the perfon and the thing might have continued to exift, without any apprehended relation of one to the other, we are in the following fections to enquire whence fuch relation may have arifen; how they are conftituted, and how they are to be verified in any particular inftance.

SECTION

S E C T.   VII.

Of the different Sources of Adventitious Rights.

BEFORE we proceed to affirm whence an adventitious right may arife, it is proper to obferve negatively, that it cannot arife from any act of injuftice or wrong ; nor be conftituted where the thing is impoffible or not real.

Injuftice or wrong has reference to a perfon injured or wronged, who may defend himfelf ; and to a perfon committing an injury, or doing a wrong, who, inftead of reaping benefit from his wrong, expofes himfelf to fuffer whatever may be neceffary to repel his injurious attempt ; or whatever may be neceffary to obtain reparation of the harm he may have done.

This negative propofition were too obvious to need being formally ftated, if it were not neceffary to correct a common folecifm in language, by which we are told of the *right of conqueft,* arifing from a fuccefsful application of mere force, without re-
                                                        gard

gard to the juftice or injuftice of the caufe in which that force was employed.

Where conqueft is matter of right, there muft be fuppofed a previous title to the fubject conquered ; and, if fuch title be verified, the conqueft amounts to no more than a juft poffeffion obtained by force.

To this negative propofition, that right cannot arife to an injurious perfon from the wrong he has committed ; we may fubjoin what is equally evident, that no title can arife to what is not poffible or not real.

Where either the thing or the perfon has no exiftence, there cannot be any relation. Upon this ground, we fhall have occafion to obferve, that although parties ftipulating what is impoffible may, by fuch proceeding, give rife to fome claim in the one againft the other, yet that there cannot be any obligation to the performance of any fuch article, however directly ftipulated.

In treating the hiftory of adventitious rights, there are two queftions which may be feparately difcuffed. The firft queftion relates to things which, prior to the origin of the right in queftion, had not become matter of right to any one * ; and the object of fcience is to afcertain by what means a thing till then open to the firft occupier, may have become a matter of exclufive right to fome particular perfon. The fecond queftion relates to the transfer or conveyance from one perfon to another of a right previoufly fuppofed to exift in the perfon by whom the conveyance is made.

Vol. II.   C c   To

---

* Res nullius.

To the firſt of theſe queſtions we may anſwer in general, that things belonging to *no one* may become matter of right to *ſome one*, either by mere occupancy, or in conſequence of labour employed to improve or accommodate the ſubject to uſe. To the ſecond queſtion, we may anſwer, in like general terms, that a right may be conveyed from one perſon to another by *convention* or *forfeiture.*

We are, therefore, in the following ſections, to define the titles of *occupancy, labour, convention,* and *forfeiture*; and to apply the law of acquiſition, founded in theſe ſeveral titles, to the ſpecific rights originating in this law or determinable according to this rule.

SECTION

S E C T I O N   VIII.

Of Occupancy, and the Species of Right that may result from it.

OCCUPANCY is the relation of a perfon to a thing, fuch, that no other perfon can ufe the fame thing without moleftation or detriment to the occupier.

PART II.
CHAP. III.
SECT.VIII.

In this manner a perfon may occupy the unappropriated ground on which he repofes himfelf, the fpring at which he drinks, or the cover to which he has betaken himfelf as a fhelter from the ftorm. In any of thefe inftances, an attempt to ufe the fame thing may harm or moleft the occupier. He may therefore defend himfelf againft any fuch attempt; or in other words, he has an exclufive right to the fubject in queftion, fo long as he continues to occupy it, or retains his poffeffion.

This right, however, does not extend to the prohibition of any act by which the occupier is not any way difturbed or aggrieved: So that the occupier cannot juftly refift another ufing the fame

C c 2

thing

thing with himself, if this may be done without any detriment to him. Every one may breathe the air of the atmofphere, enjoy the light and heat of the fun, pafs on the highway, and navigate the high fea with mutual freedom from harm or moleftation.

The right that refults from occupancy is no more than that of poffeffion, beginning and ceafing with the act of occupying the fubject to the extent defcribed : So that, as this right does not extend to the prohibition of any act by which the occupier is not aggrieved, it evidently does not preclude any one from refting on the fame ground after the firft occupier has removed from it; nor preclude a fecond perfon from drinking of the fame fpring, after the firft has ceafed drinking ; or from having recourfe to the fame cover, after it has been abandoned by a former occupier.

As the effect of occupancy, therefore, ceafes with the actual ufe, it does not amount to *property*, or to any right fuppofed to continue during the intermiffion of fuch actual ufe.

No right in one perfon to *command* the fervices of another can arife from any title of occupancy, fuppofed to take place without the confent of the perfon whofe fervices are required. To occupy the fervice of another without his confent, implies the ufe of force to obtain fuch fervice. Force fo employed amounts to an injury; and, inftead of conftituting a right, may be refifted on the moft evident principles of the law of felf-defence.

It is juftly held to be a public intereft, that fair poffeffion in every inftance fhould be as little precarious as poffible ; and upon

this

this account mankind willingly enter into conventions, by which
fair poffeffion of a certain duration is admitted as property.

The duration of fuch poffeffion in the laws of different countries is termed prefcription, and was unequal in the jurifprudence of different nations, and in refpect to the occupancy of different fubjects. By the antient law of the Romans, refpecting fome fubjects, a fair poffeffion of three years amounted to prefcription. In our law and refpecting the fubject of land eftate, forty years fair poffeffion is required to the fame effect.

It is a maxim in the law of nature felf-evident and uncontroverted, that all fubjects unoccupied and unappropriated are open to the firft occupier. If, therefore, by the ftate of nature, it be meant to defign a ftate in which nothing is yet occupied or appropriated ; or if we hold the negation of any right to be an equality of right, as if we fhould fay, that the dead are all equally alive, or that fuch as have nothing are all equally rich ; the maxim of Mr Hobbes may be admitted, fo far as it relates to matters of adventitious right : " *That in the ftate of nature all men had* " *equal right to all things.*"

There could be no rule, by which to fettle any rights which did not exift ; but, with refpect to the exifting rights of the perfon coeval with human nature, there certainly was an exifting rule, *That no one was entitled to injure or moleft his neighbour.* To this rule mankind have at all times reforted ; and by this rule they have generally been governed, notwithftanding the occafional irruptions of force and violence. When they are at any time in a ftate of war, this proceeds not from the want of an amicable rule, by which to decide their differences, but from the influence

of

of paffion or error, which inclines fome one or more of the parties to infringe the rule.

Mr Hobbes feems to make the ftate of war to confift, not fo
much in actual hoftility, as in the want of any rule by which
differences could be amicably terminated, and in the neceffary reference of parties to the decifion of force alone : But it is evident
that the ftate of war thus defined did never actually exift ; and
that, in the midft of hoftilities feemingly the moft implacable,
nations refer to a ftandard of right, according to which they plead
that the quarrel fhould be amicably terminated in their own favour.

Mankind, in every ftate, not only had original rights of the
perfon, but could not continue to exift without proceeding to occupy and poffefs the means of fubfiftence and accommodation ;
and without being engaged in tranfactions which amounted to
fome fpecies of convention or bargain : So that the fuppofition
of a ftate, prior even to the origin of adventitious rights, muft
have been of fo fhort a duration as to refemble an abftraction of
the mind, in which co exiftent circumftances are feparately conceived ; rather than a period of hiftory, during which they actually exifted apart.

SECTION

SECTION IX.

Of Labour, and the Species of Right that results from it.

LABOUR, confidered as the origin of a right, is an effort, by which a perfon may, for his own ufe, fabricate, procure, or improve any unoccupied and unappropriated fubject.

It is evident that, by the law of nature, a perfon is not permitted to labour on a fubject occupied, becaufe his labour may be a detriment to the occupier ; nor is he permitted to labour on a fubject appropriated without the confent of the proprietor.

Under this title of labour is fuppofed an effort productive of fome permanent effect, fome fruit of invention, of fkill, or of power any way applied ; and the labourer having, by the law of nature, an original right to the ufe of his talents or powers, has, by evident confequence, a right to the effects produced by any of their applications.

I

As

As the right of poffeffion continues during the continuance of occupancy, fo the right acquired by labour continues together with the fubject produced, and belongs to the producer, until he himfelf fhall confent to forego, or transfer it to another.

The right, therefore, which is thus acquired, comes up to the idea of property. It is a right, in the labourer, to the exclufive ufe of his powers, and of their lawful effects, even during the intermiffions of that ufe.

The right acquired by labour does not determine with poffeffion : This may be difcontinued during any period, and may be refumed again : If the fubject be moveable, and during any time miflaid, it may be recovered wherever it is found; if in the poffeffion of another, that other may be lawfully forced to reftore it.

It may be argued, however, that as the right of property thus originating in labour is limited to the actual effect which that labour has produced ; and, as it is not in the power of man to produce any fubftance, he cannot by his labour acquire a property in any fuch fubject whatever. Human labour may combine materials together, or give to a fubftance fome new modification or form; and fo far the right of the labourer extends : But, as the fubftance itfelf is not an effect of his labour, whenever he fhall ceafe to ufe it, the fubftance fhall be open to the firft occupier.

If any difficulty be fuppofed to arife from fuch fubtilties of argumentation, it may be removed by obferving, that, although
the

the right of a labourer may extend only to the form, modification, or improvement, he has made, not to the fubject or fubftance
which exifts independent of his labour ; yet, if no one can occupy
that fubject or fubftance, without encroaching upon his right to
the modification or improvement, it is evident, that, in defending
his right to the modification, he may exclude every perfon from
occupying the fubftance of which the form or improvement is
his property.

The favage who has wrought a piece of wood into the form of
a bow, in maintaining his right to the form, necessarily excludes
every other perfon from the ufe of the wood. The hufbandman,
who, in breaking up uncultivated land, has acquired a right to the
fruits of his culture, muft, in order to preferve his right, exclude
every other perfon from occupying the earth or ftone of the foil
to which his culture has been applied, although he has not in
reality produced thofe fubftances.

The plea of right refulting from labour is limited to the right
of property alone. When applied to any other fpecies of right,
whether a right of poffeffion, or a right to command, it is either
not neceffary, or not adequate. It is not neceffary to conftitute a
right of poffeffion ; nor is it adequate to eftablifh the claim of
one perfon to a right in the fervices of another.

Poffeffion is valid, becaufe the occupier muft not be difturbed,
although he may not have beftowed any labour on the fubject in
poffeffion. Labour, therefore, is not neceffary to eftablifh this
fpecies of right.

As to the fecond, or the right to *command* ; if it be
VOL. II.   D d   afked

afked, whether this may not refult from labour? We muft anfwer in the negative; for, although one perfon may have taken pains to qualify another for the performance of fome fpecific fervice; yet we muft contend, that no right to his fervice can be founded on this plea. Labour employed by one on the perfon of another, without his own confent, may be an injury, and cannot be the foundation of a right. If applied with his confent, but without any ftipulated conditions, the perfon to whom any new art is thus communicated, retains all his perfonal rights, and cannot juftly be forced to work for another. " If you taught me an art, might " fuch a perfon plead with his inftructor, without having ftipu- " lated that I fhould employ it for you, it muft be underftood " that I am free to employ it for myfelf." Gratitude may incline him to make fome return to a benefactor; but the demand of a return may cancel that obligation; and, in anfwer to fuch a demand, the apprentice may plead: " If you taught me an art, " that I might employ it for yourfelf, you cannot plead a benefit " intended to me, nor lay claim to my gratitude; or, if you in- " tended a benefit to me, you muft leave me to enjoy its fruits."

A perfon may innocently labour upon the property of another, without knowing it to be already appropriated. He may give a new form; he may compofe a mixture, of which the materials, either entirely, or in part, belong to fome other perfon. In all thefe inftances, the decifion of the law of nature is clear and peremptory, that no one is bound to fuffer a diminution of his right from the act of another, however free from guile or finifter intention.

As the party, acting however without guile or malice, cannot be charged with injuftice, the law of nature awards, that the
right

right of any other party concerned fhould be preferved or reftor-
ed, with the leaft poffible detriment to the fair and innocent deal- er : And this is wifely provided for, in the conventional law of every well ordered community. But the rule that is adopted, in adjufting the relative claims of parties, on fuch occafions, may vary at the difcretion of thofe on whom the practice of law de- pends. According to the law of the Romans, property thus brought in to difpute, was fometimes made to follow the original fubject, and fometimes the fpecification or form beftowed upon it. When the materials, as in the cafe of bullion wrought into plate, could be reftored to their priftine form, the property was awarded to him to whom the bullion belonged. Where the fpe- cification, or new form, was of a certain value compared to the fubject on which a work was performed, as in the cafe of a picture, compared to the canvas on which it is painted, or in the cafe of a writing compared to the paper or vellum on which it is executed, there the material, from favour to the art which was practifed upon it, was adjudged to be the property of the artift. Where fubjects, belonging to two or more different perfons, were unwarily mixt by either of them, and could not be again feparated, it was awarded, that the mixture fhould be di- vided among the parties concerned, in proportion to the fhare of materials which each had in the compofition or mixture ; and the leaft inconvenient manner of terminating a difpute was, in this manner, intended, or provided for in thefe different inftances.

Labour conftitutes a right to property in the effect, which that labour has produced. Although there may have been labour, therefore, in any particular cafe, if there be no permanent effect, there is no fubject of property. Mariners may have navigated the fea ; they may have traverfed new and unappropriated iflands ; but, if the land is no way changed by their labour ; the earth, no more

than

than the tracklefs ocean, can become a fubject of property to the perfon by whom it is merely traverfed.

It is neverthelefs a cuftom of fome ftanding, among the nations of Europe, to claim the dominion of newly difcovered lands or iflands, as founded in prior difcovery, and confirmed alone by fymbolical forms or acts of poffeffion; fuch as the erecting of columns, with dates and infcriptions recording the claim of the fovereign, in whofe behalf it is made.

So far as any number of nations have been in practice of claiming and acknowledging rights, founded in fuch forms as thefe, they muft be underftood to have entered into a fair convention refpecting fuch fubjects. A mere fymbolical occupancy is valid againft thofe who have repeatedly availed themfelves of the fame plea, and who are therefore come under an obligation to give way to it in their turn. It is a plea fufficient to exclude thofe who have agreed to be excluded by it, but not to exclude any ftranger who is not a party to any convention in the cafe, whether exprefs or tacit; much lefs a plea fufficient to deprive the native, however rude or barbarous, of the inheritance or poffeffion to which he is born.

The right of the claimant, therefore, among the nations of Europe, upon the ground of difcovery or fymbolical poffeffion, is matter of convention merely among fuch nations; and cannot be derived, either from the principle of occupancy, or the principle of labour, at leaft, until the fubject is actually occupied, or, from the labour beftowed upon it, has received fome actual change or improvement.

3   Such

Such are the ways in which a fubject, the right of *no one,* * may become the right of *fome one*; either while he occupies it, or in confequence of the effect he has produced in it by his labour.

It remains, that we confider by what means the right of one perfon may be transferred to another, as in convention or forfeiture.

* Res nullius.

SECTION

S E C T I O N   X.

Of Contract, or the Principle of conventional Obligation.

PART II.
CHAP. III.
SECT. X.

A CONVENTION, or contract, is the mutual confent of parties to conftitute, transfer, or reduce a right.

Where two or more perfons, therefore, are confenting to the fame or to mutual articles of agreement, they come refpectively or mutually under the obligation of contract.

This obligation, in the cafe of mutual confent, is univerfally acknowledged, or univerfally pleaded by thofe who exact the performance of a bargain: Infomuch, that even they who overlook every other foundation of right, acknowledge compact as fufficient to fupport all the claims of juftice in civil or political fociety.

The obligation of compact, therefore, muft either be felf-evident, or muft be derived from fome very obvious and felf-evident

I   principle.

principle. Mr Hobbes denies the exiſtence of any right prior to convention; but, it moſt be owned, that if in this, his opinion bears hard upon human nature, in denying the original rights of men, he is exceedingly prompt to ſuſtain the effect of convention in creating every right which men have occaſion to plead in ſociety; and his proceeding is to the following purpoſe.

The firſt requiſite, according to him, in eſtabliſhing any principle of law with which men are bound to comply, is: " That every " man diveſt himſelf of the right he hath to all things by nature *; " or, as he himſelf interprets, the ſuppoſed right of all men to " all things, it being in effect, as he acknowledges, no *better than* " *if no man had a right to any thing* †." The firſt requiſite, in eſtabliſhing a law of nature, is, that all men conſent mutually, that for the future there ſhall be ſuch a thing as *right*; " but," continues he, " as this conſent were utterly vain and of none effect, if this " alſo were not a law of the ſame nature, that every man is ob- " liged to ſtand to and perform theſe covenants he maketh ‡;" it appears neceſſary to eſtabliſh this obligation in general, before the conſent of parties can be ſuppoſed to eſtabliſh it in any particular inſtance.

The breach or violation of covenants, according to this celebrated writer, is the *firſt ſpecies of injury*; but, to a perſon who denies the previous exiſtence of injury, in the harm that may be done to the perſon of a man; it may be difficult to ſhow how injury commences in this form, and no other. If he deny that, prior to
convention,

* De Corpore Politico, Part 1ſ, Chap. iii. Sect. 1.

† Ibid. Sect. 2.

‡ Ibid. Chap. iii. Sect. 1.

convention, there is any obligation to abftain from harm; if he admits that the violent may wound with his fword; that the infidious may enfnare with his cunning; why not that the faithlefs may, to procure an advantage to himfelf, betray the confidence he has been able to obtain.

To folve this problem, he has recourfe to the following procefs of reafoning : *Not to perform what is contracted for, being what all men call an injury,* he proves performance to be binding, *becaufe non-performance is an abfurdity in action, as felf-contradiction is an abfurdity in argument* : " For, as he which is driven to contradict " an affertion by him before maintained, is faid to be reduced to " an abfurdity, fo he that through paffion doth or omitteth that " which before he promifed to do, or not to omit, is faid to com- " mit injuftice, and there is in every breach of covenant a con- " tradiction fo called.—He that violateth a covenant, willeth the " doing and not doing of the fame thing at the fame time, which " is a plain contradiction *."

Here, it muft be confeffed, the argument is diftinctly ftated; the obligation of contract, and with it, according to this author, all the pofitive rights of men, are made to reft on the merit of confiftency, in preference to inconfiftency or felf-contradiction. It were irrational to fay and unfay the fame thing; therefore, rational beings are bound in their actions to be confiftent with their fayings; that is to fay, *they are bound to obferve their contracts.* To do otherwife, would be to unfay in their actions, or in neglect of performance what they had previoufly faid, in terms of a bargain, or in expreffions of confent.

Such

* Ibid. Sect. 2.

Such reafoning but ill accounts for the indignation with which a breach of faith is univerfally confidered by mankind. He who breaks faith may incur the charge of inconfiftency it is true ; but how different from the charge of *perfidy* or *treafon.* The traitor next to the murderer is reckoned the moft odious among criminals, and the argument now ftated from Mr Hobbes is the lefs fit to fupport the obligation of contract, or to account for the fentiments with which breach of faith is reprobated, that it would equally apply to evince an obligation where none is admitted, and to fix a criminal imputation where the paffions relent ; and where a perfon once inclined to the commiffion of a crime fhrinks from guilt and returns to innocence.

Thus, upon the principle of confiftency, as ftated by this author, a perfon having once expreffed an intention refpecting a matter in which he himfelf alone is concerned, would be bound to fulfil his intention, whatever reafon or confideration may have occurred to the contrary. If a perfon, for inftance, has one propofed in his own mind, or mentioned in his talk an intention to carry his goods to market, he is no longer at liberty to withhold them. If he has threatened to kill his neighbour, his benefactor, or his parent, he is not at liberty to retract or to change his mind. In any fuppofed cafe of this fort, however, mankind would confider the threat as a crime, and the failure of performance, not as a breach of faith, but as the relenting of a mind which had yet fome remains of ingenuity, a fenfe of innocence, and fome difpofition to atone for the guilt of having ever entertained fo atrocious a purpofe.

In this account of moral obligation collected from the ordinary

E e fenfe

fenfe of mankind, we find a clear apprehenfion of right and wrong prior to convention.   We find an acknowledgment, that convention itfelf may be wrong ; the completion of it worfe ; and the breach of it right.   As he who has engaged or bargained to commit a murder incurs a certain meafure of guilt in the bargain he has made ; this meafure of guilt he would greatly augment by preferving confiftency, or by proceeding to fulfil his bargain ; and under fuch an unhappy engagement his duty manifeftly is to become inconfiftent, and to decline the performance.

Some writers who have employed their ingenuity to a better purpofe, and who think more favourably of man's phyfical ftate than the laft we have mentioned, feem willing, neverthelefs, to reft the obligations of men in fociety more upon convention than is neceffary ; and to reafon from this topic of contract, in cafes to which the great injunction of natural law to abftain from harm is at leaft equally obvious and equally applicable.

Society itfelf is by fuch writers confidered as the refult of a bargain, and the relative duties of men in fociety are traced up to a fuppofed original compact, on the articles of which volumes have been written*. The intention of writers, in this form of their argument, is no doubt favourable to mankind, and the hypothefis of a conditional obligation is by them recurred to, merely in order that none of the parties in civil fociety may pretend a right to enjoy his peculiar advantage, without fulfilling alfo the condition to which he is peculiarly bound, or without contributing what is due from himfelf, in return for what he expects to receive from another.   Thus, allegiance and protection being ftated, as the reciprocal

* Vide Contrat Social of Rouffeau.

ciprocal ftipulations of magiftrate and fubject, the one is not to
expect allegiance, without adminiftring protection, nor the other to
expect protection without the proper returns of allegiance and duty.

Were we to enumerate all the obligations of men in fociety, we
fhould find many, no doubt, which arife from convention exprefs or tacit; but, it is far from being neceffary or expedient
to refer the whole to this title. The obligation to abftain from
harm, and the right of every individual, to the utmoft of his
power, to defend himfelf and his fellow creatures, are prior to
convention, and are indeed the foundation upon which conventional obligation itfelf is eftablifhed.

Whoever has power may employ it in defending the innocent;
and fo far, the magiftrate having the fword in his hand need not
enquire whether the criminal that offends againft the peace of his
country, has agreed to abftain from crimes, or has agreed to fubmit to punifhment. In repreffing the crimes, and in giving examples to deter others from the commiffion of them, the magiftrate does no more than what every other perfon, prior to convention, and to the extent of his power, is entitled to do.

But, when the magiftrate affumes to himfelf alone the prerogative
of employing force for the repreffion of crimes; when he tells the
injured, that he muft not attempt to do himfelf right, but muft have
recourfe to the protection eftablifhed by law; when he requires the
fubject to part with his fubftance, to defray the expence of a public
fervice; when he affumes the right to pofitive command, in requiring the innocent to ferve his country, as well as in requiring the
injurious to abftain from harm; there, no doubt, he muft be able
to plead a fpecial inftitution or convention, to which the people
have agreed.

E e 2

Laws

PART II.
CHAP. III.
SECT. X.

Laws and inftitutions, in every community, contain articles of agreement entered into by the parties with whom they originated, and by their pofterity who accede to them ; but fuch agreements are all of them pofterior to the exiftence of fociety, and not the foundations upon which fociety was originally erected. The ef- fential obligations of men in fociety are founded in what nature has done for them, not in what they themfelves have agreed to perform ; and fuch obligations can receive no confirmation or fanction from the fuppofition of a contract which is merely fic- titious, or which did not exift.

The humane author of the treatife on crimes and punifhments *, founding even the right to punifh crimes on a fuppofed original compact, and applying a well known maxim of law, that com- pacts are to be ftrictly interpreted, denies any right in the magif- trate to inflict punifhments more fevere than are neceffary to ob- tain the purpofe for which parties contracted; that is, more fevere than is neceffary to reftrain crimes, and to keep the peace of fociety. For this being the object of parties in forming their compact, fo far, he argues, every perfon in fociety may be fuppofed to have acceded to the contract, and no farther. This, however, is no more than a circuitous way of afferting, that the ftate or its ma- giftrates have no right to punifh any crime, farther than is necef- fary for their own defence, or the defence of the caufe entrufted to their charge ; a maxim that does not require confent to make it binding, but is implied in the firft principle of natural law, which limits the means of defence within the bounds of what is neceffary for the prefervation or recovery of a right.

ɪ   If

* The Marquis Becaria.

If we muſt admit the ſuppoſition of an original compact, like a
bond of copartnery, conſtituting the foundation of ſociety, and
the firſt charter of rights to its members ; as there is no record
of the articles originally framed, theſe muſt now be inferred
from the principles of natural right; for we have no other ſource
from which to derive information of what men were likely to
have ſtipulated or agreed to perform in a period of which no veſ-
tige remains.

In the firſt treaty of peace, by which men agreed to live in ſociety together, we are told, accordingly, that they muſt have ſtipulated to abſtain from harm. But whence this information, we
may aſk ? Not from the record of any ſuch ſtipulation! Nay, but
it may be aſſumed from the manifeſt equity and reaſon of the
ſuppoſed article. This is, firſt, to alledge that a perſon is bound
to be juſt, becauſe he has bargained to be ſo; and, next, to
preſume that he has bargained to abſtain from harm, becauſe it is
juſt that he do ſo.

If we are to ſuppoſe, with Mr Hobbes, or as is, in ſome meaſure, implied in his reſting all the obligations of men in ſociety
upon a ſuppoſed original compact, that there is no right and no
obligation prior to convention; it will be difficult, ſurely, as the
example of Mr Hobbes himſelf will ſhow, to find a foundation
upon which the obligation of contract itſelf may reſt. If contract
be the ſole foundation of right, all that is commonly ſaid of an
inherent right in every perſon to defend himſelf, or of an obligation correſponding to this right on every perſon to abſtain from
harm, muſt be renounced. The diſtinction, ſuppoſed between
rights original and adventitious, muſt be dropt. All the rights
of men, whether perſonal or real, are adventitious, and begin
with

with the confent of one man not to difturb the poffeffion of another; and, in fhort, no man is obliged, even in the lateft hour of
fociety, to abftain from harm, except fo far as by fome fpecies
of compact he has bound himfelf fo to do.

Such confequences, however, are fufficiently abfurd to juftify
our rejecting the principle on which they are founded; and are
probably far from the thoughts of many, who affume the focial
compact, as a *fiction of law*, upon which to reft their decifions in
particular inftances. To this principle, at any rate, we cannot have
recourfe in fixing the grounds of conventional obligation.   That
a compact may be binding, we muft fuppofe fome previous foundation upon which its obligation may reft, whether the confiftency to which Mr Hobbes refers, or the original right of every perfon to defend himfelf, to which we have fo often referred in thefe
difquifitions.

If the rule that forbids the commiffion of harm, or the principle of nature, on which is founded a right of defence, can be applied to the cafe of parties, fo far pledging or accepting a *faith*
which is pledged to them, as that, by the breach of this faith they
may injure or be injured; it will follow, that they ought to refrain
from that injury; or may repel it, by obliging the party contracting
to fulfil the terms of his contract.

By the law of nature, every party may defend his eftate
from every invafion that is made to impair it.   Of the ftate
which may be thus defended, men derive part from the hand of
their Maker, which is accordingly to them matter of original right;
part from their own act and deed, as in the cafe of occupancy or
labour, already recited; and we may now fubjoin, that they

I

derive

derive part of their ftate alfo from the engagements in which others
are bound to them ; or from the faith that others have plighted.

The fervant is fecure in the engagement of a mafter to pay his
wages; the mafter relies for his accommodation on the engagement of the fervant to do his work.   The landlord is rich in the
engagement of tenants to pay his rents; the tenant beftows his
labour, and fcatters his feed, trufting to the leafe he has received
from the landlord.   Even the mifer himfelf, who is difpofed to
hoard up his wealth, may not have a fingle penny or article of value in his poffeffion.   He is rich in the capacity merely of a creditor, and in holding others obliged to pay the principal and intereft, in which they are indebted by bond to him.

Such credit, in one man towards another, is a part of their focial nature ; and the perfon who is difpofed to abufe his credit
may wound or deftroy, by means of that inftrument, no lefs than
by the arm of violence, or the fword which he wields in his
hand.

If it be admitted, that men are by nature difpofed mutually to
give and to receive information; that where they have no fpecial
caufe of diftruft, they rely on the informations, affurances, or
promifes which they receive from others ; and that great part in
the conduct of every perfon is determined by informations or affurances fo received.   If the bewildered traveller, in the dark,
turns confidently to the right, when he is told that there is a
precipice on the left, it muft evidently follow, that to miflead
him, or to occafion his harm, by any mifinformation, would be
equally criminal, as to occafion that harm by any other means.

Hence

Hence we may conclude, that a perfon being made to rely on the confent of another, to conftitute or to reduce a right, is not bound to fuffer by the other's breach of faith ; but may proceed on the principle of felf-defence, to force the performance of a pro-mife which makes a part of his ftate; and the principle upon which a perfon, who has come under any engagement, may be forced to fulfil that engagement, is the fame with that maxim, on which he may be forced to abftain from injury, or harm of any other kind; infomuch, that the firft principle of compulfory law, which is in appearance merely prohibitory, may branch into a variety of duties or obligations *to do*, or *to omit* to do, whatever may be a fit matter of ftipulation betwixt any two or more parties con-cerned.

To fail in the difcharge of fuch duties is, on many occafions at leaft, termed *perfidy* or *breach of faith*, and confidered with a higher degree of abhorrence, than even the injuries that are done by open force. This may, no doubt, proceed from circumftances peculiar to fraud and deceit. The traitor muft have carried the mafk of innocence to have obtained credit; he has ftolen an ad-vantage which he had not the courage openly to force. The con-traft of fraud with the mafk of innocence, which it wears, the cowardice which is imputed to the perfon who affumes that mafk in order to wound, combine together in awakening the peculiar fentiment of indignation and hatred, with which perfidy or breach of faith is confidered ; and which, though they do not make any addition to what is at prefent the object of our difcuffion, namely, the right of every perfon to defend himfelf againft fuch wrongs; yet
they

they tend greatly to evince that the fource of conventional obli- Part II.
gation is much more deeply laid than the mere confiftency of Chap. III.
words and actions, upon which it is founded by the philofopher Sect. X.
now mentioned.

SECTION XI.

Of the Laws of Convention derived from the foregoing Principle.

FROM the account which has been given of conventional right
and obligation, it appears that compact, in every inftance, implies
a plurality of parties, one at leaft who comes under an engagement, and one or more to whom the engagement is made, and
who accept of it. The firft may be termed the party *contracting*,
the other the party *accepting*.

In many bargains, the parties may be mutually contracting and
accepting; as when one party binds himfelf to convey a property, accepting a price, and the other binds himfelf to pay the price,
accepting the property. But it is not, at prefent, or in the profe-
cution of this argument, neceffary to confider the parties to a
compact in this double capacity.

From the principle ftated, it is evident. that to give a fuppofed
compact the effect which we have afcribed to it, in conftituting

a

a right, on the part of one, or an obligation, on the part of another, it is neceffary that the accepting party fhould be made to
expect a performance, and that the contracting party fhould have
intentionally done fomewhat fufficient to give fuch expectation.

Without an expectation formed, there is no object of exaction;
and, without a perfon who has intentionally given caufe for that
expectation, there is no one againft whom the exaction may be
enforced.

Agreeably to this decifion, it appears, that, although the contracting party may have done what was fufficient to create an expectation, yet if the other party fhould not, at the fame time, do
what is fufficient to make known his acceptance, there is in reality no obligation to perform.

The tranfaction, upon this laft fuppofition, amounts to no
more than an offer ; and, as the party offering has no intimation
of its being accepted, he is at liberty to change his mind, or may
have recourfe to fome other party willing to accept of the offer he
has made.

It follows, alfo, that as a fuppofed contracting party is not bound
to performance, where acceptance is not fufficiently notified, no
more is he bound to fulfil any falfe expectations for which he
has not laid a foundation.

Upon the principle of convention, fo explained, we may ground
the following law :

That, *To conftitute a valid contract, is required the mutual confent
of parties, acting freely, and in the exercife of their rational faculties;*
and

and with such means of communication as are sufficient to make known their thoughts and intentions.

In the municipal law of different countries, the forms of convention are prescribed, as in *bonds, bills, or promissory notes,* which constitute a debt ; *deeds of conveyance, articles of sale,* and so forth. So that, upon the disagreement of parties, the question at issue may be determined by a third party ; that is, by the judge before whose tribunal the reality of the obligation may come to be tried, and who must collect the sense of parties from the form in which they were pleased to express their agreement. But, as the prescribed form may sometimes have been observed, where there is neverthelefs sufficient cause to set aside the contract, such cause may be taken into consideration, under the title of an exception, and is often sufficient to repel the plea of the party, who claims the performance of an article, however stipulated in the legal form.

Such exceptions, in the municipal law of any country, are or may be enumerated under the titles of *incapacity, force, fraud, injustice,* and *impossibility.*

Incapacity may be pleaded against the validity of an obligation, when it appears, that the party, supposed to have confented, was not in the exercise of his reason at the time. *Force* may be pleaded, when he was known not to act freely ; and *fraud,* when he was known to be deceived ; more especially if the force or the fraud had been employed by the perfon who afterwards claims performance of the article so obtained.

Thefe exceptions are matter of just and neceffary consideration in courts of law, as a judge, if directed merely by the forms
prescribed,

prefcribed, might be mifled to fuftain an obligation where it is not properly conftituted. But, in difcuflions of the law of nature, where a contract is fuppofed to confift, not in any prefcribed form or mode of expreffion, but in the mutual affent of parties, acting freely and in the exercife of their reafon, the exceptions of force and fraud are precluded in the definition itfelf; and, where the fact does not correfpond to the definition, what we contend for is not an exception, by which to fet afide a contract fuppofed to fubfift, but is a negative plea, by which we deny that any contract ever did exift.

The infane or incapable can raife no expectation. A perfon forced or deceived into a bargain, cannot be expected to fulfil that bargain, when he is at liberty, or has detected the fraud that was employed to miflead him. He may confider the perfon who employed fuch means to circumvent him, as guilty of an injury; and may think himfelf entitled to reparation, inftead of being bound to perform the articles of a bargain fo obtained.

There may, however, be a real affent of parties to an article of compact which may afterwards appear to be either injurious to the right of fome third party, or in the nature of things impoffible; and in every fuch cafe, there is a real ground of exception, even upon the general affumptions of the law of nature.

The exception of *injuftice* may be pleaded to ftop execution of an article injurious to a third party, and that of *impoffibility* to fave the party contracting from fruitlefs attempts to perform what cannot be done.

Under thefe titles of *injuftice* and *impoffibility*, confidered as exceptions to a contract, a variety of cafes may be fuppofed.

3 1*ft*,

1*ſt*, That neither party, at the time of ſtipulating, was aware of the *injuſtice* or *impoſſibility*. In this caſe the deciſion is, that both parties are bound to drop their petenſions as ſoon as the exception is known.

A ſecond caſe may be ſuppoſed, where only one of the parties, at the time of ſtipulating, knew of the exception. If the contracting party alone knew that he was engaging himſelf to commit an act of *injuſtice*, he is injurious to the party againſt whom the wrong is directed. If he alone knew that the performance was *impoſſible*, he is unjuſt to the party accepting, in whom he has endeavoured to raiſe a vain expectation.

If the party accepting alone, knew that the performance would be unjuſt, he is, in accepting the offer, injurious to the party likely to ſuffer. If he alone knew that the performance to which he engaged another, was in the nature of things impoſſible, his acceptance of ſuch engagement was an injury to the perſon whom he induced ignorantly ſo to engage himſelf in fruitleſs attempts.

A third caſe may be ſuppoſed in which both parties knew of the exception at the time of making their agreement. If the article ſtipulated was by both parties known to be injurious to a third party, the agreement amounted to a conſpiracy againſt the perſon concerned. If the article was known by both parties to be impoſſible at the time of ſtipulating, there may have been a purpoſe, by ſuch ſham tranſaction, to impoſe upon ſome third party, or elſe the proceeding muſt be judged altogether irrational and abſurd.

In every contract muſt be ſuppoſed a ſufficient mode of communication municasion between the parties. *Language*, whether in fpeech or writing is the moft common, but any other means of ex- preffion, fuppofed to be mutually underftood, will be equally fufficient upon the principles of the law of nature, to eftablifh a conventional, *obligation*, or *right* ; geftures of any fort underftood as figns of declaration or affent; a continued courfe of action ; even fingle actions may, upon this principle, not only be conceiv- ed to exprefs a meaning, but are actually fuftained as fufficient expreffions of affent before the courts of law in every civilized nation.

Hence the effect of cuftom every where admitted as part of the common or the municipal law. Hence the obligation contract- ed by a fhopkeeper, to fell the goods in his fhop to thofe who will pay his price, and the obligation of a perfon who takes the goods, to pay that price. Hence the obligation of an inn-keep- er to accommodate paffengers ; and the obligation on paffengers to pay their bill ; although neither one nor the other made any verbal declaration to that effect.

In the ordinary courfe of things, we look to the future as a con- tinuation of the paft, and confider the cuftom of the country in which we refide, as an affurance of the terms on which we live with the people of that country.

It is evident in particular, that cuftom may be pleaded againft thofe who take the benefit of it, where it is favourable to them- felves ; and who, therefore, may be reafonably fuppofed willing, in their turn, to comply with it, where it is favourable or bene- ficial to others.

I   In

In this manner conventions are tacitly formed, and the laws of every country confifts more of cuftomary practice, eftablifhed by repeated decifions, than of ftatute or exprefs conftitution of any fort.

It is a maxim of natural juftice, that every party obferving a cuftom, in thofe refpects in which it is burdenfome to himfelf, is entitled in his turn to expect the obfervance of it alfo in thofe refpects in which it is beneficial. A perfon bearing the public burdens of the ftate, is entitled to its protection ; and a fovereign, granting protection, is entitled to allegiance and fupport.

Convention, though not the foundation or caufe of fociety, as implied in the *term* of *original compact*, may be fuppofed almoft coeval with the intercourfe of mankind. Men do not move in the fame company together, without communications of mind or intention. Thefe communications become objects of mutual reliance, and even that party may be charged with breach of faith who has belied the expectations he gave by his amicable looks or pacific behaviour. From the firft fteps, therefore, that are made in fociety, conventions may be fuppofed to go on accumulating in the form of practice, if not in the form of ftatute or exprefs inftitution.

Political eftablifhments, in many inftances, originate in force, and prerogatves are affumed which in the firft exercife of them were manifeft violations of right. Men neverthelefs in procefs of time, or at leaft in the fucceffion of a few ages, acquire the habits of their fituation ; and fucceeding generations may be reconciled to forms that were forced on their anceftors. They adopt as a cuftom, and willingly fubmit to conditions which owed

ed their firſt impoſition perhaps to violence. In ſuch caſes, we are not always to look back to the origin of a cuſtom or prac- tice, in order to judge of its validity. If it be ſuch as the mind of man may by habit be reconciled to, and willing to adopt, it becomes binding on thoſe who have availed themſelves of the cuſ- tom, where it is favourable to themſelves ; and are therefore fair- ly underſtood to adopt the conditions of it, where theſe conditions are reciprocally favourable to others.

Succeeding generations of men are ſuppoſed to be compre- hended under certain legal eſtabliſhments, by the deed and inſti- tution of their anceſtors. This is not ſtrictly true. Every citi- zen, as he comes of age, enters upon a ſcene which his anceſtors had prepared for him, but of which the conditions as binding on him cannot be ratified by any one beſides himſelf. He mixes in ſociety, where theſe conditions are already ratified by others; and he himſelf in complying with them, and in reaping the benefit of them, gives ſuch aſſurance of his willingneſs to accede to the terms already preſcribed in his country, as amounts to a ſufficient ratification of the ſame terms on his own part. So that citizens, in every regular community, are bound, not by the inſtitution of their anceſtors on which they were not conſulted, but by the conſent which they themſelves have given, by availing themſelves of the benefits which reſult from ſuch inſtitutions.

To the queſtion, therefore, whether perſons of one age can bind their poſterity in ages that follow? we may anſwer in the nega- tive: But ſuccceeding ages, nevertheleſs, become bound in acced- ing to the terms on which they live with their fellow citizens.

In

In judging of an inftitution, we may repeat, that we are not fo much to look to its origin as its actual nature. Compliance extorted by force does not amount to convention; but juftice itfelf fometimes needs to be enforced, and the wifeft inftitutions, at the time of their firft admiffion, may have been the fruits of compulfion: But, if in the fequel, an eftablifhment be found acceptable, and favourable to the interefts of mankind, they do well to abide by it, and, while they do fo, no individual can remain in his country, and take the benefit of its laws, without being bound to obey them in his turn.

Thus, it becomes evident, that as it were abfurd in fcience, like Mr Hobbes, to overlook the original rights of men; fo it were no lefs abfurd, like vifionary theorifts, in any queftion of law or ftate, to refer to mere original rights, as the fole ground of decifion. It were abfurd, after a perfon had bought an eftate, to reject the conveyance that was made to him, in order to judge of his title, on fuch principle of right merely as may be fuppofed to precede the inftitution of property.

But, if want of confent, in one age, will not preclude the obligation of compact on fucceeding ages, or on thofe who in the fequel voluntarily accede to a practice, no more will the confent of anceftors, with whom a practice originated, bind their pofterity, or thofe who in the fequel refufe their affent; and, if an inftitution, however willingly adopted by a former age, prove in the fequel a mere abufe; if it be a continued exercife of injuftice and wrong, fupported by force on the one part, and a continued feries of fuffering and reluctant compliance on the other; fuch practices, however long continued, as they are never ratified by confent, they are never eftablifhed on the foot of cuftomary

I   practice,

practice, nor do they obtain the force of convention. The op- PART II.
preffed, even after any indefinite period of oppreffion are free to CHAP. III.
SECT· XI.
procure relief by fuch means as they are enabled to employ for
that purpofe.

SECTION

SECTION XII.

Of the specific Obligations and Rights that result from Contract.

PART II.
CHAP.III.
SECT XII. MEN may bind themselves by contract to do, or to omit to do, whatever is within the compass of their will, and not contrary to the right of any other person; *but* in matters, concerning one person, which no way depend on the consent of another, compact were misplaced, and cannot have any effect.

In seizing upon things which are open to the first occupier, the consent of others is not required; or, in other words, the right of possession results from occupancy alone, apart from any consent.

Possession is short of property; because, if the possessor should cease to occupy a subject, he has not any right to exclude another from its use. When relinquished, it is open again to the first occupier, whether the person who formerly possessed it, or any one else.

This

This defect, in the right of poffeffion, may be in part fupplied by the confent of all the parties, who had accefs to the fubject, at the time it has ceafed to be occupied. And thus, a right of property in one perfon, may be pleaded againft all thofe who confented to forgo their right of occupancy. With refpect to fuch as confent to the property, it is matter of convention; and the perfon, in whofe favour they have given their confent, has fo far acquired an exclufive right, that, upon any difcontinuance of the ufe, he may refume it, or even recover his fubject, if found in the poffeffion of thofe who refigned their right of occupancy in his favours.

But this right, which is exclufive with refpect to thofe, whether few or many, who have confented to exclude themfelves, can never of itfelf amount to an abfolute property, or be exclufive with refpect to all mankind.

Were we therefore to admit the principle affumed by Mr Hobbes, that originally all men had equal rights to all things, and that compact alone could give exclufive right to any thing, it fhould follow, that univerfal confent was neceffary to give abfolute property, or to conftitute a right fpecial and exclufive in any one to the fole ufe of the fubject to which he laid claim; and we might infer, on the fame principle, that, as no fuch univerfal confent has ever been obtained, no right of property is yet fully conftituted: Moreover, that as fuch univerfal confent never can be obtained, we might alfo infer, that the exiftence of a right, in any one perfon, exclufive of all other men, is impoffible and that men ftill remain, and muft for ever remain, in that original ftate, in which *all men had an equal right to all things*; and are actually in a ftate of war, to which they are condemned by the want of any amicable rule by which to adjuft their differences.

Although.

Although the idea of univerfal confent be altogether vifionary, yet no one will deny that there is fuch a right as property, which may originate in the labour beftowed upon a fubject unoccupied and unappropriated. And that when property has thus accrued to any one, it may by compact be conveyed to any other, and continue to pafs through any indefinite number of hands.

With refpect to property, therefore, the effect of compact is not the inftitution of a right, but the conveyance from one to another of a right previoufly inftituted.

Property determines on the death or dereliction of the proprietor. In either cafe, the fubject is open to the firft occupier.

Among rude or favage nations, property being attached, for the moft part, to moveable articles, as *arms*, *furs*, *drefs*, or *utenfils* of any fort; and the principal fign of property being the actual ufe of the fubject in which it is conftituted, fuch articles, when found in the abfence of any perfon who claims the ufe of them, are readily treated as *res nullius*, or as things open to the firft occupier. Hence, much of the rapacity or injuftice which is imputed to men in this ftate.

A conveyance of property implies dereliction, but is not complete, without delivery into the hands of the perfon, in whofe favour the conveyance is made. Were a fubject merely relinquifhed, it would become open to the firft occupier. The perfon, for whom the property was deftined, might have an action againft the former proprietor for not fulfilling his deed of conveyance;
but

but not againſt a third party, who, proceeding to occupy the ſubject relinquiſhed, had not come under any obligation to deliver
it to him.

Upon this ground it is obſerved, that the mere law of nature will
not ſupport a legatee, in claiming the poſſeſſion of an inheritance
from any third party, who may have occupied it on the death of
the teſtator.—His action could lie only againſt the perſon, whoſe
conſent he could plead ; but that perſon is no more, and, upon
his demiſe, the ſubject in queſtion became open to the firſt occupier, who may not have conſented to put the ſuppoſed legatee
in poſſeſſion.

But ſuch queſtions, in the ordinary courſe of things, are for the
moſt part precluded. Even among rude nations, where property is
leaſt eſtabliſhed, the family of a perſon deceaſed are naturally the
firſt occupiers of his effects ; and inheritance gets a footing, not
upon any principle of right excluding the firſt occupier, but upon a principle of fact, that the family of the deceaſed are, for the
moſt part, actually in poſſeſſion.

Among nations more advanced in the progreſs of property and
of arts, the will of a perſon deceaſed is admitted as a ſufficient
ground of conveyance to the legatee. This favour is due to the
induſtry, with which property is acquired ; and it has a ſalutary
tendency, among commercial nations, to reward and encourage
that induſtry. Upon this footing, the effect of a laſt will is derived from convention, ſuch as the living have admitted ; not
from the deſtination of a perſon who is no more, and againſt
whom no action at law can be raiſed.

A claim of right, founded in compact, is valid only againſt the
party

party *contracting* ; and the right pertains only to the party *accepting*. Such only as have at once a right, in the fubject of compact, and power to difpofe of it, are competent to an effectual act of conveyance.

As every perfon may perform what *fervices* he thinks proper, and has power to difpofe of his fervices by previous confent ; *perfonal fervice* is the principal and immediate object of conventional obligation.

The *right to command* we have obferved, cannot arife from *occupancy* or from *labour* beftowed. It may arife by *confent* fo far as one perfon may, by compact, bind himfelf to obey the commands of another. Thus the artizan has right to the fervice of his apprentice upon the ground of his indenture. The mafter has a right to the labour of a fervant he has hired, and perfons ftipulating the performance of any tafk or the fupply of any commodity, have a right to all the effects of their contract.

In the fame manner, we are told that the right of government is founded in the *confent of the people* ; and this though true in many refpects is not true in all. It is true in refpect to all the pofitive fervices and contributions due from the fubject. If in thefe the rights of government are queftioned they muft be evinced on the principle of *convention exprefs* or *tacit* : For on that principle alone the right of command can be eftablifhed. The confent of thofe by whom government was firft acknowledged is frequently exprefled in formal capitulations, charters or ftatutes ; and the confent of thofe over whom it continues to be exercifed, though tacit, is no lefs real from age, to age in the continued acceptance of protection in return for allegiance and political duties. But a
right

right to protect the innocent or to reftrain crimes, which the magiftrate by his power, alone, is in condition to exercife, he is likewife
entitled to hold on the principle of the law of defence alone, and
need not recur to any fuppofed confent of the people to abftain
from crimes.

Amidft the relations in which mankind are placed, by agreement either exprefs or tacit, it may be afked, whether upon the
principles of the law of nature the relation of mafter and flave,
can be juftly admitted ?

This relation is underftood to be the fame with that of proprietor to the fubject of his property, * and feems to have originated in violence or force, and not in confent. Barbarous nations make war to enflave their captives, and difpofe of them at
market, like cattle or other fubjects of property.

Violent inftitutions, we have obferved, if they be fuch as men
in the fequel are reconciled to, and willingly adopt, may become
matter of fair convention and be eftablifhed in cuftom. How
far the inftitution of flavery may come under this defcription is
the queftion which we are now confidering.

It cannot be doubted, that perfons may be found under the
denomination of flaves, as much in appearance reconciled to their
ftate, as men are ever obferved to be in any other condition of
Vol. II.　　　　　H h　　　　　life:

---

* In the language of the Roman law a flave was faid to be a *thing* and not a per-
on. *Servus non eft perfona fed res.*

life: Shall we therefore fuppofe them to have given their confent to fervitude in the full extent of that term ?

To this queftion, we may anfwer in the negative, for manifold
reafons.

Firft, If the nominal flave may in fact be reconciled to the fpecific command or treatment he has experienced ; and, if he be fuppofed by tacit confent to have agreed to fubmit to fuch treatment, the mafter muft be fuppofed alfo to have agreed not to
change that treatment for any other.   The flave has not yet experienced, nor has the mafter yet attempted, all the ufes that may
be made of a property ; and what has not at all been practifed,
cannot be juftified upon the foundation of cuftom.   What has
never been tried, cannot be matter of ufage.   So much for the
condition of flaves, who are in appearance reconciled to their
lot.

In other inftances, it is well known, that flaves, tho' under good
ufage patient and tractable, are yet by extreme feverities driven into a
fenfe of injury and refentment, which is inconfiftent with the fuppofition of affent to the pretended condition of unlimited fubjection.
The injured feels himfelf to be a *perfon*, and not a *thing* ; and, tho'
he may feem to confent in terms to put his *fervices*, his *perfon*, and
his *life*, at the difcretion of another, yet he cannot abide the effects of capricious cruelty, without a pungent fenfe of his wrongs,
and a juft effort of nature to defend himfelf.   Such fentiments
are in reality what characterife a *perfon*, and place him in contradiftinction to a *thing* or fubject of property.

The

The contract of master and slave, if any such were supposed to exist, is such, on the part of the slave, as is not consistent with free will or the exercise of reason. It is the resignation of every thing, in exchange for nothing.

If any one should formally stipulate to forego his right of defence, and debase his mind to the sufferance of every act of injustice, this were to betray the want of reason, or at least to betray ignorance of the sense in which terms were employed to ensnare him. If such a compact therefore, were pleaded as the ground of an obligation to unlimited servitude, it should undoubtedly be set aside under the exception of *fraud* on the part of the supposed master, or of *insanity* on the part of the supposed slave.

But what is still more than this, a slave, according to the definition adopted, where the institution of slavery took place, and agreeably to the practice of purchase and sale, established in the market for slaves, is considered as a *thing*, and not a *person*. The supposition is impossible, and cannot be realized by the consent of any party, even relating to himself. He may consent to do what another commands, within the limits of possibility; but must continue to be a person, having original if not acquired rights, and inspired by nature with a disposition to revolt, whenever he is galled with the sense of insufferable injury or wrong.

The claim of a master or proprietor is founded, perhaps, with more plausible appearances, on the supposed forfeiture of personal rights, when the reparation of a wrong may support the exaction of servitude: A title which yet remains to be considered, and is the subject of the section that follows.

H h 2

In

In the mean time, the references which we have repeatedly made to the *prerogatives* of government, and the allegiance of subjects, may seem fit rather to start questions, and form difficulties, than to solve them: And we ought not perhaps to dismiss this question, relating to the specific obligations and rights that result from compact, without endeavouring to bring into some clear point of view the several questions that may arise, respecting the rights and obligations of men, under any form of subordination or political institution.

In the first place, we may venture to reject the idea of an *original compact*, as it is assumed, either in the formation of society itself, or in the establishment of any actual government: For men must have been already together in society, in order to form any *compact*, and must have been in the practice to move in a body, before they can have concerted together for any purpose whatever. And we are justified, by the history of mankind, in assuming, That, some species of government being necessary to the peace of society, Providence has kindly ordained, that wherever there is a society, there should be government also, subject to such correction as the grievances, men experience under it, may lead them to apply *.

It is nevertheless a manifest principle in the law of nature, that a right to command or an obligation to obey, beyond what is required to the mere prevention of harm, can be founded in consent alone. The powerful have a right to command any person to abstain from harm ; but not to do any positive service. There may be a power, therefore, without any right of command to this extent ; and, where any such power is exercised it may, in the

languag

* See History of Political Arts, vol. 1st.

language of Englifh law, be termed a government *de facto*, though not a government *de jure.*

There is indeed, by inftitution of Providence, and by an original diftinction of dependance and power, in every fociety, a government *de facto.* And the fame may become a government *de jure,* alfo, if the parties concerned, upon trial of the fituation in which they find themfelves placed, agree to the conditions which are required in the exercife of government. If the fubject, for inftance, agree to accept of protection, in return for the pofitive contributions and fervices required to public fafety ; in order to make fuch agreement binding on every individual, it is true that each, on his own part, muft have actually given his confent: For, by the law of nature, no one is engaged by compact, without a confent given by himfelf in perfon, or by his agent commiffioned for this purpofe.

We may be afked, then, under what government did the people affemble in a body, to give the confent neceffary to found fuch a plea of right to command them? We may anfwer: *No where.* And yet this is the only plea upon which the right to command can be fupported. We are therefore bound to verify the plea, before we can urge it in behalf of any government whatever.

The confent, upon which the right to command is founded may not be prior to the eftablifhment of government; but may be obtained under the reafonable exercife of an actual power, to which every perfon within the community, by accepting of a cuftomary protection, becomes bound to pay the cuftomary allegiance and fubmiffion. Here is a compact ratified by the leaft ambiguous of all figns, the whole practice, or continued obfervance of an ordinary

2   dinary

dinary life. The conditions here are ratified, in every age, and by every individual for himfelf; not merely ftipulated, in any remote age, and for a pofterity over which the contracting party had not any controul.

It may ftill, however, be afked, to what length the acquief-cence of parties will carry the rights and obligations, whether of the governing or governed. May the fubject be fuppofed to ac-quiefce in difcretionary power, or the magiftrate entitled to claim unlimited fubmiffion? The anfwer here is the fame as was given to the queftion of property in a mafter over his flave. Agree-ments made known by cuftomary practice can extend only to fuch practice, and will not juftify any violent acts of difcretion of ei-ther fide. And even with refpect to practice, if any act of injuf-tice were ever fo often repeated, it is not in the nature of things, that the injured fhould confent to be wronged, or agree to place himfelf at difcretion in the power of the injurious. And, if inju-ries are committed, the continuance of injuftice is a mere accumu-lation of wrongs, not a form of procedure, upon which any right can be founded.

No confent can be pleaded for the exercife of difcretionary power in the magiftrate over the fubject, any more than for the exiftence of property in the mafter over the flave; becaufe neither can be fuppofed to know the condition to which he confents; and the compact, in either cafe, would imply an act of infanity, or a re-fignation of every thing in exchange for nothing. As acts of dif-order and licence, on the part of the fubject, cannot be juftified on the precedent of any actual diforder, no more can acts of tyr-rany and oppreffion, on the part of government, receive any fanc-tion from any previous practice or abufe of the fame kind.

Here

Here, then, we reft the fpeculative doctrine, which is no more than this, that every party in fociety may, by mutual practice, acquire a right to whatever is practicable, and a matter of fair agreement ; but not to what is wrong, or inconfiftent with the fafety of mankind. And it is the wifdom of nations, fo far to define every right by actual ftatute, as in every particular queftion to exclude as much as poffible, the influence of paffion or partial intereft, whether of the governing or governed. PART II. CHAP. III. SECT. XII.

The claim of a right to govern at difcretion, or of a priviledge to obey at difcretion, before either have any effect, is a mere form of words. And, if exercifed only in acts of beneficence and duty, the difcretion in either cafe, would be applauded and loved ; but, in acts of diforder and outrage, becomes the claim of a right to do wrong, which is a folecifm in terms, and abfurd.

SECTION

SECTION XIII.

Of Forfeiture, and the Species of Right which refults from it.

BY the law of nature ; when a wrong is apprehended, it may be prevented ; when an injury is offered, it may be repelled ; and, when a damage is incurred, reparation may be exacted from the injurious party: So that; as a perfon may bind himfelf by confent or compact to do; or to omit to do whatever is fpecified in terms of agreement, fo a perfon, having done an injury, may become bound, in terms of the law of defence, to do, or to fupply to the injured party, whatever may be neceffary to repair the damage he has done.

This obligation, on the part of the perfon who has done a wrong, may be termed forfeiture ; and the party having incurred this obligation may become bound to furrender to the injured party, under the title of reparation, what was before his own right.

In purfuing the object of defence, the party attacked or aggrieved is entitled, by any means effectual and neceffary, to preferve

ferve or to recover his ftate. He has a right to the ufe of means which are effectual, but not to the ufe of means which exceed what is neceffary, in one cafe, to repel the attack, that is made upon him, or, in another cafe, to repair the damage he has fuftained.

Thefe limitations, in the right of defence, are evidently found-ed in the law of nature; although it may be difficult, in particu-lar inftances, to fix or to afcertain their application by any precife rule.

A perfon, whofe right is invaded, may think it neceffary to em-ploy all his powers in their utmoft extent, to repel the invafion; and he may have incurred an injury in his perfon, in his honour, or in his reputation, of which it may be difficult to eftimate the meafure, or to adjuft the reparation. Even in the cafe of trefpafs, on fubjects of real right, as in matters of poffeffion or property, the alarm may not be proportioned to the value of the fubject in-vaded, nor can the meafure of injury be always afcertained by the quantity of lofs fuftained. The intention or mind with which an attack is made, is often more alarming than the material lofs to be ap-prehended; and infult, in the manner of invafion, may be more injurious than the phyfical harm it occafions.

With refpect to the variety of cafes that may thus occur, we muft be contented to obferve, in general, that a perfon may be bound, to replace, from his own property, the lofs he may have occafioned in the property of another; and that, in cafe of any material damage, he may be bound to render perfonal fervices, where he has not effects to anfwer his forfeiture.

If the injury he has committed affect the good name or reputa-

VOL. II. I i tion

tion of another, he is bound to retract his calumnies, in the manner moſt effectual to repair the wrong he has done.

If he have not only impaired the ſtate of the perſon wronged, but given juſt ground of alarm, alſo, on the ſubject of his future behaviour, he is bound to admit of ſuch precaution, as may be ſufficient to guard againſt the danger of which he has given a juſt apprehenſion. And the injurious, in particular inſtances, is juſtly expoſed to ſuch puniſhment or ſuffering, as may be neceſſary to deter himſelf or others from repeating the offence.

Nature has happily inſpired the mind of man with indignation or reſentment of wrongs; and this ſentiment may quicken the arm of public juſtice: But to render the exerciſe of public vengeance, and the infliction of puniſhment agreeable to the principle of natural law, it ought not to exceed the allowable means of defence; or be any other than a reaſonable expedient for the ſuppreſſion of crimes; and this principle contains in itſelf the rule upon which a juſt gradation of puniſhment ſhould be accommodated to the variety and gradations of guilt.

In the firſt place, as the terms right and wrong are correlative, it may be obſerved, that where a perſon has not done a wrong, he cannot be ſaid to have forfeited a right; or in other words, as wrong implies ſome culpable action, no forfeiture can enſue where there is no culpability or blame.

Agreeably to this maxim, involuntary or caſual incident, of any ſort, although it may be the cauſe of harm to any one who is placed within reach of its effects, yet is it to be conſidered, not as a wrong, but as a misfortune, equally an object of regret to the doer, as to the ſufferer; and to both equally an object of future

ture

ture precaution. If a perfon, for inftance, fhould, by falling from a height, hurt or damage the perfon or property of another, in the way, it is evident, that by fuch misfortune he might become an object of pity, but not of refentment, that the damage fuftained could not be imputed to him, nor the reparation of it in juftice be exacted from him. So that, although there may be damage, if there be not a crime, there is no juft occafion for the infliction of punifhment.

In the Roman law, a perfon was refponfible for the trefpafs committed by his beaft, as well as for a trefpafs committed by himfelf; but this is juft fo far only as the damage fuftained from a beaft, otherwife lawfully kept and ufeful, could be imputed to neglect or culpable inattention, on the part of the owner.

It was admitted, that the owner ought to guard againft fuch trefpaffes as it was the nature of his beaft ufually to commit. Thefe he might forefee, and was bound to prevent: But, if an animal fhould depart from the ufual track of his nature, and trefpafs in a manner that was not to be expected from him; if a cow, inftead of a trefpafs on the pafture or ftanding corn of a neighbour, fhould, contrary to the natural inftinct of fuch animals, become carnivorous, and devour the young of a neighbouring herd: Here the damage could not be imputed to the owner, as the prevention of it could not fall within the province of any ordinary or reafonable degree of care or attention.

The decifion of law, in this cafe, evidently proceeds upon a principle, that forfeiture is proportioned to the degrees of demerit, and we may add, that meafures of punifhment, authorifed by the law of nature, ought to be regulated upon the fame principle.

PART II.
CHAP. III.
SECT.XIII.

I i 2 To

To crimes which originate in malice, or in any deliberate purpofe of guilt, fufficiently ftrong to break through the reftraints of
confcience or of public repute, a proportional defence and correction muft be applied. Where fociety is alarmed by overt
acts of malice or deliberate guilt, fufferings may be juftly inflicted that may ftrike even the obdurate with awe and terror; or,
if the life or liberty of the guilty perfon fhould be inconfiftent
with the public fafety, he may no doubt, be juftly removed by exile or by death.

Offences that arife from fudden gufts of paffion, may be reftrained or corrected by punifhments of inferior degree.

Faults of ignorance or inattention may be corrected by better
information, admonition, or even by the experience of an evil
thereby incurred.

One order or defcription of men may be reftrained by the fear of
fhame or difhonour; to reftrain another pecuniary fine or bodily
fufferings may be requifite; and it is not at all neceffary, that we
fhould recur to convention, in order to reft upon this bafis the
obligation of the magiftrate not to confound unequal meafures
of guilt or public alarm in the promifcuous application of extreme
punifhment to offences unequally heinous, or unequally incorrigible; nor is it neceffary to recur to convention, in order to found
the right of the fubject to plead his exemption, in every cafe where
unneceffary or difproportional degrees of feverity are employed a-
gainft him.

We have ftated forfeiture among the fources of adventitious
rights; and, in confidering what fpecies of right may refult from
thence, may proceed to obferve, that forfeiture cannot, like occupancy

pancy or labour, give title to a fubject, in which no one before had
any right. The perfon forfeiting muft forfeit only what was his own, fome poffeffion or property which he may be forced to re-fign, or fome fevice which he may be forced to perform.

It is farther evident, on the principle of the law of nature, that nothing can be lawfully feized or forced, under the title of for-feiture, except it be of a nature fit to repair or to compenfate a damage done, and that more cannot be exacted than is neceffary for this purpofe. This is implied in the general claufe of the law of nature, which limits the means of defence to what is ef-fectual and neceffary.

A lofs of property may be repaired, by an equivalent in pro-perty or fervice performed. Even injuries which cannot be re-paired in kind, as the lofs of a limb or bodily organ, may receive fome compenfation; and alarms may be quieted by fome ade-quate meafure of punifhment, having a tendency for the future to reftrain fuch crimes. But it is evident, that, in the claufe now cited is implied a prohibition of cruelties or ineffectual feve-rities, which have not a tendency to repair or to compenfate the damage fuffered, nor to reftrain the repetition of guilt.

From hence alfo we may conclude, that although a perfon may have forfeited his poffeffion, his property, or his labour, to any a-mount, yet no one can forfeit all his perfonal rights, or from a *perfon* become a *thing* or fubject of property. Criminals, accord-ingly, in the policy of fome nations, are condemned to labour, or to confinement for life. In this, however, it is not pretended, that their nature is changed from a perfon to a thing, or to a fub-ject of property. Capricious cruelties having no tendency to

prevent

prevent or to redress a wrong, are unlawful even with respect to those who have trespassed on the rules of justice.

Among nations of old, captives or prisoners of war were generally sent to the market, or retained as slaves; and from hence was derived the maxim of the Roman law, that a person might become a slave, upon the principle of the law of nations *.

We may admit, that those nations justly considered individuals as involved in the guilt of their country, as often as a just reparation of wrongs was withheld. But, even upon this supposition, they greatly over-rated the forfeiture; or condemned their captives to a privation, which they had not incurred. They had undoubtedly a right to detain them during the continuance of a war, that they might not return to strengthen their enemy. They had a right to exact from them any useful service, which they were in condition to perform, towards repairing the wrongs done by their country: But as this proceeds upon a supposition, that their country had committed an injury, and refused to make reparation, the case of every captive was not the same; and the injurious, who enslaved the subjects of a nation they had injured, were doubly in the wrong.

We may admit, perhaps, that a person, either in the wrongs done by himself, or as involved in the wrongs done by his country, may incur a forfeiture, such as, that after he has bestowed the labour of a whole life in endeavours to repair it, the effect may

still

---

* Servus fit jure gentium.

ftill be inadequate ; and we may admit as an inference from this fuppofition, that the claim of right acquired on the part of the injured, and the obligation incurred on the part of the injurious, may amount to fervice for life ; but an obligation to fervice for life is yet far fhort of flavery.

In the firft place, it is limited to fuch ufeful performance, as the captive is able to render, and excludes the infliction of capricious feverities, that have no tendency to repair the damage done.

In the difcharge of his obligation, the captive is ftated as a perfon and as a moral agent, who, if he be not willing, may be forced to do what is neceffary to repair the wrong committed, but nothing more.

In the next place, as the law of nature fuppofes the perfon ferving, yet poffeffed of all thofe rights, of which the forfeiture has no tendency to effect the reparation in queftion, it is implied in the fame law, that, as often as thofe rights are invaded, he is entitled to repel the aggreffion, and to defend himfelf.

It is ftill more evident, that no one can be a flave by birth ; for, even if he were bound to remain in the ftate of his parent, yet the ftate of the parent does not appear, upon any principle of the law of nature, to amount to flavery, or the privation of every perfonal right; but, even if this privation could be fuppofed to have been incurred by any convention or forfeiture, on the part of the parent, the child at his birth is innocent or difengaged, and born to the poffeffion of all his perfonal rights.

From the whole, then, we muft conclude, that the relation of
3   mafter

mafter and flave is the refult of violence, and cannot have arifen, like poffeffion, property, or lawful command, upon any juft title of occupancy, labour, convention, or forfeiture.

A perfon condemned to fervice may accommodate himfelf to fuch fervices as he has been made to perform, and to fuch treatment as he has been ufed to receive: But this cannot be interpreted as the conceffion of a right to impofe unlimited burdens, or a right to treat him with boundlefs feverities.

One order of men may plead the expediency of holding another in fervitude; but men have not a right to impofe upon others whatever is expedient to themfelves; and we muft ftill conclude, that as no man is by nature the property of another, no more can he become fo in any of the ways in which the right of property is acquired.

The conditions of men may be unequal, to any extent; and it may, in various ways, become the lot of one to render fervice to another: But the law of nature ever prefcribes limits of juftice or humanity, to the advantage which any one may take of the relation in which he ftands to his fellow creature.

So far we have enumerated the rights of men, whether original or adventitious, and have enumerated alfo the fources from which adventitious rights are derived or begin to exift, and the means by which they may be conveyed from one to another. It remains that we confider the law of nature, in refpect to the fecond part of its applications, that by which it is propofed to regulate the defences of men.

2　　　　　　　　　　　　　　CHAP.

C H A P. IV.

Of Jurisprudence,

Part Second, Respecting the Defences of Men.

S E C T I O N I.

Of the Means that may be oppofed to Injuftice in general.

HAVING fpecified a variety of *rights*, under the different titles of *perfonal* and *real*, of *original* and *adventitious*, with the different ways in which rights of the latter denomination may be acquired, we proceed next to confider the means by which a *right* may be *defended* or mantained.

Part. II.
Chap. IV.
Sect. I.

K k   Under

Under this title, the laws of war among nations will form a principal object of confideration and difcuffion; but as every perfon having a *right*, is entitled to fome adequate means of defence, we fhall ftate the law in its moft comprehenfive form, in which the rights and defences of fingle parties and of fellow citizens are included, no lefs than thofe of nations or feparate communities.

We have obferved, as the firft and moft general ftatement of the law of nature relating to this fubject; that a right may be maintained; or, in other words, that a wrong may be prevented, an affault repelled, and damage repaired, in any way, that may be effectual and neceffary againft the injurious party.

In the farther application of this law we are to confider the variety of perfons and circumftances to which it may relate.

Varieties of perfons may be comprehended under the titles of *perfons fingle, ftrangers to one another*, and *unconnected*; under the title of *fellow citizens*, and *feparate nations*, or the members of which feparate nations are compofed.

The circumftances under which a right is expofed or invaded, may direct us to the means of defence which may be refpectively proper or fufficient on fuch occafions. In one fet of circumftances, or on one occafion, *perfuafion* may be fufficient; in another it may be required to employ *deception* or *ftratagem*; ; and in a third it may be neceffary to employ *force*, at any hazard of fuffering to the injurious party. The means of defence, therefore, may be enumerated under the titles of *perfuafion, deception,* and *force*. The firft may take place among friends; the two laft

2   are

are lawful only upon the fuppofition of enmity, and are termed *hoftilities.*

Perfuafion confifts in the ufe of argument, reprefentation or rational inducement of any fort, to obtain the confent of the party with whom it is employed. To diftinguifh perfuafion from deception, it is neceffary that it fhould be limited to the ufe of confiderations founded in truth, or believed by the perfon who ufes them to be of real moment in deliberating on the fubject refpecting which they are offered. To difguife or conceal the truth, to mifreprefent any important circumftance relating to it, or to impofe with fallacious argument, is rather to deceive than to perfuade.

Under this limitation, *perfuafion* may be employed to obtain a favour no lefs than to defend or maintain a right; and as they who may be perfuaded to do right are not to be confidered as injurious or malicioufly inclined, they are not objects of punifhment, whether punifhment be confidered as an example to deter the injurious, or as a precaution to guard againft any future criminal attempts.

Perfuafion is amicable; but where amicable means are not fufficient to preferve a right, *hoftilities* no doubt are lawful; and among thefe *artifice* or *deception* where fufficient, may be chofen as the leaft hurtful to the perfon againft whom it is employed.

Deception or mifinformation, in the nature of things, even apart from diftant confequences, is pernicious; and to employ it without neceffity is an injury. The perfon againft whom it is fo employed has fubject of well-founded complaint; or may demand

K k 2

information

information of the truth as his right. Even a perfon who is put upon his defence, may reject the ufe of difguife or deception, as difhonourable means of fafety to himfelf: But we are not enquiring, in this place, what is the moft honourable part for the injured to act, but what the fuppofed injurious perfon may claim as a right, refpecting the ufe of means to be employed againft himfelf.

It is admittted, among the modern nations of Europe, that requifition of right, *manifefto*, and folemn *declarations of war*, fhould precede *hoftilities*, or the actual ufe of force. Difguifes and artifices, neverthelefs, in certain negociations or tranfactions of ftate, are employed to gain an advantage, perhaps, without any fuppofed infringement of this rule.

There is, indeed, a general difpofition to reprobate *artifice* or *deceit*, even when employed to repel an injury, or to fruftrate a malicious intention. This proceeds upon an affociation of bafenefs or cowardice with every act of diffimulation or falfehood, which we accordingly reprobate under the denomination of *treachery* : But this appellation no more applies to the ufe of ftratagem in repelling an injury, than the term murder applies to the ufe of a fword or deadly weapon in repelling an affault on the perfon or property of an innocent man. If a perfon, acting in his own defence, may receive an affaffin on the point of his fword, how can it be fuppofed, that he may not withhold information from him, or even by mifinformation miflead him from the execution of his malicious purpofe.

The affaffin who purfues an innocent perfon, in order to murder him, may no doubt be lawfully told, that the perfon he feeks

is

is gone to the right, when he is actually gone to the left. In this
manner, deception or ftratagem is univerfally admitted as juft on
the principles of the law of nature; and, although perfons who
confult the reputation of bravery may think that open force is
preferable to deception or difguife of any fort; yet, upon the general principle, that rights are to be defended by means the leaft
hurtful to the perfons againft whom they are employed, deception and artifice is in general to be preferred to the ufe of actual
force.

The ufe of *force*, it is true, may not always be more fevere or
deftructive in its effects than the ufe of deception; but, as force
repelled by force is likely to proceed to the higheft extremities, it
is juftly placed as the laft refort of the injured in defending their
rights, and not to be employed where it is fafe to rely on perfuafion or ftratagem.

Under this title of *force* may be included not only the ufe of
arms and actual violence, forcible reftraint, and the infliction of
punifhment, but even threats, or the denunciation of violence,
which may operate on the fears of thofe againft whom they are
employed.

Such being the gradation of means, that may be employed in
defence of a right, the law of nature is modified, in particular
circumftances, by a regard to the choice which is to be made of
fuch means, according to the degree in which they are feverally
effectual or neceffary.

In the applications of this law, alfo, regard muft be had to the
defcription and relation of perfons, whether *ftrangers* and *uncon-*

3   *nected,*

nected, fellow citizens, separate nations, or the *members* of which *separate nations* are compofed.

Of the law, as it applies to the cafe of perfons fo diverfified, it
is propofed to offer a few of the moft neceffary obfervations, in
the following fections.

SECTION

S E C T I O N   II.

*Of the Law of Defence, in the Cafe of fingle Perfons, Strangers and
unconnected.*

THE parties to whom the law of defence is to be applied in this
fection, are termed *fingle*, becaufe we mean not to .confider peculiarities incident to collective bodies, confidered as fuch.   They
are termed *ftrangers* and *unconnected*, becaufe we mean not, in de-
ciding any queftion that may arife between them, to take into our
account the effect of any previous convention either exprefs or
tacit.

In fuppofing fuch parties, we abftract from all the peculiarities
which occur in the cafe of fellow citizens, under the effect of their
municipal laws, civil or political inftitutions.   We abftract from
the peculiarities which diverfify the cafe of feparate nations, modified as it is by previous treaties, claims, or conventions, or by
the mode in which collective bodies are made up of the members
which feverally compofe them.

The

The cafe, then, which we are now to confider, is fuppofititious, and a mere abftraction. So that, in this point of view, the circumftances of a cafe, which in nature are joined with many other particulars, are to be ftated apart, and feparately confidered. Such abftractions are ufeful in argument ; but muft not, or ought not to be miftaken for matters of fact.

This caution has not always been obferved, in treating of the abftraction which we have now made. The cafe of parties, ftrangers and unconnected, has been termed the ftate of nature, and even miftaken for hiftorical fact : But, in applying the law of nature to this fuppofition, it is not by any means neceffary to admit, that the whole of the human fpecies ever confifted of parties unconnected, or that men ever exifted in a ftate of individuality, or in a ftate of eftrangement of one from all mankind. The purpofe of fcience is effectually ferved, by fuppofing two or more parties fo unconnected, although neither be fuppofed unconnected with the whole fpecies.

The term, *ftate of nature*, as equivalent to the abftraction which we now make, has been employed by writers, who do not by any means feem difpofed to favour the affumption of eftrangement from his kind, as the natural ftate of man. Dr Blackftone, among others, has made ufe of that term in the following paffage : " If " a man," he fays, " were to be in a ftate of nature, unconnect- " ed with other individuals, there would be no occafion for any " other laws than the law of nature and the law of God ; neither " could any other law poffibly exift." But he afterwards fubjoins : " Man was formed for fociety ; and, as is demonftrated
" by

" by the writers on this fubject, is neither capable of living alone,
" nor indeed has he courage to do it *."

The ftate of nature, then, according to this learned and judicious
writer, is not the natural ftate of man, but a mere abftraction made
for the fame purpofe for which abftractions are commonly made
in the purfuit of fcience ; that we may have a diftinct view of
certain confiderations feparately taken, before we proceed to view
them as combined in the aggregate forms under which they are
actually prefented in nature.

Man, even in his phyfical ftate, exhibits a fum of many fimultaneous circumftances, whether original and coeval with his being,
or, what is nearly the fame thing, immediately confequent upon
it. He has occupied fomething that is ufeful to him, and has
a right of poffeffion ; he has laboured to fome purpofe, and has a
right of property ; he is a father or a child, the member of a family or fome larger fociety ; and the fimpleft movement he can
have made with his fellow creatures, may amount to convention, or fome adventitious modification of his original obligations
and rights. So that we fhall find no actual period of hiftory in
which we can apply the reafonings of this fection to the fpecies
at large, or to any confiderable numbers of men.

We may fuppofe two perfons, at the fame time, caft afhore on
fome defert ifland, and fuch is perhaps the only poffible cafe
in which our fuppofition can be realized ; and our queftion at
prefent with refpect to it is not, what would be mutual inclina-

Vol. II.   L l   tion

* Comm. on the Laws of England. Introd. Sect. 2.

tion of fuch perfons at their firſt meeting, whether to co-ope-
rate as friends, or to encounter as enemies ? This queſtion is no
doubt of confequence in forming our notion of man's deſtination,
whether to peace or to war, to fociety or folitude : But that the
decifion in fuch a cafe might apply to human nature in its fimpleſt ſtate ; it might be neceſſary to fet apart any previous effects
of experience or habit, by which either of the parties feparately, or
both, might be previouſly difpofed to act a part which nature
would not have fuggefted to them prior to fuch experience or habit.

It cannot be doubted, that in fo forlorn and difaftrous a ſtate,
each would rather meet with a friend than an enemy, and each
would rather make a friend of the perfon he cafually met than an
enemy. There is, however, reafon to believe, from the principle of
caution with which human nature is endowed, even in child-
hood, and which experience may direct, but does not remove,
that fuch perfons would approach one another with mutual circumfpection and caution, each rather with fear of what he himfelf might fuffer, than with any difpofition to annoy his fellow
creature ; and univerfally it may be aſſumed perhaps, that the ear-
lieft fenfation of human nature, as Montefquieu has obferved, is
rather a feeling of weaknefs and a need of fupport, than a feeling
of ftrength or a difpofition to provoke animofity.

But whatever may be the folution of this or any fuch phyfical
queſtion, our object at prefent is not to determine, what the parties in fuch a cafe might be inclined to do, but what each would
have a right to do for his own prefervation and defence. We
would ftate the decifions of the law of nature on a fuppofition of
the fimpleſt cafe, in which parties are vefted merely with their
original rights and the means of defence with which they are accompanied:

3

companied: Our decifions, therefore, upon this fuppofition can
be little more than a repetition of what has been already ftated in
the general enunciation of the law ; whether refpecting the rights
of which man is born in poffeffion, or which he is competent to
aequire, and the general permiffion of means effectual, fo far as
they are neceffary for the prefervtion of fuch rights.

Together with the original appurtenances of human nature,
life, *limb*, and *faculty*, we muft likewife admit all thofe rights,
which, even acting feparately and unconnectedly, the individual
may acquire for himfelf. We muft fuppofe him entitled to defend not only his organs and powers, but the fruits and effects
of them alfo ; entitled to defend his poffeffion, as firft occupier of
any fubject that accommodates him ; or his property in a fubject, as having employed labour to meliorate or to procure it : So
that, together with his rights of original poffeffion, he is entitled
alfo to defend his right, to make acquifitions by labour, convention, or otherwife.

If, in the midft of rights fo defined, one party fhall commit
an injury, or give juft caufe of alarm to another, this other is
entitled to his defence and is not reftrained in the choice of
means, by any confideration befide the general provifion of
the law of nature already ftated ; a provifion which admits that
effectual means may be ufed, but in which unneceffary acts of
cruelty or feverity, with refpect to thofe againft whom fuch
means may be employed, are ftrictly prohibited.

Upon the fuppofition of a difference fubfifting between parties
otherwife ftrangers and unconnected, or what is called the ftate
of nature, it is fometimes afked, who is to judge or to decide

L l 2

beween.

between parties in this state? This in effect is first to suppose, that parties having no convention are amenable to no jurisdiction inferior to the tribunal of God, and afterwards to enquire to what human jurisdiction such parties are subject.

They may or may not submit to an arbiter at pleasure; and, though nature has limited the means of defence to those which are necessary, the observance of this limitation, together with the exercise of every other right, would in fact depend on the discretion and candour of the parties themselves; a case in which no provision being made against the passions or mistakes of men, applications of the law of nature, however clear in theory, might be very lame and imperfect in practice; and such condition of parties, if ever realized, should be deplored as calamitous, or exposed to much inconvenience and evil.

The inconvenience would suggest, for its remedy, recourse to the judgement and arbitration of some third party, more impartial than either of the persons more immediately concerned. The utility of some permanent recourse of this sort, would naturally lead to political institution, and the establishment of ordinary jurisdiction and protecting power: So that, while we suppose men to be associated from their birth, or otherwise cast into groups together, every difference or dispute would suggest the necessity or utility of political establishment.

Society is the natural state of man, and political society is the natural result of his experience in that state of society to which he is born. This is not the experience of single persons, or of single ages. It is an experience, which began with the commencement of every society, and can end only with its final extinction. Political

litical eftablifhments, accordingly, which began to be formed in
in the firft and fimpleft ages, continue in a ftate of gradual formation, as the experience of every age directs, to the lateft period
at which ftates or communities, in the courfe of things, are allowed to arrive.

The people in republics, in the laft as well as the firft ftage of
their political union, are devifing rules by which to govern themfelves.

The monarch continues to fettle terms, on which he propofes
to diftribute rewards and punifhments, honour or difgrace, among
his fubjects. And the defpotical mafter continues to make known
the advantage he propofes to himfelf or his people from the exercife
of his power; whether in the gratification of a divine benevolence,
that of Antoninus; or in the gratification of a brutal appetite like
and paffion, like thofe of Caligula and Nero.

SECTION

SECTION III.

Of the Case of fellow Citizens.

THIS case is indefinitely varied in the multiplicity of political forms. Our object, with respect to it, is to enumerate, in general terms, the principal parties of which every political society consists ; and to state the obligations and rights, which are essential to their relation, as members of the same community.

Civil society is not improperly termed a state of convention ; for, although men are actually in society together, before they enter into any form of bargain or compact ; yet, every step that is made, in the concourse of numbers, tends to convention. Every practice continued into custom, is fairly interpreted as the faith of parties plighted for the observance of it ; and the members of every society, even of the shortest duration, become invested with rights, or subjected to obligations, founded in some species of contract express or tacit.

But

But we now ceafe to enquire in what form the civil or politi- PART II.
cal compact is ratified, whether by practice, capitulation, or fta- CHAP. IV.
tute. Thefe are the proper ftudy of profeffional lawyers, to SECT. III.
whom the fupreme authority of their refpective communities is
the ultimate rule in adjufting the obligations and rights of men.

To the citizen of every particular community, the fpecific law
of his own country is the tenure by which he holds his rights, and
the meafure of obligations which he is bound to fulfil; but, however the civil inftitution, in any particular inftance, may appear
to depart from the law of nature, by adopting modifications,
which in their firft affumption were optional to the parties concerned; yet, as fuch modifications are founded in convention,
there is not any fpecies of obligation or right actually valid in a-
ny community, that may not be traced to this its foundation in
the law of nature.

There are certain relations of men effential to every fociety or
community confidered as fuch; and there are certain obligations
and duties which may not only be traced to their foundations in
the law of nature, but which are to be confidered as immediate
objects of that law, and placed, as we now propofe to place them,
among the cafes to which the law of nature is immediately applicable.

Under every political eftablifhment, there is a relation of *magiftrate* and *fubject*, and a relation of *fellow citizens*, which, however diverfified in particular inftances, are neverthelefs in a certain
abftract point of view common to every eftablifhment, and effential to the nature of political fociety itfelf.

It

It is our object, at present, therefore, to state the relative conditions of magistrate and subject, and the relative condition of fellow subjects in the most general terms, so as to comprehend the obligations and rights which enter into the nature of political society itself considered as such, without attempting to specify the peculiarities, by which the relations of men, in different instances, may be diversified.

It is the condition of the magistrate, in his most abstract point of view, to govern and to protect the subject: It is the condition of the subject to be governed and protected.

It is the mutual condition of fellow citizens, in the same abstract point of view, to be vested with rights, in regard to which they are to one another reciprocal objects of consideration or respect: It is implied, in the character which is common to them all as fellow citizens, that, if any difference arise between them, they recur to the judgement of the magistrate, and that, whereever his interposition can be obtained, and may be effectual for the prevention or redress of wrongs, they are to refrain from any application of force on their own part, and to acquiesce in such means of defence, as the magistrate is duly bound to employ for their protection.

The citizen, therefore, in preserving his rights amidst the collisions of different claims and pretensions, resigns into the hands or the magistrate the weapons of defence, which, upon the supposition of *parties strangers* and *unconnected*, we found the individual entitled to use for himself. And the magistrate may not only employ the authority with which he is vested, so as to defend the innocent,

3   cent,

cent, but lies under an exprefs obligation, fo to employ it: whilft
every other citizen, whatever be the means of defence with which he is cafually furnifhed, is reftrained from the ufe of them, provided the interpofition of the magiftrate can be obtained for his fafety.

Thefe are conditions implied in every political eftablifhment, and without which fociety either cannot be preferved, or cannot be faid to have received any political form.

In thefe conditions, however, the *obligations* and *rights* of the parties, fo general and fo neceffary, are derived from convention alone. The magiftrate has agreed to protect the fubject, otherwife is not bound to this any more than to any other act of beneficence which he may perform at difcretion. The citizen has agreed to abide by the judgement of the magiftrate, and to refrain from any attempt to do himfelf right, where the interpofition of the magiftrate can be obtained for that purpofe; and, although the form, in which fuch agreements are entered into in different communities, may vary indefinitely, yet the compact, in refpect to its general refult, is the fame in every inftance; and the parties may equally plead their conventional rights and reciprocal obligations in every community.

We have already had occafion to obferve, that the right of the magiftrate to interpofe in the defence of the innocent, or in the repreffion of crimes, does not need the fanction of compact, in order to eftablifh it; for this right is common to him, with every other perfon having power, in whatever manner that power may be conftituted, whether in the ftrength of his arm, or in the cooperation of numbers that obey his commands.

M m

In what, then, we may be aſked, is the right of the magiſtrate conventional and peculiar to himſelf? It is conventional and peculiar, in ſo far as he alone is entitled to employ his power to this effect, and ſo far as every other perſon is reſtrained from like application of power, wherever recourſe can be had to that of the magiſtrate. In the abſence of the magiſtrate, or where his aid cannot be obtained, the ſubject may defend himſelf and his fellow citizens; and every individual man, to the utmoſt of his power, may interpoſe in the prevention of crimes.

The right of the magiſtrate, therefore, to repreſs crimes, and to protect the innocent is prior to convention. His obligation, at the ſame time, not to employ means unneceſſarily deſtructive or ſevere, even againſt the perſon who has incurred his oppoſition or his cenſure, is alſo prior to convention; and there is, as we obſerved upon the foundations of the law of nature, prior to any concert or agreement of parties, a rule for the application of various reſtraints, and the gradation of puniſhments.

Crimes, we have obſerved, are unequally pernicious and dangerous, and unequally alarm the community. The more forcible efforts of defence are juſtified by the higher degree of alarm which the crime is naturally fitted to give. Some diſorders are more eaſily reſtrained than others; and to theſe an inferior meaſure of puniſhment being ſufficient, the magiſtrate is not entitled, by the law of nature, to employ puniſhments of ſuperior degree.

Different deſcriptions of men, we have obſerved, are governed by different motives. The law of nature will not authoriſe, with reſpect to any one claſs or order of men, an higher meaſure of puniſhment,

2

nifhment, than is fufficient to reftrain them. The fear of torture
or death may be neceffary to reftrain thofe who are infenfible to any other confiderations ; while fhame, or the fear of difgrace a- lone, may be fufficient to reftrain, or to reclaim another order or clafs of the people.

As nations, by ftatute or cuftom, are found to depart from the conditions which the law of nature, prior to convention, has im- pofed ; fo they have feldom been found to obferve any regular gradation of punifhments, or at leaft to remain within the bounds which fimple juftice, in every particular cafe, would prefcribe. They have departed from the law of nature, in the terms of their convention or practice ; and, in the refult, fometimes find them- felves engaged in forms of adminiftration no lefs inexpedient than cruel and unjuft.

If, to the maxims of ftrict law we may be allowed to fubjoin confiderations of expedience, it is evident that, by withholding diftinctions in the meafure of punifhment, we inure the minds of men to confound the higher and lower meafures of guilt. And, if a criminal be to incur the higher meafure of punifhment, even for crimes of a lefs heinous nature, his cafe, in proceeding to infringe the law, is the fame as if no punifhments were to be inflicted for the higher crime ; and he will therefore prefer it to the lower, if his temptations incline him fo to do.

By the law of nature, a magiftrate, in reftraining a crime, may proceed to the ufe of means that may be neceffary for that pur- pofe ; but this law, inftead of being ftrained to the utmoft pitch of feverity, ought rather to give way to confiderations, which hu-

manity

manity no lefs than expedience, in many inftances, will fuggeft.

The conceptions of men, on the gradations of demerit and cri-
minality, may be greatly affected by the promifcuous application
of punifhments.   And, although the principle of defence, ftrictly
applied, would juftify that meafure of punifhment, whatever it may
be, which is neceffary to reprefs the crime, yet prudence, as well as
humanity, would in fome inftances reject this authority, and reprobate the application of a punifhment, againft which human
nature would revolt more than even againft the crime itfelf.

A licentious intercourfe of the fexes is highly pernicious, and
the higheft meafure of punifhment might perhaps be neceffary,
and ftill ineffectual to reprefs it entirely ; but it is evident that,
if the punifhment of murder were to be applied in this cafe, the
remedy or the antidote might be more fhocking to human nature,
and even more pernicious to mankind, than the evil itfelf.

It may be more difficult to reftrain a theft committed under the
preffure of famine or want, than one committed for gain. It may
be more difficult ftill to reftrain a theft committed for the relief
of a perifhing family, than one committed for the fupply of perfonal want; yet human nature muft revolt at the fuppofed application of ftrict law in fuch cafes ; and indeed it is admitted, in
the ordinary jurifprudence of all nations, that the extreme neceffity of one perfon may fo far fuperfede the right of another, as to
difarm the power that is provided in civil fociety to enforce this
right.

To fucceed in eftablifhing a juft gradation of punifhments, we
muft

muſt come with reluctance to the uſe of extreme ſeverities and a-
void a precipitant application of puniſhment in the treatment of
the lower offences.   When ſlight offences are puniſhed too ſevere-
ly, it becomes difficult properly to increaſe the meaſure of puniſhment for the higher crimes. When under the Roman empire,
for inſtance, a ſarcaſm on the perſon of the emperor was puniſhed with death ; it was not poſſible to find a proportionate degree
of ſeverity for the crimes of perfidy or murder.

But whatever may be the gradation of puniſhments adopted,
it is evident that the higher meaſure of ſuffering, may on occaſion, be neceſſary, and cannot be replaced by the lower or any
intermediate degree.   There may be crimes, we have obſerved,
bearing evidence of a diſpoſition ſo depraved, and in appearance
ſo incorrigible, that it may be neceſſary, by exile or death, to
remove the criminal from the ſociety whoſe peace he alarms.
And even, according to the circumſtances of his crime, it may
be neceſſary to diſtinguiſh this ſacrifice with peculiar marks of reprobation and horror, to operate as an example againſt the indulgence of ſimilar diſpoſitions in other men.

It is no doubt poſſible in the application of puniſhments to err
on the ſide of remiſſneſs as well as rigour.   Mercy to the aſſaſſin
is cruelty to the innocent, who may be expoſed to ſuffer by the
commiſſion of his crimes.

We hear of ſovereigns to whom the executive powers of law
are committed, who, either from miſtaken lenity, or from an
apprehenſion of ſomewhat too ſacred in the life of man to be taken
away by any human authority, have declared againſt capital puniſhments ; or reſolved for a time to ſuſpend the uſe of them.   The
object

object of government, in the mean time, is not mercy to criminals, but the repreffion of capital crimes which indanger the life
as well as other rights of the innocent.   And there is furely no
wifdom in declaring that criminals alone, for the future, fhall
take the life of a fellow creature.   If the life of a man is too facred to be taken by any human authority, what is the innocent
traveller to do, when attacked on the high way with weapons that
threaten his life ? what is the ftate to do, when invaded by a foreign enemy, who forces his way by the deftruction of all that
oppofe him ? What is the foldier to do, when he finds himfelf
under the neceffity to kill, that he may not be killed ? In fhort,
what is the magiftrate himfelf to do, when he finds the lives of
innocent fubjects in danger from the profligacy of diforderly perfons, who are ready to facrifice the peace of their country to the
gratification of their vicious paffions ? If a life muft be expofed,
either that of the innocent at the difcretion of criminals, or that
of criminals at the judgement of the magiftrate, it is furely evident on whom the choice fhould fall.

We plead for a juft gradation of punifhment, not that the guilty may efcape, but that the innocent may be fafe, and that no
one may be expofed to greater feverity than he has actually incurred by his crimes.

From the whole of this argument, then, it appears, that the
law of nature, where there is no convention to the contrary,
limits the right of the magiftrate to the ufe of fuch means as are
neceffary to the defence of the innocent or the prevention of
wrongs ; that all reftraints or feverities, employed beyond thefe
limits, are unlawful ; and that, even prior to convention, a rule
may be found upon which to erect a juft gradation of punifhments.

Although

Although convention be not neceſſary to authoriſe the magiſtrate in the diſcharge of his duty for the repreſſion of crimes; it is by convention that he alone is inveſted with the excluſive prerogative of interpoſing at all times in defence of the innocent. In every well ordered community his powers are acknowledged or inſtituted expreſsly for this purpoſe, and fellow citizens are underſtood to have agreed to refer their differences to a judge, to forgo the uſe of force in themſelves, and recur to the magiſtrate for protection.

This fundamental convention of fellow citizens is that which eſſentially diſtinguiſhes their caſe from that which was conſidered in the laſt ſection. It is that which conſtitutes the ſpecific advantage of thoſe who have the benefit of political eſtabliſhments.

The citizen, even when injured, muſt not do himſelf right; but muſt have recourſe to the protection of the magiſtrate for this purpoſe.

There are, however, exceptions to this ſalutary rule; either where, in the nature of things, the interpoſition of the magiſtrate cannot be obtained to prevent a wrong, or where the injury, once ſuffered, cannot be repaired by the utmoſt exertions of his power. In every ſuch caſe the ſpirit of political inſtitution, which is inſpired by a concern for innocence, requires, that the innocent ſhould be allowed to defend himſelf. If this were refuſed him, the ſociety to which he has recourſe for protection would in fact become a ſnare, in which he would be expoſed to ſuffer without any hopes of redreſs.

It is admitted accordingly, that any one aſſaulted in his habitation

bitation, or in his perfon has a right to repel the affault. The maxims of law in different countries may be unequally favourable to this act of defence, requiring unequal degrees of caution in proceeding to the laft extremities. In fome it is required, that a perfon affaulted fhould endeavour to efcape before he repels force with force : But as an attempt to efcape may in fome circumftances augment the danger to which the perfon affaulted is expofed, it appears unjuft and cruel to expofe him to this additional hazard; and the humanity which feemed to take part with the aggreffor, is indeed more properly due to the perfon attacked, who ought certainly to be indulged in defending himfelf at any neceffary hazard to the perfon who affails him.

A woman who is forcibly attacked in her chaftity, or a man who is put to the trial of perfonal eftimation or honour, may receive an injury, which the utmoft power of the magiftrate cannot afterwards repair. The exception is accordingly admitted, in favour of the private right of defence, on fuch occafions.

Among thefe modes of attack, there is a fingular fpecies of injury, owing its effect to the caprice of manners in modern times; but of which the effect is extremely fevere and injurious, not fufceptible of any legal meafurement, nor repairable by all the power of the magiftrate.

In confequence of this fingular caprice, altogether unknown to the celebrated nations of antiquity, not only afperfions of character, but any fingle term of reproach, or gefture of infult, fo far impairs the eftimation or credit of the perfon who fuffers them; that if the breach be not repaired, in the way which caprice alfo directs, he becomes an outcaft from the fociety, in which his condition

dition depends on the esteem in which he is held. Applications to the courts of justice, for reparation, would only increase the dishonour. False aspersions may be removed by the clearest evidence of truth; but this would not remove the dishonour of having suffered them to be made. An accusation may be known to be true or false; its effect, however, in this case, does not depend upon the degree in which it is believed, but upon the degree of tameness with which it is received. Even calumny hurts, not by the imputation of any criminal charge, but rather by the imputation of cowardice, implied in the manner of receiving it; and the defence which caprice has provided for this mode of attack, is a display of courage, not a refutation of any false accusation. The accusation may be true; but the courageous vindicates his honour: The accusation may be false; but the coward is overwhelmed with disgrace. Even the injured is denied the use of stratagem or surprise, in his own defence. He must meet his antagonist, however injurious, upon equal terms; and, if he would preserve his honour, must pass through the hazard of a single combat for that purpose. His character for integrity may be blasted or entire; but his estimation, in point of honour, is independent of either condition.

In this example, the deviation from reason is monstrous; but the dignity of justice is made to stoop to the caprice of fashion; and, so long as the private injury is suffered to have its effect, and the petulance or folly of one person may drive another from his place in society; so long as the magistrate cannot preserve the citizen in his state; so long the injured citizen must be allowed to defend himself, and to adopt the only means which are effectual for that purpose.

VOL. II.   N n   To

To reform this abufe, has been juftly considered as an object of great importance in the policy of modern nations: But attempts to this purpofe have begun, perhaps, at the wrong end, by denunciations of feverity againft thofe who, finding their honour invaded, take the ordinary way of preventing or repairing the wrong with which they are attacked. If men are by vulgar caprice made acceffible to an injury of the moft ferious nature, to an injury which the magiftrate cannot repair, it is by no means juft to reftrain them from the only means of defence that is left in their power. This being evident to the general fenfe of mankind, the only effect of feverities denounced by the law, in moft countries, againft the injured, as well as the aggreffor, has been to oblige courts of juftice to fall upon meafures to evade the rigour of that very law they are required to apply.

If any thing could be done, to deprive unmerited affronts of their efficacy in the opinion of thofe who determine what fhall be a gentleman's reception in the world, the evil might probably foon give way, and the fenfibility of honour be changed into a contempt of offences which are now admitted to have the moft fatal effects.

We fometimes congratulate ourfelves on the influence of this practice, as it tends to polifh our manners, and reftrain the violent from offenfive brutalities, to which paffions may lead in the intercourfe of fociety. We do not confider, however, that we owe our fenfibility to fuch offences to the imputation of cowardice, which is made to accompany the fufferance of them; and that, without this imputation, unmerited infults would pafs in fociety, like the noife of a fcold, in which no one is ever pleafed

to

to think himself affronted, and which he therefore hears with
contempt or indifference.

Crimes that proceed from the affectation of bravery, are not to be repreffed by the fear of punifhment. The threats of law, in fuch cafes, give the quarrelfome a double opportunity of diftin-guifhing himfelf. He braves his antagonift, and he braves the law. Even if he fhould be punifhed, his fuffering does not degrade him in the opinion of the people; for the people, like himfelf, admire bravery, even where it tends to difturb the public peace.

Abfurdity is more likely to cure itfelf, by being fuffered to incur its extreme, than by being kept within certain bounds, which ferve to conceal the extent of its folly; and duelling, like other fafhions, is likely to wear itfelf out when it becomes an affecta-tion of the vulgar, and ceafes to diftinguifh thofe who are termed men of fafhion.

If there be in our times a progrefs towards this point of reformation, we have reafon, in the mean time to regret the condition of thofe, perhaps the leaft deferving of any fuch fate, who may fuffer under the prevalence of a folly, of which they cannot always avoid the effects.

Were the law to diftinguifh the *aggreffor*, in the firft approach to a quarrel, juft marks of difgrace affixed to the perfon in whom the offence originated, might perhaps infpire every party with caution to avoid a quarrel, and have better effects than any forcible reftraints applied to check the affectation of courage. It is not va-lour to brave difgrace; and, if the law fhould condemn an ag-greffor to fome fpecies of infamy, the fafhion of feeking for ho-

N n 2 nour,

nour, by rafhnefs in giving provocation, might be reftrained by the profpect of an oppofite effect.

It might be difficult, indeed, in many cafes, to fix the charge of aggreffor upon either of the parties in a quarrel : But the beft effect of law is not merely to give the decifion where an occafion of trial has arifen, but to prevent fuch occafions, from an apprehenfion of a decifion that may be given. All that the law, indeed, can do, is to lay down a rule, and leave juries to apply it to the beft of their judgement, on the circumftances of every particular cafe. The rule, even before it is applied, would have its effect on the minds of thofe who are expofed to get into quarrels, and who, by avoiding the imputation of being the firft aggreffor, might prevent the firft fteps towards an offenfive difpute.

Juries, too, in fome inftances, might be able to fix the charge of aggreffor, fo as to increafe the effect of the law by real examples of ignominy and difgrace. We pity the perfon who is forced into a quarrel, to vindicate his honour; but we deteft the bully who is ever forward in giving rife to fuch quarrels; and any difgrace which the law might award for fuch characters would be fupported by the general opinion and confent of all reafonable men.

Thefe are queftions of political wifdom, rather than of ftrict law; but are ftated with advantage, when the laws to which they refer are under confideration.

Such, then, we may conceive to be the prerogative of a magiftrate, in reftraining crimes and offences. It is in part prior to convention, and a concomitant merely of his power. It is limit-

I

ed

ed to him alone, by the convention of fellow citizens, in which they have agreed to wave their right of perfonal redrefs, and recur to eftablifhed tribunals for judgement in their differences, and to the power of the magiftrate for his protection, in maintaining or in recovering a right; a convention, the articles of which, in whatever form they be ftipulated, whether of ftatute or cuftomary practice, are effential to the relation of fellow citizens in every cafe whatever; ftill admitting, indeed, the exceptions we have mentioned in cafes to which the interpofition of the magiftrate cannot be effectual, or cannot extend.

Members of the fame community are thus underftood to have their conventional obligations, relating not only to matters of right and wrong that may come into queftion between them, but alfo in relation to certain pofitive duties which they owe to the community, and of which the magiftrate is appointed to infpect the performance.

Political eftablifhments cannot fubfift without the fupport of their members, contributing either by their means or by their perfonal fervices to the public defence, or to the arrangements which may be neceffary for public profperity. In the very nature of political fociety, therefore, convention to this amount is implied.

Under this general title of political convention, may be included every law and eftablifhed cuftom relating to the prerogative of the magiftrate, whether fupreme or fubordinate, or relating to the privilege of the fubject, of whatever rank or condition.

There

There are, in moſt communities that have made any progreſs in political arts, certain primary articles, which may be termed fundamental laws of the conſtitution. In theſe articles the deſcription of the ſovereign power, whether a King, Nobles, or majority of the people, is either given or aſſumed. The powers to be exerciſed, and forms of proceeding are aſcertained. The immunities, as well as the duties of the ſubject, are ſpecified.

Such fundamental laws, or conventions, are neither the foundations upon which ſociety was originally formed, nor do they always follow ſoon after its firſt inſtitution. They come in the ſequel of circumſtances into which men have paſſed, without any view to political eſtabliſhments, as in the ſequel of caſual ſubordination of ranks, ariſing from perſonal *qualities, birth, education,* or *fortune :* They are ſometimes the reſult of amicable deliberations, and ſometimes ſuch as prevaling parties may have obtained by force. Mankind are known to live for many ages in ſociety together, before they are ſenſible of the inconveniences, whether ariſing from the abuſe of prerogative or the abuſe of privilege, for which political law is intended as a remedy. The evils have ſometimes taken a deep root, before the attempt is made to remove them ; and civil war is frequently the prelude to the eſtabliſhment of order upon any permanent footing. Thus the great charter in England; many of the political capitulations in Germany, the pacification of parties at Rome, and what may be termed the fundamental political law in the inſtance of many other ſtates, was the reſult of war or contention that aroſe after many ages of ſociety had elapſed.

Political eſtabliſhments in ſome inſtances appear to have no other foundation than cuſtom, or a ſucceſſion of acts which imply,

I   that

that parties acquiefce, in the ftate of their country, or in the forms according to which its affairs proceed ; and in juftifying the exertions of government in fuch inftances for promoting the public welfare, we feldom look farther than to the actual tendency of adminiftration to the public advantage.

It is a part in the focial nature of man, to hold the action of a fellow creature, as juftified on the principle of benevolence, made known in acts of public utility ; but any claim of right to extort benefits, cannot, prior to convention, be admitted, without leading to confequences extremely dangerous and hurtful to the caufe of fociety. If benefits were to be enforced, beneficence would ceafe to be known as a virtue, and what ought to be a voluntary act of good will would become the effect of mere compulfion.

The ufe of compulfion, upon the principle of mere utility, would become a very dangerous precedent. The powerful could eafily obtrude this plea, wherever they thought proper to exert their violence, and under pretence of extorting public benefits, the greateft of public evils might arife in a want of fecurity to thofe very rights which government itfelf is eftablifhed to maintain. The people is not fafe, if the magiftrate may not only, reftrain crimes and diforders, but alfo exact contribution and actual fervice, beyond what he is authorifed to demand by fpecial contract, ftatute, or cuftom.

Any right in the magiftrate or fovereign to exact contribution, or pofitive fervice of any fort, from the fubject, being founded in convention alone; we may confider the different conftitutions of government as fo many compacts diverfified in the *terms*; or as fo many bargains in which the parties are varioufly bound, or in which,

in

in return for what they are engaged to perform, they accept of unequal conditions. The terms may be unequally expedient; unequally favourable to any of the parties, or to human nature in general. They may have been fuggefted by the relation in which
parties were occafionally placed, as when the prerogatives of monarchy or ariftocracy arofe by degrees from the continued diftinction of families, and the advantage of hereditary poffeffion.

The terms to which fome of the parties fubmit may have even
been impofed by actual force; but in all communities, fo far as
a right to enforce the performance of public fervice is fuppofed,
we muft be able to derive this right, either from the original
principle of felf defence, or from the principle of contract, on
which alone one human creature is bound or may be forced to
ferve another.

It may afked, then, on what principle of juftice are we to reft
the exercife of compulfory law, in the cafe of governments which
are known to have originated, and which continue to fubfift, in
force or violence alone? On this foundation it is admitted, that
no conventional right can arife. But it is well known in the
hiftory of nations, that at one time the leader has forced his followers to fubmiffion; that at another time the follower has extorted privilege from his leader; that conditions fo obtained have
been expreffed in ftatute, or gone into cuftomary practice; and
that the effects of compulfion have thus become articles of a legal conftitution, of which the validity is never queftioned by any
of the parties concerned.

The poffibility of fuch a cafe has been already ftated, in confidering cuftom as one of the forms in which conventional obligations

tions arife. A condition, at firft impofed by force may be
fuch, it was obferved, as that men fhall be reconciled to it, continue to obferve it willingly and freely, infomuch, that a perfon
conforming to it, on his own part, has the moft reafonable expectations of a fuitable return in the conduct of others.

This reafoning, however, will not apply, where any party in
fociety affumes to itfelf an advantage, or fubjects any other to inconvenience of fuch a nature, as that, although compliance may continue to be forced; yet the fufferer is not reconciled to his condition, nor ever willingly confents to the obfervance of it.
He does no more than he is forced to do; and the violence to
which he fubmits, in every fubfequent period of a mere impofition, has the fame character of ufurpation which it had at the
firft. Such, no doubt, is the character of defpotical tyranny, by
whatever party it be affumed, or exerted in difcretionary acts of
injuftice or cruelty, over the perfons and properties of other men.

Under this title of continued ufurpation, we have already ftated the claims of a mafter, refpecting his fuppofed property in
the perfon of a flave; a claim which, we obferved, cannot be
founded on any principle of juftice acknowledged in the law of
nature.

A people, in the fame manner, from confiderations of danger,
may fubmit to the claims of tyrany, whether ufurped by the leader
of a military band, or by the majority of a diforderly people, and
they may acquiefce in one fpecies of evil from the apprehenfion of a
worfe; but fuch government, whether of long or of fhort duration,
we may obferve, in anfwer to any of the queftions now or formerly
ftated, is not founded in any maxim of right whatever. The

principles of human nature, however long ftifled by violence, are ever repugnant to fuch ufurpations; and, like the force of a fpring wound up, ftill exert a preffure againft the power that reftrains them.   Hence, in perfect confiftence with natural juftice, though not always with prudence or expedience, we may vindicate the fudden or gradual reform of abufes, which for ages may have poffeffed in appearance the authority of law and political inftitution.

When we look back to the origin of government, as there is no where an original right of one perfon to command another, except fo far as is neceffary to reftrain him from harm, we have recourfe to convention as the only principle upon which a right to command can accrue to one, or an obligation to obey can be incurred by another.

Prior to fuch convention, we fay, *that fovereignty is lodged in the multitude*; but, when we bring thefe words to the teft of any rational application, they amount to no more than this, that, prior to convention, every one has a right to difpofe of himfelf, fo far as is confiftent with the fafety of others: And that the multitude have this right, becaufe made up of individuals, each of whom is poffeffed of it; but, in what form the multitude is to exercife it, as a collective body, muft depend on agreement to which individuals affent.   Prior to convention, the majority has not any right to command the minority, more than any one individual has to command another.

In the abftract decifions of natural law, refpecting the obligation of reciprocal contracts, the failure of one party diffolves the obligation of another.   So far, the matter is adjufted, in words even between the fovereign and fubject.   In practice,

2   too,

too, the fovereign has a ready provifion made to enforce the rights of government againft the refractory fubject, and the rights of one individual againft the wrongs of another; but, when the prerogatives which are given for protection, are employed to opprefs, what new power can be found to redrefs the grievance? It is neceffary, perhaps, that law fhould be filent on this head, or take its precautions in wife limitations of government rather than propofe to refift its abufe.

This is accordingly the great problem of political wifdom, and a principal teft of national felicity : But after all that can be contrived, or deliberately thought of, for this purpofe, fomething muft be left to the powerful inftincts of nature. When the multitude, whofe interefts fo much it is to have a fettled government, tear down the power by which themfelves are protected, we muft fuppofe that they are either feized with madnefs, or that by wrongs they are driven to defpair. In either cafe, maxims of fcience and reafon, or principles of juftice are inculcated in vain. The reafoner is every where furrounded with precipices. If he maintain, that the people, in every cafe, fhould obey, he delivers over the fubject to be opprefled and injured at difcretion.

If he admit that the people, in any cafe, may refift; as there is none but the party himfelf to judge of the cafe, all government will feem to be held at the difcretion of thofe who ought to obey it.

So far are we from being able to ftate any fpeculative or abftract pofition that may not be abufed. And fo far are we left to the powerful inftincts of nature, for our direction in matters of the greateft moment. When the ftorm threatens, the benighted traveller will take fhelter wherever he can find it; and, when the roof cracks over his head, he will fly from under it into the

midft

midſt of the ſtorm. He need not recur to any maxim of law for this purpoſe: The power of neceſſity is ſuperior to law; and the inſtinct of nature drives to its end, with a force which ſpeculative maxims can neither withſtand nor direct.

Attempts to find any regular counterpoiſe to the weight of deſpotiſm, when every ordinary form is warped to the purpoſe of injuſtice, have perplexed the moſt ingenious minds, or ſometimes ſuggeſted a doctrine which can ſcarcely be applied beyond the form of words in which it is ſtated. That, as power originates with the multitude, that is, with the individuals of whom the multitude is compoſed, they have a right to reclaim it, wherever it is abuſed; or, if they are bound by the terms of a political contract, to ſubmit to government; theſe terms are reciprocal, and the contract may be broken of either ſide: If on that of the ſovereign, the power is again that of the multitude, and may be recalled.

Such maxims in ſpeculation coſt nothing but the words in which to expreſs them; but, in practice, we muſt remember, that, as the multitude never can be aſſembled, this maxim in effect puts the ſword in the hands of every individual, to employ it for himſelf. And the fate of mankind, in ſuch inſtances, muſt depend on what we term accident, or the character of thoſe who gain the aſcendant, or are able to preſcribe new forms of proceeding, after numbers are tired of the diſorders which have attended the ſuſpenſion of the old.

SECTION

SECTION IV.

Of the Cafe of Nations.

THE human fpecies, though difpofed to affociate, is difpofed to feparation alfo. It is ever found in divifions and compartments, under the denomination of families, tribes, nations, or hordes. And of thefe the very leaft are rarely, without compulfion, or fome urgent confiderations of fafety or expedience, made to co-alefce in greater numbers, or, beyond the ties of acquaintance or confanguinity, fubmit to act under any common direction.

There is, however, in the nature of things, fufficient provifion made to affemble the fpecies, or to form the combination of indefinite numbers.

Men are, by their difpofitions and their faculties, qualified to make the neceffary arrangements for the conduct of fociety however enlarged. And, however reluctant in every fucceffive ftep, they actually pafs over the bounds of perfonal acquaintance or

PART II.
CHAP. IV.
SECT. IV.

2   perfonal

perfonal relation and numbers, however unknown to one another, fuffer themfelves to be formed into nations and empires of the greateft extent.

But, with refpect to the objects of our prefent diffcuffion, *any feparate company or fociety of men acting under a common direction*, may be termed a *nation*: For any plurality of men fo united, in the language of lawyers, is an artificial perfon, having power to act, and rights to defend.

In the intercourfe of feparate nations there being no government or common magiftrate to whom they are fubject, their cafe is, or may be nearly the fame with that which was fuppofed in a preceding fection under the relation of parties *ftrangers* and *unconnected*. They are fubject to the law of nature alone, however it may be modified by fpecial conventions, and the law of nature for this reafon is alfo termed the law of nations. In their differences or difagreements they may appeal to the judgement of neutral powers ; but if a difference is not otherwife removed, they may have recourfe to *war* and the decifion of *arms*.

The law of nations, which proceeds upon the fuppofition of peace when their is no exifting offence, proceeds upon the fuppofition of war when differences arife that cannot be otherwife reconciled ; and is therefore, relatively to fuch occafions, termed alfo the law of peace and of war.

The laft of thefe titles is that under which the learned Grotius has treated of the law of nature ; and perfons who have recourfe to this author will have occafion to felect from his redundancy what is neceffary rather than to feek for additional information on the fubject. Poffeffed of the juft principle of compulfory law,

he

he has applied it in a moſt ample detail, but ſo intermixed with
quotations from the cuſtom and practice of different ages, with confiderations of duty, as well as right; that his work becomes a ſyſtem of ethics, and the hiſtory of opinions and cuſtoms, rather than a ſimple deduction and application of the principles of com-pulſory law. His quotations, indeed, are intereſting, ſo far as we are concerned to know what men and nations have thought and practiſed, on the ſubject of their mutual obligations and rights; although their opinions are not of ſufficient authority in eſtabliſhing the principles, or in directing the applications of juſ-tice.

The moſt admired nations of antiquity were erroneous in their doctrines, and unfortunate in their practices relating to this im-portant ſubject. In war, the hoſtilities they practiſed were often unneceſſarily deſtructive; and the ſervitude to which they deſ-tined their captives was altogether unfounded on any principle of juſtice. So that, what we have to learn from the example they have ſet in theſe particulars, is rather what we ought to avoid, than what we may imitate or quote as authority in deciſions of natural law.

We are, in this reſpect, certainly more happy in modern times. War is made with little national animoſity, and battles are fought without any perſonal exaſperation of thoſe who are engaged: So that parties are, almoſt in the very heat of a con-teſt, ready to liſten to the dictates of humanity or reaſon; and there is no branch of practical juſtice, which we may recom-mend with more hopes of ſucceſs, than that which reſtrains na-tions at war, from unneceſſary ſeverities againſt one another.

The

The artificial perfons, of whom we are now to treat, confidered internally, or in refpect to their conftituent members, confift
of fellow citizens, magiftrates, and fubjects : Confidered external-
ly, or in refpect of one nation to another, they have their feparate
rights, whether original or acquired ; may avail themfelves of fuch
rights ; and guard them, by fuch means as are in their power, a-
gainft any fpecies of infringement or wrong.

Among the rights of nations, acquired or adventitious, may be
reckoned the ftipulations of treaty, or the conditions of acknowledged cuftom.   Thefe feveral articles of right, every nation lies
under an obligation to obferve, refpecting its neighbour, and is
entitled to maintain refpecting itfelf.   In their difputes, they
may have recourfe to perfuafion or reafon ; but, if reafon fhould
fail, their final refort is to ftratagem or force.

Such is the ftate of war between nations ; a ftate in which it is
allowed, that former conventions ceafe to be binding, and that
a nation aggrieved may avail itfelf of every means in its power to
obtain redrefs ; but, if the grounds of war be lawful, on the fide
of the one party, they muft be unlawful on the part of the other ;
and all that we fay, concerning the rights of war, in the application of force, is true only upon the fuppofition that the grounds of
the war itfelf are juft : Infomuch that, in ftating the maxims
of law, on this fubject, we endeavour to exprefs only the rights
of thofe who are entitled to plead the juftice of their caufe.

Wars may originate in *rapacity, emulation,* or *malice,* in *error* or
mifapprehenfion of right ; they may be of indefinite continuance,
or even form the ordinary ftate of contiguous nations.   The fact

in

in thefe refpects, is matter of hiftory, and admits of indefinite variations; but we are, in this place, to confider merely upon what fuppofition the act of hoftility, in any one nation, may be juft; to what extent lawful hoftilities may be carried, or within what limits they are circumfcribed, even to nations who are entitled to ufe them in the higheft degree : But, before we proceed to this principal object of difquifition, it is proper to confider queftions which relate particularly to the cafe of nations, as they are, in their manner of acting or fuffering, diftinguifhed from fingle men.

As the perfons of whom we are now to treat, include a plurality of individuals, having each a principle of will and activity centered in himfelf, as well as a common caufe, in which the members compofing the community may jointly act, or fuffer in a body; two principal queftions may arife concerning them: Firft, what actions, proceeding from the members of a community, are to be confidered as acts of the community itfelf? And, fecondly, In whofe perfon may the community be fuppofed to receive an injury; and from whom, in cafe of an injury received, may the community exact repation?

To the firft queftion, we may anfwer, That the fovereign of the ftate, of whatever defcription, whether a monarch or national affembly, is ever fuppofed to act for the community, and his actions are ever chargeable as actions of that body of which he is the head. In his title of fovereignty is implied a general fubftitution of his acts, for acts of that nation, of which the fupreme direction is committed to him. To this we may add, that the action of any individual, if employed by the fovereign, or commiffioned by the public fo to act, or if generally underftood to act for his country, will alfo involve, as a party in all his proceedings, the community to which he belongs.

But, as private citizens may offend againft the peace of their own country, as well as againft that of a foreign nation, ftates are not anfwerable for the offence of particular fubjects, farther than they previoufly authorife their conduct, or avow and protect the offender after the fact. Thus, pirates committing depredations on the high feas, are confidered as private criminals, and amenable to the penal laws of their own country, whilft letters of marque, or private fhips of war, authorifed by public commiffion, or publicly received into port with their prizes, and protected in the ufe of them, are juftly confidered as involving their country in the hoftilities they have committed, whether *unlawful* or *juftly provoked.*

To the fecond queftion, we may anfwer, That a nation may receive an injury in the perfon or effects of any citizen: That, in the cafe of wrongs fo received, the injured party may exact reparation, and make reprifals on the perfon or effects of any fubject or member of the injurious nation: And, in refpect to both queftions, it is evident, that as a nation may be chargeable with a wrong committed by any of its members, whether authorifed or merely protected, fo the injurious nation may be coerced or forced to make reparation by means that immediately affect the private intereft of any of its citizens, as well as by means that affect the community at large; infomuch, that the law of defence, in its application to the cafe of nations, will bear, that a community injured, whether in any of its public interefts, or in the

perfon

perſon of any of its members, has a juſt claim to redreſs, and may make reprıſals on the public, or on the perſons and effects of any or all the members of the offending nation.

SECTION

S E C T I O N   V.

The same Subject continued.

A S national councils are compofed of members differing in their opinions and difpofitions; and often fluctuating in their refolutions, according to the influence of contending parties, communities cannot be known to one another, as individuals are known, under any permanent character of tried affection and fidelity.   Nations are, therefore, almoft in every inftance, mutual objects of jealoufy and diftruft; and muft think themfelves fafe fo far only, as they are feverally in condition to maintain their refpective rights. They muft keep a watchful eye on the powers by which they may be annoyed from abroad, no lefs than attend to the means of defence with which they are furnifhed at home.   Their independance muft ceafe to exift, the moment it is held at the difcretion of any foreign power : what a neighbour, therefore, is about to gain, may be to them no lefs a fubject of alarm, than what they themfelves are about to lofe; and a war may be juftly under-

I   taken,

taken, by one ftate, to check the dangerous progrefs of another;
as well as to make any other provifion neceffary to its own prefervation.

This may render the queftion of right and wrong between nations extremely complicated, and fufpend or perplex the decifions
of juftice refpecting the caufe of a war.

In cafes of manifeft aggreffion the right of nations, like that of
individuals, to defend themfelves is obvious, and injuftice in the
firft ftep of the war communicates a like character of wrong to
every fucceeding operation in the conduct of it; but in queftions
of mere caution or diftruft, it is difficult to determine how far one
nation may juftly oppofe the progrefs of another, and in doing
fo be fuppofed to act on principles of mere defence; or at what precife
point they may be faid to act offenfively, and to become aggreffors
in any quarrel that may arife between them.

The Romans may have been vindicated in requiring the Car-
thaginans to evacuate Sicily and Sardinia, but not in taking poffeffion themfelves of thofe iflands, much lefs afterwards in requiring the Carthaginians to remove their city to an inconvenient
diftance from the fea.

In queftions of this kind men of the greateft integrity may be
partial to their own country, and fuch is the force with which
nature has directed rival nations to pull againft one another, that
it would be dangerous in the councils of either to effect an impartial part; while an enemy is ftriking, the fword of a friend
moft not be held in fufpence.

In

In the quarrels of nations, therefore, much allowance is to be made for the miſtake or miſapprehenſion of parties, and even for the caution with which it is proper, in national councils, to guard againſt the claims of a rival, even if he ſhould appear to be ſupported by juſtice. ,

If one nation employ force in ſupport of its claims, however juſt, the nation attacked is entitled to reſiſt every attempt to reduce it under the power of another ; and is not ſafe, even in making a juſt conceſſion, while its powers of defending itſelf are brought into hazard.

For theſe reaſons, we may wave the queſtion of juſtice, in the cauſe of a war, as depending on the actual circumſtances of the particular caſe, and conſider nations, acting without guile or premeditated malice of either ſide, as entitled to the privileges of a fair defence.

The means of defence were, in a former ſection, referred to three ſeparate titles, *perſuaſion, ſtratagem,* and *force.*

The firſt, it was ſaid, may be employed among friends, and in obtaining a favour, as well as in repelling an injury. In caſes where it may be uſed with ſucceſs, or where it may be ſafe to warn an enemy of a claim, that may be ſupported by force againſt him, it is no doubt required, that proper repreſentations ſhould be made, as the leaſt hurtful means that can be employed in urging a claim of right.

The Romans, for the moſt part, by previous complaint and requiſition of their right, propoſed to ſanctify their cauſe, and to

I

give

give at leaft an appearance of juftice to the hoftilities which they Part II.
were about to commence. The manifefto and declaration of war, Chap. IV.
which generally precedes hoftilities in modern Europe, may be Sect. V.
practifed with the fame effect; but they are not ftrictly required
by the law of nature, in every cafe whatever. A nation that has
taken the advantage of furprife, in committing an injury, cannot
complain if the fame advantage be taken of itfelf in making reprifals.

Declarations may operate merely as a warning to put the injurious party on his guard, and enable him the better to perfift in
the wrong he has done, a fuppofition on which the practice is
not at all neceffary, or derivable from any principle of natural
juftice.

Among nations, however, like thofe of Europe, in which the
fubjects of different ftates are involved together in commercial
connexions, and though innocent of any public wrong, are fo
much expofed to fuffer by the errors of thofe who govern their
refpective countries, it is at leaft humane, if not in ftrict law required, that a certain warning of their danger fhould precede the
actual hoftilities by which they are expofed to fuffer, and of the
caufes of which they are perfectly innocent.

This confideration, it is hoped, may long recommend the practice of declaring war before the actual commencement of hoftilities, among the modern nations of Europe, who, indeed, by the
continuance of it, and by cuftom, have given the expectation of
it in fome meafure the authority of convention or compact.

Stratagem

Stratagem, implying fome fpecies of *deception*, is more the refort of an enemy than of a friend. It may be employed in mifleading the injurious from his aim, or in obtaining from him
conceffions which he might not otherwife be willing to make.

On this fubject, we have already confidered the fcruples that
may arife refpecting the ufe of *deception*, and the preference which
the *brave* may give to the ufe of open force, even in obtaining
redrefs of their wrongs ; but we did not find, that the injurious
can take any juft exception to the ufe of *ftratagem*, or complain
that he is *deceived* when the effect is merely to counteract the
wrong he commits. There is, however, one form in which deception is reprobated by mankind in general, even in the midft
of hoftilities, and under the utmoft animofity of a national conteft.

Although it be allowed to miflead an enemy by falfe appearances,
and even by falfe informations, it is not allowed to enter into illufive treaties, or to ftipulate articles for the fake of an advantage
to be gained by a fubfequent breach of faith.

It is allowed that hoftilities cancel the obligation of preceding
conventions, but not the obligation of treaties that may be entered into after commencement of a war. Hence the facred regard
that is paid to cartels, refpecting the treatment or exchange of
prifoners, the capitulations or treaties of furrender which take
place in the midft of military operations, the quarter granted to
an enemy who lays down his arms, or the freedom that is given
to a prifoner, upon his parole of honour not to ferve until he is
fairly exchanged.

In

In all thefe inftances, the faith plighted, though even to an enemy, and under the operation of force, is held, by the general confent of all civilized nations, to be facred in the higheft degree.
The obligation, though poffibly not founded in the principle of
ftrict law, certainly refts on a principle of humanity, abfolutely
neceffary to the welfare of mankind, as without it, the calamities
of war, once begun, could fcarcely ever be brought to an end.
Peace itfelf refts upon the faith of a treaty concluded, while nations were yet at war; and, if it were admitted that fuch treaties
could be entered into, and concluded merely to deceive an enemy,
and draw him into a fnare, it is evident, that the only means left
to mankind, by which to ftop the iffues of blood, without the final extermination of an enemy, would be cut off, and two nations at war would be obliged to perfift in hoftilities to the utter
deftruction of one or the other.

On this ground, breach of faith, even during war, is reprobated among civilized nations ; and indeed, the advantage that
might be derived from it, in any particular inftance, would be
more than counterbalanced by the general diftruft which the faithlefs would incur, in cafes where it might be their intereft to have
credit given to their declarations or profeffions.

Force is the ordinary and ultimate refort of nations who cannot
fettle their differences upon amicable terms.   But, even in this
laft refort, the law of nature, we have obferved, directs a choice
to be made of fuch means, as being effectual, are leaft hurtful to
the parties againft whom they are employed.   The effect to be
aimed at is the redrefs of a wrong; and any harm done, even to

an enemy, beyond what is neceſſary to this effect, we have obſerved, is itſelf a wrong, and by the law of nature forbidden.

In applying this maxim to the caſe of nations at war, or in de-termining what may be lawful in the choice of hoſtilities, we are to conſider the object in view, and the ſtate into which it is pro-poſed to reduce an injurious party, in order to obtain the ends of juſtice.

Whatever may have been the ſubject in conteſt, the immediate object of hoſtilities employed by either party, is to reduce an anta-goniſt to a ſtate of conceſſion, ſo that he may no longer reſiſt what is claimed as a right. This is the ſituation into which one party is reduced by a defeat; and the advantage gained by it ac-crues to the other, by having vanquiſhed his enemy.

The firſt or immediate object of military operations, then, be-ing to obtain the victory, a ſecond is, to employ the advantage gained, ſo as to preſerve, ſecure, or recover the right which was originally in queſtion. And the ſtate of war between nations may may be divided into two periods; the firſt, that which precedes; the ſecond, that which comes after the victory. In the firſt pe-riod, parties are ſtill contending; in the ſecond, one or other is in condition to enforce his demands, or both, tired of the conteſt, wiſh for an accommodation.

With reſpect to the firſt period, or during the conteſt of par-ties, it is evident, that as hoſtilities are lawful only in preſerving a right, or in obtaining reparation of a wrong; ſo, in the choice of hoſtilities, ſuch only are to be deemed lawful as are neceſſary to obtain the victory.

3

This

This maxim in fpeculation is abundantly clear, but in practice it is often difficult to apply it; for, while one party refifts or preffes with all his force, and takes every opportunity to ftrengthen himfelf and to weaken his antagonift, the other party will think himfelf juftified in employing every means in his power to counteract operations, of which he knows not the precife extent.

Contending nations, for the moft part, thus urged by an apprehenfion of what an enemy may be devifing againft them, proceed at once to extremities; ufe weapons and engines the moft deftructive, and employ means the moft likely to reduce their enemy to fubmiffion, without any fcrupulous enquiry into the degree in which fuch means may be neceffary, provided they are likely to be effectual for obtaining the purpofe to which they are employed.

It is happy in the practice of nations when means of a deftructive nature, fuch as the ufe of poifoned weapons, infecting the fprings or fupply of provifions, breach of faith, or any other deftructive meafures, tending to furprife an enemy, without giving him the option of fubmiffion, are fo far reprobated, as that neither party thinks of employing them, nor apprehends that they are ever to be employed againft himfelf. In favour of fuch practice the law of nature is clear and peremptory: That the party attacked ought, if poffible, to have open before him the extent of his danger, as that alone may be fufficient to obtain the conceffion which conftitutes the end of the war.

Qq 2

During

During the period of conteſt, to whatever extremity an enemy that reſiſts may be urged, it is evident, from the general principle which limits the operations of war to ſuch means as are neceſſary to obtain the victory, that an enemy who ſubmits or yields, is thereby entitled to quarter. The end of the war, with reſpect to him, is already obtained; and to refuſe quarter, is juſtly conſidered amongſt civilized nations as an object of deteſtation and horror.

Priſoners taken in the courſe of a war are, agreeably to the dictates of natural law, diſarmed and ſecured, that they may not return to ſtrengthen the enemy: But as cruelties practiſed towards them have not any tendency to procure or to haſten the victory, it is not lawful to withhold ſubſiſtence or reaſonable accommodation in the manner of treating them.

The expence of ſubſiſting priſoners of war may indeed become an addition to the damage already ſuſtained from an enemy, and may accordingly become a juſt matter of charge againſt the party whoſe wrongs give riſe to the conteſt; but againſt whomſoever this queſtion may be decided, it is evident, from the general obſervations already made, relating to the faith that is to be kept even with an enemy, that cartels or treaties of any ſort, for the mutual accommodation of priſoners, are matters of ſtrict obligation.

We ſpeak not now of the regard which brave men and virtuous citizens mutually have for one another, though engaged on oppoſite ſides of a national quarrel. This is an article not of ſtrict law, but of perſonal generoſity, of poliſhed manners, or of candour,

2   dour,

dour, honourable for thofe who obferve it rather than matter of
right, which may be always exacted by thofe towards whom it is
obferved.

It is a well known maxim in the law of nature, that injurious
parties have no right to exact the performance of any promife
they may have extorted in purfuance of a wrong previoufly done.
Thus a robber, who has taken a traveller's money on the high
way, if he fhould extort a promife of fecrecy, has no right to exact the performance of fuch promife.

Upon this principle it fhould feem, that, in the courfe of a
war, engagements contracted with the injurious party are not
binding ; or do not beftow any right on fuch injurious party to
exact the performance.

Notwithftanding the evidence of this maxim, nations, moved
by the confideration of its fatal confequences, have almoft univerfally confented to forego the exceptions of force or injuftice
otherwife valid, to repel the obligation of treaties entered into
during the continuance of a war, and have confented to hold the
faith of fuch treaties equally, if not more facred than that of convention even between nations at peace. It is on the faith of
this confent, that the afperities of war are foftened towards individuals, that the prevailing party, on every particular occafion,
may refrain from unneceffary feverity towards an enemy, may
fpare the vanquifhed, and releafe the captive. Upon the faith
of this maxim, even during the animofities of war, a way is kept
open for the return of peace; and the party aggrieved, even having an enemy in his power, is prevailed upon to fheathe the
fword, and rely upon a promife of that enemy to repair the
wrong

wrong he has done, and to preferve the peace undifturbed for the future.

It is evident, in the abftract point of view, that while parties are at war, it is lawful to affift the innocent ; but, that any perfon giving aid to the guilty, becomes an accomplice in his crime. Upon this principle, parties at war, afferting their claim of right againft an enemy, have an equal claim againft the auxiliary, or a-gainft any nation giving refuge, protection, or fupport to an enemy ; but parties, unconcerned, may repel the attempts which are made to engage them in a quarrel, refpecting which they are difpofed to preferve their neutrality.

Neither of the parties at war may lawfully feize the effects of a neutral perfon, in order to employ them againft his enemy ; but, if the effects of a friend are deftined for the ufe of an enemy, and are fuch as may enable him the better to carry on the war, they may be lawfully feized.

If an enemy receive protection in the port or fortrefs of a neutral power, he may be lawfully purfued, and forced even in that retreat. With refpect to fuch matters, however, contiguous nations having frequent intercourfe, whether in peace or war, by their ordinary practice, give fanction to cuftoms, in fome inftances unequally agreeable or difagreeable to the original tenets of natural law.

Accordingly, among the modern nations of Europe, the effects of a friend going to an enemy may be feized, if they are fuch as would enable that enemy the better to carry on the war ; and the

effects

effects of an enemy may be feized on board the fhip of a friend, provided the fhip is reftored with freight and other expences.

In the operations of war at land, an enemy may be purfued into the territory, and forced to furrender in the fortrefs of a neutral power; but, in the operations of war by fea, neutral ports are held to be facred, and the protection they give is extended to fome indefinite diftance, at which their fignals can be underftood, or to which guns from the fhore may be fuppofed to reach.

In this diftinction, which is made between the liberties that may be taken with the land fortreffes and fea ports of an enemy, the rule is no doubt capricious, and the reverfe of that which the law of nature feems to inculcate. By the maxims of this law, an injured party may purfue his redrefs by any means which are confiftent with the fafety of others who are not concerned in the wrong of which he complains. There is, or may be, evident reafon to bar his entrance into the territory of a neutral power, or to bar his laying fiege to a fortrefs in which an enemy may have taken refuge, as this cannot be done without damage to the territory on which he enters, or demolition to the works he would force; but there is no reafon why he may not approach the coaft or enter the port of a neutral power, and there force his antagonift, by means which no way affect the intereft of the neutral party in queftion. The only probable reafon that can be affigned for the origin of this diftinction is, that neutral powers are better prepared to keep the peace of their ports againft the force of intruders by fea, than they are prepared to keep the peace of their territory againft the force of great powers collected to make war on their frontiers; that therefore they urge their right in the one cafe, and forgo it in the other.

Such

Such are a few of the principal points to which the law of nature applies, in what we ftated as the firft period of a war, while
parties yet contend for the afcendant or the victory. If the e-
vents of the war nave been fuch as incline either or both parties
to make the conceffions neceffary to an accommodation, they are
come to the fecond period, in the fequel of victory, which was
fuppofed to be the firft or immediate object of hoftilities.

In this ftate of parties, the victor has acquired a power to enforce his right, but, refpecting the caufe or fubject of the quarrel, does not become vefted with any right that did not originally fubfift, or that has not arifen in the way of additional claim of
compenfation for the damage fuftained in the courfe of the war.

The victorious, if his general claim be juft, is now in condition
to enforce it; he is in condition, alfo, to enforce compenfation for
whatever he may have fuffered in vindicating his right; and may
lawfully require fecurities, or take precautions for his future fafety. But, as the fuccefs of arms cannot change wrong into right,
and as the innocent is not lefs entitled to juftice, for being unable
to refift the violence that is offered to him, any fuppofed right of
conqueft, arifing from the fuccefs of a war, is a mere folecifm in
language, and the reverfe of any juft tenet of natural law.

The fortune of war is fometimes favourable to the injurious,
and may place either of the parties concerned in poffeffion of advantages which they have not any right to retain either in virtue
of their original claim, in virtue of compenfation for damage fuftained in the war, or as fecurities required to their future fafety.
On thefe fuppofitions, conqueft can beftow no right; and it is fortunate

tunate in the practice of nations, when, either from a principle
of moderation, or from an apprehension that neutral powers might interpose to check the abuse of their advantages, they employ their conquests only to secure themselves in the possession of their rights.

Among other advantages of civilization and public justice in modern Europe, we have reason to congratulate ourselves upon this, that conquests are seldom undertaken, and acquisitions seldom retained, except upon the ground of some plausible or probable claim, on which the subject in question was originally seized or demanded.

C H A P. V.

Of Moral Action, and the Characteristics of a Virtuous and Happy Life.

S E C T I O N I.

Of Virtue, as diftinguifhable from the Effects of Compulfory Law.

IN fome fuch manner, as has been attempted in the two laft chapters, we may trace the outlines of jurifprudence or compulfory law from a firft principle in nature, as we purfue a feries of mathematical theorems from an axiom or definition previoufly affumed or underftood. Our theories, in either cafe, no way affect the the phyfical ftate of things otherwife than they are applicable

R r 2

plicable

applicable by aſſumption of circumſtances, or by ſome degree of approximation in the caſes which actually take place.

The object of compulſory law is defence; and to obtain this end *force* is perfectly adequate : But the object of morality in general is different : It is to inſpire virtuous diſpoſitions, and render that ſtate of the perſon we would defend not only ſecure, but otherwiſe eſſentially happy.

When the law is thus conceived, as divided into two ſeparate tables; the one containing a prohibition of wrongs, the other requiring poſitive acts of beneficence, the ſanctions are ſuppoſed to be diſtinguiſhable alſo, under titles of perfect and imperfect obligation. The uſe of words is no doubt in ſome meaſure arbitrary; but it ought not to be implied in any words we employ, that a rule, merely becauſe it may be enforced, is in any degree more binding than the conſideration of what is in itſelf an article of wiſdom, as conſtituent of good to mankind.

Juſtice is ſaid to be the object of compulſory law; and it is ſo, no doubt, in reſpect to many of its external effects : But, conſidered as an article of ſupreme felicity to the perſon who willingly obſerves it, juſtice is no leſs above the reach of compulſion, than is the whole of that guardian affection, which renders man towards his fellow creatures not only unwilling to be the cauſe of harm, but active alſo in yielding the fruits of beneficence. The perſon who abſtains from harm, merely becauſe he may be forced to do ſo, is in no degree comprehended under any deſcription of virtue, and in reſpect to the good at which morality aims, may be conſidered as a wretch and an outcaſt from mankind.

3

Force

Force may operate in practice, by prefenting evils which deter from iniquity ; but vice itfelf is a greater evil than any that force can inflict ; and the obligation to humanity and candour, therefore, is as perfect as the fear of evil or the confideration of human felicity can make it. A perfon who deliberates on the choice of his conduct, will not always find himfelf more powerfully determined to refpect what may be called the right of one fellow creature, than he is to relieve the diftrefs, or cordially to embrace the merits of another *. An orphan, it is faid, was found almoft naked, lying on the grave of his parent, of whom he had been recently deprived ; the perfon who found him, we fhall fuppofe, was paffing to an appointment, at which he was about to difcharge a debt : But this object fixed his mind ; he employed his money in procuring relief and protection for him ; and his creditor for the time was difappointed. Will any one reprobate this act of humanity, as interfering with a matter of more perfect obligation ? Even the courts of law, as we have had occafion to obferve, can admit the extreme neceffity of one perfon as valid to fufpend the right of another. Thus, a perfon about to perifh for want of food, is allowed to fave himfelf by recourfe to the property of another ; and the plea of humanity is held to be more facred than that of an abfolute and exclufive right. Why fhould not humanity therefore be enforced ? If it be the primary good incident to human nature, why fhould it not be obtained by any means the moft effectual for this purpofe ? There is not, indeed, any reafon why it fhould not be effectually obtained ; and if force could be effectual to infpire benevolence,

PART II.
CHAP. V.
SECT. I.

even

---

* Vid. Prix diftribués et propofés par la Societé Royale d' Agriculture, dans fa féance publique tenue a Paris le 23 Decembre, 1791.

even the fword and the mace fhould be employed to make men love one another. But benevolence is a modification of will, which no application of force can procure: Even the external effect, if obtained in this manner, would lofe the character of virtue. A beneficent action, which, when free, is liberality or charity on the part of thofe who practife it, would, under the application of force, be changed into extortion or robbery on the part of thofe who fhould fo exact the performance of it for their own advantage. To beftow the felicity of a willing mind, force is not only inadequate, but, by alienating the affections of thofe againft whom it is employed, would have a contrary tendency.

All that the magiftrate can do in this matter is, by fhutting the door to diforder and vice, to endeavour to ftifle the ill difpofitions of men; and by fecuring the paths of integrity, and marking them with confiderations of diftinction and honour, to facilitate and encourage the choice of virtue, and to give fcope to the beft difpofitions which nature has furnifhed, or which the ingenuous mind is able to cultivate in itfelf.

We are now to confider not the applications of force, but the felicity of a willing mind. What is the beft and moft happy condition of human life? What moft agreeable to the law of God and the general fenfe of men ingenuous and well informed? The confiderations which lead to this choice, if benevolence be fuppofed to need any excitement to its own purfuits, have been already enumerated under the titles of *confcience, religion,* and *public repute.* But thefe may not be fufficient without all the other accompaniments of a well informed, as well as benevolent mind.

Confcience, indeed, for the moft part will approve the acts of
3   beneficence

beneficence and reprobate the effects of malice : But prejudice, on particular occasions, may assume the name of conscience. And men are not always virtuous in doing what they themselvs conceive to be right. A person who has incurred a mischivous error, may have his own approbation, while he is in reality an object of just detestation and horror ; and the merit he assumes to himself in the face of better information, argues a mind depraved at once in its judgements as will as affections. Even the furious zealot who is pleased to inculcate his doctrines under terrors of the rack and the fire, may think that he is active in the cause of truth, or in propagating a faith which is necessary to the salvation of mankind. Or the Mufsleman, who thinks it a duty, when the standard of Mahomet is erected, to plunge his dagger in the breast of any Jew or Christian that is within his reach, may flatter himself that he has the sanction of conscience for the outrage he commits on humanity and justice.

Under the title of *public repute*, or a deference to the sense of mankind, we may in general be directed to a harmless and beneficent course of life ; but not always securely to this effect. Vain glory and mean popularity are sometimes grafted on this principle, and as often mislead the conduct of men, or embitter the moments of life with jealousy or disappointment. In private the silence of fame is often the best repute, as at Athens, that woman was said to merit the highest praise of whom no rumour either good or bad ever went abroad *. And to the father of a family also, who, by the constitution of his country, is neither a
statesman

* Vid. Thucidides lib. ii. c. 45. Rex vixit male qui natus morienfque fefellit.

ſtateſman nor a wariour, nor placed in any public profeſſion, the ſilence of fame is itſelf a laudable diſtinction *.

Under the title of *religion* we admire and love the conceiveable perfections of the ſupreme Being : But bigotry and ſuperſtition may aſſume the name of religion, and ſubſtitute acts of oppreſ-ſion and cruelty towards men for acts of duty towards God.

We muſt not therefore truſt to whatever may bear the name of religion or conſcience, or to what may have a temporary vogue in the world for our direction in the paths of a juſt and manly virtue. Every advantage of a benevolent mind and well informed underſtanding are conducive to this purpoſe, and the characteriſtics of a virtuous life, frequently revolved in the mind may have a ſalutary tendency to the ſame effect. To delineate the features of virtue is an agreeable taſk, and, when happily performed, is favourably received by man-kind. Even they who in practice are leaſt obſervant of the models preſented to them, nevertheleſs bear witneſs to the truth of an obſervation which Cicero has quoted from Plato. *That if virtue could be rendered manifeſt to the eyes of men, it would excite the*

* Nec vixit male qui natus morienſque fefellit.

Upon this idea of a virtue retired in modeſt ſilence and indifference to fame, there is wanting for the inſtruction of mankind, a biographical collection containing exam-ples of men who have been able to fill up the years of a happy life with occupations and duties which gave continual ſatisfaction, without any wiſh to extend their celebrity. It might be difficult indeed to collect materials for ſuch a work, and few are enough lovers of mankind and indifferent to fame to be qualified for the execution of it. If Mr Addiſon had betaken himſelf to this taſk, his country that owes him ſo much would have owed him ſtill more than for any of his actual ſervices.

the moſt wonderful paſſion of love and deſire of wiſdom *. Its leſſons are happily received through the channels of ingenuous literature and the fine arts, no leſs than in the way of formal inſtruction. Of the firſt, there are many proofs in the works of diſtinguiſhed genius, whether, ancient or modern in which qualifications which ſerve to accompliſh the author ſerve alſo to inſtruct the world *. Of the other, there are alſo valuable remains of antiquity in the Memorabilia of Socrates ; the Ethics of Ariſtotle ; the offices of Cicero ; and ſtill more in the remains of Epictetus and Marcus Aurelius. In our own language alſo there are many valuable compoſitions on the ſubject. Some on that of manners, and the ordinary concerns of human life, having appeared periodically at different times of this century, ſtill continue to be read with more than the pleaſure of novelty. Others that have been delivered by perſons in holy orders, and in the diſcharge of their ſacred functions. With theſe, in any inſtance, I do not compete : But in my attempt to touch this copious ſubject, of which I cannot by any means hope to fill up the detail ; I am ambitious to ſhow that there is a ſcience of manners or of Ethics, no leſs than of Juriſprudence or of Politics, and for this purpoſe

S s   would

---

* Forman quidem ipſam, Marce fili ; & tanquam faciem honeſti vides, quæ, ſi oculis cerneretur, mirabiles amores, ut ait Plato, excitaret ſapientiæ, *Cic. de Officiis*, lib. i. c. 5.

---

* Scribendi recte ſapere eſt et principium et fons.
Rem tibi Socraticæ poterunt oſtendere chartæ,
Verbaque proviſam rem non invita ſequentur.
Qui didicit patriæ quid debeat et quid amicis ;
Quo ſit amore parens, quo frater amandus et hoſpes ;
Quod ſit conſcripti, quod judicis officium, quæ
Partes in bellum miſſi ; ducis ille profecto
Redere perſonæ ſcit convenientia cuique.

would willingly point out a method, bywhich to derive the offices or duties of a virtuous life from principles at once fo comprehenfive and unqueftionably evident, as to enable every perfon to fill up the detail for himfelf.

SECTION

SECTION II.

Of the Occasions and Characters of Human Action in general.

WE have laboured in former sections, to have the characters, whether good qualities, or defects of mind distinctly conceived, as constituting, on the one hand, the happiness and good, or, on the other, the misery and ill, of intelligent being. In these characters of the mind subsists the distinction of good and evil. Corporeal actions are distinguished only as their effects and external expressions.

So much to be observed is perhaps necessary to a right understanding of the subject. At the same time, it must be admitted, that any individual mind, however possessed of its highest perfections, if, without means of communication with other minds, would be no more than a single and separate existence, not a member in any community of beings; not active to any beneficent purpose; nor even having any scope for the exercise of its best dispositions and faculties.

PART II.
CHAP. V.
SECT. II.

S s 2

The

The Author of nature, fo far as we know, has not fo disjoined individuals from one another in any part of his works. There is an affinity and combination of minds, as well as of material fubftances. The chain of communication extends from one to many, from fpecies to fpecies, and even from world to world, throughout the intellectual as well as material fyftem of nature. In our limited views of the intellectual world, there is a medium, through which individuals give and receive intimation of their meaning, and on which they jointly work with mutual difpofitions to concert or oppofition. How this chain of communication may be formed, betwixt intelligent beings different from man, or how it may be fupplied in a ftate any way different from the prefent, we know not; but, in the prefent condition of man's intelligent being, his communication with other minds is effected by means of his animal frame. Through this medium, minds mutually know and are known to one another. Among the fubjects that affect the animal nature, they find conftituents of intereft or felf prefervation, on which they are induftrious. They encounter with one another in the fame or oppofite purfuits, and find materials that may be employed as means of beneficence or harm, of co-operation and oppofition, according as they are difpofed to act the part of friends or of enemies.

We have already indulged the idea, that this fcene of animal life, is but the opening of a boundlefs courfe, in which man is deftined to purfue the objects of his intelligent nature: By means of animal perceptions, the firft rays of information or knowledge are made to dawn upon his foul; he is made to perceive the world in which he is a part; and, in the edifice of nature, in which he is

lodged

lodged is not, like the other animals, merely an indweller; but is partly let into the reafon of its contrivance, not merely urged by inftinct, but qualified to deliberate on the choice of his actions, whether in obtaining a convenience to himfelf, or in procuring a benefit to his fellow creatures.

Thefe occafions of action, making fo material an article in the hiftory of the human fpecies, have been already ftated; and the purfuits or exertions of mind, to which they give rife, have been enumerated under the refpective titles of arts, *commercial, political,* and *intellectual.* The firft are employed on fubjects required to fupply the wants and neceffities of animal life; the fecond relate to the order of fociety, or the relations of men acting in collective bodies; and the third relate to the exercifes and attainments of mind, in the ufe and improvement of its diftinctive powers.

When, in the fequel of this ftatement, we confider how far the intellectual powers of man are fhort of the degrees which he himfelf is able to conceive, we were naturally led to fuppofe, that there are, in the univerfe of God, much higher forms of intelligence than his. At the fame time, we cannot but think, that even he is of no mean rank in the fcale of being; for to him is allotted one of the primary planets, and what, under this title, may be reckoned a feventh part of this folar or planetary world. Here, then, is a mighty apparatus made for his accommodation; and our beft way of reconciling fo much confequence in the fyftem of nature, with fo much littlenefs in the prefent attainments of man, is, by fuppofing this terreftrial fphere which he occupies, and probably many fuch, to be nurferies for the great world of intelligent being: And in this fuppofition we may learn to refpect the prefent fcene of things, however feemingly frivolous, as a prelude to the

3

the higher parts of a drama, for which men are deftined to prepare in paffing through the offices, employments, and duties of the prefent life.

Under one or other of the titles now mentioned, and formerly treated more at large, we may fuppofe the prefent occafions of human action to be comprehended ; and, if it be good for man to act his part, it is certainly required, in conftituting that good, that the occafions of action fhould be attended to, and well under-ftood. The external fituations of men may be varied indefinitely, by the unequal poffeffion of things conducive to convenience or felf prefervation, or by the unequal diftribution of materials on which the powers of wifdom and goodnefs may be employed; and we may know that happinefs or mifery is not proportioned to the meafure in which fuch things are poffeffed, but to the right or wrong ufe of them, and to the wifdom or folly of the part which is acted with refpect to them. Yet, as the work is not likely to be well executed where the materials are neglected, philofophy, which bids us attend to our duty, as the principal object in hu-man life, has no tendency to make us overlook or neglect the oc-cafions to which the propriety of our conduct relates.

In general it is fuppofed, that means are fubordinate to the end for which they are employed; and from this rule it fhould fol-low, that the induftry and ingenuity, the fobriety and fortitude, practifed by a man in the purfuits of fortune; that the benevo-lent affection, exercifed in acts of liberality or charity, fhould be of inferior confideration to the wealth which he means to acquire in the one cafe, or to the favour and relief which he means to beftow in the other. In the eftimate of human concerns, how-ever

ever, the contrary is true. Where human virtue is the means, and external advantage the end, we know from experience, that the means are of more value than the end, and conftitute the happinefs of human life, in whatever meafure the end be obtained, or even where in the event it is fruftrated. To this purpofe, it is obferved by Cato, in Cicero's dialogue concerning the fupreme good, that, although human action is directed to certain external ends of accommodation or fafety, which he enumerates, yet that, from the action itfelf there refults a confideration of much greater moment, than the end or purpofe to which the action itfelf was directed *. In the productions of men, materials are of lefs value than the ingenious defign and execution of the work. And in acts of good will to mankind, the external effect is inferior to the affection of a generous and beneficent heart.

The great object of reafon, however, in thefe obfervations, is not to detach men from a proper attention to the occafions of action, but to qualify them, however the fcenes may differ, to act their part with propriety, or to prevent them from thinking that their good confifts in mere fituation, or in the materials they employ, and not in the nature of the part which they themfelves are free to act, in every fituation, and with refpect to any material.

To few it is left to determine what courfe of life they fhall purfue. The conduct of patrimonial interefts, the cares of family, the duties of public or private ftation, are to moft men fufficient to mark the line or direction in which they are to pafs

through

* Cicero de Finibus, lib. iii. cap. 6.

through life.   But, to bear the characters of an ingenuous or happy mind, it is not neceffary that the fituation or line of life fhould
be fpecifically adapted.   This bleffing is attainable in every fituation, and is the gift of God to every rational creature who knows
how to difcharge the prefent duties of his ftation with diligence,
benignity, and courage.

Different inftitutions of fociety engage their members in different purfuits.   Under fome inftitutions, it is the prevailing object of
paffion to become rich; in others, to obtain precedence and titles, or
to make a fhow of rank and fortune derived from anceftors.   In o-
thers, it is the prevailing paffion to be diftinguifhed in the claffes
of ftatefmen, of warriors, or orators.   But in the fcene of human
life, be it conftituted by whatever direction of public opinion, the
wife, the ingenuous, and the beneficent will ftill find their place ;
and it were dangerous or abfurd to wafte, in vain expoftulations,
the fpirit, which ought to operate in the beft ufe of our fituation,
whatever it may be.

In a little village of the Alps, the attendants of Cæfar could
perceive that even there, as well as at Rome, there might be parties and a conteft for rank : And he himfelf could there alfo apprehend the ufual objects of his ambition, fuperiority of power,
in refpect to which, he would rather be the *firft in that village* than
the *fecond at Rome*.   In every department of human life, if there
be a vice to be fhunned, there is alfo a virtue to be practifed ; and
what every man is chiefly concerned to know, is that, even in his
village, or in his place, there is occafion to exercife the character
of a noble and ingenuous mind, as well as a danger to be incurred on the fide of folly and of vice.

Philofophers

Philofophers would varioufly teach us; fome to refer our actions, and to limit our views, to private or feparate gratifications; to court an exemption from care and folicitude on the concerns of other men; and to fill up the moments of life with the leaft poffible trouble or avocation from our own perfonal ftate and enjoyments. But nature feems to require that we feek for the interefting fcenes of human life; that we confider our own, and the caufe of mankind, as common; that we confider our fociable difpofitions as the better part of ourfelves; and that we willingly feize the occafions which exercife the powers of a wife and beneficent mind.

Reafon, pretended or real, may thus difpofe or indifpofe us for the fcene which providence has opened before us. But nature has provided, that the individual can no where fhake himfelf loofe of his fpecies, and that if he does not bear his part in fociety as a friend, he muft fuffer as an enemy.

The veffel, on board of which all men are embarked, muft be managed and wrought by the common fkill and labour of the crew, and none can be indulged in exemptions, which, if all were to plead and obtain, would end in the ruin and deftruction of the whole. " I would reap," fays Ariftippus, " what other people " fow, I would enjoy my pleafures in a city which others have " built, and labour to preferve". This confidered as the choice of an individual may be cunning; but offered as a fcheme of philofophy for mankind, is more abfurd than language can ex- prefs. If the flothful mariner, in his wifdom, fly from the helm, or fhrink from his watch on the deck, what is to become of the veffel in which he is embarked, and in which the fcene of his

VOL. II. T t private

private enjoyments, or interefts, however real, is likely upon this plan to be of fhort continuance.

Animals are obferved to have their native propenfities, from which there refults a diftinctive afpect and manner of life. This obfervation will apply no lefs to man. He too is diftinguifhed from his birth. He is deftined to know himfelf, to obferve and to chufe among the ends of purfuit, and his afpect is different according to the choice he has made, and according to the ability or temper with which he perfifts in that choice.

Every fituation may try the fkill of the perfon who is placed in it; may try his difpofition to beneficence, or his neglect of other men, his fortitude and his application to objects that merit the principal fhare of his attention. *Skill, difpofition, application*, and *force*, are accordingly the qualifications to which we referred, as requi-fites in the formation of an active character. And, with a view to which, morality has been divided into a correfponding num-ber of parts or branches, which are termed the Cardinal Virtues, to wit, *prudence* or *wifdom, goodnefs* or *juftice*; temperance and *for-titude*. This arrangement of the fubject is familiar in common language, as well as in the fchools of morality, and points out a method in which we may continue to purfue what remains to be obferved on the external characteriftics of a virtuous life.

Wifdom is the virtue or excellence of the underftanding, by which a perfon is fkilful in the choice of his objects, and in the means of obtaining his end.

Goodnefs is the excellence or virtue of a good difpofition, from which men venerate the rights and feel for the fufferings of their
fellow

fellow creatures, from which they are averſe to be the authors of harm, from which they are ever faithful and true to the expectations they have raiſed, and ever ready, by acts of kindneſs and good will, to prevent even the wiſhes of thoſe who by nature or accident are made to depend on their will.

Temperance is the proper choice of our purſuits and applications ; or ſuch a meaſurement and regulation of inferior gratifications and deſires as is conſiſtent with the higher and better occupations of our rational nature.

Fortitude is that ſtrength of mind which enables the virtuous man to withſtand oppoſition, to contend with difficulty, and to poſſeſs himſelf in the midſt of danger. It is the foundation of magnanimity, which, when a perſon is called upon to perform any of the more arduous duties of life, inſpires a courage ſuperior to the conſideration of inferior intereſts or concerns. Its principle in the mind is an eſſential conſtituent of happineſs; not only as it qualifies men to encounter with eaſe any real difficulty, diſtreſs, or danger, but as it is an antidote to thoſe imaginary fears and miſ-apprehenſions which conſtitute weakneſs, and a principal article of meanneſs or ſuffering.

Such being the *cardinal virtues*, forming what we may conſider as the firſt and moſt general arrangement of the moral duties, we proceed to conſider their conſequences, or the more particular habits and exertions in which they ſeverally conſiſt. In doing this, the firſt or moſt general title in each diviſion will ſerve as a principle, from which the inſtructions of moral propriety relating to the ſeveral parts may be drawn.

T t 2

SECTION

SECTION III.

Of the Characteristics of Prudence or Wisdom.

WISDOM being a difcernment of the ends which we ought to purfue, and of the means moft effectual for the attainment of them, it fhould feem to include every virtue. For, on the fovereign direction of a mind perfectly apprifed of its good, and of the manner in which that good is to be fecured, we may fafely rely for the rectitude and propriety of our conduct in every inftance.

Wifdom was accordingly fo confidered by the antient philofophers; and, in the imaginary defcription of a wife man, every conceivable perfection of human nature was included.

We are thus difpofed, for the moft part, to fimplify our conceptions, and to feek for fome fundamental principle from which, if we fecure it, every other requifite will follow; but the reality of any fuch principle, even in the government of human nature,

may

may be doubted. The love of mankind, which we have affumed as the neareft approach to a general principle of virtue, requires the direction of wifdom and the fupport of courage. Wifdom alfo requires the reality of a benevolent affection, which even the beft difcernment of what ought to be done, on particular occafions, cannot fuperfede.

Among the happieft effects of wifdom, we may reckon the proper direction which a benevolent difpofition itfelf may receive towards the attainment of its end ; but if in this, wifdom or prudence is fubfervient to goodnefs, the benevolent affections are often the beft fecurity that judgement itfelf fhall not err : For they often lead to the genuine point of integrity and honour, when a cold difcernment of what is proper for the occafion might fail of its aim.

Wifdom, ftated as one among the cardinal virtues, refers chiefly to thofe duties which refult from reflection, and which terminate in preferving the ftate and character of the individual unimpaired. Such are *decency, propriety, modefty, oeconomy, decifion*, and *caution*.

Thefe being the characteriftics of prudence, and the external marks of a confiderate mind, or the effects of habit acquired, together with experience in the progrefs of reafon, they are among the virtues which the Duke de la Rochefoucault fuppofes to owe their merit to reflection, and to embellifh a character the more for being acquired. But, even here, there is a partiality to natural, parts, of which, under the notion of fuperior genius or great ability, men court the reputation, even where they incur its neglect or acknowledge its abufe. It is that which is fuppofed to give to

the

the ftatefman or warrior his fuperior luftre; that which elevates the orator, the poet, and fine artift of every defcription, above the ordinary ranks of men; and we have the folly frequently to efti-mate a merit which ought to confift in a proper ufe of our facul-ties, by the mere poffeffion of a talent, with too little regard to the falutary effects which it ought to produce.

The value of wifdom, however great, is more evident perhaps in its contraft with folly, than when feparately ftated. " A fool," fays La Bruyere, " cannot look, nor ftand, nor walk like a man " of fenfe. The contraft thus appears in the moft trivial, as well " as moft important occafions of human life, in every feature of " the countenance, and every action and gefture of the body. " The fool is mortified in being told of his folly, and feels the " imputation of it as a grievous reproach."

What then are thefe characters. When we attempt to a-nalyfe them, the diftinction, fhould appear to arife, on the one hand, from a difcernment of what ought to be done, and from a habit of doing it; on the other, from a miftake, or want of difcernment of the object, of the occafion, and of the place, or from a habit of being occupied on occafions of ferious bufinefs with objects of inferior value. Such is the folly of the coxcomb, the vain-glorious, the avaricious, the fpendthrift, and the prodigal, the contemptuous, and the proud.

Wifdom is the difcernment of what a man ought to wifh for himfelf, for his friend, for his country, and for mankind. And fuppofing a difpofition to act well in all thefe relations, it is the ability with which he may acquit himfelf well on the different occafions

occasions to which they give rise. It has, in every person, a particular reference to the conduct of his own affairs. He may, indeed, consider his benevolence, or good will towards others, as one
of the most important articles in the predicament of what belongs
to himself; but such affections belong more properly to their separate articles of goodness or justice.

Decency, considered apart from every other principle of moral
obligation, though an article of wisdom, is that of which the external or physical effects are of least moment to human life. It is
directed chiefly to save appearances, and gives evidence of a mind
cautious to avoid what is evil, in matters which, either by opinion, custom, or natural sensibility, are rather offensive than hurtful to others. Its rules, therefore, are prohibitory and its offices
sometimes consist in avoiding before others, what, when alone,
may be innocent, or perhaps necessary.

There are men, who, under an affectation of being superior to
trifles, suffer themselves to trespass on the rules of decency; but
offence unnecessarily given to our fellow creatures, whatever be
the manner of it, is not a trifle; and the poet has justly observed
that " Want of decency is want of sense." The observance of
this duty, as it is dictated either by the instincts of nature, or by
the custom of our country, is important, as the presence of one
man is important to another, and the reception which a person
meets in society is important to himself.

The objects of prohibition, which come under this article, might
be summed up under three titles, *nudity, filth,* and *obscenity*; but
of these the boundaries are sufficiently marked in the custom or
manners of every nation or age; and to go into any detail with respect
to

to them would be, in some measure to offend against the duty which we mean to enjoin.

Propriety is the suitableness of action to the person who acts; to the occasion; and to the place: so that, although it comprehends decency, because what is proper is also decent, it proceeds upon a principle yet more extensive and less depending on local apprehensions and customs. Indecency is chargeable only in the presence of others; impropriety may be incurred by a person when alone, as often as he neglects what is due to himself or to his fellow creature, or as often as he incurs what is unsuitable to the part he has to sustain, either in respect to *rank, profession,* or *age.*

There is a propriety, as well as decency, in all the external effects of virtue: In all the effects, for instance of good sense, benevolence, and resolution, these are proper to human nature as such, and constitute the principal graces or recommendations of the human character; but it is proper to limit our observations on this article of propriety, to particulars which are derived from this consideration alone.

Among the proprietes of high rank, we may reckon the conditions which are peculiarly requisite to preserve respect; that *reserve* which avoids improper familiarities; that *candour,* which guards against *petulance, contemptuousness, affectation,* or *scorn.*

It is proper, that the claim to superior respect should be supported by superior accomplishments of manners and candour; by a superior steadiness and moderation in all occasional emotions and passions, whether of *sorrow, anger, mirth,* or *joy.*

I

The

The genuine expreſſions or effects of reſpect conſtitute the proprieties of inferior ſtation, in its relation to that which is ſuperior.

Reſpect naturally carries a mixture of good will and affection, which breaks forth in the well regulated plainneſs of truth, rather than in flattery or continual aſſent. There is a certain ingenuity required to render a perſon capable of affection and reſpect. It begins with giving a dignity to the manners of thoſe who are poſſeſſed of it, and its attentions bear the moſt honourable teſtimony to the elevation of thoſe towards whom it is directed.

The conceſſions of the ſervile are the effects of *baſeneſs*, *intereſt*, or *fear*, and are proper objects of *diſtruſt*, not of *predilection*, or *favour*.

In the ſociety of ingenuous men, however unequal in point of rank, there is a candour, which, in reſpect to freedom, in reſpect to the diſpoſition to oblige, to receive, and to give information, tends to bring the parties on a foot of equality. It is indeed impoſſible that, in the ſocieties of men, actual advantage of any ſort ſhould ceaſe to have its effect; but, in the company of the wiſe, there is no formal intention to extend, nor any jealous anxiety to ſupport that effect; and the diſtinctions of rank appear more in the attention of the ſuperior to encourage, and in the inferior not to abuſe that freedom of converſation, which conſtitutes the charm of ſociety.

Profeſſions too have their proprieties, which are ever required, not only in formal and profeſſional appearances, but even in the

moſt

moſt familiar and unguarded moments of life. This might be illuſtrated by referring to the ſentiments of men reſpecting the proprieties of character, in different inſtances ; but the example of what is commonly required to the propriety of manner, in thoſe who are veſted with holy orders, may be ſufficient. While others are indulged in harmleſs levities, perſons of this profeſſion ſhould be at all times not only innocent, but conſiderate to avoid even the ſlighteſt approach to offence.

Among the proprieties of age we may reckon, that diffidence is proper to youth, reſolution to manhood, and tranquillity to the laſt ſtages of life. The young are yet learning to be men, and ought not to aſſume the confidence of manhood, until they have laid the foundations on which it may ſecurely reſt.

In manhood, it is proper that a perſon enter on his part with deciſion and reſolution.

In old age, the vivacity with which paſſions operate in youth or manhood being impaired by the experience or the decline of years, objects appear in their comparative meaſures of importance ; and the deliberate mind of the aged is better prepared to inform and to adviſe than to act.

Modeſty ſeems to be akin to diffidence, and they are ſometimes miſtaken one for the other ; but they are plainly diſtinct. The deciſive and reſolute may be modeſt, but are not diffident.

Modeſty is the proper meaſure of our claim or pretenſion to conſideration or preference relatively to other men. It is a guard

gurad which wifdom fets over the conceptions of perfonal importance, in which every perfon apart is apt to affume too much for
himfelf.

This conceit or conception of importance, when not properly
reftrained, is, in the language of a neighbouring country, termed *felf love* *. From this motive, the fool is at all hazards inclined to bring himfelf forward into view, and not only to avail
himfelf of any advantage he may have, but to affect more than
is real. He is ready to abate of the candour which he owes to
others, while he exceeds in the meafure of confideration which he
claims for himfelf.

Modefty is founded in natural difpofition, as well as in reflection or reafon, and therefore holds a middle place among the different kinds of virtue diftinguifhed in the paffage that has been
formerly quoted from the Duke de la Rochefoucault. The natural difpofition to this virtue, as well as to juftice, is benevolence or the love of mankind. Hence men owe to nature their
difpofition to receive with favour the pretenfions of others, and to
rejoice at advantages fuperior to their own; while they learn
from experience to guard againft the effects of partiality to themfelves, and to avoid intruding their own advantages, however real,
upon the attention of others.

Self-defence, in the cafe of an attack, will juftify the modeft
in a fair and manly reprefentation of their rights, but does not
authorife unprovoked or unneceffary oftentation of what they
poffefs; of what they have done; or of what they have fuffered;
much lefs the affectation of fentiments or qualities by which they

U u 2   would

* Amour propre.

would deceive the world into a belief of their own confequence, beyond its real meafure or degree.

Oeconomy is the proper ufe of what fortune has beftowed, whether in the fruits of labour or inheritance.

The term is fometimes employed as fynonymous with parcimony or frugality; and thefe, indeed, are the œconomy of certain conditions, but no more than a particular form of this virtue accommodated to fmall refources. In great fortune, the proper œconomy is not parcimonious, but fumptuous and liberal.

In every eftate, no 'doubt, it is proper œconomy to accommodate expence or confumption to the fupply which fortune affords. The moft ample fupply may be exceeded by a wafte that is not reftrained within proper limits: So that, whether to the poor or to the rich, the neglect of œconomy will have its pernicious effects. If, to the poor, fortune be no more than the means of fubfiftence, a frugal ufe of fuch means is neceffary to felf-preferation. If, to the rich, it conftitute rank and power, a proper adjuftment of expence to the meafure of fortune is in their cafe neceffary, to avoid dependance and degradation.

Moralifts have talked fo much of the vanity of fortune, and of its inefficacy to happinefs, that they may be fufpected of encouraging a dangerous neglect of affairs; a neglect by which the labourer may incur indigence and beggary; the trader incur bankruptcy; and thofe of the higheft rank incur much embarraffment, or fink from their ftation.

It

It were indeed far from wifdom not to avoid fuch confequences ; but if, notwithftanding every reafonable effort of diligence to avoid them, they fhould be incurred, wifdom no doubt
has its offices in that as in every other emergency. In every
event, diligence, equanimity, and fortitude, continue to be the
higheft meafure of happinefs of which any given ftate is fufceptible.

Whether any one has ftrength fufficient, as the philofophers
of old conceived or feigned of the *Wife Man*, to be as happy
under a difagreeable reverfe of fortune as in the higheft profperity, may be queftioned ; and every one may anfwer from
an eftimate of the ftrength of his own mind : But it cannot be
doubted that the wife will endeavour to avail himfelf of his faculties, of his temper and refolution, in the manner moft likely
to fupport him, and to repel this or any other caufe of diftrefs
to which he may be expofed But if philofophy have taught him to
believe, that virtue alone is happinefs, he muft not forget upon any
event which befalls him, that the proper ufe of his fortune is a virtue, and therefore a part, at leaft, in that very happinefs on which
he is taught to rely ; fo that whoever neglects the proper œconomy of his affairs, whether he err with the mifer in penury, or
with the fpendthrift in prodigality, cannot plead the authority of
philofophy for the folly he commits in either extreme.

The folly of the mifer confifts in the admiration of riches, without availing himfelf of their ufe, whether in accommodation to himfelf or in benefit to others, or rather it confifts in facrificing every advantage of wealth to the paffion of merely fecuring the poffeffion.
The folly of the fpendthrift proceeds from the oppofite defect ; from a
difpofition

difpofition to wafte in the gratifications of vanity and fenfuality or from a difpofition to rifk in hazardous adventures, whether of bufinefs or play, the means of fubfiftence, the fecurities of independance, or rank, and the materials of beneficence.

The vain expend their fortunes, and part with them in order to prove the poffeffion. The fenfual multiply expenfive contrivances to procure an enjoyment which palls on the fenfe the more it is courted, or which, carried to extremes, impairs the faculties of the mind, and begets inattention to affairs. In thofe who depend on their labour for fubfiftence, fenfuality is an improper confumption of what they acquire : It occafions a wafte of time and forms a habit of indolence and floth, the reverfe of that induftry on which the fuccefs of their labour depends.

The wants of nature are eafily fupplied, and the gratification of uncorrupted appetite is fully confiftent with the higher and better purfuits of human life : But the voluptuary in acquiring habits inconfiftent with thefe purfuits, is debauched by his imagination rather than by the force of his appetite, or by the folicitations of fenfe. Appetite is confined within narrow limits, and would leave the mind at leifure to employ itfelf otherwife, if it were not prevented by the fruitlefs project of feeking for continued enjoyment where it is not to be found ; and in which imagination, becaufe it never is gratified, is always infatiable.

Next to vanity and fenfuality, dangerous adventures in bufinefs or play are moft likely to mar the difpofition to œconomy, or lead to the improper ufes of wealth. The produce of chance is generally fudden, and, when great, takes the minds of ordinary men unprepared for the proper ufe of what they may have gained. The
tranfitions

tranfitions of fortune in fuch adventures are fometimes extreme as well as fudden. When favourable they intoxicate, and eafily plunge thofe on whom they have fallen into farther and ftill more inconfiderate adventures ; and fcarcely admit of any bounds to their courfe, fhort of fome fatal reverfe, which cuts off the fource even of any farther adventure, and leads to defpair.

In the enumeration of virtues which belong to the underftanding, or to the fuperintending exercife of wifdom, were mentioned *decifion*, and *caution*, habits of a feemingly oppofite tendency, but equally neceffary to obtain the ends of prudence.

Decifion is a feafonable and refolute choice of what the occafion requires. In the defect of this virtue, and by improper delays, every opportunity is loft, and every meafure comes too late. Wavering and fluctuation in the execution of any purpofe are equal to a total inaction, or, by improper delay until the occafion is paft, incur the double difadvantage of a labour beftowed, and of its difappointment or lofs.

Every art may have its deliberations, and the artift will decide with advantage in proportion to his fkill in the particular department to which he is bred. The decifion which wifdom requires is a part in the bufinefs of mankind ; *æque pauperibus prodeft, locupletibus æque* ; and although a certain felicity of decifion in great affairs is the peculiar character of fuperior genius, yet the fteps of integrity that do not waver in the conduct of human life, are attainable by fuch faculties of reafon as ordinary men poffefs.

Cicero apprehends, that the queftions on which we may hefitate in our ordinary conduct may be extended to five in number;

ber ; of which only three had been mentioned by Panetius, whofe
method he profeffes to follow in treating this fubject of offices
or moral duties. The firft queftion is, Whether the action propofed be right or wrong ? The fecond, Whether it contribute to
our intereft ? And the third may arife where intereft feems to in-
terfere with duty, if it fhould be made a queftion which to prefer ? To thefe three he fubjoins the two following ; firft: Of two
things that are praife worthy, which fhould be preferred? 2d, Or,
of two things fuppofed to be ufeful, which is moft for our intereft ?

In queftions of the firft kind, relating to right and wrong, confcience is the arbiter, and is for the moft part ever ready to decide. Benevolence will lead us to aim at effects which tend to
the good of mankind ; and a principal object of deliberation in
fuch cafes is to diftinguifh with judgement, in what we may actually ferve our fellow creatures, by contributing to their fafety,
their welfare, their inftruction, and the good order of the focieties
to which they belong.

Queftions of comparative utility, whether refpecting our own
.advantage or that of other men, are often more problematical
than mere queftions of juftice or right. Such queftions occur in
private and in public affairs, in the tranfactions of merchants, in
the conduct of armies, in the deliberation of fenates and councils
of ftate. In all thefe departments genius or natural ability is
confpicuous ; but in every meafure of natural ability, there is recourfe to experience ; and inftruction, which being neceffary even
to the moft able, may bring acceffions of wifdom alfo to thofe
who are by nature of inferior capacity.

The

The queftion, of a choice to be made betwixt interfering con-fiderations of intereft and duty, is not to be admitted upon any principle of morality ; and although we fometimes feel for the prefon who is required to make great facrifice of intereft to the obfervance of his duty, we acknowledge the evidence he gives, in making that choice, of decided integrity and virtue ; but fhould fcarcely admit of an excufe if he had acted otherwife.

As to the additional queftions propofed by Cicero, they coincide nearly with the two firft queftions which had been propofed by Panetius the original whom he profeffes to follow. Upon the fame principle, by which we determine what is right in con-tradiftinction to what is wrong, we may determine what is moft ftrictly binding when we are preffed by calls of duty, of which only one in fome particular circumftances can be anfwered. And in queftions of comparative utility, we muft proceed in determin-ing what is moft ufeful, upon confiderations which lead us to diftinguifh the oppofite meafures of profit and lofs.

Difficulties of choice are often great in queftions that admit of delay and of the moft deliberate difcuffion, but ftill greater in cafes that come by furprife and require immediate decifion. Thefe are the trials of fuperior genius, requiring even together with that natural advantage the proper ufe of experience ; and as experience is neceffary in the exertions of the higheft capacity, fo it may be ufeful to the loweft, and furnifh that meafure of prudence and wifdom of which ordinary men are fufceptible. From the experience of the paft, men are qualified to forecaft what is likely to happen in the future. And may thus be prepared for difficulties, or ready to decide upon them before they arrive.

Events,

Events, indeed, in the courfe of human affairs, are never determinable in the fame manner with the events that regularly
fucceed one another in the mechanical fyftem of nature. We
know precifely at what hour the fun will rife to morrow, but
what action the caprice of thought and paffion may lead a human creature to perform, at that or any other hour, is more
than human forefight can reach, with any confidence above that
of mere conjecture.

Where events are contingent, it is an object of prudence to
admit into our account the different emergencies that may poffibly happen, and to fettle what our judgement and refolutions
fhould be on the different fuppofitions which our experience may
lead us to make; fo that even in cafes of apparent furprife we
may, in fome degree, have the advantage of premeditation and
deliberate choice.

Caution confifts in a proper attention to the difficulties likely to
arife in any bufinefs or purfuit in which we are about to engage.
It is a principal feature of prudence, and what indeed in a great
meafure engroffes the name. We forecaft the difficulty and expence of an undertaking, that we may not engage in what is a-
bove our ftrength. We attend to the characters of thofe with
whom we are about to act, or whom we are about to employ;
that we may not confide in perfons who, either from want of
capacity or good faith, are unfit to be trufted.

The paths of human life are ftrewed with difficulties, and the
cautious endeavour to forefee them, not that they may in every
inftance avoid, but that they may be the better prepared to encounter them. The virtue which they practife is to be carefully diftinguifhed,

guifhed, from the weaknefs by which the timid or irrefolute de-
clines every duty, and in proportion as it appears to be hazardous
or difficult. Caution is, in contradiftinction to this weaknefs, a
refolute purpofe of action, and a collected ftate of the mind in
which difficulties are forefeen, and proper meafures are taken to
furmount them.

As it is virtuous and noble to proceed in our duty, undifmayed
by difficulty or danger, fo it is wife to forecaft the circumftances
in which we are about to engage, that we may be prepared to
acquit ourfelves properly. In this refpect caution is not an attribute
of fear, but is connected with intrepidity, conftancy, perfeverance,
and a temper undifturbed in the courfe we have chofen to purfue, in all matters alike, whether trivial or important.

Such is the leffon which Epictetus would teach us to apply on
occafions, however trivial, that may poffibly try the temper. As
an example, he refers to the public baths which were generally
crouded at Rome by a promifcuous concourfe of people. " When
" you are going about any action," he fays, " remind yourfelf
" of what nature the action is . If you are going to bathe, re-
" prefent to yourfelf the things which ufually happen in the
" bath; fome perfons pufhing and crouding, fome dafhing the
" water, others giving abufive language, and others ftealing;
" and thus you will more fafely go about the action *"

The object of caution, according to this celebrated moralift, is
not to prevent our engaging in actions that are proper for us to
perform, but to enable us to conduct ourfelves properly in the

X x 2

.duties

* See Mrs Carter's Tranflation of Epictetus.

PART II. duties to which we are called by juftice, humanity, expedience
CHAP. V.
SECT. III. or neceffity, however attended with difficult, hazardous, or dif-
agreeable circumftances.

SECTION

SECTION IV.

Of the Characteristics of Goodness, or Justice.

As *Wisdom* is the specific atrribute of Intelligence; *Goodness* is the attribute of mind also beneficently difpofed towards others.

We may conceive intelligent beings employed on the fubjects of thought, either without encountering any objects of affection; or, without having any concern in the ftate of fuch objects, farther than to afcertain their reality; to diftinguifh their qualities; and to clafs them under general or fpecific appellations: In either cafe, this fupreme order of intelligent nature would prefent but a partial view of itfelf. But, if we fhould fuppofe an individual who is part of a community, yet indifferent to the character of his fellow creature, or indifferent to the good or the ill of which they are fufceptible; in fuch a perfon, we fhould ftill not perceive any thing to be loved, and fcarcely to be admired, even in the poffeffion of the higheft meafures of penetration, memory, or other conftituents of intellectual power.

Or

Or if we fhould proceed from the fuppofition of indifference to that of malice and cruelty, or if we fhould fuppofe intellectual ability employed to devife mifchief, and to fport with the afflictions of others ; intelligence itfelf, or ingenious device, thus perceived only in the abufe of it, would be an object not of indifference, but of deteftation and horror.

Intelligence on the contrary, that is bufy in obferving juft objects of affection, and poffeffed of a fenfibility, to which no being fufceptible of happinefs or mifery is indifferent ; a mind, which is ingenious in performing acts of beneficence, bears that character of goodnefs of which the veftiges are fo deeply marked in the order of nature itfelf, and of which the participation is fo effential to that virtue of which we would now enumerate the branches or effects.

This in the idiom of our language is termed, the virtue of the *heart*; in the language of a neighbouring nation, joined with a juft elevation of nature, it is termed the noblenefs of the *foul*; (*La beauté de l' ame* ;) and is indeed the principal grace of the human character ; whether in the conduct of life, or in the productions of genius. Hence the fovereignty of Homer among the poets of every age ; the high rank of Efchylus, Sophocles, and Euripides among the tragic poets ; of Tacitus among the hiftorians ; of Shakefpeare, and Milton among the poets of our ifland ; of Plato, Antoninus, and Montefquieu among the philofophers of every age.

To thefe may be emphatically applied the adage of Chremes, in Terence ; *I am a man, and nothing human is indifferent to me*[*].

Wherever

* Homo fum; humani nihil a me alienum puto.

Wherever men of this genius touch on the concerns of man-kind, the moſt lively colours of good and evil are brought into view; and what they themſelves feel on the ſubject, is, without any formal recommendation communicated to others †. Without this advantage, the brightneſs of mere wit however dazzling, is but tranſient; and ſeldom outlives the period of its novelty : With it works of ingenuity keep poſſeſſion of the heart, and retain their powers undiminiſhed from age to age; in theſe the innocent and the juſt can recognize his patron, or his friend; and enjoys a par-ticipation of ſentiments, in which he finds his nature raiſed to a ſpecies of godlike benevolence to the world around him.

Goodneſs in the conduct of life, is an averſion to be the cauſe of harm; it is veneration and love to the worthy; it is candour, and a deſire to redeem the moſt defective; it is pity to the dif-treſſed, and congratulation to the happy; it is that diſpoſition, from which a man, obſerving the rights of his fellow creatures, ſhuns every violation of them with the moſt ſacred regard; from which he feels for their ſufferings, and is ever ready to relieve them; from which he is faithful and true to his profeſſions, or engagements, and ever ready, by acts of kindneſs and good will, to

prevent,

---

† To him the mighty mother did unveil
Her awful Face : The dauntleſs child
Stretched forth his little arms, and ſmiled.
This pencil take, ſhe ſaid, whoſe colours clear
Richly paint the vernal year :
Thine too theſe keys immortal boy :
This can unlock the gates of joy;
Of horror that, and thrilling fears,
Or ope the ſacred ſource of ſympathetic tears.

Gray'e *Ode on the Progreſs of Poetry*.

prevent or to outrun the wifhes of thofe who by nature or accident are placed within reach of his influence.

The duties of goodnefs, confidered in refpect to their principle, may be claffed under two divifions; of which the one includes all the modifications of *Innocence*, of which we have fuppofed the fanction to admit the applications of compulfory law ; the
other comprehends all the modifications of *Beneficence*, from which
the applications of compulfory law are excluded.

There is a certain magnanimity with which the noble minded, in refpect to the good offices required from their fellow creatures, limit their own pretenfions to the mere effects of juftice
and of truth; but in performing fuch offices on their own part,
confider the higheft acts of generofity and kindnefs as no more
than the difcharge of a debt that is due to mankind. While they
confider as benefactors to themfelves, and fully entitled to e-
fteem and gratitude, the perfon who is cautious of harm, and who
refpects the rights of his fellow creatures, they are ever ready to
prevent the defires, or anticipate the wifhes of thofe who are
placed in their way.

In referring to the offices of goodnefs, as they may be feparately
comprifed under the titles of *Innocence* and *Beneficence*, we may
confider *Fidelity*, *Veracity*, *Candour*, and *Civility* as modifications
of the firft; *Piety*, *Perfonal Attachments*, *Gratitude*, *Liberality*,
Charity and *Politenefs* as modifications of the fecond.

And in extending this title to all the offices of civil and political fociety, it will include the reciprocal duties of magiftrate
and fubject, as well as the duties of the citizen towards the community

munity of which he is a member. Thefe may be termed the public offices of goodnefs; and to compleat the enumeration of its branches or parts will come to be ftated in their place.

With refpect to *fidelity*, confidered as an article of mere innocence, we may refer to what has been already obferved on the principle of convention; that to break faith is an injury to the perfon with whom it was plighted. And it is an injury which the innocent will avoid, from motives of mere humanity, without regard to the fanction of compulfory law, or the force that may be juftly applied to obtain the performance of a contract. The faithful, accordingly, carry the obfervance of this duty into many tranfactions which the arm of the magiftrate cannot reach. They would feel themfelves chargeable with guilt if they neglected to fulfil, fo far as may be in their power, any expectation which they have occafionally raifed, or if they fhould fail in the difcharge of a truft for which any one has been reafonably made to rely on them.

As error and miftake are in the nature of things pernicious, as they weaken or miflead the mind, and in the conduct of life may produce indefinite mifchief; *veracity* too, as well as fidelity, is to be reckoned among the neceffary conditions of a virtuous life. This duty is to be obferved not only where the immediate effects of miftake are detrimental, in refpect to the eftate or fortune of the perfon deceived, but even where by mifreprefentation or exaggeration it tends to affect the mind with falfe conceptions of things whether momentuous or trivial. The innocent abides by the truth, becaufe it would be a crime to deceive any one to his hurt. A man of fenfe will not deceive, becaufe it were folly to

VOL. II.　　　　　　　Y y　　　　　　　difcredit

discredit himself; and if fiction were indifferent to any of these effects, it is at least impertinent and idle.

This duty of veracity, however, does not exclude the use of fable, parable, or supposition, employed in illustration of any moral or physical truth, nor does it preclude the use of professed fiction, as in poetry, to multiply agreeable and rational conceptions of the imagination, without any intention to obtrude fable for truth, or fiction for reality.

It is not necessary to observe perhaps that the innocent, whose veracity is guarded by the single consideration, that it were injurious to mislead the conceptions of other men in any case whatever, will refrain with detestation from the least approach to calumny or false aspersion on the name and reputation of his neighbour. Aversion, to be the author of harm, will not only restrain him from propagating invidious reports, but will inspire him with mercy even to those of whom the conduct may have been offensive; he will not press down the load of reproach even where it has been incurred, and will strive to hide the error that is past, or the fault that may in the future be corrected.

Candour also is truth, but it is the truth that proceeds from humanity and fairness of mind; it is the just allowance which is given to the pretensions or merits of other men, even in circumstances, which to the uncandid would render them objects of hatred, as well as opposition.

The candid would conduct competition, and even resentmen itself, with the least possible detriment to those who are the ob-t jects of either. He will admit a fact, even where it is unfavour-

I   able

able to his own claims. He will be more guarded in cenfuring PART. II.
an opponent than even an indifferent perfon.—Where it is not CHAP. V.
neceffary to blame, he will be filent; where praife is due, he SECT. IV.
will acknowledge it; and will diftruft any prepoffeffion in himfelf
by which he may be inclined to exaggerate the faults of an enemy.

At the fame time, unfincere and affected commendation of
thofe we inwardly hate or defpife, is not entitled to the praife of
candour. This virtue is an effort of truth and veracity as well
as beneficence. It fpurns the unworthy, and fcorns the affectation of lenity that is affumed from weaknefs, or employed by
cunning, the better to enfnare or circumvent an opponent.

In competitions of intereft, the generous and the humane are
feldom vehement; in competitions of efteem, they are not apt to
be jealous; and the fecurity with which the candid proceeds, is
generally proportioned to his magnanimity, and his defire to poffefs the conftituents of real merit in himfelf, rather than to derive, whether in reputation or profit, the external fruits or effects
of confideration from others.

Civility is a guarded behaviour to avoid offence even in the inferior concerns of human life. It is commonly joined with politenefs in the character of good breeding, and thefe virtues or
accomplifhments are fo far connected as they are both the effects
of goodnefs, obferveable in matters fuppofed to be comparatively
of fmall moment. They are however frequently and not improperly diftinguifhed. The civil avoids to give offence, or any pofitive moleftation in the ordinary concourfe of men; the polite
endeavours to furnifh matter of fatisfaction and pleafure. The

Y y 2 firft

firſt therefore is an article of mere innocence, the other aſpires to effects of beneficence and poſitive ſervice.

The civil are careful not to offend by any effects of inattention or neglect, by any contemptuous reception of what others think or feel ,whether by contradiction unneceſſarily harſh, by any inſult of vanity, affectation of precedence, or ſuperiority of any ſort. When ungracious office is neceſſary, they endeavour to perform it in the leaſt painful manner, and qualify accidental offences with the moſt unfeigned deſire to atone for them.

Where good underſtanding and good diſpoſition are united, ci-vility will not be wanting. It is not the excluſive appurtenance of any rank or condition, but the feature of conſiderate huma-nity, wherever it be found: It diſtinguiſhed the keeper of the priſon at Athens, in adminiſtering the poiſon to Socrates *, no leſs than the great emperor Aurelius, in his ordinary manner : To him nothing was indifferent in the conduct of life; and even a leſſon of civility he had received was rec-koned among the favours of Providence ; not rudely to cri-
ticiſe

---

* The particulars here alluded to, are told by Plato in the Phædo nearly as follows,

After Socrates came from the bath, he was ſeated, and continued ſilent, when the keeper accoſted him in theſe words, " I know Socrates, that you will not blame me ; " but thoſe who are in fault, and whoſe orders I am bound to obey. In you I have " always met with humanity and mildneſs of temper, very different from moſt of " thoſe who are ſent to this place. In doing my duty, I am commonly treated with " rage and curſes ; but, I have not this to expect from you ; I truſt you know what " my orders are ; it is now time to take the draught ; and ſo farewell, be recon-" ciled as you may to what cannot be helped." In ſaying this, he turned about to depart, and burſt into tears. How civil the man is ! ſaid Socrates, It was thus he would frequently come to amuſe me with his talk, and ſtrove to oblige me ; and now how kindly his tears are ſhed : But let us mind his directions. Do Crito, if the draught be mixed, cauſe it to be brought.

" ticife any folecifm or impropriety of expreffion or pronuncia-
" tion; but in continuing the converfation, to pronounce the word
" again, in a proper manner, either by way of anfwer or enquiry ;
" or as if to confirm what was faid, and not as anxious about the
" expreffion; or in fhort, by fome other fkilful addrefs to fet the
" perfon right *." But, with whatever degree of fimplicity it may
operate, it is ftill perceptible to thofe who can diftinguifh the genuine, tho' feemingly feeble or negligent expreffions of a benevolent mind. The ingenious peafant is civil, no lefs than the well
educated gentleman, if together with a difpofition not to offend,
there be underftanding to diftinguifh what would be offenfive: But
where either of thefe qualifications is wanting, men are apt to
meafure the obligations of duty by the mere external effect, and
either do not know in what they are rude, or think themfelves
entitled to do or to fay whatever does not materially affect the
perfon or property of thofe with whom they converfe.

Civility is a habit very generally acquired in the practice of fociety,
where experience and knowledge of the world confpire to enforce
the duties of good fenfe and of innocence. Here it may be confidered as artificial, and they who are difpofed to violate the rules
of good breeding accordingly charge the well bred with infince-
rity or falfehood. In their opinion, rudenefs alone is fincere ; and
a mannerly attention not to offend in trifles, a mere mafk of hypocrify.

The rude who are fo apt to think an attention to others the effect
of hypocrify or falfehood, are equally inclined to confider the ci-
vilities which are paid to themfelves, as a tribute of confideration
due

* Vid. Grave's tranflation of Antoninus, l. I. c. 10.

due to their perfonal importance or fpecial merit ; but the crimes of rapine and murder are not a more certain, though a more pernicious evidence of a bafe and ungenerous mind.

Civility, confidered merely as the habit of avoiding offence, is the firft and moft indifpenfible part of good breeding ; and may give to a converfation in which there is no folicitude to pleafe, or defign to flatter, all the form which is neceffary to render it highly agreeable as well as inftructive.

So far this branch of goodnefs, confifting in reluctance to be the author of harm, may appear to be a mere negation of evil, an exemption from malice, or any of its external effects ; but when we confider, among the general duties of candour, what a guard is neceffary to fecure the mind againft the formation of prejudices; to fecure it againft the effects of real or apparent provocation ; or what force of mind is required to preferve it untainted with jealoufy or envy, in the competitions of men, as well as to prevent any external effect of thefe malignant difpofitions ; it is evident, that the modifications of innocence are not to be fupported without high meafures of regard, and good will to mankind.   It is even eafier on many occafions to perform the moft fplendid acts of beneficence, than it is upon all occafions to maintain this uniform tenor of an innocent and unoffending life.

Beneficence, neverthelefs, is fuppofed to be raifed a ftep higher in the fcale of the virtues than mere innocence, which terminates in refraining from harm.   The catalogue of the bleffed is accordingly made up by the poet, of fuch, as by pofitive efforts of
benevolence

benevolence or magnanimity have promoted the progress, or contributed to the welfare of mankind. *

Among the modifications of benevolence, *piety* to Almighty God, is justly entitled to the first, and the highest place.

This affection of mind is susceptible of indefinite gradations, beginning in this its highest pitch, modified by veneration only, without the possibility of any beneficent effect towards its object, and descending from thence, to what may be considered as its ordinary tenor among created beings, where the object, though esteemed or respected, may also on occasion inspire tenderness, or move commiseration and pity.

Wherever true benevolence operates, and the being of God is perceived, there piety to him must operate also; not as a principle of beneficence towards its object, but as the first and most essential form of an affection, of which the objects are wisdom and goodness in the degree, whether supreme or subordinate, in which they are conceived to exist.

This affection constitutes religion in the human mind, and has its external expressions and effects also. It is naturally expressed in terms, and in rites of adoration. " What else can I, " says Epictetus, a lame old man do, but sing hymns to God. If " I were a nightingale, I would act the part of a nightingale: " If I were a swan, the part of a swan. But since I am a rea- " sonable creature, it is my duty to praise God. This is my bu- " siness; .

* Hic manus ob patriam pugnando vulnera passi,
Quique pii vates, et Phœbo digna canebant,
Inventas aut qui vitam excoluere per artes,
Quique sui memores alios fecere merendo.
Virgil, Lib. 6to.

" finefs, *I do it.* Nor will I ever defert this poft as long as it is " vouchfafed me; and I exhort you to join in the fame fong *." It has a natural effect in rendering man the friend of mankind, being the family of a common parent, to whom the higheft duty, that can be rendered is beneficence to the creatures he has made: So that the man who ftates himfelf as a willing inftrument in the hand of his Maker for the good of his fellow creatures, is he whofe piety renders the moft acceptable fervice to God.

Although piety in its proper acceptation is a fentiment of religion, the term is neverthelefs, by a kind of figure, employed to fignify any high meafure of veneration or love which we pay to any of our fellow creatures who are raifed above the ordinary rank of men in our veneration or efteem. Thus it is *piety* in the child to love his parent. It is piety in the dutiful citizen to love and refpect the juft and beneficent magiftrate who, more by his wifdom and his care than by his power, appears to be the vice-gerent of God.

But in every inftance of good will to men, the effects of a benevolent difpofition may reach the object of it in beneficent and pofitive fervices; and may be confidered among the characte-riftics of a *focial attachment*, upon whatever ground of connection it be formed.

Under this title we may confider the relations of confanguinity, of neighbourhood or acquaintance, as well as attachments of predilection and choice, more properly termed the connection of friends.

In

Mr s Carter's tranflation, Book 1. c. 16.

In the relation of confanguinity men are not at liberty to chufe their objects. They may be affociated together without efteem, affection, or confidence : yet there are certain duties which God and nature feem to require in the benevolent towards his kindred, although he may not apprehend any perfonal merit on which to ground any particular efteem or affection.

The child cannot chufe what fort of parent he would have, nor are the wifhes of the parent always gratified in the character of his child. Brothers are placed in the fame rank together by the appointment of nature, in which their choice is not confulted ; yet in all thefe inftances there is a duty which nature has impofed, and in exemption from which, even the plea of demerit in the perfon to whom the duty refers cannot be admitted. The parent muft not abandon or neglect even his profligate child, nor the child fail in attention and refpect to the parent, even of whofe failings and weakneffes he is moft fenfible. Brothers muft not fhrink from one another, even in cafes of high demerit, nor leave, as a ftranger might be left, even the guilty to perifh unaffifted under the effects of his guilt. The ties of confanguinity feem to be intended by nature as a fpecial bond of fociety by which the dulleft of men are mutually pointed out to one another as objects of confideration, even if they fhould not be fenfible to the ties of humanity or merit under which they are placed to other men.

This principle, indeed, is perhaps more frequently abufed as a fource of undue partiality to thofe of our own kindred, or as a fource of uncandid animofity to others or neglect of their merits, than it is ever entirely wanting in the difpofition of individuals towards the family of which they are members, and in whofe fate they are themfelves in fome meafure involved.

Among the examples of perfonal attachment, that which proceeds on the fympathy of affections directed to the fame worthy objects ; on the predilection of merit and unlimited confidence, is that which peculiarly merits the appellation of *Friendſhip*, and in which the parties may be faid figuratively to have but one heart, one mind, and one intereft.

In forming this connection the higheft meafures of probity are required. Virtue, operating in the minds of different men, may concur in all its external effects, but folly and vice are jarring and incongruous principles, which, in the degree in which they take place, render men unworthy and incapable of this facred connection.

Intimacies of a different kind, confifting merely in acquaintance, or in a habit of affociating together, are commonly enough known under the title of friendfhip : But the maxims or precepts which are applicable to one meafure or degree of connection cannot be fafely or properly transferred to another. There cannot be any referve, for inftance, in that entire affection and confidence which we fuppofe betwixt friends, and no limit to their friendly exertions, without a breach or forfeiture of the rights which friendfhip implies. In connections of inferior degree, it may be fufficient not to offend or not to neglect the duties of humanity which occafions prefent. In this inftance, a more active principle is required, and the occafions of perfonal fervice not only taken when offered, but induftrioufly fought for.

We

We are told of a maxim which fome of the wife have prefcribed, and others have reprobated : " *Live with your friend as with*
" *one who may become an enemy*". This maxim is prudent in the
occafional co-operations of intereft or party. The perfon who
fupports me to day, becaufe it is his intereft to do fo, may wifh
to overthrow me to morrow, if an oppofition of intereft fhould
take place. It may be prudent, therefore, not to furnifh him as
a friend with arms, which he may afterwards turn againft me as
an enemy. But this maxim, applied to the cafe of parties united by mutual conviction of unalterable worth, entire affection,
and unlimited confidence, would be altogether prepofterous, and
cannot be adopted without difcontinuing the connection of
friendfhip, or ftifling the affection in which it confifts.

Friendfhip or intimacy, of whatever degree, prefuppofes acquaintance or fome occafional connection, in which the parties
have an opportunity of being mutually known. Among fuch
connections, *Confanguinity* no doubt is one, under which parties
have occafion to give the moft fenfible proof of the degree in
which they are mutually or feverally qualified to become objects of
confidence and affection. Nature has given to the parent a predilection for his child, which affections of the pureft friendfhip
may equal, but cannot exceed ; and the return on the part of the
child, being the natural recoil of the moft tender affection, is fcarcely avoidable ; but ftill fentiments of this nature are diftinguifhable from the attachments founded in the preference of efteem
and the freedom of choice. The friend who has miftaken his
object, and become attached to a perfon unworthy of his affection,
may become cold and indifferent as foon as he has detected his
error ; but the parent weeps when he has made fuch a difcovery

Z z 2

refpecting

respecting his child, and the child is abashed when he cannot vindicate the character of his parent.

The fortunes of men are sometimes involved in those of their kindred : Although we distinguish therefore the specific principle of consanguinity from indiscriminate affection and good will to mankind, yet it appears. that nature in planting the instinctive affections which unite the members of a family together, and which may extend to a numerous kindred, has in this manner sown the seeds of a boundless society. Or seeming only to connect individuals of a narrow circle together, has formed a chain, whose links being continued in every direction, extend far beyond where personal acquaintance or choice would reach.

Happiness, we have had occasion to observe, is an attribute of the mind, and benevolence, in the several forms of which it is capable, is a principle constituent of this attribute or condition of mind. It is happy to meet with an object of affection. It is happy to perceive the returns of confidence and love. The external effects and expressions of such reciprocal dispositions in the minds of men are highly agreeable, and may be of the greatest use ; but still, in estimating the happiness of friendship, we return to the mutual affection itself which takes place between friends, and is the principal constituent of its value. The external effects of benevolence may be intermitted for want of occasion, but the affection itself cannot grow cold without causing the enjoyment it brings to cease.

In considering connections of choice, the first subject of casuistry or moral instruction must relate to the choice itself, or the discernment of its proper object.

As

As the proofs of merit may be flowly collected, it is evident, that confidence of the higheft degree is to be cautiously given, and in the refult of time and continued experience. The firft re-quifite in the character of a friend, doubtlefs, is probity and good intention. Intimacy with the profligate is a fnare to the innocent.

PART. II.
CHAP. V.
SECT IV.

A fecond quality, and likewife in a high degree neceffary, is underftanding, or what is commonly termed good fenfe. The fociety of fools is the accumulation of folly. Whoever is defi-cient in point of judgement or underftanding may hurt where he means to ferve, and often from mere weaknefs of mind, without any intention to betray, fails in the truft which is repofed in him.

The ingenuous will value the affection of his friend more than any of its external effects; but in gratifying the fenfe of his own mind, will be ever attentive to obferve in what manner he may be ufeful to his friend, and it is in bearing the important charac-ter of a beneficent and trufty affociate, that perfons are moft likely to win the affection and confidence of thofe with whom they are deftined to act.

The worth of a man is made known by its external effects; and though external effect is fubordinate in value to the affection of mind, yet neither this nor any other connection in the minds of men could exift otherwife, than by means of the external effects, and appearances which caufe them to be mutually known.

To a young man, who complained that he had no friends, and
was

was generally neglected, "Confider," faid Socrates, "what
" are your own merits. Are you of fuch value to mankind, as that
" any one fhould fingle you out as an object of predilection and
" friendfhip ? If you were of fuch value, the world knows its in-
" terefts too well, to neglect or overlook you. Shew yourfelf a-
" ble and willing to act the part of a friend, you will find many
" to folicit your favours, and fome who will deferve your high-
" 'eft confidence."

A perfon, who in the manner of this young man laid claim
to the attention and friendfhip of others as matter of intereft to
himfelf, was very properly called upon to confider in what degree he beftowed upon the intereft of others that confideration
which he required to his own; but the fires of affection and benevolence, which are kindled in the human breaft on occafion of
external marks of affection and good will, greatly furpafs in value
thofe external occafions on which they are kindled.

Gratitude, the third article in our enumeration of the characteriftics of beneficence, is in the mind of the grateful the fenfe of
a benefit received, and among the external duties of life it is an
effort to repay with affection the favours which have been done.

Benefits may take place between ftrangers and perfons unknown, and may proceed from any occafional emotion of good
will or compaffion, as well as from eftablifhed fentiments of perfonal attachment. But wherever an act of kindnefs is done, a proper return is conceived to be due; it is conceived to be due to a
ftranger or perfon unknown, who has done a good office, even
more than to a relation or a friend.

As the fenfe of an injury done to ourfelves is different from the
I   fentiment

fentiment of indignation at wrongs in general, fo the fenfe of a benefit received is different from the general approbation or ef- teem of beneficence ; and where actual favours are conferred, we conceive a fpecies of debt to be contracted by the perfon who has received the obligation; we fometimes pafs from the idea of a debt of gratitude, as it is fometimes called, to the requifition of penal ftatutes by which we would enforce the difcharge of it. Such we are told was the policy of fome ancient nations, who in their wifdom, "highly worthy of imitation," did not neglect to punifh the ungrateful, any more than thofe who were guilty of any other crime pernicious to fociety.

There is not however fufficient reafon to believe, that fuch was ever the actual policy of any nation whatever. Such a policy would tend to place the relation of parties who beftowed or ac- cepted a benefit upon a very different footing from that upon which beneficence and even gratitude are fuppofed to proceed. Where the law would enforce the returns of good will, it would be difficult to diftinguifh an act of kindnefs from an interefted loan ; or the acceptance of a favour from the contracting of a debt. For this purpofe of law the precife value of a benefit ought to be fixed, in order to eftimate the return; and the pro- fpect of gain, or the neceffity of compliance, fubftituted for kind- nefs in the exchange of good offices, would totally alter the na- ture both of the benefit and of the return. A benefit offered might be confidered as a fnare to be carefully fhunned, until the meafure of the expected return was afcertained; and in this manner, what ought to be the fpontaneous effects of benevolence could not be diftinguifhed from the traffic of intereft.

In

In refpect to this duty of *gratitude*, therefore, as well as in refpect to every other act of beneficence, the neceffity of keeping diftinct the fanctions of morality from thofe of compulfory law is extremely evident. We enforce the payment of a debt, that perfons in poffeffion of property may be fafe to lend ; but we only commend or enjoin the duties of gratitude, that the benevolent affections may have their natural fcope in the focieties of men.

Whoever ftrives to enhance the value of a benefit which he himfelf may have done, and urges the claim of gratitude too far, offends a-gainft the moral principle of beneficence, not lefs than he who appears infenfible of the kindnefs he has received, and there is not in the nature of things furer evidence of a mind that deferves no return, than that of upbraiding others with the benefits which we fuppofe ourfelves to have conferred.

Liberality is a character of unreferved beneficence in matters agreeable or obliging to others. It is a natural effect of difintereftednefs or cordial affection, but is obferved to be unequal in perfons perhaps originally of equal good difpofitions, when warped by different habits in different conditions of life. Men become illiberal in a ftate of dependence, under perfonal awe and under the neceffity of attending to fordid or trivial confiderations. They efcape this defect in oppofite circumftances, of independance, freedom, or exemption from fordid concerns : And there is a certain force of mind above it in all fituations.

The effect of external condition is to give fcope to original difpofition, not to infpire it. The country gentleman, without any uncommon degrees of generofity, furrounds his dwelling with
pleafure

pleasure grounds, and substitutes ornament for gain. He would
make every one feel, in the manner of expending his fortune
how little he regards the returns of profit. And yet, even in
this, he retains what may be termed a sordid predilection for
subjects which he is pleased to call his own. Beauty is no man's
property, and may be made to pervade the face of a country
without regard to this circumstance. The liberal may bestow
it on subjects of public concern, on high-ways, bridges, barren
hills covered with wood, and public places adorned with mo-
numents of distinguished men or distinguished events ; and all
this without expecting any returns of admiration or profit.
As the Almighty makes his sun to shine on the evil and on
the good, the liberal is not checked by any supposed want of
merit in mankind; he can restore a plantation which the mischie-
vous idler has destroyed, restore its number on the mile-stone
which has been defaced, or repair the parapet which has been
broke down.

Such might be termed the luxury of a liberal mind in great
wealth : But liberality is not, as we are sometimes inclined to
suppose, peculiar to the rich, nor limited to the bestowing of
gifts or the conferring of favours. A person may be liberal in
his commendations of merit, in his concessions to a rival, in his
manner of treating an enemy, in his neglect of petty advantages,
in his impartial and indiscriminate attention to persons entitled
to his regard, and in the general frankness of manner with which
he transacts any business, without jealousy or mean distrust, and
without any harsh interpretation of the words or actions of those
with whom he is concerned. He may be liberal in doing with
a cordial alacrity even what the law would oblige him to do.
The character of liberality, in short, is that freedom and noble-

VOL. II.   A a a   ness

nefs of manner with which the ingenuous upon every occafion do what is right; not as a part they have ftudied, or a tafk to which they fubmit, but as a part which is natural to them, and as a pleafure in which they indulge themfelves without defign or reflection.

The proceedings of a liberal mind at the fame time are the ex-preffions of an upright intention; and far from being indifcrimi-nate in the choice of their objects, the liberal fpurn and awe the unworthy with the fame irrefiftable effect that they gain or encou-rage perfons of an oppofite character; they appear indeed to be fecured from miftake in the choice of their objects, only by a kind of inftinctive difcernment, without difficulty, hefitation, or anxious reflection.

Charity is the character of beneficence exhibited in relieving the diftreffed. It proceeds from that fpecific form of benevolence which is termed commiferation or pity. As the diftreffes of men are various, the motives of humanity in the different tranf-actions of life may operate to a variety of effects. From fuch mo-tives the generous victor may fpare the vanquifhed and releafe the captive, as the charitable will feed the hungry, clothe the na-ked, or vifit the fick.

In the variety of diftreffes incident to human life, the rich may have their fhare and their claim to relief as well as the poor; though in the common ufe of this term, it is limited to thofe acts of beneficence which the rich are peculiarly in condition to perform, and of which the poor may receive the benefit.

Wherever

Wherever property is eſtabliſhed, it comes of courſe to be un-equally diſtributed. It accumulates in the poſſeſſion of ſome, and is entirely wanting to others. As this inequality may be traced to its origin in the unequal diſpoſitions of men to induſtry and fru-gality, as well as more caſual advantages, ſo it ſerves to main-tain, in the moſt proſperous and wealthy ſocieties, ſome remains of that neceſſity which nature has intended for the ſpecies as a ſpur to their induſtry and incentive to labour. If the wealthy are relieved from the neceſſity of toil, or may chuſe the objects of their purſuit, the poor ſtill remain ſubject to this neceſſity; and few are exempted from every application that may contri-bute to enlarge the ſtock or promote the welfare of their com-munity.

The inferior ranks of men, even where they are not urged by neceſſity, are, by ambition, and by ſtriving to gain for themſelves the advantages which they obſerve in the poſſeſſion of the rich, excited to promote or increaſe the wealth of their country.

As we may venture to aſſume that the wealth of nations con-ſiſts in the labour of the poor, or in the induſtry and ingenuity of thoſe who are deſirous to make for themſelves acquiſitions of fortune; ſo to the poor, health, ſtrength, and whatever elſe quali-fies men for daily labour and ſucceſsful purſuits, are the inheri-tance which nature has provided, and the uſe which they make of that inheritance is the ſource of wealth and proſperity to the community of which they are members.

If the uſe of induſtry or labour could be entirely ſuperſeded in any ſociety, or, in other words, if the poor could be ſupported gratuitoufly, this would be to fruftrate the purpofe of nature, in rendering toil and the exercifes of ingenuity neceffary to man; it would be to cut off the fources of wealth, and, under pretence of relieving the diftreffed, it would be to reject the condition upon which alone Nature has provided, that the wants of the fpecies in general fhall be relieved.

For thefe reafons, poverty alone is far from being a fufficient recommendation to charity, and the undiftinguifhing practice of this virtue would be highly pernicious; as by enabling the poor to fubfift in idlenefs, it would deprive them of one great prefervative of their innocence, and a principal conftituent of happinefs, the habit of regular induftry; and deprive the community of its beft refource, the labour of its members.

It is a wife maxim therefore in every well ordered fociety, that no perfon able to earn his bread, fhould be maintained gratuitoufly; that the feeble fhould be affifted in fupporting themfelves, but that they only who have no bread, and are unable to earn it, fhould be maintained by charity. This indeed is a condition to which the induftrious poor, or fuch as depend for fubfiftence on their daily labour are frequently reduced; whether by old age, difeafe, or misfortunes. In every fuch cafe, they have a claim not only upon the humanity and compaffion of the rich, but upon the juftice and good policy of their country alfo.

Their claim upon the humanity of thofe who have it in their power to relieve them, is doubtlefs irrefiftible; but it is of too ferious and important a nature in the view of good policy, to reft the provifion of the neceffitous poor entirely upon this principle.
                                                                        As

As the labour they beſtow when able to work, may be conſidered as employed in the public ſervice; it is but juſt, that the public ſhould charge itſelf with the care of thoſe, who by age or miſ-
fortunes are become unable to ſubſiſt themſelves.

In whatever manner public proviſion is to be made for the ne-
ceſſitous poor, whether by Hoſpitals and places of public reception,
or by diſtributing the ſupplies of neceſſity to the private habitations
of thoſe who are entitled to receive them, is a queſtion rather of
public œconomy and good policy, than of moral duty.

We may however obſerve on this ſubject, that where the public has provided moſt effectually for the relief of ſuch neceſſities
as are publickly known, ſtill much remains to be done in private
charity; there muſt ſtill be many perſons who, although they
cannot or will not eſtabliſh their claim to a public ſupport, may
be ſo well known to individuals, as to entitle them to all the attention which humanity and compaſſion can beſtow. In ſuch
caſes frequently the benevolent have an opportunity to taſte the
ſweeteſt fruits of beneficence, where it is at once proper to beſtow,
and to conceal its effects.

Beneficence, under moſt of the characters we have now mentioned; whether *friendſhip*, *gratitude*, *liberality*, or *charity*, may
be ſuppoſed productive of ſome material effect, and be ſenſibly uſeful to thoſe who are the objects of it. The benevolent affections,
however, may ſubſiſt where ſuch effects are ſeldom wanted, and
where good will, eſteem, or the manners they produce, are nevertheleſs the principal ſource of enjoyment: And goodneſs may o-
perate with ſignal advantage, where the effect is no more than
the expreſſion by which the beneficent intention is known.

Goodneſs,

Goodnefs, we have obferved, in the form of civility, may be confidered as an article of mere innocence, or the effect of a difpofition to avoid offence.   In the form of politenefs, it is a pofitive
difpofition to oblige; a difpofition, in the exercife of which the benevolent find occafion of good offices, where neither the profit,
nor the fafety, nor the perfonal accommodation of parties are at
ftake.   It my operate on every occafion, in efforts of attention,
good will and refpect; when we confer, or when we withhold
the objects of choice or requeft.   The firft is done with a liberal
promptitude, the other with an unaffected regret.

The polite is attentive to the habits, expectations, and feelings
of thofe with whom he converfes: He would prevent their re-
quefts, by anticipating the effects; and would conceal his own
wants, where the knowledge of them might importune or diftrefs
thofe to whom he is unwilling to be troublefome.

The duties of politenefs, compared with thofe of other virtues,
carry the idea of flight obligation.   They are termed good
manners, becaufe we confider the manner more than the effect,
and they are fuppofed to terminate in fome trifling forms, which
any one that is willing may acquire by rote.   There are no doubt
fome pretenfions to good breeding, of which thefe obfervations are
true, but confidered as an article of beneficence, there is not any
duty in which good fenfe, fincere benevolence, and candour are
more neceffary.

Without difcernment, the affectation of politenefs becomes a
fource of moleftation and trouble; without benevolence, it is a
mere oftentation of fuperior breeding.   Its forms, like the words
of

of a language, may have been arbitrary in the original ufe of them, but when eftablifhed, convey the meaning of perfons, who fpeak, in a way that entitles them to efteem and confidence, or, on the contrary, renders them objects of difguft or offence.

As the language, fo the manners of particular focieties may differ; and as a perfon may not be able to fpeak with propriety where the language is foreign to him, fo he may not appear with accomplifhed politenefs where he is unacquainted with the ordinary forms of behaviour, or where he is altogether unpractifed in the obfervance of them.

Whatever the habits of fociety may be in fuch matters, they are no doubt fooneft and moft effectually acquired where the intercourfe of men is moft clofe and frequent; and the manner of this intercourfe, confidered apart from any actual effect, is fuppofed moft important.

From this confideration it appears that the name of politenefs, both in Greek and in Latin, took its origin from an idea, that to be polite was to have the manners of the town, in contradiftinction to thofe of the country *.

Apart from the confideration that the feelings and wifhes of men may be better underftood in the habits and manners of one fociety, than they are in thofe of another; it is certain, that where focieties differ in point of manners, on whichever fide the advantage of fuperior intelligence may lie, perfons of the beft difpofition

* In Greek the polite was termed Αστειος, and in Latin *Urbanus*; and from the latter of thefe terms, we confider urbanity in contradiftinction to rufticity.

position may appear defective in politeness, where the manner of shewing it is not familiar to them; but this no more incapacitates the peasant for politeness in the city, than the citizen for politeness in the country. If the peasant appears rustic in the town, the citizen may appear frivolous, ignorant, or affected in the country; and of the two that person is most deficient in breeding, who is farthest gone in the mistake, that the local habits of a society to which he himself is accustomed, are the standard of good manners to mankind.

The real standard of manners, so far as it can be collected from external expressions, is the ingenuity, candour, and disposition to oblige, from which those manners proceed.

The habits which the mind may have acquired in those important respects, may be traced to the objects of estimation, which men in different societies have been led to adopt. In societies where men are taught to consider themselves as competitors, and every advantage they gain as comparative to that of some other person, the conscientious may be faithful and true to his engagements, in what he is pleased to think matters of real concern; but the emulation in which he has been nursed is a fretful passion; and politeness, under its influence, cannot be any other than an effect of disguise. The interested and sordid make no allowance for good or ill offices that neither fill nor empty the pocket. With such persons as these, even virtue itself is illiberal, and kindness unmannerly.

For this character of goodness, which is distinguished in the offices of mere good breeding, it should seem, that we must resort to the company of those who are least actuated by sordid

cares,

cares, by perfonal jealoufies, or by any confideration of intereft which in the ordinary fociety of men can be brought into queftion. In company of this fort, men are accuftomed to lay a proper ftrefs on the effects of good fenfe and benevolence, however little their fortunes may be affected by them. Whilft in focieties of a different defcription, they run the hazard of an oppofite character; may be juft and beneficent in what they term articles of moment, but from an affected indifference, or real infenfibility to what they confider as matters of inferior value, are fullen, contemptuous, or negligent on may occafions, on which benevolence and good will might contribute effentially to the happinefs of human life.

Men are thus likely to be polite where the habits of life are likely to be liberal; that is, where benevolence is not ftifled by fordid cares, oppreaffed with dependence, awed by fubjection or mean apprehenfions of danger. We are to look for this character, therefore, in the higher ranks of life, or to hold the defect leaft excufable if it be wanting there. It is not indeed a neceffary accompaniment of riches or luxury; it is found amidft the poverty of rude nations, and in the fociety of men leaft acquainted with the arts of accommodation. There ignorance of the ordinary conftituents of intereft fecures the mind from the meannefs of fordid and illiberal competitions, and the very favage, exempted from the teafing regards of perfonal vanity by his paffion for the real and fuperior diftinctions of courage and fortitude, preferves, we are told,* in the fociety of his equals, a good breeding and refpectful attention that is not excelled in the higher circles of polifhed fociety. It is part of his dignity to remain unmoved by novelties, to be ferious and courteous in his ordinary manners,

Vol. II. B b b and

* Vid. Charlevoix's account of the original Natives of North America.

and he is no lefs agreeable and infinuating in the character of a friend, than he is terrible and dangerous in that of an enemy.

To need nothing and to poffefs every thing are, perhaps, equally favourable to that liberality and politenefs of manners which we commonly confider rather as the polifh, than as the effential conftituent of goodnefs. The naked inhabitant of the Pelew Iflands accordingly appeared to poffefs all the attention to oblige, and all the reluctance to intrude or importune, which, in the polite circles of Europe, diftinguifh the accomplifhed gentleman.

To what purpofe then, it may be afked, fhould we know all this; if the models of good behaviour may be taken even from thofe who are leaft inftructed in the ufe of them.

Men are happy fometimes in the abfence of incentives to evil: But where evil obtrudes, it is the nature of man to act from what he knows to be good, and in oppofition to what he conceives to be evil. Where he cannot be ignorant, it is proper he fhould not be deceived, and where his virtue is in queftion, he fhould be accuftomed to revolve in his mind the real conftituents of a virtuous life.

The obfervations now made on the characteriftics of juftice and goodnefs, relate to human nature at large, in whatever relation of fellow citizen, or alien, of magiftrate, or fubject. As the benevolent will be humane to his fellow creature in every relation, in that of fellow citizen he will be candid and beneficent; in that of magiftrate he will be diligent and inflexibly juft; in that of fubject he will be refpectful and orderly.

To

To thefe we allude under title of the public offices or duties
of juftice and goodnefs, comprehending protection on the part of
the magiftrate, allegiance on the part of the fubject, and public
fpirit the common duty of citizens in every rank or condition of
life.

PART II.
CHAP. V.
SECT. IV.

The relations of men in fociety, confidered in refpect to their
origin, are frequently cafual. In their progrefs they acquire the
force of convention; and as conftituting the form on which the
peace and wellfare of fociety depends, are to the benevolent the
moft real and the principal objects of attention and refpect.

The dutiful and juft citizen may on occafion confider what he
has a right to enforce, that he may exact no more; but does not
fo much confider what he himfelf may be forced to do, as what
in goodwill to his fellow creatures, he ought to perform.

On the part of the fubject, and under the title of *Allegiance*, are
included *Fidelity*, *Deference*, and *Submiffion* to the will of the Sovereign or Magiftrate. This is the head of the fociety, and is
therefore an oftenfible or principal object of that affection we bear
to the fociety itfelf; his virtues are the fecurities and bleffings;
his authority is the fource of peace and good order to the whole.

Unhappy is that fubject, who can miftake for *Liberty*, a difre-
fpect to the perfon of the magiftrate; and who can perceive no
beauty in the gradation of influence, or diftinction of ranks, in
which providence has made the order of fociety to confift.

B b b 2

Equally

Equally unhappy on the other part, is that magiſtrate or ſovereign, who can miſtake the inſtitutional powers of his ſituation
for a conceſſion of property to him in the perſons, effects, or ſervices of the people.   He has power indeed to do harm, as well as
good ; but this is not peculiar to him ; the robber and the aſſaſſin
partakes in it with him, and with this ſingle difference, that the latter in his attempt to do wrong expoſes himſelf more ; and where
the miſchief is equal, is to the whole amount of his courage the
better man.   But as the actions of men in every relation are mutually important, and as every one has it in his power, ſo no one
is exempt from hazard or riſk in his attempt to do harm. The tyrant is fearful in the midſt of his guards, and many of his cruelties are mere acts of precaution againſt the reſentment he has already incurred.

But if power be ſometimes obſerved to corrupt thoſe who are
entruſted with it, the benevolent magiſtrate or ſovereign has greater advantages towards forming his mind to humanity and juſtice,
than thoſe of more private ſtation.   The concerns of his fellow
creatures are more immediately his own : The commonwealth
upon one account or other, is ever preſent to his mind : The
proſperity of the people is proſperity to him ; and the diſpoſition
moſt natural for him to feel, is that of a parent towards the family in whoſe welfare his own is involved.

The force with which he is armed, is that of the community, and reminds him of the uſe to which it ſhould be employed.
If there be a law of Nature or State on which he founds his prerogative, the ſame law is no leſs ſacred in its application to the
privilege or protection of the meaneſt citizen.

Public.

Public fpirit, or the preference of public to partial confideration, is a duty incumbent on every member of the community
alike.

Under every form of a fociety, the individual does a real fervice
to the public by the reafonable and proper care of his own prefervation, by attention to the welfare of his family, and by a diligent
obfervance of what belongs to his rank, his profeffion, or condition of life. An immediate view to the public is unequally required under different conftitutions of government; moft under
democratical governments; and leaft under abfolute monarchies,
where public deliberations are limited to the councils of a Prince.
But wherever juft precautions are taken in the national eftablifhment for the fafety and wellfare of the people, it is happy for e-
very individual to know and enjoy the advantages of his own
fituation, without giving way to that reftlefs fpirit, which in the
abfence of any real grievance would aim at fanciful refinements of
Law or State.

SECTION

SECTION V.

Of the Characteriſtics of Temperance.

THIS virtue, in the general deſcription of it, implies that diſen-
gagement from mean purſuits and gratifications, which gives to
the mind full command of its faculties in the preferable occupations of a rational nature. It is the peculiar attribute of a being, in
which animal and intellectual powers unite, and is the proper ad-
juſtment and effect of ſuch power in the general tenor of a happy life.

Mere animals when compared to man, we have obſerved, proceed more by regulated inſtincts leading to the ſpecific materials
which they have occaſion to uſe, and terminating in a meaſured
application or enjoyment of theſe materials. They ſeldom err in
the choice of their objects, and ſeldom exceed in the meaſure of
their gratifications; whereas the principle of animal appetite in
human nature, though inſtinctive alſo, and equally correct in the
end for which it is given, is leſs circumſcribed in the uſe of means,
or is more ſubject to err under the influence of imagination or o-
pinion; theſe when miſtaken for reaſon, ſerve only to miſlead
the

3

the animal difpofitions, which they affect to guide: Infomuch, that when the conceptions of mind are falfe, the animal appetites are the more apt to go wrong for being joined with an intellectual principle.

To man therefore, neither the firft conceptions of his mind, nor the inftincts of his animal frame are a fufficient guide to the courfe of life he ought to purfue. Thefe conceptions and inftincts are themfelves a province fubjected to the fuperintending power of intelligence, and requiring to be governed with circumfpection and caution.

This mixt nature of man is beautifully allegorifed by Plato, under the image of a Team, in which animals prone to the earth, or wild beafts of a fpirit, fiery, reftive, and unruly are yoked together with courfers of a celeftial breed: Thefe ftruggle to maintain a better or more elevated courfe, than that into which they are dragged, whether downwards or aftray, by the others with which they are combined in the team.

To whatever length we may purfue this allegory, we muft ob-ferve, that among the animal appetites there is not any one fu-perfluous, nor any one which fhould be entirely fupprefled. The frame of nature is beautifully conftructed, and its movements make an admirable part in the order of things. There is no rea-fon to reprobate any of its enjoyments merely as fuch.

Mankind indeed, in different ages or nations have varied in their conceptons on this fubject. They would reprefs one fett of animal enjoyments, and authorife another. If in one quarter of the globe, the gratifications of the table are left at difcretion, thofe of the fexes are reftrained. Or if under the fanction of religion, certain meats and the ufe of fermented liquors are prohibited;

polygamy

polygamy, or a kind of fyſtematic debauch of the ſexes, is admitted as a privilege of the true believer.

Whether men derive their apprehenſion in ſuch matters, as they ſometimes derive their conception in other ſubjects, from the ſuggeſtion of occaſions which we do not perceive, and which we therefore, term caprice ; or whether they are led by conſiderations of expedience and utility peculiar to their climate, or manner of life, the conceptions themſelves, when generally entertained, give riſe to maxims of decency which are no doubt to be treated with that reſpect which individuals ever owe to the manners of their reſpective times and countries. And although men of reflection may diſtinguiſh what is arbitrary in the manners of thoſe with whom they live, they are not on this account by any means entitled to neglect the obſervance of them.

The informations of reaſon are not ſufficient to direct the ſteps of ordinary men; nor are the marks which cuſtom has affixed in particular ſituations to give warning of the dangers to which morality is expoſed, altogether ſuperfluous, even to men of ſuperior diſcernment and wiſdom.

It is however proper to obſerve in characteriſing the virtue of temperance, that in the general application of its rules to mankind, it is not limited by the local or temporary apprehenſion of any nation or age : That it is not to be defined by the peculiar reſtraint or indulgence which is adopted in the Eaſt or in the Weſt, but is ſuch a freedom of mind from the dominion of inferior appetites and habits, as enable the perſon poſſeſſed of it to purſue the better occupations of a beneficent and intelligent mind.

The

The cardinal virtues, we have obferved, may be comprifed under the denominations of *fkill*, *difpofition*, *application*, and *force*. *Wifdom* is the fkill of the virtuous to obtain the ends of beneficence; *Goodnefs* is the difpofition to purfue thefe ends and fo far as the animal appetites unreftrained might impede the mind in its better purfuits ; *Temperance* may be confidered as effential to the application or diligence required in performing the duties of a virtuous life.

Under habits of fenfuality, whether in devifing the means of enjoyment, in urging enjoyment itfelf to fatiety, or in attempts to reftore the fatiated appetite, there is a neceffary wafte of time. And in the diminution of health, or intellectual faculty impaired by debauch, a difqualification enfues for any better application of mind : So that man, without a proper guard upon himfelf in this particular, might be entirely diverted from the objects of his rational nature, deprived of his underftanding, or funk into a ftate of brutality more diforderly than is any where elfe exhibited in the animal kingdom.

Mere forbearance or afcetic feverity, however, is not fufficient to prevent or to correct this evil. Abftinence may be extreme, and no lefs than the oppofite vice of excefs, enfeeble the living frame and impair the energy of the rational powers ; nor is mere fobriety, however regulated, fufficient in this important refpect to complete the merit of a virtuous character. The mifer is fober from penury, or that he may fave his money ; the fhaper is fober, that he may fucceed in fome ftroke of his art, and overeach or circumvent thofe who are lefs guarded in their manner of life.

To have the merit of temperance, it is neceſſary that the ſuppoſed receſs from animal gratifications ſhould be employed in a
better way ; in a diligent diſcharge of ordinary duties ; in purſu-
ing a rational courſe of life, and in the exerciſes of intelligence
which lead to the attainments of wiſdom and promote the progreſs which human nature is deſtined to make.

Temperance, therefore, may be conſidered as conſiſting of two
branches, ſobriety or reſtraint from exceſs, and application or a
proper direction of mind. To the firſt are oppoſed *Debauchery*
and *Senſuality* ; to the ſecond *Diſſipation* or *Sloth*.

To a perſon appriſed of the higher enjoyments and occupations
of a rational nature, it is not difficult to reſtrain the mere animal appetites within reaſonable bounds. Their gratifications are
not in their nature calculated to occupy a long or improper portion
of time. When their purpoſe is obtained, they ceaſe to importune ; nature gives warning of approaching exceſs in feelings of
ſatiety, diſguſt, or of poſitive pain ; and although the glutton,
without attending to theſe admonitions, may hurry his meal into ſurfeit or fatal exceſs ; yet, in general, mere appetite is not
the ſource from which intemperance is moſt likely to ariſe.

Senſuality is a diforder of the mind ; it reſults from the imagination, and is a project of obtaining a continual enjoyment
where nature has given no more than a capacity of occaſional and
temporary pleaſure.

An agreeable ſenſation is fitted by nature to allure the animal to perform the functions which are required for the preſervation

vation of her work. But attempts to prolong or to accumulate
such pleasures, for the most part wear out or impair the very faculty by which they might be enjoyed at their reasonable periods ;
or if this effect should not follow, the intervals of mere sensual
gratification require to be supplied by some amusement or pastime of a different kind, as conversation, exercise, or play: So
much, that if the voluptuary appears to pass his time agreeably,
his principal enjoyments are of a nature very different from those
of any mere sensuality, and actually consist in applications or ex-
ercises that amuse the mind.

Under this imposition of fancy, or misapplication of language,
which refers all human as will as animal enjoyment to sense, it
is not uncommon to call that a life of animal pleasure, which is
in fact a life of mental occupation or social amusement ; and although the specific enjoyment of human nature on many occasions
consists in its being rationally employed, it is common to consider the more serious engagements of life as an oppression or
interruption to pleasure.

In consequence of such misapprehensions men are doubly mis-
led, they are turned away from that which constitutes the merit
and felicity of their nature, to objects which are inadequate to
their purpose ; and which, to fill up the moments of human life
agreeably, must be pieced out with what they term amusements,
and which are in reality mental engagements, though of a value
inferior to those which they reject as a burden.

The disposition of human nature in the mean time is favourable to the attainment of proper habits, if we are successful in
removing those which are improper. An exemption from sloth
necessarily implies activity : We can scarcely refrain from one

set

set of pursuits without betaking ourselves to some other ; so that mere relief from the habits of sensuality, or the longings for animal pleasure, may of itself lead to better applications of mind. Many circumstances concur to recommend beneficence, and to interest men in the welfare of their fellow creatures ; and if they be not debauched by habits of a different tendency, they are likely to move in the track of their duty as the most natural path in which they should go.

The greatest danger to which the ingenuous are exposed in making a choice of their active engagements, is that of neglecting business for the sake of mere amusement or pastime, in which, without sinking into sloth or sensuality, they form habits of dissipation equally fatal to the higher and better engagements of the mind.   They lose the faculty of serious exertion, and shrink from any thing that has the aspect of business, as the sickly stomach loaths the appearance of wholesome food.

As it is difficult to ascertain the distinction betwixt amusement and business, the one by a very natural figure is easily substituted for the other.   Thus " *Business*," says Sir William Temple, " *is the diversion of man ;*" and there is no doubt, that persons who betake themselves with alacrity to any serious occupation, thereby are more effectually amused or diverted than those who affect a life altogether composed of dissipation and pastimes.

The human mind is not amused without an object, and the nearer that its object, in the interest it creates or the ardour it excites, approaches to what are termed the important affairs of life, the more effectual the amusement or pleasure it brings The dissipated, accordingly, while they fly from business as an application of

too

too ferious a nature, find fome other intereft or paffion to command their attention ; and are in fact the more entertained, that their faculties are intenfely employed, and their affections warmly engaged.

The gamefter hazards his fortune, or the hunter expofes his life; and both, in order to be amufed, require the higheft meafures of exertion, of eagernefs, and agitation of mind. When familiarity with an object has leffened the ardour it brings, they feek for occafions to renew their intereft, and to awaken their paffion: They ftrive to do for themfelves what nature has fufficiently done for the whole of the human race; they create a neceffity of labour, and an occafion for the exertion of their powers. Of this fort, the huntfman may obferve that nature has ftored human life with abundance of game; and the gamefter may obferve, that fhe has proffered to mankind in every fituation, a ftake for which they may play; and if they are pleafed to join the fatisfaction of promoting the welfare of others with that of preferving and accommodating themfelves, they will find little occafion to rack their invention for paftime or concerted amufements; nor will they be led to imagine any thing more pleafant to be done, than that which they are in the prefent moment, and by the proprieties of their ftation called upon to do.

This were the genuine refult of temperance; a well directed activity of mind, exempted from the dreams of the voluptuary, or the diffipation of the idle. It would confift in a proper ufe of what is prepared for the purpofes of animal life, and in the habit of applying to what are the proper engagements or occupations of a rational nature.

In

I

In youth, we are for the moſt part unwilling to apply to any thing that does not promiſe immediate gratification or pleaſure : And this diſpoſition, if indulged, leads to a habit of diſſipation for life : It lays the foundation of a frivolous manhood, and a wretched old age, about to depart from the paths of this mortal ſcene without leaving any honourable track behind. It were happy, if in youth we could be perſuaded, that the care of parents and tutors to give proper habits of application, though at firſt diſagreeable, is in the way to future ſatisfaction and pleaſure ; or if we could be made ſenſible at this time of life, that we are not more intereſted to acquire knowledge, or receive information, than we are to form habits of diligence, and a juſt direction of the mind to the purſuit of thoſe pleaſures, which are at once honourable, permanent, and juſt.

SECTION

SECTION VI.

Of the Characteristics of Fortitude.

TO the requisites of an active character, which we have been considering, it is necessary to subjoin that of a forcible or resolute mind : Under this title, *Fortitude* is required to fill up the sum of the virtues.

In mere body, there is a force constituted by resistance to change; in animal life, it is courage and muscular strength; in free agents, it is a determinate choice of conduct unaltered by difficulty, suffering, or danger.

It is not required that the resolute mind should be insensible to the warnings which, in the form of pain, nature has given of the ills to which the animal nature is exposed, nor does it require the neglect of such warnings, or of the means that may be employed for safety in consequence of them; but as the duties of human life frequently call upon the virtuous to pass through inconvenien-

3

cies,

cies, and to incur danger or pain in the conduct of some worthy purfuit, the quality of a mind poffeffed of itfelf, and undiflurbed in the exercife of its faculties is required to complete the character of virtue.

In this fcene of difficulty and danger, the actor cannot proceed with a mind that is deficient in fortitude, any more than the archer can fhoot with a bow that wants elaflicity or flrength.

Among the principal characteriflics of this virtue may be reckoned *Refolution, Intrepidity, Patience,* and *Conflancy.*

In all thefe inflances, no doubt, force of mind, like flrength of body, may be employed to an *ill,* as well as to a *good* purpofe ; but as mere abflinence from animal pleafure, without a proper application of mind to better purfuits, does not conflitute temperance, fo neither does exemption from fear or impatience conflitute the virtue of fortitude.

The ignorant are fometimes fearlefs, becaufe they know not their danger. The criminal is daring, from the force of fome vicious paffion ; but fortitude is the flrength of integrity that is foflered by a confcience void of offence, and is as far removed from the audacity or impudence of the profligate, as it is from the bafenefs of the coward.

Refolution is the courage with which the virtuous proceeds in his courfe of beneficence towards his friend, his country, or his fellow creature, in any circumflances that require his aid. It was nobly expreffed by the three Ifraelites, in anfwer to the king of Babylon who threatened to caft them into the midft of a burning

ing fiery furnace, if they did not worfhip the golden image which
he had fet up: And who is that God, he faid, " that fhall deliver " you out of my hands?" " We are not careful, they faid, Ne- " buchadnezar *to anfwer thee in this matter: If it be fo, the God* " *whom we ferve is able to deliver us from the burning fiery furnace,* " *and he will deliver us out of thine hand, O King ; but if not, be it* " *known unto thee, O King, that we will not ferve thy Gods nor* " *worfhip the golden image which thou haft fet up*". Here was a refolution expreffed not in the confidence of efcape or fafety, but in the fentiment of a daring integrity which no menace could fhake. And the benevolent is refolute when a friend or an in- nocent fufferer requires his aid, becaufe affection or commifera- tion is more powerful than intereft or even felf-prefervation. And the fame virtue of fortitude may be known, though with lefs evidence and on flighter occafions, by the voluntary hazard of fuffering, or inconvenience in the difcharge of any duty what- ever.

Intrepidity is tranquillity and prefence of mind in the midft of danger. It is oppofed to that perturbation of *fear* or *terror* by which the weak minded are difqualified to acquit themfelves properly or to extricate themfelves from the dangers in which they are involved. Without intrepidity, enterprife is rafhnefs, and ferves only to lead the feeble minded into fituations in which they are not qualified to act.

As the intrepid continue to poffefs themfelves or to have the ufe of their faculties in the midft of danger, intrepidity is not only an exemption from the fufferings of fear or terror, but is the beft fecurity alfo againft the evils with which any danger is fup- pofed to threaten. It enables the perfon alarmed to take the beft

D d d meafures

meafures for fafety, or to employ the beft and moft vigorous means of refiftance.

In proportion as we are ardent in the caufe of our fellow crea-tures, we are lefs apt to be difturbed by confiderations of inconve-nience or danger that affect ourfelves ; fo much that a generous or tender affection is itfelf in fome meafure a principle of forti-tude, and prepares the mind for a courageous difcharge of its duty. The female parent, even in the moft timorous fpecies of animals, is obferved to be bold and fearlefs in defence of her young.

> *For the poor wren,*
> *The moft diminutive of birds, will fight*
> *(Her young ones in her neft,) againft the owl *.*

And it is under a fenfe of indignation at the commiffion of ini-quity, or in the ardour of enthufiafm for the good of their coun-try, that men are obferved to make the greateft efforts of intre-pidity and courage : In fo much, that as fortitude is a neceffary fupport in every virtuous enterprize, the confcioufnefs of integri-ty, and a generous refolution, is the true incentive to courageous and ardent exertion of mind.

Patience may have a reference to any actual fuffering from which there is not an immediate profpect of relief. The patient endures what cannot be helped without exafperating the fore with the fruitlefs irritations of a peevifh and fretful difpofition.

In

---

* Shakefpeare in Macbeath.

In the order of nature, and in directing the animals to the means of their own prefervation, pain is employed perhaps with more power and efficacy even than pleafure. External caufes that threaten to wound or to hurt, give warning by the infliction of pain: Difeafes that announce the profpect of Death give an alarm in the fame manner; and the fuffering is made to increafe while the danger continues, or is not to be removed but by a removal of the caufe that annoys.

According to this general law of nature, no living creature is exempted from pain ; but to acknowledge the beneficent purpofe for which it is inflicted, and to employ the mind without peevifhnefs or difcontent, to obtain that purpofe is a principal characteriftic of that virtue of fortitude which we are now confidering.

Patience in fuffering, like intrepidity in danger, is the beft alleviation of the evil to which it refers, and that which enables the mind to make the moft fuccefsful efforts in obtaining relief.

The effect of pain in caufing diftrefs is in a great meafure proportioned to the apprehenfion with which it is received. The timorous patient fhrinks from the furgeon's knife before it has touched his fore, and has already fuffered in imagination before the fenfe could be affected. The fearlefs on the contrary are hardy in bearing what they difdain to fear. The mind, it is well known, under any vehement emotion of affection or paffion is infenfible to wounds or pain, and even the diftreffed may be diverted from their fufferings by any object that warmly interefts the

D d d 2

mind.

mind. Patience therefore, we may believe, is greatly aided by an exemption from fear. And this virtue is impaired by melancholy or other peevifh and fretful paffions, even more than by any defect of firmnefs or ftrength in the animal frame.

Sentiment and occupation of mind, fufpend the effect of mere fenfation, while a certain vacancy of thought, and habitual indifference to objects that give any ardour to the mind, leave it entirely to be occupied by the flighteft feelings of bodily fenfe.

To correct the foul therefore of its weakneffes, whether fear or melancholy ; to fet the order of nature in its proper light ; to occupy the mind with this and other objects of a juft affection, appear to be the proper means to ftrengthen it in bearing the inconveniences and pains to which human life is expofed.

Patience, it muft be confeffed, in many inftances appears to be the gift of nature ; but in whatever meafure it be given, it may ftill be improved by thofe who are fenfible of its value, and who do not eafily forego what they admire and wifh to poffefs. The martyr and the hero are no doubt fupported in feeming paroxyfms of fuffering, by the fenfe of honour they have attached to the part they perform.

Conftancy is that force of mind by which we perfevere in purfuits properly begun, or engagements properly made. It is oppofed to wavering or unneceffary fluctuation of choice.

An ill choice ought no doubt to be corrected. But in order to prevent the neceffity of change, proper caution ought to be employed before we form our engagements. There is a time for
deliberation,

deliberation, and then it is proper to give every confideration its due regard. A choice well made is the proper antidote to wavering and inconftancy, which proceed from the want of any fixt conception of the object at which we aim ; and which conftitutes a weaknefs of mind fubject to difguft or wearinefs from any difficulty or difappointment for which we are not fully prepared. The inconftant are known to drop even the purfuits in which they are fuccefsful in order to exchange them for fomewhat elfe, which they have not tried, and of which the principal recommendation is that of being new. They are of courfe by too frequent a change of their objects unable to effect any valuable purpofe whatever.

To perfift in our engagements is often a material article of juftice, and a matter of right which the parties concerned are entitled to exact. To perfevere without wavering or difguft in purfuits which are properly chofen is neceffary to the fuccefs of them. For this reafon, even if a better choice fhould appear than that which we have actually made, it is feldom wife to change a purfuit in which we have made any confiderable advance, to begin another in which all our labours are again to be renewed.

But this virtue of fortitude, which lays the foundation of all the proprieties we have mentioned, whether, *refolution, intrepidity, patience,* or *conftancy,* has a value in itfelf, independant of the purpofe which it enables the perfon poffeffed of it to purfue and obtain. It is, in many inftances, an exemption from fuffering or an alleviation of pain. It opens the mind to the influence of its beft affections, and gives it the poffeffion of itfelf and its faculties on trying occafions.

Fear

Fear next to malice is the greateſt bane to the human heart; it is a ſtate of ſuffering, degradation, and weakneſs, or a diſqualification for the practice of any virtue. The coward is too anxious for himſelf to entertain any generous affection for others, and too feeble in his reſolution to give any adequate effect to the purpoſe he forms. He is mean and abject in adverſity, inſolent in proſperity, and cruel in urging the effect of his jealouſy or fears againſt any object of theſe paſſions, which he may have got in his power.

There are no conditions of the mind that appear more evidently in the perſon, than thoſe oppoſite characters of a reſolute and cowardly nature. The one bears the aſpect of elevation, even in the retreats of modeſty, or in the midſt of adverſity; the other is preſumptuous, or abject, merely as the occaſion gives or withholds the advantages of fortune, which he is ever ready to feel and to abuſe. The prepoſſeſſion of mankind, therefore, in favour of courage, and in contempt of cowardice is well founded in nature; the firſt no doubt may be abuſed, and the latter may ſerve on occaſion to render men tractable and ſubmiſſive to the powers by which they are governed; but, as we are not to reject a bleſſing merely to avoid the abuſe of it, neither are to adopt a great evil for the ſake of a trifling convenience.

Courage, it is true, may be abuſed; it is neverthelefs, though not an abſolute ſecurity againſt ill diſpoſitions and vicious habits, an aptitude for all the nobler affections of the human heart, as well as a force by which the mind is enabled to ſupport itſelf in the purſuit of its worthieſt objects.

We

We have obferved, that a generous affection is in fome meafure a principle of courage; the converfe alfo is true; the courageous, in proportion as they are fecure upon their own account,
have minds fufceptible of a proper concern for others; and the
benevolent become infenfible of perfonal inconvenience or danger, in proportion as they are engaged in the exercife of beneficent affection towards their fellow creatures : Infomuch, that the
characters of generofity and courage are in their nature allied,
and in their exertions mutually ftrengthen or confirm each other.
Magnanimity is the joint refult of both, it is the effect of goodnefs
and probity, raifed above the confideration of interefts, of dangers,
or fufferings, which are apt to embarrafs the conduct of ordinary
men. The magnanimous fteer through impediment or danger,
at which the ordinary pilot would lower his fails; they turn upon an enemy, from whom the ordinary warrior would retreat;
they fpare the vanquifhed, whom the ordinary victor would facrifice to his fears or refentments; they commend an oponent, to
whom an ordinary rival would not allow any merit; and that e-
levation of mind which they poffefs, is, at once, a principal foundation and a fupport of all the virtues.

The ingenuous, by afpiring to what is noble, is led to practife
the virtues which conftitute the excellence of human nature, and
by his refolution and force of mind fupports the efforts, and perfifts in the courfe of life into which he is led by his beft difpofitions.

SECTION

SECTION VII.

Concluding Obſervations.

WE have thus, in purſuance of the method propoſed at the outſet of this work, attempted to ſtate the actual diſtinction of man
in the ſyſtem of nature; his powers of diſcernment and choice;
his purſuits and attainments, the progreſs he is fitted to make,
and of which the direction and effect for the preſent is committed
to himſelf; but of which the final termination is, we truſt, far
removed from his view.

We have inquired, how far any diſtinction of moral good and
evil is manifeſt to ſuch powers of perception as ours, and coin-
cides with the diſtinction of enjoyment and ſuffering, of perfection and defect, of which our nature is ſuſceptible; and laſt of
all have conſidered in what form the diſtinction of good and evil
ſhould operate in the choice and external actions of men; from
the whole of theſe facts and obſervations ſtriving to evince, that, as
there is in the frame of man a ſtate of *Health*, *Strength*, and *Beauty,*

I

ty, eligible upon its own account; fo there is in the form of his intelligent being, and in the purfuits of his active life, a fcheme of *Wifdom, Goodnefs, Temperance*, and *Fortitude*, which, apart from any confideration of the paft or the future, is in the prefent, and in every moment of his exiftence the preferable ftate of his nature.

But in return for fuch labours as thefe, we may be told, that we only perpetuate the miftake which is common to many, who, in amufing themfelves and others with fuch inquiries, have formed fchemes of perfection, to be admired indeed; but far above the reach of mankind. That, as in our general account of perfection we far exceed what human nature is fit to attain, fo in the detail of our precepts and rules, we would fubftitute a concerted manner, for the principles of benevolence and wifdom, which when prefent fuperfede the neceffity of rules, and when wanting, are ill fupplied by any ritual or external forms of behaviour: That in talking fo much of virtue, we ftand aloof from the world in which it ought to be practifed, and affume the importance of wifdom in mere words and technical forms of expreffion. It was thus, we may be told that philofophers in antient times affected a language, a manner, and drefs peculiar to their refpective fects; and hung out the fuppofed colours of wifdom, with little regard to its real poffeffion or ufe.

This charge may be true of many, and the error pointed out in it is a juft object of caution to every one who would avail himfelf of the fruits of a fcientific education, without incurring its abufe. The ancient fects in philofophy, have been likened to the modern fects of religion rather than to the varieties of opinion in matters of philofophy that have been entertained in modern times. Sectaries are ever ready to value themfelves more on their profeffion of faith, than on their practice; and are

E e e   fonder

fonder of any myftery or paradox they have adopted, than of the plaineft and moft important dictates of reafon or good fenfe. We muft not however confound under this cenfure thofe examples of fublime and accomplifhed virtue, which fhone forth amidft the pretenfions and ridiculous formalities with which philofophy in the perfons of many of its profeffors may have been difgraced. It was in the reign of Aurelius, that Lucian gave loofe to his fatire on this fubject, and it was by this philofopher, in return for his ingenuity, that he was protected and employed in the provinces.

It muft indeed be admitted, that to erect philofophy into a profeffion, of which the votary is diftinguifhable from the reft of mankind, otherwife than by a fuperiority which good education may give in any department of life, and by a blamelefs or beneficent intercourfe with other men, is to miftake its nature. In the fchool, and in our attempts to think comprehenfively and juftly, we are led into fyftem ; but in reaping the fruits of a culture thus applied to the mind, it may be expected that on every particular occafion we fhould acquit ourfelves properly, without any formal difplay of our general knowledge. It were piteous indeed, to carry nothing with us from hence into the world, but formal pretenfions and technical terms. To this the manners of the world are fortunately repugnant, and perhaps lead to an error in the oppofite extreme, that of affecting indifference to confiderations of virtue, which we inwardly and juftly efteem. To talk of morality in the fafhionable world*, is faid to be quoting the ten commandments. And pretenfions are fo far from being received as merit, that perfons of the moft honourable nature do well to avoid any unneceffary parade of their principles or fyftem of action.

A

---

* Here the author alludes to what was a fafhion in his own times, although it may now perhaps be changed.

A perfon who has learned his exercifes, may be known by his carriage, without retaining the ftiffnefs or formality of the fchool; and his movements, when moft graceful, appear to be the effects of mere inattention and negligence. Nor need we fcruple to carry this obfervation by analogy into the moft ferious confiderations of a manly and beneficent life. Virtue itfelf is then moft perfect, when it does not appear to have been learned or affumed as a merit; but is fuch as the perfon who practifes it cannot depart from, e-ven in the moft negligent moments of life: This, however, we muft not fuppofe to be the fruit of actual neglect or indifference to what is right: The mafter artift, in every inftance, derives the accomplifhed freedom of his calling, not from the negligence with which he feems to practife it, but from an accomplifhed under-ftanding of its graces, and a habit of correctnefs carefully acquir-ed in practice: And the manners of an accomplifhed man in be-neficence and candour, however little it may be neceffary to dif-play the fyftem he has formed on thefe fubjects, muft not be entrufted to chance.

Perfection is no where to be found fhort of the infinite mind; but progreffion is the gift of God to all his intelligent creatures, and is within the competence of the loweft of mankind. There needs not the genius of Hannibal or Scipio to detect the falfe no-tion of happinefs, of honour, or perfonal diftinction, which mif-lead the fool and the coxcomb. Men of humble capacity may learn to think juftly on thefe fubjects: And as far as wifdom de-pends on a juft conception of familiar objects, it is the nature of created mind in the courfe of experience and obfervation to im-prove its fagacity, and to make continual approach to the high-eft meafure of intellectual ability of which it is fufceptible. The

world

world is far from being so unreasonable, as to expect from every individual the utmost perfection of which human nature is susceptible; nor of any individual, in every action of his life, a full display of all the good qualities of which he himself is possessed. But the virtue of goodness, whether operating in mere innocence, or in beneficence, is surely improveable, if not actually acquired by habit.

It is that which we commonly enough express in the distinctive denomination of a gentleman, when employed as a term of praise; it implies a certain caution to avoid what is hurtful, or offensive to others, liberality, and humanity, or attention to oblige, and to anticipate the wishes of the modest and unassuming. The conversation of gentlemen is accordingly a scene of satisfaction and ease, not of strife, and competition for superiority: And this we impute to their breeding, and to the lessons of a dignified rank, not to any original difference of disposition or temper.

The attainments of men are actually unequal, and the individual differs from himself, at different periods of his life.

Whether the inequalities of men, as some have alledged, may be traced to mere casual circumstances, engaging them in different efforts and pursuits, may be left undetermined. Or without venturing an assertion so little susceptible of proof, we cannot doubt, that if the same person differs from himself at different times, it is in consequence of the efforts he makes, or neglects to make, and of the habits of thinking or of acting he has formed. Good offices conciliate the minds of men; and to have lived with the beneficent and the candid, tends to inspire benevolence and candour.

It

It is a vulgar obfervation, that we are inclined to love thofe on whom we have conferred a benefit, more than thofe from whom we have received one. And the interpretation of this fact is fomewhat malicious ; to wit, that we are more tenacious of the obligations we have laid upon others, than of thofe which have been laid on ourfelves. -But in whatever way it be underftood, the fact is important. Every one has it in his power to do a good office, though not always to receive one ; and according to this obfervation therefore, has that in his power which is moft effectual to his own happinefs, or the goodnefs of his own difpofitions.

Fortitude and temperance grow upon the mind, in the continued practice of thefe virtues. The veteran becomes calm in the midft of a hardfhip, or danger, to which he is accuftomed. And the ftrenuous mind, in any worthy purfuit, becomes fuperior to the allurements of pleafure, or the languors of floth.

We have thus, on the fuppofition of an improveable nature in man, endeavoured to fpecify what he has to wifh for himfelf, for his friend, and for mankind. And the model propofed for him cannot be improper, if it lead him to fhun any evil to which he is actually expofed, or to attain any good which is placed within his reach.

It ftill remains for a fubject of feparate inquiry, to confider *what the citizen has to wifh for his country*. And what is that public good, which in every community ought to be the object of political inftitution, and which, when obtained, ought to reconcile every individual to his ftate in fociety, whether it be his lot to govern, or be governed.

CHAP.

CHAP. VI.

OF POLITICS.

———————

SECTION I.

Introduction.

WE have already confidered fociety and government, or na- PART II.
tional eftablifhments, in refpect to their origin and their progrefs, CHAP. VI.
we are now to confider them in refpect to the good and evil of SECT. I.
which they are fuceptible, or the comparative advantage in refpect to which they are unequal.

I

Under

Under this notion we may treat of *Population, Manners,* and *Wealth,* of *Civil* and *Political Liberty,* with all its accompany-ments in raifing the character and genius of a people.

Opinions on the fubject of public, no lefs than of private good are of much importance to mankind.   As error and miftake, re-lating to the one, involve the mind in folly, fuffering, and diffap-pointment; fo, in relation to the other, they would involve whole nations in diforder and riot, or in fcenes of degradation and op-preffion.

SECTION

SECTION II.

Of the People confidered in Refpect to Numbers.

THE goodnefs of God is manifeft in the form and extent of his works. Of thefe, fo far as they are known to us, the moft excellent is man, exhibiting the effects of Divine Goodnefs in the multitude of his fpecies, and in the laws of nature, which are e-ftablifhed for their prefervation, accommodation and increafe.

PART II.
CHAP. VI.
SECT. II.

The number in which we fhould wifh mankind to exift, is li-mited only by the extent of place for their refidence, and of pro-vifion fufficient for their fubfiftence and accommodation; and it is indeed commonly obferved, or admitted, that the numbers of mankind in every fituation do multiply up to the means of their fubfiftence.

To extend thefe limits is good; to narrow or contract them is evil; but although the increafe of numbers may be thus confi-dered as an object of defire, and although we may wifh, in every

VOL. II.   F f f   inftance, instance, that the people should multiply, yet it does not follow, that we ought to wish the species thus indefinitely multiplied, to be united also into one and the same community.

The formation of families, and the continuance of their members together for a certain time, are physically necessary to the preservation of the human race ; but the union of numberless families into one society, is so far from being equally necessary, that the number of families so united may be reduced indefinitely, in a perfect consistence with every advantage of the mere social life.

But nature, in giving to man the highest place in the scale of active existence has multiplied the occasions on which he is to exert both his animal and his intelligent powers. Besides the physical wants and necessities, which are left for him to supply, besides the advantages which are left to be gained by his industry and his application, the very vices and follies incident to one part of the species, create employment for another, and the divisions of men mutually furnish objects of caution, and occasions of action, from which no part is exempted, and on which every separate society must regulate its establishments, and estimate the value of its numbers.

Mankind are exposed to dissention and quarrels, whether from the influence of irregular passions or mistaken apprehensions of right and wrong. And as the possibility of discord and war is thus entailed upon human nature, no nation, however inoffensive in its own purposes, or however wise in its measures, is entitled to think itself exempted from the common lot of mankind ; or

to

to fuppofe that its rights are fafe without the precautions that are neceffary to fecure them.

In this point of view, we may confider the increafe of the human fpecies not only as an object of general benevolence, but as a matter of expedience alfo in the cafe of every particular ftate. We may wifh that our country fhould be populous ; or increafe in numbers indefinitely, the better to fuftain the national contefts in which they may be engaged.

In every nation, the people may be confidered in two refpects.

Firft, as forming the object for whofe fake the fociety is inftituted, and for whofe fake it ought to be preferved.

And next, as affording the means by which the fociety is fo formed and preferved.

In the firft point of view, *Salus populi, fuprema lex efto*, is the fundamental principle of political fcience. If the people be happy, we have no title to enquire to what other purpofe they ferve, for this itfelf is the purpofe of all human eftablifhments.

At the fame time, the people may be confidered as the ftrength and fupport of their community ; and although, in the firft point of view, every intereft is fubordinate to theirs, yet in this fecond point of view, they muft accommodate themfelves to the interefts of ftate ; and if there be any paradox in this manner of ftating the fubject, it arifes from our confidering the end of political eftablifhments, and the means of obtaining that end, as feparate or diftinct, whereas they are in this cafe the fame.

F f f 2

Eftablifhments

Establishments are meant for the good of the people, and the people also serve to support their establishment. The greatest measure of happiness bestowed on the people, is that by which they are the means of making a happy community; and if the members of a community accommodate themselves to what is best for the state, this is no more than to be, and to do, what is most for their own preservation and welfare.

If the citizen on occasion must submit to personal hardship for the benefit of his country, such in fact is to him the occasion on which he is to reap the happiest fruits of his nature, magnanimity, benevolence, and fortitude. It is good for his country to be safe, and it is still more so for him to be an instrument in obtaining that safety. If it be the lot of the vine to bear a fruit for its owner, fertility and abundance of clusters is the prosperity and beauty of the plant that comes so loaded to the vintage.

The people considered as the vital blood of a nation, if they are fitted by their character to supply that part, have a value proportioned to their numbers; or if the numbers be given, we are to estimate their value, from the measure of life and of strength, which they bestow on their country.

SECTION

SECTION III.

Of the Manners, or Political Character of the People.

WE are not under this title, to repeat the general descriptions of virtue and vice. These we observed, may operate in any situation, or on any materials : They may operate in public or in private life, in prosperity or adversity, respecting matters of *property* or *estimation*, matters of *private* or *public concern*.

To distinguish the political from the moral character, we must recollect, that although a man may be virtuous or vicious in any situation, and conversant in any materials, yet there are, in relation to circumstances and manner of life, certain habits which enable those who are possessed of them to give to their virtues the proper effect in their particular case, or in the treatment of matters, in which they are particularly concerned. A scholar or a merchant, may be each in his way a person of great sense and integrity; but the one is not therefore qualified for a counting room, nor the other for a place at college. Where habits proper to the political state are ob--tained,

3

tained they conftitute the value of a political character ; or where the people are by contrary habits difqualified to maintain the political form of the community, or to purfue the objects of ftate ; their numbers may be great, but they are not of proportional value to the nations they conftitute.

I m ay be obferved, that mankind in the refult of the political arts to which they are led by the exigencies of fociety, arrive at different eftablifhments, whether fimple or mixt. They are led by their fituation alfo to purfue a variety of objects, in which the pacific or military arts may prevail, and the eftimable character of the people in the political point of view is their fitnefs to reap, to preferve, and to improve the advantages of their own inftitutions; and to fuppprt their country in purfuit of its refpective objects. Under eftablifhments, therefore, in which the people are differently governed, or have formed themfelves into a governing power ; and in nations differently occupied, whether in commerce, or war ; and engaged in the practice of fpecific arts, whether lucrative or liberal, fuitable habits, though various in different inftances, give to the people a political value proportioned to their numbers.

In ftates of a democratical form, and fmall extent, where the people may be deftined to govern and to defend themfelves, the habits of the ftatefman and the warrior are required as ordinary accomplifhments of the citizen; and the individual is entitled to eftimation, only in proportion as he poffeffes thefe habits. Authority and power are entrufted in the hands of particular perfons, but every citizen equally retains his claim to fuch occafional truft. There is a fpirit of equality therefore, an attention and

I

zeal

zeal for public concerns, which make an eſſential part in the habits of ſuch a people.

If the citizen under a democratical government ſubmit to re-
ſign his pretenſions, he betrays the right of every other perſon in
the ſtate, while he ſurrenders his own. If he aim at any aſcendant, or ſuperiority of fortune, different from the effect of ſuperior ability and virtue, his pretenſions become inconſiſtent with
public order and ſafety.

In proportion, therefore, as we ſuppoſe individuals in ſuch inſtances not qualified to preſerve their ſtation, not diſpoſed in their
turns to obey without meanneſs, and to command without inſolence ; the community, inſtead of increaſing its ſtrength by multiplying its numbers, actually tends to its ruin. Want of numbers might expoſe ſuch a ſtate to be overwhelmed by an external
power ; but the want of a fit character, in public ſpirit, ability,
and vigour, prepares the ſtate from within for immediate ſubver-
ſion, as a fabric is prepared to tumble or fall into ruin by the
weakneſs or decay of the parts that compoſe it.

The manners of men may vary without inconvenience in republics of a different deſcription. In ariſtocratical or mixed government,
for inſtance, certain caſual or hereditary diſtinctions of fortune being admitted, the inferior may yield and the ſuperior aſſume a comparative advantage in perfect conſiſtence with the order eſtabliſhed. Nay, in proportion to the inequalities acknowledged, there is
a habit of the perſon fitted to the rank, and in every condition a
ſuitable character or manner. The habits of ſtation are neceſſary
to qualify the citizen to ſuſtain the part which is aſſigned to himſelf. Elevation and dignity are ſuited to the rank in perſons of
one

one condition, deference and refpect are fuited to the rank in thofe of another; and without fuitable diftinctions of character different orders of men would be difqualified for their fituations, and a community fo made up of difcordant parts would be unfit to maintain the eftablifhment in which the public order confifts. The utmoft to be expected among citizens in this ftate of difparity is that the fuperior fhould, by his noble qualities, merit the refpect which is paid to him; or earn the returns of affection and gratitude by the good he performs.

Under monarchies, whether abfolute or mixed, the fcale of fubordination may be farther extended; or the extremes of high and low much farther removed from each other than they are in republics of any fort; while the interval between thefe extremes is filled up with many flow and infenfible gradations. Under fuch inftitutions, accordingly, equality may be altogether unknown; the habit of individuals may be in every inftance either to yield or to affume a fuperiority. And thefe habits of fubordination, of precedence, or deference, are neceffary to give the people their value in the different ranks they are deftined to hold.

Under all or any of thefe varieties, a people difqualified to preferve the political form of their country, nobles without beneficence, elevation or dignity, inferiors without refpect or fubmiffion; inftead of giving national ftrength proportioned to their numbers, would prove the immediate fource of weaknefs, or lead to revolutions of uncertain or dangerous iffue.

But while we thus contend for propriety of manners adapted to the conftitution of ftate, it muft be obferved, that, if there

be

be any political eftablifhment raifed upon a plan of injurious ufurpation on the part of thofe who govern, and proceeding upon a debafed and abject fpirit of fubmiffion on the part of thofe who are governed, it were abfurd to afcribe any merit, under the notion of a political value, to the habits which might be required to preferve fuch a fyftem. The form itfelf we muft confider as an abufe or a calamity, and for the fake of mankind muft contend, that manners fuited to preferve it are evil. That manners, on the contrary, which difpofe the people to revolt, and overthrow fuch governments at the expence of any temporary hardfhips, are neceffary to obtain or reftore the bleffings of national peace difturbed by the continual, though unrefifted wrongs to which the fubject is expofed.

This defcription is perhaps too nearly verified, where the relation of fovereign and fubject is conceived on the models of mafter and flave, where the one is conceived to be a property and holds his poffeffions and his life, not upon conditions that may be fuppofed merely unequal; but without the obfervance of any condition at all, and at the will of the other, by whom the difcretion is frequently abufed. The value of the people, in fuch inftances, is to be eftimated from their qualifications to repel fuch pretenfions, and from the energy with which they recur to a form more confiftent with juftice and the good of mankind.

Amidft the varieties of political character, nations differ alfo in refpect to the objects on which they are chiefly intent: One nation is intent upon commerce, or bufied with the arts of fubfiftence and accommodation: another has its exiftence to contend for at the edge of the fword is therefore intent upon the arts of war, and the advantages to be gained or loft in the conteft with its neigh-

bours. In either cafe, the fitnefs of men to promote the profperity, or to watch over the fafety of their country, is an ef-
ential circumftance in eftimating the political value of their
numbers.

Commercial natious have not any intereft in the increafe of population, except in fo far the people are induftrious, or poffeffed
of fome profitable art. The idle, the profligate and the prodigal become, in proportion to their numbers, a fource of public diftrefs and calamity.

Warlike hordes, on the contrary, would multiply warriors,
not traders or pacific inhabitants. The Romans, in the firft
ftate of their principality or republic, haftened their population
by the indifcriminate admiffion of ftrangers to a participation of
all their political rights. They had no occafion to make any
felection of thofe, they were to admit on the rolls of their people;
for all the hordes in their neighbourhood from which their numbers could be fupplied were warriors like themfelves, and every
acceffion to their number from the nations around them, was
an addition to their military lifts.

While ftates are thus intent upon any particular object, they
appear to eftimate the character of their people upon a partial model ; and fo far, no doubt, it is partial as they limit their notions
of virtue to the tranfactions in which they themfelves are engaged,
or to the forms according to which they themfelves are accuftomed to proceed : But to fuch partialities we muft fubmit in eftimating the comparative merit of nations, and in judging of the luftre
which individuals may have caft around them in their refpec-
                                                            tive

tive ages. Human nature no where exifts in the abftract, and
human virtue is attached, in every particular inftance, to the ufe of particular materials, or to the application of given materials to particular ends.

SECTION

SECTION IV.

Of the Wealth of the People.

WE may confider national wealth in refpect to the purpofe it ferves, while in the poffeffion of the people ; or in refpect to that which it ferves, in the form of a revenue to the ftate employed to defray public and national expences of government, defence, or chargeable inftitutions of any fort.

Wealth, as it may be referred to the firft of thefe purpofes, and is in the poffeffion of the people, is the fubject of this fection ; as it may be referred to the fecond purpofe of revenue to to the ftate, will be the fubject of that which follows.

The firft and moft effential purpofe of wealth is the fubfiftence and accommodation of ufeful men; and its value is to be eftimated from the numbers it will ferve to fubfift and accommodate ;—furnifhing. at the fame time, the means of lucrative enterprife for the accumulation of more wealth, or the reproduction

duction of that which is neceffarily confumed. Thefe are purpofes which it ferves beft, not in the coffers of the ftate, or at the
difpofal of thofe who are fuppofed to act for the community, but
in the management of the frugal and induftrious proprietor ; or
laid out on the principle of private intereft, and with a view to
private gain.

In refpect to national wealth, ftates may rate their profperity,
not fo much by the fums they are enabled to levy in the form
of revenue, as by that wealth which, in confiftence with public fervice, they are enabled to leave in the hands of the induftrious citizen. In his hands it is employed to its beft ufes,
the rearing of a family, the eftablifhment of manufacture, the
purchafe of materials and other articles, in the outlay of a lucrative and profperous trade.

The conftituents of wealth are more or lefs quickly confumed
in the ufe. The fulleft granary and the ampleft ftore of commodities are, within a limited period, exhaufted in the confumption
of a people ; and their wealth is to be eftimated, not from the
ftate of their magazines or ftores at any particular time, but
from the fources of reproduction and continual fupply, by which
the abundance they enjoy is increafed or perpetuated.

The fource of fupply which nature has provided for man, in
any given fituation of climate or foil, is labour. Without this, in
refpect to him, the land is every where barren, and materials of e-
very fort are too rude for his ufe. The wealth of the citizen is
meafurable by the quantity of labour he can employ. If he
can command the labour of others, he may difpenfe with his own;
but, to enable one perfon to obtain the labour of another, it
is

neceffary that the one fhould be able to pay the hire of that labour; and that the other fhould be in need to receive that hire.

If all men were equally rich, every one might be willing to
pay the hire of labour, while no one would be willing to labour
for hire: But, as labour is neceffary to fupply the confumptions
of life; on the fuppofition of equal riches, every one would be
reduced to labour for himfelf; and thus a fuppofed equality
would reduce the fortune of every perfon to the fruit merely of his
own labour, and, in fact, would be to render every perfon alike
and equally poor.

The antient republics, amongft whom it was propofed, in fome
inftances, to equalize the fortune of citizens, had recourfe to the
labour of flaves, and the object, without this provifion, would
have been altogether chimerical and wild.

Nature feems to have ordered, that, in proportion as men fhall
depart from their original poverty, they fhall depart alfo from
that original ftate of equality, in which it was neceffary for every
individual to labour for himfelf.

The unequal capacities and various difpofitions of men; covetoufnefs and frugality, in one; neglect and diffipation, in others;
unequal ability, application, and fuccefs in the practice of the lucrative arts, have ever, in the progrefs of wealth, been accompanied
with a diftinction in the fortunes of men; fo that, while fome
are in a condition to command the labour of many, others remain
without any other poffeffion than the immediate fruits of their
own.

From

From a difference of fortune there refults a difference of eftimation and rank; and to thofe who would emerge from the lower ftation, there is a motive of ambition joined to that of neceffity, in promoting the practice of arts: So that nations who are forward in the accumulation of wealth, proceed in it with a double ardour from the effect of advances they have already made; and thus owe, in a great meafure, to the inequalities of fortune, what fprang originally from neceffity, the application of that labour by which articles of confumption are reproduced, and the fources of wealth are enlarged.

In this ftate of unequal fortune, one man has the means of projecting and executing a lucrative enterprife; numbers of others feel the neceffity of committing their labour to his direction; and what he gains, even while it remains in his own poffeffion, goes into the mafs of national wealth.

Skill, experience, and a fleight in the application of labour, contribute greatly to the fuccefs of it, or to the accumulation of its fruits. To promote thefe advantages, the divifion and the fubdivifion of tafks are highly conducive: A perfon who has to work but in one fingle material, will foon come to underftand his department better, than if he had to do with a number of different fubjects that would tend to diftract his attention, and embarrafs his thoughts. Whoever operates but to one fingle effect, and obtains that effect by repeating without variation one fingle movement of the hand or the foot, will become mafter of his tafk in a fhorter time, and will practife it with lefs interruption, than if he had to pafs through a variety of operations; were obliged frequently to change his tools; and at every fucceffive part of his work were required to practife a different fpecies of fkill.

Among

Among the circumftances, therefore, which were formerly mentioned, as attending the progrefs of commercial arts, none is of more confequence to their advancement, than the feparation of callings, and the fubdivifion of each into a convenient number of different branches. This leffens the difficulty of every apprenticefhip, and greatly increafes the produce of any given number of hands. A fit affortment of perfons, of whom each performs but a part in the manufacture of a *pin,* may produce much more in a given time, than perhaps double the number, of which each was to produce the whole, or to perform every part in the conftruction of that diminutive article. But to this feparation of tafks, as well as to circumftances in the original lot of man, it was obferved, that *commerce,* or the exchange of commodities, was neceffary. A perfon who performs but one fpecies of labour, and obtains what is not the whole or perhaps is not any part of his own confumption, muft have a facility in exchanging what he has produced for the other commodities which his occafions require, but which he is not equally in a condition to fabricate for himfelf.

With the benefit of commerce, or a ready exchange of commodities, every individual is enabled to avail himfelf, to the utmoft, of the peculiar advantage of his place; to work on the peculiar materials with which nature has furnifhed him; to humour his genius or difpofition, and betake himfelf to the tafk in which he is peculiarly qualified to fucceed. The inhabitant of the mountain may betake himfelf to the culture of his woods, and the manufacture of his timber; the owner of pafture lands may betake himfelf to the care of his herds; the owner of the clay-pit to the manufacture of his pottery; and the hufbandman to

the

the culture of his fields, or the rearing of his cattle: And any one commodity, however it may form but a fmall part in the whole accommodations of human life, may, under the facility of commerce, find a market in which it may be exchanged for what will procure any other part, or the whole: So that the owner of the clay pit, or the induſtrious potter, without producing any one article immediately fit to fupply his own neceſſities, may obtain the poſſeſſion of all that he wants. And commerce, in which it appears that commodities are merely exchanged, and nothing produced, is neverthelefs in its effects very productive; becaufe it miniſters a facility and an encouragement to every artiſt, in multiplying the productions of his own art; thus adding greatly to the mafs of wealth in the world, in being the occaſion that much is produced.

In trade, the profit of one is not, as fometimes fuppofed, neceſſary lofs to another; or rather, commerce being the exchange of what may be fpared for what is wanted, and this a mutual convenience to all the parties concerned, is equally gain and profit to all.

The principle of trade is private intereſt, the fartheſt poſſible removed from public fpirit, or any concern for a common caufe; yet, fo far as wealth, in the poſſeſſion of the people is a benefit to the ſtate, private intereſt in trade operates with the leaſt erring direction for the public benefit, and is fecure of its purpofe, where public councils would miſtake or mifs of their aim.

The trader, no doubt, may err in the purfuit of his gain; but the principle from which he acts is fo exquifitely fenfible to the experience of profit or lofs, that the leſſons of that experience

feldom need to be repeated: The firft lofs is fufficient to correct
the error of the trader, and he runs with irrefiftible avidity
wherever it appears that profit is to be made. The ftate may do
much to protect, or even to aid him, but not in the way of excit-
ing his ardour, or in directing its application.

It is a primary object of government, on this and many other
accounts, to fecure the property of its fubjects, to protect the induftrious in reaping the fruits of his labour, in recovering the
debts which are juftly due to him, and in providing for the
fair decifion of queftions that may arife in the intercourfe of
trade.

For the encouragement of commerce, in particular, it is wife to
facilitate communications by commodious high ways, inland and
fea navigations, and every other conveniency that tends to leffen
the difficulty of removing commodities from the place in which
they are produced to that in which they are wanted. This is
the principal aid which commerce requires. Minifters of ftate
have had their predilections; fome for manufacture, others for
agriculture; fome for foreign, others for domeftic trade, and it is
not uncommon to imagine, that either is profitable only in proportion as the commodity of the merchant brings money, or filver and gold in return.

In fpeculation we wifh to fimplify our objects, and would propofe to fet the whole machine of human life in motion, by touch-
ing fome key, or by pulling a particular ftring. Some would encourage manufactures, in order to furnifh the hufbandman with
a ready market for the produce of his farm; and take this way
to encourage the culture of land. Others are inclined to adopt
I   the

the converfe of this expedient; or increafe the produce of land, in order to feed the manufacturers at a cheaper rate: At the fame time, it is evident, that, if the ftate can procure any fpecial aid or inftruction to either, that this aid ought to be directly applied where it is fuppofed to be of ufe, and not left to wait the recoil of encouragement or inftruction from a different quarter.

Errors of adminiftration are ftill more pernicious, as a late ingenious author has fully demonftrated *, where, apart from any confideration of public fafety, they tend to check one article of trade in favour of another, or act upon a principle of predilection for exportation or importation, in preference of one to the other.

With refpect to the comparative importance of the home and foreign trade, it is evident, that a perfon having a redundancy of any commodity, and not able to find what he wants in exchange for it, in the dwelling of his neareft neighbour, muft go farther, and even if neceffary to the territory of a feparate fovereign.

A market that is not to be found in the neighbouring village may be found in fome city or diftrict at a diftance; and a commodity which can neither be produced nor vended in one latitude, may be produced or find its market in a different one. If in the fearch of this market, the trader is led to the dominions of a fovereign different from his own, he is faid to go into foreign trade. If all the parties live in the territories of the fame fovereign, the commerce between them, however remote from each other, is ftill domeftic or internal. But this circumftance, it fhould feem, does not affect the preference to be given to one branch of

• trade

* Smith on the Wealth of Nations.

trade over another, farther than as a preference is due to the neareft and readieft market; as being attended with the leaft expence
of labour or carriage, and the leaft delay of returns.

It is evident that, where a redundant commodity cannot be
difpofed of at home, the producer is interefted to have it carried
abroad, or prefented wherever he can find a market; that, where
the commodity he wants cannot be obtained at home, he is interefted to have it from abroad, or from whatever quarter it can be
procured. But the neceffity of foreign commerce, in either way,
may diminifh as the territory of the ftate extends; fo that fmall
ftates may be in continual need of commerce with foreigners, while
great empires, like the globe of the earth itfelf, have a fufficient
range for every fpecies of trade within themfelves.

Where filver and gold, or money, is more wanted than other
commodities, commerce will naturally take its direction to the quarter in which thefe are to be had in return; but, where other commodities are more wanted than gold or filver, thefe will be fent
for a fupply of the more preffing neceffity; and there would be
no profit in retaining them if other commodities are more ufeful
than they are.

One article of policy connected with commerce, and in which
the authority of ftate is fuppofed to be neceffary, is the effay and
coinage of money, to ferve as a ftandard of valuation and medium of exchange. Commerce may originate in what is termed
barter, in which the parties mutually give and take the articles
which they have to fpare, in exchange for thofe they want. The
hufbandman may have given his meafure of corn in exchange
for the yard of the manufacturer's cloth, without any ftandard
of

of valuation befides what is affixed by the want or exigency of the feveral parties. Even where the parties in trade recur to a particular commodity as a common ftandard of valuation in their various tranfactions, they may themfelves eftimate the quantity and quality of the ftandard, as well as that of the commodities they are to appreciate by a reference to its value; but many inconveniences are avoided by felecting the precious metals as the ftandard of valuation, and ftill farther inconvenience is avoided by the juft interpofition of government to afcertain, by a mark of public authority, the finenefs and quantity of the fpecies which is to pafs in circulation. This is the object of coinage, and a principal article in the policy of nations, relating to commerce or the operations of trade.

It is well known that even the precious metals, however fitted to reprefent a great value in fmall bulk, neverthelefs may become too unwieldy for quick circulation, and for repeated transfers of property, when the tranfactions of commerce come to be widely extended, and great remittance of money required in payments. That, in this cafe, where public or private credit is fufficiently eftablifhed, promiffory notes, or obligations to pay, may pafs through many tranfactions, and for a time fuperfede the neceffity of actual payment, while the money lies ready to anfwer the demand, at the place from which the promiffory note was iffued.

In this matter, it is a facred object of policy to keep faith with the creditor; and, where the credit of ftate is interpofed, and to give ready protection to the citizen where any abufe in the circulation of paper or promiffory notes can be dreaded.

2

Here

Here then, or in refpect to the accumulation of wealth, we may venture to reft the eftimate of national felicity : Firft, on the labour of the people, or the degree in which that labour is productive ; next, on the fpecies of commodity produced, and its fitnefs to fubfift and accommodate the greateft number of valuable citizens and ufeful hands ; and, laft of all, on the freedom of trade, and the equal protection given to the people in every branch of commerce unreftrained and unforced, with this fingle exception, that where in the courfe of trade advantages may arife, or inconveniences be incurred, refpecting the fafety or defence of the commonwealth, in every fuch cafe, fafety is to be preferred to profit ; and the public defence being a primary object of public attention, and an object for which ftates muft be prepared to incur indefinite expence, it is an object for which alfo they muft be willing on occafion to forgo their profits, and to embrace the lefs profitable branch of trade in which men are formed for the public fervice, in preference to the more profitable branch in which this advantage is not to be obtained.   Hence the wifdom of encouraging feamanfhip in maritime nations, and the wifdom of guarding, in every ftate, the manners of a brave and ingenuous people, in preference to their numbers or wealth.

SECTION

S E C T I O N V.

Of the Revenue of the State.

THE wealth of the people, according to the obfervations of laft fection, like other articles in the fyftem of nature, is a fluctuating quantity, continually perifhing, and continually reproduced. Its fources are the labour employed in agriculture and manufacture. Its iffues are the confumption made by the people, and the expences incurred by the ftate. Its increafe or diminution depends on the proportion which the fupply bears to the wafte or confumption.

The firft and principal ufe of wealth is the fubfiftence and accommodation of the people: But there is another, if not included in this, at leaft neceffary to obtain its end ; the fupport of government in the difcharge of its neceffary functions, as in difpenfing the law, in preferving the peace at home, in guarding againft danger from abroad, or in any other object of adminiftration calculated for the general benefit of the community.

In

In what manner a public revenue is to be conftituted for thefe purpofes is matter of very important concern. It is underftood to come into the management of thofe who are intrufted with government, and is that on which the fpirit of liberty has moft caufe to be jealous; in which the fuppofed interefts of the governing and the governed are fooneft at variance; and in which the tyrant has moft immediate occafion to abufe his power.

In rude and barbarous hordes, numbers of men appear to be united merely as making up the train of a leader. Whatever be their purfuits or refources, the leader is fuppofed to prefide in the one, and to enjoy a principal fhare of the other.

In the firft wars of the Romans, every citizen kept the field at his own expence, or ferved the public from the fame ftock with which he fupported himfelf and his family. If the leader, in conducting the public fervice, incurred a greater expence than any of his followers, he was enabled to difcharge that expence by means of the fame advantages which procured him the afcendant he enjoyed. And in his cafe, to employ the fpoils of one enemy, in waging war with another, was at once to have a public revenue, and to be entrufted with its application.

In the firft diftribution of property, individuals are likely to fhare in proportion to their power. The leader or fovereign of the community, together with his power, has a claim to what may enable him to fupport his rank, and to difcharge its functions; and the demefne appropriated to him is underftood, at the fame time, to be his private eftate, and the revenue of the commonwealth.

Some

Some republics, as well as principalities, have had part of their PART II. public revenue conftituted in fubjects referved for the communi- CHAP. VI. ty, or fet apart from the property of any individual, for this pur- SECT. V. pofe. Such were the mines which were wrought for the ftate of Athens; the pafture lands of Campania, and other fubjects which were let for the republic of Rome.

The kings in Europe have their forefts or demefne lands, which are fo many remains of the funds from which the ftate of a feudal fovereign was maintained, as that of his vaffals was fupported from their refpective fiefs.

In the progrefs of nations, however, the demefne of the fovereign has been found ftill lefs and lefs adequate to the public expence. While other fubjects of property in private hands are improved or rendered productive ; the royal foreft in their neighbourhood continues to be wafte ; and government, taught to rely on other and more copious refources, has long confidered the demefne of the fovereign as a mere article of ftate and pleafure to the prince, or as the means of liberality towards thofe in his favour.

As private intereft is the great principle of lucrative arts or accumulation of wealth, it is material to the profperity of nations, in this article, that every fubject fufceptible of improvement fhould be appropriated or pafs into private hands, who may turn it to the higheft account : Infomuch that the idea of a public demefne, as men advance in fkill and induftry, is juftly exploded, or exchanged for a contribution, or taxes to be levied from the labour or eftates of the people.

It

It is juft, and in every community matter of tacit, if not of exprefs agreement, that every one who partakes in the benefit of a
public eftablifhment fhould bear a part in the expence it incurs.
On this principle is founded the obligation of the fubject to contribute his fhare to the revenue of the ftate; and, on this principle,
a revenue wifely conftituted may, in the progrefs of national
wealth, without any public oppreffion, be made to keep pace
with the growing exigencies, the growing numbers, riches, and
frugality of the people.

Taxes, for this purpofe, may be laid in different ways, and
follow the rates of property in different fubjects and effects.

They may be laid in the form of affeffment on the rents of
land, or other fources of private returns: They may be laid on
goods as they pafs in commerce; or they may be laid on articles
of confumption in the actual ufe.

In judging of the abfolute or comparative expedience of taxes
diverfified in any of thefe ways, the following maxims may be affumed.

Firft, That the real exigencies of the ftate are to be provided
for at any hazard or expence to the fubject. The interefts of the
ftate and of the people, when well underftood, are the fame. The
firft intereft of the people is that every one fhould be protected;
and the firft intereft of the ftate is, that it fhould be in condition
to afford protection. Whatever may have been in fact the origin of government, upon this principle alone, the folicitude with
which

which it is adminiſtered, and the reſpect that is paid to it by the people are founded.

Secondly, it may be aſſumed, That the private eſtate of the ſubject is in no caſe to be unneceſſarily taxed, under pretence of a public concern. The eſtabliſhments of a great people may contain a variety of departments, and lead to applications of revenue uſeful and proper, in a variety of different ways; but beyond theſe limits, it is evident, that, to tax the people were to rob them of their property, to take from induſtrious hands what may go into the hands of the prodigal; or, inſtead of a ſource of farther wealth to the community, prove an occaſion of abuſe or a waſte, for which the commonwealth is to receive no compenſation or ſupply.

In the third place, it may be aſſumed, That, as it is a principal object of government to ſecure the property of the ſubject againſt every invader, care ſhould be taken, in the form of taxation, to fix the limits of public exaction, ſo as no way to impair the ſecurity of the ſubject, in the poſſeſſion of what he has left; that, while he is required to contribute a part of his labour to the public expence, the extent of this demand ſhould be well aſcertained, and no admiſſion be given to arbitrary impoſitions, which might render the fortune of the ſubject in any degree precarious. It is in the confidence of a ſecurity of property that the labourer toils to obtain it, and chearfully contributes a part of his gains to enſure the remainder.

It is difficult to obtain ſecurity on this point wherever the ſovereign, conceiving his own intereſt as diſtinct from that of the

people,

people, is at the fame time empowered to impofe taxes by his own prerogative, and without their confent.

A prerogative of this extent, wherever it be lodged, whether in the hands of a monarch, a fenate, or democratical affembly, except fo far as bodies of the two laft defcriptions are fuppofed to to tax themfelves, is not confiftent with the liberty of thofe over whom it is exercifed. In a monarch, it leads to the defpotifm of one ; in a fenate, to the defpotifm of a few ; and, even in a democratical affembly, when exercifed over fubject-provinces, is the defpotifm of many ; and, for this very reafon, is the more oppreffive and the lefs reftrained, than it is in either of the two former inftances. Thus the Athenians oppreffed their allies, or fmaller ftates in dependance upon them, under pretence of exacting the quota of each in fupport of the common caufe ; and the Romans, while they exempted themfelves from taxes, fuffered their provinces to be oppreffed with every mode of vexation.

In the fourth place, it is evident, that no tax fhould be laid on in fuch a manner as to drain the fource from which it is derived. The labourer ought not to be interrupted or difabled in the performance of his labour. The trader ought not to be robbed of his ftock ; nor the landholder difpoffeffed of his land. Each may be required to contribute a part of his returns ; but this fhould be done in perfect confiftence with the fafety of that fubject from which his returns are derived.

In the fifth place, it may be affumed, That not only every real grievance, but every apparent one alfo, and whatever is likely to be felt as fuch in the impofition of taxes, is to be avoided.

The

The public and its members ought to be confidered as parties in the fame common caufe, and fharers in the fame common adventure. It is the intereft of the ftate, that it fhould be chearfully ferved and fupported; that nothing fhould take place in the exactions of revenue or of public fervice which has a tendency to alienate the minds of the people; that, in the choice of taxes, thofe ought to be preferred which are leaft likely to be felt as a grievance. For this reafon, probably, the moft profperous ftates have indefinitely varied the forms of taxation, fo that by raifing fome part, though not the whole, from any particular quarter, they have avoided laying a burden to be felt as a grievance, upon any particular clafs or order of the people.

Cuftoms fall ultimately upon the confumer of the goods for which they are paid. Perhaps all taxes fall ultimately upon thofe who may themfelves be made to pay, but who have not the means of recovering any part of what they have paid, by impofing any terms for that purpofe upon others. Whoever lives on his rent, and buys every article of confumption, without having ought to fell, comes under this defcription. It is contended, therefore, in fpeculations on public oeconomy, that taxes of every kind, however immediately conftituted, fall ultimately on the produce of land. This is probably a miftake; for every other perfon that lives on a taxable income, and by the confumption of taxable goods, without having any to fell, muft bear a proportional part of the burden, as well as the perfon whofe rent is from land. But, even if the reverfe were admitted, it would be far from expedient to apply to the landholder directly for the fupply of a whole revenue to the ftate. Were this meafure to be taken, the whole burden would apparently, as well as really, lie upon one clafs of

3   the

the people; and even if the load ſhould continue to be ſupported by this claſs, it would neverthelefs, from its immediate preſſure and apparent partiality, be conſidered as an inſufferable grievance, and become a continued ſource of complaint.

It is material, therefore, in conformity to the maxim now ſtated, that taxes, wherever they may ultimately fall, ſhould be diverſified in reſpect to the ſubjects taxed, and the tax gatherer have immediate recourſe for payment to all orders of the people, that the whole may, at leaſt in appearance, if not in reality, bear a proportional ſhare of the burden.

In this manner, and through a ſucceſſion of ages, a revenue of the greateſt extent may be raiſed gradually and almoſt inſenſibly, ſo as ſcarcely to occaſion any complaint of a grievance but from thoſe who induſtriouſly ſpeculate on the whole amount, and indulge apprehenſions of what may be the ultimate reſult of its progreſs.

The policy to which this maxim refers has been adopted by ſovereigns of almoſt every deſcription, whether they meant to charge their people with heavy burdens in the moſt artful manner, or to provide for the real exigencies of ſtate in the manner that would be leaſt felt as a grievance. This conſideration, while it may influence the choice of a tax, ought to influence alſo a choice of the manner in which taxes are to be levied, or made effectual, with the leaſt cauſe of complaint on the part of the ſubject.

Taxes, we ſuppoſe, may be levied, either by officers in the pay of the public, or by perſons who farm the revenue at a determinate

nate rate. In general it has been obferved, that taxes let to farm
are more oppreffive than thofe which are levied by public commiffion or revenue officers.

It is not difficult to perceive whence it fhould arife, that a revenue let to farm is more oppreffive than one that is collected by
officers in behalf of the public. A farm of revenue is commonly let to the higheft bidder. The fovereign ftipulates for a certain
fum to be paid into the public coffers, without any rifk from the
negligence or failure of thofe who are employed in the collection,
or from the infolvence of thofe from whom it is due. The far-
mer rents the fubject but for a limited period ; and acts in that
period under the impulfe of a temporary intereft, and at the hazard of exhaufting the fource of future revenue, while he reaps
the prefent. He naturally proceeds with the illiberal feverities
of a private concern, having in his view to obtain fome adequate
return for his rifk and trouble, as well as to make up the fum he
is bound to pay to the ftate. His concern in the matter is temporary, and he labours to make immediate gain for himfelf, however it may affect the permanent interefts of the public. He calls
upon the fovereign to fupport his exactions, under pain of fuffering him to fail in performing his engagements; and, under this
pretence, the public authority is of courfe employed to enforce
the vexations of private rapacity.

Where, on the contrary, officers are employed with fixt falaries,
to collect the duties which are required by the public, thefe officers being reftrained from exacting more than the public has impofed, and though called to a ftrict account of what they have received, anfwerable only for the diligent and faithful difcharge of
3   their

their own duty, they are not interefted to urge the public exactions to any cruel or oppreffive extent.

Taxes are of different denominations, taken either from the
fubjeƈt on which they are impofed, or from the manner in which
they are levied.   They may be reduced to five titles, *capitation, affeffment, monopoly, cuftoms,* and *excife.*   The two firft are exaƈted
from the perfon or the eftate of the fubjeƈt; the other three are
exaƈted from commodities in fale or confumption.

Capitation is a tax on the perfon, and when not modified by any
diftinƈtion of poor or rich, is fuppofed to fall equally on both.
This may be the firft rude device of an arbitrary mafter, who, not
being willing to embarrafs himfelf with diftinƈtions, would arrive at the end of his government in the fhorteft way *.   It were
abfurd to exaƈt no more from the rich than the poor can pay.
And it would be cruel to extort from the poor as much as the
rich may without inconvenience afford.   Capitation were in either way unjuft and impolitic, either unproduƈtive or cruel.   It
has indeed feldom or ever been exemplified in this extreme.   The
moft arbitrary and inconfiderate mafter is aware of its defeƈts,
and aims at fome diftinƈtion, by which he would make the wealthy contribute in fome proportion to their means.   In a plan of
capitation, for inftance, projeƈted for a neighbouring kingdom, it
was

* The Turkifh governor in the ifland of Cyprus levies a poll tax from every inhabitant, without diftinƈtion of perfons ; and, by way of additional revenue, fometimes repeats the exaƈtion from perfons of a particular name, whether *George, James,*
or *Thomas.*   And, we may believe, when fuch is his humour, may add a name or two
more. The labour of thinking feems to be the principal diftrefs from which thefe officers
fhrink.

Mariti's Travels into Cyprus and Syria.

was propofed to range the people into fix claffes, and to fix a pro-portional rate for each. Such an arrangement, however, would ferve only to diminifh the evil, not to remove it entirely. Within each of the claffes confiderable varieties of fortune muft have been admitted, and great injuftice would ftill take place in the exaction of equal rates from perfons of unequal wealth, though of the fame clafs.

Were we to fuppofe a capitation or poll-tax to be freed of all its defects, by a perfect adjuftment of the exaction to the means of thofe on whom it is laid, this in fact would be to change it into that form of taxation which we would exprefs under the name of affeffment.

Under this title we may include every fpecies of tax, in which a due proportion to the means or eftate of the fubject is aimed at. Such, in particular, is the nature of the land tax in Great Britain.

The rent of land is of all others the moft palpable fubject of affeffment; but this form of taxation may with great juftice be made to comprehend the rent of houfes or tenements of any fort, which yield an ordinary return to the owner.

Property in money or ftock is lefs eafily afcertained. The very attempt, in the cafe of a merchant, might be attended with much inconvenience, or improperly difclofe the fecrets of trade. His ftock is fluctuating. It is rifked upon uncertain events; and, at particular times, it may be doubtful whe-ther his fortune is not greatly reduced, or whether he is not upon the eve of recovering his rifk with great profit. Free and trad-ing nations, therefore, may wifely forego the application even of

VOL. II.   K k k   affeffment,

affeffments, where the indifcriminate extenfion of fuch a tax might check the efforts of trade, on which the increafe or prefervation of national wealth fo much depends.

Monopoly is the exclufive privilege of buying or felling a commodity, from which it is propofed to levy a tax.

Whoever has the fole privilege of buying may buy at his own price, and will give no more than what enables the feller to bring his goods to market. If he alfo have have the fole privilege of vending, he will exact as much as the confumer can be made to pay, without difcouraging him entirely from the ufe of the commodity. With thefe advantages, the dealer may make indefinite profit in the refult of his trade. When the fovereign takes fuch a monopoly to himfelf, or lets it to farm, as has been done in many ftates, refpecting falt, tobacco, and other commodities, he obtains by fuch means a confiderable revenue, limited only by his regard to what the people may fuffer from an immoderate exaction upon a commodity of general ufe, or by the danger of fuppreffing that ufe altogether, if the profit attempted to be made amounts to a prohibition. The Roman ftate, at a very early period of its hiftory, took or let to farm the monopoly of falt The fame meafure has been repeated in different nations of Europe and Afia, and is extended to a variety of other fubjects.

Among the objections to this mode of taxation may be reckoned the neceffity with which fovereigns of almoft every denomination muft feel themfelves, being obliged to farm their monopolies, and thereby expofe their people to all the vexations which accompany this mode of levying a tax, joined to the peculiar vexation
of

of being prohibited from fupplying themfelves with an ufeful or neceffary article, at the eafieft rate.

The effect of monopoly, otherwife, may be the fame either with that of a capitation tax, or of a fair affeffment. A monopoly of the mere neceffaries of life, or of any commodity which the poor muft confume, at leaft, equally with the rich, has all the cruel effects of indifcriminate capitation or poll tax; whereas the monopoly of any commodity of which men proportion the ufe to their means of procuring it, fuch as are matters of luxury or fuperfluous accommodation, has the effect of affeffment fo as to fall chiefly on the rich ; or, if it fall upon perfons of unequal condition, it may do fo in juft proportion to their fortune, or to their confumption of the article taxed.

But, in general it may be obferved, that, if commodities are to be taxed, the form of cuftoms or excife is preferable to that of monopoly.

The revenue of cuftoms confifts in certain rates exacted for goods as they are paffing in commerce. They are exacted at toll-bars, at the entry to markets, at the gates of cities, or at fea ports.

The exaction of cuftoms, no doubt, is an interruption to commerce, and as fuch is avoided by nations whofe principal trade confifts in the carriage of goods.

Cuftoms are commonly advanced by the merchant, but confidered by him as a part in the coft of his goods, and to be recovered with profit in the fale of his commodity ; fo that taxes of

this

this fort actually fall upon the confumer. By either merchant or confumer, however, they are lefs felt as a grievance than any other form of taxation. The merchant fubmits to pay cuftom, becaufe he hopes to recover that and every other part of his advance with profit. The confumer is almoft infenfible of it, becaufe it is paid as a part of the price of the commodity, which he freely buys, and from the ufe of which he is free to refrain whenever he becomes unwilling to pay the price.

As goods in commerce pafs through a number of hands, and are paid for, fuccefsively by different traders, it is evident that the earlier any cuftom is paid to the revenue, in the tranfmiffion of articles from the hands of the producer to thofe of the confumer, the heavier will that duty fall on the latter, as he will be made to refund with profit the advance which every intermediate trader has made ; and the more will what he is made to pay, in confequence of a duty fo early advanced, exceed what actually paffes into the coffers of the ftate. To obviate this and fome other inconveniences, fuppofed peculiar to the revenue of cuftoms, the duties of excife have in fome cafes been preferred.

The excife, when ftated in contradiftinction to cuftoms, is a duty exacted from commodities in the actual ufe, and paid, not by the merchant, in any ftage of the trade, but by the confumer.

In this form of a duty, all interruptions to commerce are propofed to be avoided, and the duty fimply exacted from the confumer, without any accumulation of impofitions on the coft of the article. In nations, however, where the fubject is fond of his immunity,

nity or exemption from the controul and infpection of government, it is difficult to inftitute a revenue of excife, in the perfect
form of its definition, as *a tax levied from the confumer*. The
citizen expofed to fuch exaction would be aggrieved, in having
his dwelling always laid open to the intrufion of the revenue officer, and his manner of life fubjected to infpection. To avoid
thefe inconveniences, the excife in Great Britain is no more than
an approximation to the model propofed under this title. It is a
duty exacted not from the confumer, but from the producer or
laft vender of the commodity; who, on account of the profits to
be made by his trade, may fubmit to the inconvenience of having
it infpected.

Another occafion of diflike, which, in this ifland, is taken to the
revenues of excife, is more accidental. The firft duties of this
kind, that were fettled on the crown, were given in lieu of certain feudal rights which the king was entitled to exercife at difcretion; and it was thought reafonable that their equivalent
fhould be adminiftered in the fame manner with that part of
the former revenue for which it was fubftituted. It is accordingly adminiftered by a revenue board; and queftions that arife with
refpect to it, are decided by commiffioners, without admitting the
fubject to a trial at common law. The excife laws, accordingly,
being fuppofed lefs favourable to the people than thofe by which
their rights are adminiftered, in other inftances, are confidered
with peculiar diflike.

But apart from thefe confiderations which are peculiar to the
free fpirit of this conftitution, the merit of excife, like that of any
other tax impofed on commodities, whether levied by monopoly
or cuftoms, is meafurable by the nature of the commodity on
which

which the duty is paid.   It may be a tax either on the poor or on
the rich feparately, or on all the different ranks and conditions
of men, according to the degree in which they confume the commodity taxed.

No revenue can be confiderable, that is derived only from a few,
or from a particular clafs of the people.   In the choice of articles
to be taxed, therefore, fubjects of very general confumption, if
made to pay what even the poor can afford at the rate of their own
confumption, and which in the greater or increafing confumption
of the rich may amount to a payment proportioned to their fortunes, is no doubt the preferable object of taxation, whether in
this form of excife or any other.

SECTION

SECTION VI.

The fame fubject continued.

IN whatever manner a public revenue be conftituted, whether in all or any of the ways now mentioned, a queftion ftill remains, In what manner the public refources are to be applied to the occafional exigencies of the ftate ?

An ordinary expence is to be provided for, from fome ordinary fund ; but fudden or extraordinary occafions require fome immediate or extraordinary fupply ; and it is an important queftion in the adminiftration of public revenue, In what manner this fupply is to be obtained, whether by calling upon the fubject, at every particular emergency, to contribute proportionally to the occafion ; by having a treafure referved from the favings of an ordinary income ; or, laft of all, by anticipating a future revenue in money borrowed, and chargeable with intereft on fome public fund ?

There

There is no doubt that contributions proportioned to the occafion, if thefe could be always obtained, would be the moft proper and fafeft manner of accommodating revenue to the variable
exigencies of the ftate. In this manner, perfons entrufted with
government might be reftrained from engaging in projects of expence beyond their means or refources. Perpetual taxes would
not be impofed for temporary or precarious advantages; nor
would the errors of a paffing age leave, for a monument of its
mifconduct or misfortune, an unneceffary burden to be borne by
pofterity. But it may not be practicable, on every emergency,
and on thofe even the moft preffing, to find a fupply fully adequate to the occafion; and a nation thus trufting its fafety to
the fupply of the moment, would be expofed to much difadvantage, and even danger.

The occafions on which a people are likely to be called upon
to contribute moft largely, are the very times in which their
means are the moft likely to be impaired, or they themfelves precluded from the command of them. Such might be the cafe in
time of invafion by a foreign enemy; when lands are laid wafte;
when the ftock of the hufbandman and manufacturer is carried
off or deftroyed; or even in cafe of war at a diftance, or when the
channels of trade are obftructed or turned away from their ufual
courfe, and the returns of profit are interupted or rendered precarious. In all fuch cafes, no revenue fuddenly conftituted can
be equal to the occafion.

The provident ftatefman, therefore, we may fuppofe, would be
prepared for for fuch an emergence in one or other of the ways
we have mentioned; that is, he would manage his ordinary in-

come

come in fuch a manner as to have fome favings referved in his coffers to meet fuch extraordinary occafions ; or he would borrow upon credit from the few who are in condition to lend what the public may not then be in condition to advance ; but which it may be in condition to repay in a more favourable time.

The firft of thefe practices, in amaffing a treafure hath been adopted by fovereigns in many ftates both ancient and modern. It is peculiarly adapted to the character of a prince, who is able in ordinary times to ftretch the refources of his people to their utmoft, or who is entitled at difcretion to call upon them to contribute what he has not any immediate occafion to expend.

If indeed the ordinary revenue is fuch as the people can eafily fupply, and the faving proceeds rather from the moderation and wife oeconomy of the fovereign, than from his rapacity in extorting from the people more than is confiftent with their profperity to give ; in fuch a cafe, the formation of a treafure by public faving is unqueftionably a wife meafure, and fovereigns are entitled to refpect in proportion as they purfue it fteadily and fuccefsfully.

In purfuit of this meafure, however, it is affumed, that more may at all times be exacted from the people than there is any immediate or prefent occafion to expend; that a capital or ftock, equal to the public favings may be withdrawn from the lucrative trade of the fubject, and lie unemployed in the coffers of the ftate. But to withdraw any part of the public ftock, in this manner, from public ufe, is no doubt an inconvenience ; and it will be the more fenfibly felt, in proportion as the people are induftrious, and qua-

lified

lified to improve the stock in their hands, by employing it in the hire of useful labour.

The objections thus stated to either of the two former ways of administering a revenue, whether by making demands, on every emergency, proportioned to the occasion; or, by hoarding at one time what may be wanted at another, may be removed by adopting the method which has been mentioned in the third place, viz. that of borrowing a capital for any sudden or extraordinary case; and, by creating a fund, or imposing a tax no more than sufficient to pay the interest of the debt so contracted.

In this practice, the lender is tempted by the equitable or lucrative terms which are offered to him; the public is tempted by the convenience of obtaining great sums, adequate to the occasion, upon the credit of a small or inconsiderable tax, government, at the same time, reserving the option of paying up the capital at a convenient time, or leaving the fund allotted to pay the interest in a transferable form, all parties are fully accommodated.

The creditor, although the public debt should not be paid, may recover his capital at pleasure by the sale of his stock: But the continuance of this practice requires that the good faith of the public should be known, and a perfect confidence established in the security it has given. The practice is therefore most likely to succeed, where the people, by themselves or their representatives, have a share in the government, and are consulted particularly in what relates to the revenue of their country. As their consent is required to the levying of taxes, they are likely to prefer a small tax, though with the burden of a perpetual annuity, to heavy taxes for the present, without any such burden. Un-

3   der

der fuch conftitutions of government, while the public at large become debtor, fome part of that public alfo becomes the creditor, and in this capacity is deeply interefted in having the public faith ftrictly obferved.

By this expedient, nations are qualified, on great occafions, to make exertions proportioned to their credit, and may fometimes overwhelm an enemy of fuperior ftrength, whofe coffers are drained, and who has not an equal accefs to this refource.

For this reafon nations who have ample credit will ever be tempted to employ it, and proceed in accumulating debt fo long as the increafe of their wealth enables them to provide for the fupply of funds on which the public credit may be fecurely eftablifhed.

This policy, however is fuppofed liable to peculiar objection, and is indeed threatened with evils of a very ferious nature. It opens a new fpecies of trade in the transfer of public funds attended with profit and lofs to individuals, but unlike the employment of ftock in manufacture or commerce, which tends to the increafe of national wealth, it refembles rather the viciffitudes of a gaming table, turning the induftry and fkill of thofe concerned into inftruments of mutual deftruction, by which they would prey upon one another ; fo that, whoever gains, the public is fure to lofe to the amount of a labour which is fo mifapplied. The more that the public funds increafe, the more fcope is given to this ruinous branch of traffic ; and the ftreets of a capital, inftead of the concourfe of a bufy people, who are labouring to increafe the wealth of their country, exhibit crouds of adventurers who are haftening to partake of its fpoils. They lend, not

to

to accommodate their country, but to make profit on every occafion of public expence or calamity.

The ſtateſman, in the mean time, is tempted by the facility of
borrowing to be laviſh of the public credit. The monied men
encourage him, that they themſelves may have lucrative bargains;
and they from whom a tax is to be levied prefer a light burden
in which their poſterity is to bear a part, to one more heavy, of
which they themſelves muſt have borne the intire load.

A national debt may be increaſed almoſt inſenſibly, while the
means and the ſtrength of the people continue to grow ; but no
progreſs in human affairs is infinite, and whatever may be the
ſtrength of a people, a load that is continually growing muſt o-
verwhelm them at laſt; or, to ſpeak without a figure, the intereſt
of a debt that is continually accumulating muſt come in the end
to equal, or even to exceed, all the funds which can be found for
payment of its intereſt.

Upon this account, it is a wiſe policy to eſtabliſh ſome form, in
which a debt that is gradually increaſing, by recourſe to the public credit on every accidental occaſion, may alſo be gradually di-
miniſhing, in times of reſpite from every ſuch occaſion.

It may happen fortunately for nations in which the meaſure of
borrowing is adopted, that the intereſt of money, by the accumulation of unemployed capital, may be conſiderably reduced;
and in this caſe the public, by borrowing at a reduced intereſt to
pay off the original debt, may conſiderably diminiſh the annuity
which they were originally bound to pay. In this manner, while
the capital of the debt in Great Britain was increaſing, the an-
unity,

nuity, by a mere reduction of intereſt, was kept from increaſing, in the ſame proportion. An original intereſt, in ſome inſtances, of eight *per cent.* being reduced to three, it may happen that, while the capital of a debt is doubled, the annuity receives no in-creaſe, or may even be reduced.

So far, however, it appears from the whole of theſe obſerva-tions, that ſtates, in adopting any ſpecific form in the admini-ſtration of revenue, are expoſed to peculiar inconveniencies or dif-ficulties; and it is probable, that no two ſtates can with equal ad-vantage have recourſe to the ſame expedients. One ſtate may not be expoſed to any ſuch great or ſudden emergency as may not provide for by an effort made on the occaſion; and, in ſuch caſe, it is undoubtedly expedient to accommodate the ſupply to the ſervice for which it is wanted.

As every ſtate may to a certain extent proceed in this manner, and on many occaſions find a ſupply proportioned to the exi-gence of the caſe, it is undoubtedly wiſe, ſo far as is practicable, to accompany every emergence with a ſuitable proviſion, while, at the ſame time, care may be taken to have ſome treaſure reſerved in the coffers of the ſtate, for occaſions which cannot thus be provided for by occaſional ſupplies. Thus, the Romans who had repeatedly ſuffered under ſudden invaſions from the warlike na-tions of Gaulic extraction, reſiding within the Alps, had a ſacred treaſure reſerved, which it was deemed profane to touch, but in caſe of ſome ſuch alarm from that quarter as threatened the public with immediate deſtruction.

Notwithſtanding theſe maxims, it muſt alſo be admitted that, where ſtates are fortunately circumſtanced with reſpect to credit,

I

and,

and, by means of this advantage, are able to maintain their ſtate againſt nations otherwiſe-more powerful than themſelves, it were no doubt impolitic in them, to forgo their advantage, or to ſuffer themſelves to be overwhelmed, rather than employ a ſpecific means of defence which they in a particular manner have in their power.

But, without dwelling any longer on the compariſon of different forms for the adminiſtration of revenue, we may obſerve, that the wiſdom of any public expence is to be eſtimated by the occaſion on which it is made; and public profit or loſs from any adventure is to be meaſured by the return which it brings, whether adequate or unequal to the coſt.

An expence, in whatever manner it be provided for, whether by ſavings made of the paſt, or by anticipations of a future revenue; or, in whatever manner it be diſburſed, if it either were unneceſſary, or did not bring a proper return, is to be conſidered as an article of public loſs.

On the contrary, an expence which is neceſſary to public ſafety, or which brings an overbalance of gain, in whatever manner the ſupply be obtained, may be conſidered as part in the courſe of a proſperous nation. Not only poſitive acquiſitions, but loſſes avoided, and the maintenance of a people in their progreſſive courſe of improvement, may be ſtated in account againſt the debt which is incurred, and be ſufficient to create a balance in favour of the nation by whom it is contracted. Mere debt, therefore, is not to be conſidered as an article of loſs, or even inconvenience which the national gain may not amply compenſate. Nor are

we

we rashly to conclude, that a nation is the poorer for every article of debt it has contracted, until we have considered to what
effect the money so procured has been expended, and whether the
public advantages gained by means of it are fully adequate to the
risk and the cost.

At the same time, admitting this rule to be followed in the estimate of profit and loss, whether from money spent or borrowed,
the peculiar effect of a national debt contracted is merely to
transfer existing property or revenue, from the person who formerly consumed it, to a person who now receives it in the form
of interest for his money.   In this form, the property is at once
of use and transferable with more ease than in any other form
whatever.   To the stockholder it joins the convenience of a bank
with the profit of a mortgage, and is of great benefit to the trader
at every little interval at which his money is unemployed.   We
cannot doubt, therefore, apart from the advantage of credit in the
public operations of a people, that it is a public benefit also to
have part of the national property in this transferable form: How
much, it may be difficult to determine.   It may, no doubt, with
advantage, be increased to a certain degree; but not indefinitely.
And it is wise, as the public occasions may tend to accumulate
debt, that there should be a public regulation also, tending to
diminish it *.   In this manner, the balance of universal order is
beautifully preserved throughout the system of nature †.

Where

---

* As in the commission for managing a finking fund.

† The influx of rivers is balanced by evaporation from the sea; and the projectile
impulse of planets is circumscribed within certain bounds by central forces.

PART II.
CHAP. VI.
SECT.VII.

Where the money wanted cannot be raifed within the year, it may neverthelefs be raifed within a limited period, if the fund provided fhould be fufficient not only to pay the intereft, but alfo to extinguifh the debt within a fpecified time.

SECTION

SECTION VII.

Of Civil or Political Liberty.

THERE is a meaning annexed to liberty which is highly interefting to every ingenuous mind. Its votaries are fuppofed to
have a common caufe with their fellow creatures, and ever occupy a diftinguifhed rank in the lift of the heroes. It is thus that
Pelopidas and Thrafybulus, Dion, Cato, and Brutus, rife above
the level even of eminent men. It infpires magnanimity and noblenefs of mind; at the fame time, like every other object that
greatly concerns mankind, certain mifapprehenfions of it, or falfe
pretenfions to it, give occafion to great abufe. The zealot for liberty has run into the wildeft diforders; and adventurers, under
pretence of promoting it, have found their way to the moft violent and pernicious ufurpations *.

VOL. II.   M m m   On

* To this we afcribe the Tribunitian diforders at Rome, and the ufurpations of
Cæfar and Cromwell, &c.

On a fubject fo interefting, we are deeply concerned to have
juft information; and, as the fubftitution of a falfe idol for this
object of ardent devotion has led to fuch fatal extremes, we are
no lefs concerned to reprobate the idol with horror, than we are
with fond devotion to reverence the genuine object of worfhip;
and may very properly, in our way to the formation of a juft notion of liberty, begin our refearches by obferving what it is
not.

Far fetched knowledge is not the moft ufeful, either in the formation of theories, or in the conduct of life; and it is in the common courfe of things we muft look for the rule to direct us in
either.   It is alfo in the moft common or vulgar errors we have
to dread the greateft danger to the peace and welfare of mankind.
However perfons of reflection, therefore, may think it idle to
wafte time in correcting fuch errors, we muft attend to the
common notions of men, refpecting a matter in which the
plurality of voices may often prevail over reafon and good fenfe.
Upon this account we may be allowed to obferve, in the outfet,
that liberty or freedom is not, as the origin of the name may feem
to imply, an exemption from all reftraint, but rather the moft
effectual application of every juft reftraint to all the members of
a free ftate, whether they be magiftrates or fubjects.

It is under a juft reftraint only that every perfon is fafe, and
cannot be invaded, either in the freedom of his perfon, his property, or innocent action.   If any one were unreftrained, and
might do what he pleafed, to the fame extent alfo every one elfe
muft be expofed to fuffer whatever the free man of this defcription were inclined to inflict; and the very ufurpation of the moft
                                                    outrageous

outrageous tyrant is no more than a freedom thus affumed to
himfelf.

Under this miftake, the vulgar conceive a zeal for liberty to confift in oppofition to government; take part with every refractory fubject; and feem to think that whatever impairs the power of the magiftrate muft enlarge the freedom of the people. It is material, then, to remember that every perfon whatever, no lefs than the magiftrate, if not properly reftrained, may trefpafs on the liberty of his fellow creature; and that the eftablifhment of a juft and effectual government for the repreffion of crimes, is of all circumftances in civil fociety, the moft effential to freedom: That every one is juftly faid to be free in proportion as the government under which he refides is fufficiently powerful to protect him, at the fame time that it is fufficiently reftrained and limited to prevent the abufe of its power. This is the roof under which the free citizen takes fhelter from the ftorm of injuftice and wrong; and he is no lefs concerned to know that the roof is tight and fufficient to repel the ftorm, than he is to know that it is well fupported and fecured from falling on his head.

We are fafe, then, to define liberty, the operation of juft government, and the exemption from injury of any fort, rather than merely an exemption from reftraint; for it actually implies every juft reftraint. It muft be admitted, at the fame time, that to a being whofe active exertions are a principal fource of his enjoyments, reftraint, if capricious or unjuft, may be confidered among the firft of his grievances; and there is no infringement of liberty more fenfibly felt than a teazing impofition of frivolous obfer-

M m m 2   vances,

vances, or an arbitrary reſtraint impoſed on the harmleſs purſuits of an ordinary life.

It is highly grateful to the human mind to purſue its innocent courſe undirected and uncontroulled.   It is even flattered with the imagination of romantic ſcenes, in which nature is free; not bound to any taſk; not reſponſible to any authority; not hampered by any forms; and left to purſue the object of the moment ·in the way that the preſent moment ſuggeſts.   This we conceive to be the ſtate of the ſavage in his foreſt, connected only with the ob-jects of his affection or choice; and, even in his engagements with thoſe he loves, releaſed from any ſenſe of awe, controul, or reſtraint, whatever.

From this ſtate of ſuppoſed perfect freedom, we apprehend that every ſtep which is made towards a political eſtabliſhment muſt be to the individual a ſurrender of ſome original right; but we are diſpoſed to apologiſe for the conceſſion a free citizen has made, by ſtating the ſacrifice of a part as neceſſary to ſecure the remainder.

Liberty, therefore, if moſt perfect in the condition of the ſavage, it ſhould ſeem from this account of the matter, is at leaſt inſecure; and this circumſtance overthrows the very idea of that freedom which conſiſts in the ſecure enjoyment of rights. The ſavage may, if he will, retire from the haunts of his fellow creatures, and avoid them as he himſelf is avoided by thoſe animals of which he is diſpoſed to make a prey.   But, while he lives within reach of o-ther men, he himſelf if weak may be a prey to the ſtrong; or, if individually ſtrong, he may ſtill be a prey to numbers, if per-chance they ſhould combine againſt him.   His freedom, then, is preciſely no more than a privilege to deny himſelf all the com-

2   forts

forts of a man, in order to avoid the inconveniencies of a dangerous neighbourhood: Or, if security be necessary to liberty, in what manner, we may ask, can he at once possess and secure his comforts? Only by the concert of many, mutually to defend one another, and for this purpose to act under a common direction. This, in other words, is to form a political establishment; and so far mankind universally proceed to adopt some species of polity upon the suggestion of nature, or the early lessons of experience in ages otherwise rude.

Now, it may be asked, what has the individual surrendered in coming under such an establishment? the freedom of retiring from his kind, shall we say, and of relinquishing all the comforts of society? But this he has in fact no where surrendered. This sort of freedom is still entire to the citizen of London and Paris, as much as to the original inhabitant of Canada or Labrador. But the subject of any regular government will scarcely think it a privilege that he may, if it so please him, relinquish all the comforts and securities of life under the notion of recovering the original freedom of his kind. Security, in fact, is the essence of freedom; and, if security is to be obtained under political establishment alone, there alone also is freedom obtained: and, in repairing to this shelter, when properly instituted, the savage surrenders nothing, or rather in the acquisition of security acquires every thing.

Freedom or liberty, then, we may conceive to be the genuine fruit of political establishment: But, where the fruit is wanting, the tree is justly accursed for its barrenness, or torn up by the roots for its yielding a poison instead of a wholesome food. When liberty is considered as the cause of the innocent against the guilty, or of the weak against the strong, and awakens the heart against

against infult and wrong, we may eafily account for the ardent and enthufiaftic affection with which it is embraced by every ingenuous mind. Mere reftraint, however injurious, is but one fpecies of wrong, and would form but a partial account of the e- vils which render the tyrant fo much an object of indignation to mankind.

But to the negative propofition thus ftated, that liberty does not confift in mere exemption from reftraint, we may fubjoin ano- ther, That it does not confift in the equality of ftation or fortune. In this fenfe, liberty were a mere chimera or vifion, never realiz- ed in the ftate of mankind. The nations who contended moft for the equality of citizens, in admitting the inftitution of flavery, trefpaffed moft egregioufly on the equality of mankind.

Nay, but we fhall be told, that all men were originally equal. This, in regard to property, can mean only, that, when no one had any thing, all men were equally rich: But even this is no more than fancied equality in a fingle point. In refpect to fex and age, ftrength of body and mind, individuals are deftined to inequality from their birth; and, almoft in the firft fteps of fociety, bear the diftinctions which induftry and courage give in the different at- tainments of men, and lead in the fequel to all the varieties of profeffion and fortune.

The only refpect in which all men continue forever to be equal, is that of the equal right which every man has to defend him- felf; but this involves a fource of much inequality in refpect to the things which any one may have a right to defend. As every one originally had a right to preferve himfelf in the juft ufe of his limbs, organs, and faculties, he has alfo a right to what thefe

may

may juftly procure for him ; he has a right to engage himfelf in any bargain or compact, and to ftipulate for himfelf any fair condition ; he has a right to acquire by his labour any unappropriated fubject, or any fubject appropriated with confent of the former proprietor. In the exercife of thefe rights, the conditions of men, whether in refpect to poffeffions, or in refpect to their mutual conceffions or claims of fervice, may become unequal to any fair amount; and it is not poffible to prevent the inequality of condition in the fortunes of men, without violating the firft and common principles of right in the moft flagrant manner.

Whilft we admit, therefore, that all men have an equal right to defend themfelves, we muft not miftake this for an affumption that all men muft have equal things to defend, or that liberty fhould confift in ftripping the induftrious and the fkilful, who may have acquired much, to enrich the lazy and profligate, who may have acquired nothing, or who may have wafted all they could reach. It is impoffible to reftrain the influence of fuperior ability, of property, of education, or the habits of ftation. It is impoffible to prevent thefe from becoming in fome degree hereditary ; and of confequence it is impoffible, without violating the principles of human nature, to prevent fome permanent diftinction of ranks : And, if this were poffible, it is far from expedient in the circumftances of human life. In thefe inequalites we find the firft germe of fubordination and government fo neceffary to the fafety of individuals and the peace of mankind ; and in thefe alfo we find the continued incentive to labour and the practice of lucrative arts.

As liberty confifts in the communication of fafety to all, nothing could be more repugnant to it than the violation of right in any part, in order to level the whole. It is true that great inequalities

I   of of fortune are adverfe to fome fpecies of political inftitution ; that great diftinctions of rank, founded in birth alone, to the exclufion of merit, or to the fuppreffion of all the efforts of diftinguifhed ability in public fervice, is a corruption fatal to mankind ; that unreftrained poffeffion of arbitrary power of any fort, is for the fake of liberty and juftice, to be carefully watched and ftopped fhort of the extreme to which it may tend: But, as every one has a right to the condition in which, by the ordinary courfe of human nature, he is fairly placed, in which he is no way injurious to his fellow creatures, it muft follow that liberty, in every particular inftance, muft confift in fecuring the fairly acquired conditions of men, however unequal.

Diftinctions of fortune may give rife to a feparation of ariftocratic and popular factions, or a fuppofed oppofition of interefts, in the different orders of a people ; and we will have occafion to obferve that neither is fafe without fuch a fhare in the government as may enable them to defend themfelves, or put a negative on any meafures which might be prejudicial to their refpective interefts. Both the high and the low, however, frequently afpire to the government of their country. The one is faid to contend for authority, fubordination, and power; the other for liberty, immunity, or privilege : But liberty is far from being fafe in the exclufive prevalence of either. This will not be difputed relating to the unreftrained prevalence of ariftocratic authority. But it is no lefs true, that liberty does not confift in the prevalence of democratic power. The violence of popular affemblies and their tumults need to be reftrained, no lefs than the paffions and ufurpations of any other power whatever ; and there is indeed no fpecies of tyranny under which individuals are lefs fafe than under that of a majority or prevailing faction of a corrupted people.

From

From thefe obfervations, upon the whole, it appears, that liberty confifts in the fecurity of the citizen againft every enemy, whether foreign or domeftic, public or private, from whom, without
any provifion being made for his defence, he might be expofed to
wrong or oppreffion of any fort : And the firft requifite, it fhould
feem, towards obtaining this fecurity, is the exiftence of an ef-
fective government to wield the ftrength of the community againft
foreign enemies, and to reprefs the commiffion of wrongs at
home.   Under this protection, indeed, there may be danger
from the very power which is eftablifhed to afford it ; but, without fome fuch provifion, there cannot be any degree of fafety
whatever.

In purfuing this idea of liberty, therefore, through the feveral
circumftances that may be neceffary to give it reality and effect,
we have to confider, in the firft place, what may be neceffary to
give an eftablifhment efficacy in reftraining the diforder of the
fubject : Next, what precautions may be neceffary in the inftitution of power, to prevent the abufes that may be apprehended in the difcharge of its functions.

Thefe functions, we may conceive under three feparate titles,
legiflation, *jurifdiction*, and the *execution of the law*, or *conduct
of the national force*.   And, correfponding to thefe functions,
in every political eftablifhment, three diftinct powers may be
confidered ; namely, the *legiflative*, the *judicative*, and the *executive*.   With refpect to each of thefe, liberty requires that the
powers fhould be effectual to the eftablifhment and prefervation
of order on the part of the fubject, and that it fhould be fo exer-

VOL. II.   N n n   cifed

cifed on the part of the magiftrate, as not to offer any injuftice or wrong to the people.

In farther treating of liberty, therefore, we are to confider the inftitutions of government required for the difcharge of the principal functions now enumerated, and providing at the fame time for the efficacy of power, and the fafety of thofe who might be expofed to fuffer from its abufe.

SECTION

S E C T I O N   VIII.

Of Liberty as it may be affected by the Exercise of the Legiſlative Power.

LAW is the ſovereign will to which every part of the commu- PART II.
nity muſt conform itſelf.   That power, therefore, whether ſingle CHAP. VI.
or combined of many parts, which gives law to the community, SECT. VIII.
muſt be ſupreme ; and, when its will is declared, cannot admit
of any controul, without a diſſolution of the political frame.

Upon this ground, liberty ſeems to require that every member
of the commonwealth ſhould have acceſs, before the law is enacted, to guard himſelf againſt any wrongs to which he may be expoſed from the admiſſion of any partial regulation ; or, in other
words, that the people of every ſeparate order or rank, however
diſtinguiſhed by fortune, ſhould each have an active ſhare in the
legiſlature of their country.

At

At the fame time, if this be admitted, it fhould feem to follow that liberty muft be confined to a few democratical ftates, in which alone it is poffible to comply with this condition. And fo indeed, among antient nations, liberty was fuppofed peculiar to republics, and to thofe efpecially in which the fovereignty was exercifed by the collective body of the people. Upon this ground, the republics of Greece and Italy were, with a few exceptions, diftinguifhed from the reft of the world.

But the practice of reprefentation, fo happily introduced in fome modern nations, though not of fo great extent as to admit of their people being collectively affembled, has removed this difficulty, and enabled every order of the ftate, if not collectively, at leaft by deputation, to take a part in the legiflature of their country, and to have a vigilant eye on the proceedings of the whole.

What renders this expedient, of trufting the interefts of many to a few, a fufficient fecurity to the people who rely on it, is that their reprefentative, by being a perfon of the fame mind and intereft with themfelves, and himfelf included in every act of legiflation, is likely to proceed as his conftituents would do in his place. In whatever manner the reprefentative be fingled out, if he bear thefe qualifications, human nature does not feem, in ftates of confiderable extent, to admit of any greater fecurity to liberty than this.

It may be thought that election is the moft likely, if not the only way of fecuring thefe qualifications in the perfon who is to reprefent the people; but, if the roll of the citizens be fufficiently purged of all perfons unfit or unworthy to partake in the legiflature

lature of their country, the reprefentative might no doubt without any danger be drawn by lot.

But here we may be told, " That more is required to com-
" plete the advantage of a form in which citizens act by repre-
" fentation: That it is not enough the reprefentative partake in
" the intereft of thofe he reprefents: That he ought to feel him-
" felf in the exercife of a truft committed to him by the confi-
" dence and good will of his fellow-citizens, and be led to act
" from affection in return for their efteem." This, indeed, however little it may be neceffary to fecure his regard for an intereft
in which he himfelf partakes, is the true ftate of a man and a citizen acting for the welfare of his country.

With this, alfo, it may farther be urged, " That every ftatute
" being a treaty or act of convention between the parties con-
" cerned, and, like any other compact, is binding only upon
" thofe who in perfon, or by their commiffioners, have given
" their affent; the reprefentative muft have an exprefs commiffion
" or deputation, entitling him to bind his conftituents before he
" can fubject them to any condition in the form of law; and that
" in acts of legiflation, every individual has a right to name his
" reprefentative, or, if this right be withheld from him, that he is
" not bound by any deed which may follow."

Upon this plea of abfolute right in every individual to be bound
only by his own affent, it fhould be allowed that, prior to convention, a people cannot be bound to any act in which they are not
unanimous. Where any individual diffents, he does more than
withhold his agreement, he declares a repugnance: But when a
plea thus amounts to fomething that has never been realized in the

3   hiftory

hiftory of mankind, ftill more, if its object be fuch as cannot be
realized, there is reafon not only to doubt its validity, but actually
to confider it as altogether nugatory and abfurd.

Laws are every where acknowledged to be binding on perfons
who are never called upon to give their affent, either by themfelves or their reprefentatives. And where it is propofed to have
a general affent, ftill the affemblies which are held for this purpofe are partial, and far from admitting every fubject, without
exception, for whom the law is to be made. One of the fexes,
though by nature vefted with every right; and a great part of the
other fex, upon an arbitrary diftinction of nonage *, are excluded
altogether ; many are kept away by difability of health or decline
of age; yet, it never was fuppofed, in any cafe whatever, that
thefe are to have a difpenfation from the law. Even of the few
who attend deliberative or elective affemblies, it feldom happens
that the whole is unanimous. And if the majority in fact
overule the minority, this prior to convention is a mere effect of
power, not matter of right. The majority is no more than a government *de facto*, until the people at large, finding their account
in the obfervance of fome fuch rule, and every individual, in his
turn, availing himfelf of his advantage in being of the majority,
by his acquiefcence, gives it a right of convention in the fame
manner as any other actual government receives the fanction of
compact, and becomes binding on thofe who avail themfelves
of the benefit it beftows.

3   Prior

* The period of nonage has been varied from 18 to 21 and 25 years, and is in
reality arbitrary. One perfon may have more fenfe under 20 than another at 40 or 60,
or any other time of his life ; but, as children are incapable of public truft, it is neceffary that there fhould be a rule in this matter to which all muft conform.

Prior to convention, every one has a right to govern himfelf; but not to govern any one elfe. The government of others, then, prior to convention, is not matter of right to any one; although to have government, and this purged of every perfon incapable or unworthy of the truft, is matter of expedience to every one. And under every wife political eftablifhment it becomes a queftion, who may be fafely entrufted with legiflative power? for furely the indifcriminate right of every one, whether capable and worthy, or incapable and unworthy, cannot by any means be admitted.

While we fuppofe the people, therefore, to partake in the legiflature of their country, whether collectively or by reprefentation, a variety of queftions are ftill open to difcuffion:

1ft, Who are to be admitted on the rolls of the people, and to have a deliberative or elective voice?

2d, In the cafe of a people too numerous to meet in any one body, in what divifions are they to act?

Thefe queftions, even under eftablifhments the moft favourable to public liberty, have been decided as chance would have it. In all the ancient republics, the clafs of free citizens was but a fmall part of the whole number that was fubject to the law. At Athens, the moft democratical of all the ancient republics, not a third; and at Rome, ftill in a fmaller proportion. Even the citizens, fo reduced in their proportion to the whole number of men in the community, were never in fact collectively affembled. At Athens, of about two hundred and eighty four thoufand fouls, including free citizens, aliens, and flaves, no more than five thoufand commonly met in the Ecclefia or national affembly; a proportion
rather

rather to be confidered as a reprefentation than a collective body. At Rome, the people difperfed over the country towns and the provinces were, in the fame manner alfo, cafually reprefented in the comtia by fuch as frequented the ftreets of the capital. In the cafe of Athens, fo far as concerned the free citizens, being about 84,000, the reprefentation may have been adequate and fafe : Five thoufand citizens, inhabitants of the city, cafually taken from the whole, and making laws for themfelves and the community, were no way likely to invade the rights of the multitude ; although, from their democratical fpirit, they too often invaded the rights of particular citizens, diftinguifhed by their fortunes, or even by their merit. The cafual reprefentation which took place at Rome was much lefs adequate or fafe. The diforderly inhabitants of the town gave law to their fellow citizens as well as to their fubjects and allies of the provinces.

In modern Europe, we are every where happily rid of that diftinction of free man and flave, which in antient times excluded fo many of the human fpecies at once from any means of defending themfelves, in forming the laws to which they were fubject. But even here, and where the fpirit of political eftablifhment is moft favourable to public liberty, there are ftill confiderable exclufions from the political meetings of the people, whether for police or election. Not to mention again the exclufion of women and children, there is in every country a diftinction of denizen and alien, by which many inhabitants are excluded from any fhare in the government to which they are fubject. In the little canton of Schweitz, the mafter and his fervant unyoke their team, and go to the national affembly together : But ftill the alien inhabitant muft abide by refolutions in which he has no part. In the firft attempts of the French Revolution to equalize the rights of men, a certain though

a

a very fmall *cenfus* was required, to entitle the citizen to a vote at elections. In a fubfequent appointment this cenfus was dropped; but ftill thofe who are to be governed by the law exercife their dif- cretion, and menial fervants are excluded. In Great Britain, a cer- tain cenfus * is required, together with fome circumftances of free- hold and burgefs qualification. And even, notwithftanding thefe qualifications, certain officers of the executive power, as being dependant on a part of the community diftinct from the com- mons, are, by recent laws, excluded from a vote at the election of commoners to ferve in parliament. But, notwithftanding thefe exclufions, the liberty of the fubject is more fecure perhaps than it ever has been under any other human eftablifhment. And if any one plead that, being excluded from a vote at elections, he is not bound by the laws to which the people affent by reprefentation, his plea may be admitted, and he is at liberty to withdraw from the influence of thefe laws: But, while he remains within the precincts to which they extend, and continues to take the benefit of them, he is not at liberty to counteract or to difturb the order of things efta- blifhed. The public, to avoid a fpecial difcuffion of the franchifes of every individual; and the return of fuch difcuffions, on every par- ticular occafion, have fettled general rules for the better government of the country: And, if thefe rules carry an exclufion to any indivi- dual, he neverthelefs owes to that law the fame obedience that he owes

Vol. II.   O o o   to

---

* Diftinctions of rank, for the moft part, are taken from birth or property; and we may cenfure the rule, but cannot reverfe it. It is even fortunate for mankind that a foundation of fubordination is laid, too obvious to be overlooked by the dulleft of men, or by thofe who ftand moft in need of being governed. But, though property fometimes overpower both ability and every other merit, yet there are occafions in which it muft give way to either. At elections and country meetings, men of for- tune predominate; but armies are commanded, and ftates are governed by men of ability.

to every other law of which he enjoys the effect and protection.

But, in respect to these exclusions, and in respect to other particulars, in matters of particular form, there is a considerable latitude, within which varieties are found that do not essentially affect the liberties of mankind. As to the separate divisions, in particular, in which a numerous people may assemble for any purpose of state, they have for the most part been casual; as were the tribes or Curiæ at Rome; the tythings, hundreds, parishes, counties, and borroughs, in Great Britain. Such divisions may be unequal; and yet, in perfect consistence with freedom, have equal voice in the deliberative or elective proceedings of their country. The liberties of mankind do not totter upon a single point of support: They make for themselves a large and capacious base, under a variety of forms, in which men still find themselves in condition to defend their rights. All that can be said in the matter is, that, if any people were to make up anew the rolls of their citizens, or to set off the divisions in which they were to act, the rolls ought to be made up with the fewest exclusions, and the divisions set off with the greatest equality, consistent with reason and public safety. Where people indeed act by representation, their liberty depends more upon the character of the representative, than upon the form of proceeding, or the number of persons who are admitted to vote at elections; and when this matter is settled upon any footing that is safe, stability is of more consequence than any advantage

to

* Humanum est errare.

to be gained by change. Too much fluctuation, or frequent tranſition from one ſet of rules to another, is, of all circum- ſtances, the leaſt conſiſtent with that ſenſe of ſecurity in which the poſſeſſion and enjoyment of liberty conſiſts.

SECTION

S E C T I O N   IX.

Of the Judicative Power.

PART II.
CHAP. VI.
SECT. IX.

IT is congenial to the nature of intelligent being, that the scene in which he is to act should be governed by fixed and determinate laws, either obvious, or scrutable by the faculties with which he is furnished. Such, accordingly, is the scene prepared for man in the system of nature.

It is also essential to the liberties of a people, that their rights should be defined in well known and permanent regulations, from which the citizen may know his condition, without consulting the caprice or uncertain will of any person whatever. As for this purpose there is required a legislature the most likely to form impartial laws, so also is required a judicature the most likely to give these laws their proper effect.

In

In whatever manner the powers of ftate be diftributed, that which gives law to the whole, we have obferved, muft be fupreme; and though, by this circumftance, the legiflative power cannot admit of controul, either in the application or interpretation of its own enactments, yet it is perhaps by this very circumftance, in ordinary cafes, difqualified to exercife, in confiftence with the fafety of the people, either the judicative or executive powers.

It were dangerous to allow of any latitude or any exercife of difcretion, in the application of law. This is the tenure by which every citizen holds his right; and it were nugatory to fay, that the tenure of law were fecure, if it might be interpreted and applied at difcretion. But it is impoffible to feparate the idea of difcretionary power from that of the fovereign or fupreme legiflature. Perfons invefted with fovereignty, and inured to command, will not eafily fubmit to be reftrained by rules which, though juft in the principle, may, in particular cafes, appear inexpedient. The difcretion that was exercifed in framing the law will incline even thofe by whom it was framed, under the influence of fentiments or paffions that may arife on particular occafions, to difpenfe with the rule which they themfelves had enacted. And if the law be departed from, in any cafe whatever, the citizen is fo far aggrieved, or becomes infecure of his tenure.

If the legiflature be compofed of members collected from the different orders of the community, as the fafety of thefe differeut orders feem to require, there is indeed, even from fuch affemblage of powers concentrated in the fame affembly, lefs abufe to be apprehended in the application as well as enactment of

2   the

the law.   But fuch numerous affemblies are peculiarly apt to
enter into the paffions and interefts of a particular cafe, to com-
municate paffion by contagion, and to become eager in the
purfuit of any object, by mere fympathy or participation of zeal ;
fo that one or other of the parties, to whom a law fhould apply,
in a particular cafe, may be liable to fuffer by the heat or paffion of a moment, a tenure which of all others is the leaft fecure
by which any right can be held.

A perfon may be qualified to hold a place in the legiflature of
his country, by merely partaking in the intereft or concern of the
order or clafs of men he reprefents, or of which he makes a part;
and he may provide for the fafety of his conftituents, by refufing
his affent to whatever is inconfiftent with his own : But to exercife the office of judge, more may be neceffary ; an equal concern
for the rights of all parties, and an adequate knowledge of the
laws in which thofe rights are defined.

Where the laws, therefore, are greatly multiplied, as is generally the cafe under inftitutions of freedom, the ftudy of law becomes the object of a feparate profeffion ; every one, whofe right
in a particular cafe is brought to the teft of law, has recourfe to
the affiftance of learned counfel ; and, as in the conteft of parties
each may have recourfe to partial counfel, it is neceffary that the
public alfo fhould have counfel retained for law and juftice.

Such we may conceive to be the character in which official
judges are appointed, under every well regulated government.

As judgement, in any one inftance, may be fubject to error,

2   or

or incline to abufe, it is proper that there fhould be courts of
appeal, and means of review; or, in cafe of apprehended corruption, it is proper that the official judge fhould be refponfible
to fome tranfcendant jurifdiction which may take cognizance
of his conduct, and reftrain a crime which would involve the
whole community at once in its confequences. Here the legiflature itfelf muft interpofe; and, if for no other reafon than this,
ought not, in the previous fteps of a fuit, to charge itfelf with
the functions of judicative power.

In legiflation, citizens affemble with a profeffed intention to
promote or to guard their own interefts, or thofe of their refpective orders; and, even in the exercife of judicative power, it
may not be poffible to exclude the confideration of peculiar interefts, even from thofe who fit in judgement on the rights of
fellow citizens: But, if any intereft is to be admitted in the
tribunals of juftice, it fhould certainly be no other than the general intereft of the people at large; an intereft which is equivalent to juftice itfelf; which requires that no right fhould be
violated, or that no violation of right fhould efcape punifhment.

This, in fact, is an intereft which the impartial citizen has in
every queftion of law. If crimes may be committed, and a wrong
may be done to any one, it may be done to himfelf. If an innocent perfon may fuffer under pretence of a criminal charge, fuch
a charge, in the next inftance, may be brought againft himfelf.
If crimes are not reftrained, or if criminals are fuffered to efcape,
the innocent citizen may confider every criminal fo difcharged as
an enemy let loofe againft himfelf and his family.

It

It appears, then, that a perfon fo affected is equally qualified for the judicative as for the legiflative truft : He has every inducement to judge fairly, to the utmoft of his ability, in every queftion of civil or penal jurifdiction. He may need the affiftance of learned counfel, or of the official judge, in directing the forms of procedure, in bringing queftions to iffue, or in pronouncing the fentence of law; but, where evidence is brought before him, and the circumftances of a cafe are fairly ftated, he is fully competent, as in the ordinary affairs of human life, to perceive the reality of a fact, or to pronounce of a deed that has been done, whether it be guilt or innocence.

Such, indeed, is the defcription and function of juries in the tribunals of fome modern nations, who have fortunately in this inftance refined on the practice of feudal eftablifhments, by which queftions of right or criminal charge, in particular inftances, were referred to the judgement of a few felect men from the vicinage. The occafional tribunal fo compofed is termed a Jury, becaufe its members are fworn to determine truly in the queftions which come to be tried before them. The oath of the juror may no doubt be held in part a fecurity for the truth of his verdict; and a like fecurity might be had, by adminiftering a fimilar oath to the official judge: But the fpecific fecurity which is had in this cafe arifes, not from the fanction of an oath, but from the character and condition of the juror equally interefted in civil queftions, to fupport every right, and to reftrain every wrong, and, in penal queftions, to protect the innocent, however accufed, and to punifh the guilty, however fupported.

That

That this character, indeed, may be realized in every inftance, it is proper that a lift, collected indifcriminately from the vicinage in which any queftion has arifen, fhould be purged of all partial counfel, by challenge of the magiftrate or of the parties concerned, until they who are inclofed for trial fhall be free from any exception, whether of reafon or namelefs diftruft, that may lie againft them.

PART II. CHAP. VI. SECT. IX.

Men taken, for the occafion, from the mere ordinary walks of life, may be ill qualified to unravel the intricacies of of a judicial cafe; but, in this, it is the function of the official judge to affift them. Law is devifed for the people; and as, in the accumulation of its forms, there may be introduced a number of technical terms, with which lawyers alone are familiar, it is right that in every particular trial they fhould be brought back, if poffible, to the ufe of a language which all men underftand. This is the tenure by which every citizen holds his right; and it is proper that it fhould not be wrapped up in obfcurities. The official judge partakes in the magiftracy, and may be infected with its fpecific prepoffeffions againft the fubject. If his conduct occafion any fufpicion of this fort, the power of a jury is on this account alfo wifely interpofed to prevent its effects. And upon the whole we may venture to affume, that a tribunal fo conftituted gives to the citizen, in the poffeffion and exercife of his rights, all the fecurity which it is poffible to obtain through the medium of any human eftablifhment.

After all, it is poffible that, in thus attempting to fix canons of eftimation in matters of political inftitution, we may be partial to thofe of our own country, and miftake the forms to

VOL. II.   P p p   which

PART II.
CHAP. VI.
SECT. IX.
which we ourſelves are accuſtomed for the models of reaſon and
wiſdom. It is, however, fortunate for a country to have inſtitutions which can be ſo miſtaken by thoſe who experience
their effects.

SECTION

[S E C T I O N   X.

Of the Executive Power.

WHEN a people is orderly, and affairs proceed with little interpofition of government, we may be apt to imagine that they
might do without it : But the happieft effect of government is
to prevent diforders, not to redrefs them.   And when we confider the mixture of ill difpofition, folly, or miftake, that is ever inherent to human nature, the more probable inference from the cafe
of a people at reft, is, not that government is needlefs, but that they
are well or happily governed. The citizen muft not imagine that
law is unneceffary to him, becaufe he has not had any occafion
to recur to its protection. This want of occafion is itfelf the greateft proof of its energy. Were this energy witheld for a moment, the
fmalleft leaven of depravity, in any part of the fociety, would foon
deftroy the peace of the whole ; and, by a licence to crimes on
the one hand, and to private refentment on the other, would foon
make a fcene of confufion and riot.   Even where the inclination

to evil is leaft frequent, if it actually exift in any part, the whole muft be on their guard.

Among the advantages to be reaped from fociety, therefore, one, and a principle one, is, That numbers of innocent men, by uniting their forces, may be fecure of their rights to a degree that could not be obtained by any fingle perfon acting alone for himfelf. Under fuch combination properly directed, the community is fecure againft any foreign enemy, and the individual is fecure againft any wrongs to which he is expofed from the commiffion of crimes.

To wield the national force for thefe purpofes is the office of executive power ; and the citizen knows not of any confideration more effential to his liberty, than that there fhould be fuch a power fully adequate to the purpofe for which it is eftablifhed. It is like the roof, by which thofe who take fhelter under it are protected from the ftorm: It is the moft effential part of their dwelling, and for the fupport of which the walls and other parts of the building are chiefly contrived.

It were a great error, therefore, in the zealot for liberty, to fet himfelf againft the formation of an executive government, fufficient to combine the ftrength of the people, and to enforce the obfervance of juftice in every part of the community.

At the fame time, if we fuppofe that a power which is eftablifhed for thefe purpofes were employed to violate the rights it ought to protect, there is no cafe more fatal to the liberties of the people : For, on this fuppofition, the arm which ought to defend is itfelf the force that invades. The remedy is become the difeafe;
and

and the roof, under which shelter is taken from a storm, threatens a ruin more dreadful than the storm it was intended to repel.

In respect to the executive power, therefore, in whatever form it be established, it is equally the interest of the citizen that it should be irresistible in every act of justice, and that it should be restrained in every commission of wrong. And in this consists the great problem of political wisdom for securing the liberties of the people, which are equally exposed in the licence of the subject against the magistrate, as in the licence of the magistrate against the subject.

Of the functions of executive power, some are in continual exertion; others, whether casual or periodical, are only occasional. Some require great secrecy and dispatch; others admit of being publicly known, and may be the better directed for having been publicly discussed.

Functions of so different a nature may be discharged with advantage, by powers differently constructed, and under different forms of proceedure.

Matters of an ordinary and public concern, such as the administration of revenue, or the internal policy and government of a country, may be treated of in numerous councils, and taken up at regular periods, or at any convenient times.

Affairs that may come by surprise, and that require dispatch, may be committed to single men, as they are, in republics of small extent, commonly entrusted to magistrates elected at determinate periods: And, in such cases, the abuses of power may be guard-

2

ed

ed againſt by limiting its adminiſtration, as at Venice, or by ſhortening its duration, as in other ſmall republics of Italy.

It being the intereſt of the citizen, that the executive government employed in the defence of his rights ſhould, in that exerciſe of it, be altogether irreſiſtible ; it is required, of courſe, that no other perſon within the ſtate, no faction or partial combination whatever, ſhould be able to withſtand the power of the magiſtrate when fairly exerted.

In republics uncorrupted, the elective magiſtrate is, by the reſpect which every citizen bears to the majeſty of the common-wealth, ſufficiently ſupported to enable him to ſuppreſs every diſorder to which any private faction or party may be inclined.

But, in republics greatly corrupted, faction and party often become too powerful for the legal authority, and the private citizen is ſometimes expoſed to injuries which the uſual forms of the ſtate cannot reſtrain.   To remedy the defects of government, in ſuch caſes, the people have had recourſe to the temporary eſtabliſhment of extraordinary powers, as that of the decemvirs, or of dictators, at Rome.   But, in times of great corruption, the remedy has proved worſe than the diſeaſe.   The decemvirs abuſed and attempted to prolong their diſcretionary power, and the dictatorſhip ended in the uſurpation of perpetual deſpotiſm:—An emergence, indeed, which among many others in a corrupted ſtate may appear at the inſtant to be the leaſt of its evil ; as at Rome, the uſurpation of Cæſar may have appeared a leſs evil than the dangerous tumults which were employed in the conteſts of Clodius and Milo.

2   In

In ftates of the greateft extent, the citizen, either by himfelf PartII. or his reprefentative, may have fuch a fhare in the legiflature as Sect. X. may fecure him from any encroachment on his rights in the form of law; but, without a fufficient executive power, he may not be fecure of the right which law confers upon him; or he may fuffer from the crimes which become frequent under the licence which attends a weak government.

In great empires, there is a danger of difunion and difmemberment of provinces, as well as diforder and licence of individuals; and, to preferve the peace and give effect to the laws, in every corner of fuch a dominion, it is perhaps neceffary to veft the executive power with all the prerogatives and influence of monarchy, and to take in aid of its authority whatever is fit even to impofe upon the imaginations of men, the luftre of birth, the fplendour of a court, as well as extenfive patronage, and the command of a military force. So armed, the fovereign may be able to reprefs every diforder, and to overcome the refiftance of any party, or combination that may be formed to difturb the public peace. And with thefe advantages, no doubt, he may be in condition to preferve the rights of the citizen; but he may alfo, if not properly reftrained, be in condition to invade thofe rights; and hence the difficulty of arming the executive power with adequate force, and at the fame time of referving a fufficient fecurity againft the abufe of that force, or to eftablifh fuch a relation between the executive and legiflative powers, as that neither fhall, without proceeding to violence, encroach upon the functions or rights of the other; or that, in cafe of violence, the moft daring ufurpation fhould feel itfelf weak in proportion as it ventures to fhock the general fenfe of the people.

For

For the firſt of theſe purpoſes, it is neceſſary that every branch of the legiſlature ſhould have all the power that is neceſſary to preſerve its own privileges; ſhould be perfectly free and unawed in its deliberations; and, though not in condition to obtain every article of law that may be propoſed for its own advantage, that it ſhould have a negative upon every article from which it apprehends a diminution of its rights.   So far alſo it is proper that the executive power ſhould have a voice in the legiſlature; or, in other words, that to prevent encroachments upon its juſt prerogative, or any diimnution of that energy which ought to be exerted for the ſafety of the people, it ought to have a negative upon every act that may tend to ſuch conſequence.

It is eſſential to liberty, that, in matters to which the foreſight of legiſlature can reach, the operations of power ſhould be nothing more than the execution of law.

In reſpect to this object, wherever the people of every denonomination, by themſelves or their repreſentatives, have a deliberative and negative voice in the legiſlature, they ſeem to have all the ſecurity that human nature can give: In the firſt place, a ſecurity that there ſhall be laws, according to which the executive power is to govern, and that theſe laws ſhall be equitable or juſt reſpecting the ſubject.   And ſo far we have already, in what is obſerved on the ſubject of legiſlature and judicature, pointed out the moſt effectual ſecurities againſt the abuſes of executive government alſo.

Still farther, if the people in their legiſlative capacity retain the privilege of conſtituting and granting the public revenue,

while

while they are careful to make it fufficient for purpofes of ftate they may charge it with conditions fufficient to prevent its mif-application, or even withold it entirely, when they apprehend an abufe.

In refpect to judicature, when the very perfons who are moft interefted that no right fhall be infringed, that no innocent man fhall fuffer, and no guilty perfon efcape, are themfelves the perfons called upon to interpret and apply the law, the fecurity of the citizen, whether in civil or criminal cafes, appears to be complete ; fo that, in what has been obferved on the inftitutions of judicature as well as legiflature, the moft effectual fecurities againft abufes of the executive power have been already pointed out.

But there is nothing perfect in human affairs; and all the functions to which we have referred under the titles of legiflation, jurifdiction, and execution, though neceffary to the fafety of the people, are all of them fubject to abufe, if not by their feparations rendered a mutual counterpoife, or a reftraint from the errors to which they may be feverally fubject. If any perfon or clafs of perfons, having a partial intereft, were en-trufted at once with the legiflative and judicative power, that intereft might be expected to prevail in the fpirit and tendency of every law, or warp every judgement in the application of it. And if the executive power, which is neceffarily partial, fhould have the whole legiflature and judicature, no civil liberty could poffibly exift. Partial laws, in this cafe, according to Montefquieu, would be enacted in order to be partially applied and executed; and errors committed in one form could not receive correction in any fubfequent form of proceeding in the ftate.

But

But, although fuch dangerous accumulations of power be a-voided, and the great principles of order, refulting from the juft authority of government and the privileges of the people, be admitted in form, they are not in effect fecure otherwife than as the forces of the ftate are properly adjufted to give them effect. Law without force, is no more than a dead letter; and force, if improperly lodged, will fruftrate all the precautions of a legal eftablifhment. It is not lefs dangerous in the hands of a profligate rabble who would level the conditions of men, than it is in the hands of an ufurper who would render them fubject to his will. In order to obviate the danger from either of thefe quarters, the fame guard that is or ought to be fet over the fources of the legiflative power, namely, that every refpectable order in the ftate may have a proper fhare in it, and every improper perfon be excluded from the truft, ought alfo to be fet over the diftribution of arms or of force in the community. Where the law originates, there alfo is the proper depofitary of the national force ; and whoever has not the proper intereft in the laws of his country is but ill entrufted with its defence.

In ordinary times, military fervice, like the profeffions of law, divinity, or medicine, may be entrufted to perfons who make it an honourable calling. But, it does not by any means follow, that they who have a real ftake in the prefervation of an order eftablifhed fhould forego the ufe of arms, and profefs their inability to defend themfelves or their ftate upon any emergence whatever. Or, if this fhould be thought neceffary, at any period of national progrefs, we cannot any longer be at a lofs to account for the viciffitudes

ciffitudes of human affairs, or the fatal reverfes in which the eftablifhed order of ranks is fometimes overturned *.

The magiftrate, in republican governments, is called to account at the expiration of his office; and even the monarch, whofe office does not expire but with his life, may be called to account in the perfon of his minifters: But the ultimate and effential fecurity to liberty, or guard againft the diforders which are equally fatal to the ftate of the magiftrate as to the privilege of the people, is the character to be retained by thofe who have any confiderable ftake in the welfare of their country, a character by which they are qualified, in the laft refort, to defend as well as to fulfil the ties of their ftation. Public benefits enjoyed by one order of the community, and the defence of them entrufted to another, is indeed an abufe, againft which mankind have not perhaps yet any where found a permanent guard.

Such, however, are part of the reflections into which we are led in fearch of means for the prefervation of juft government, as well as precautions, which render executive power in the moft extenfive dominions, confiftent with the freedom of the people.

Upon the faith of fuch expedients as we have now mentioned, we may venture to deny that defpotifm is neceffary to the prefervation

Q q q 2   tion

---

* The prefent order of things in Europe originated in the afcendance of perfons having arms in their hands. What was originally a cavalier or military horfeman, is now a gentleman; and, in the conftitution of our own country, members returnable from the counties to parliament, as appears from the remaining form of the writ addreffed to fheriffs for this purpofe, were to be military†; none being thought worthy of a place in the councils of ftate, but fuch as were armed for its defence.

† *Miles gladio cinctus.*

tion of order in the moſt extenſive dominions. It is indeed more difficult to preſerve liberty in great empires, than in ſtates of a moderate extent; becauſe they who are entruſted with the neceſſary powers, in ſuch inſtances, ever ſtruggle againſt the precautions of freedom as inconſiſtent with the energy of government.

For this reaſon, it is a principal intereſt of the citizen that the extent of his country ſhould remain within reaſonable bounds, acceſſible to juſtice in all its parts, without the exerciſe of a force dangerouſly conſtituted even for the authority that employs it, and too often underſtood to be turned at diſcretion againſt thoſe it is deſtined to protect.

The ſecurity of juſtice is, in every ſtate, the great intereſt of all parties, whether the governing or the governed; and whoever wiſhes to have it in his power to do wrong, whether the ſubject who would be exempt from the reſtraints of government, or the magiſtrate who would be exempt from the reſtraints of law, however little either propoſe to uſe his exemption, may, from the very deſire to poſſeſs it, be conſidered as an enemy to mankind.

SECTION

SECTION XI.

Of National Felicity.

IN this attempt to folve the political problem, refpecting what the citizen ought to wifh for his country, we have not entered into any difcuffion of the comparative advantage of different forms of government, as they are commonly enumerated, under the titles of *democracy, ariflocracy,* or *monarchy.* In the firft, the fovereignty is exercifed by a majority of the people in their collective affemblies ; in the fecond, by a part or fuperior clafs of the people, hereditary or elective ; and, in the third, by a monarch or fingle perfon, conducting his adminiftration by proper officers, and agreeably to general rules or fixed laws which he himfelf may have laid down.

PART II.
CHAP. VI.
SECT. XI.

To thefe legal forms fufceptible of juftice and wifdom, other three have been fometimes added ; namely, *Ochlocracy,* in which the people govern by tumults rather than regular affemblies. *Oligarchy,* in which a few, without any genuine title of eftimation or election, ufurp the government. And *Tyr-*

2

rany,

rany, in which a fingle perfon governs according to his occafional will, without any fixed rule or general laws. Thefe, indeed, are rather the abufes neareft to each of the regular forms, than conftitutions having any pretence to the choice or approbation of mankind in any cafe whatever.

It appears to be the will of providence, that wherever there is fociety there fhould be government alfo; and, whatever be the government, it is the nature of man to accommodate himfelf to its forms, not always indeed with perfect contentment, nor always the reverfe; but he is affected in this, as in other parts of his lot, according to the humour he is in, not according to any precife ftate of his fortune.

Monarchy has its admirers, as well as democracy; and it were vain, in moft inftances, to propofe to the fubject of either a fudden change from the one to the other. Each is beft fitted by his inclinations and his habits to the fituation in which he is educated. It may therefore be afked, to what purpofe perplex ourfelves with queftions on a fubject in which our ftate is already determined? We come with our fchemes of what is beft for mankind, like an architect with his plan after the houfe is built, and the lodger fitted to his mind. To diflodge him for the fake of eventual improvements, would be at leaft to incur immediate calamity and diftrefs, without any affurance of future advantage.

To the queftion, that may be afked in any particular cafe, To what government we fhould have recourfe, or under what roof we fhould lodge? The firft anfwer, no doubt is, *The prefent!* Nay, but the prefent government may have its defects, as the walls or roof of the building in which we lodge may be

insufficient,

infufficient, or threaten to fall on our heads. Then, fet about the neceffary repairs. In refpect to your dwelling, the walls may be renewed or rebuilt in parts fucceffively; and, in refpect to the adminiftration of government, grievances may be redreffed. But, in refpect to the one, it is a wife maxim ; *Beware you take not a-way fo much of your fupports at once as that the roof may fall in* : Or, in refpect to the other, Beware you do not overthrow fo much of your government at once as that the innocent have no protection againft thofe who may be difpofed to the commiffion of crimes.

This caution, indeed, it may be difficult to apply in every cafe. In fome inftances, it may be faid of our dwelling, that the roof is actually falling, and the whole muft be taken down: In refpect to our political fituation, that the oppreffion of a defpotic power, whether in the perfon of one or many, is incorrigible, and muft be cut fhort at once ; for, while any meafure of fuch power remains, no reform can be obtained.

It is indeed the nature of extreme evil to be furrounded with calamities on every fide ; infomuch that, in guarding againft mifchief of one kind, fome other muft be incurred. And, although it may happen that the laft remedy of a political evil, like a chirurgical operation, may be attended with more pain than was inflicted by the difeafe in any equal portion of time, ftill the operation neverthelefs is to be preferred to a perpetuity of the complaint.

As to the choice of a political eftablifhment, could we fuppofe nations acting wifely in purfuit of public order and freedom, as defined in the foregoing fections, it is probable they would proceed to fomewhat different from either of the fimple forms we have mentioned.

2   The

The members of any community have never been found in such a state of equality as not to have a diftinction of ranks, to the fafety of which it is required that they fhould have each a diftinctive fhare in the legiflature of their country. Nor is it fafe for the fubject, of any denomination or clafs, to commit the enactment, as well as the execution of the law to any fingle power. Hence we may affume, that, in purfuit of the political advantage in queftion, a fortunate people will adopt fome mixed rather than any of the fimple forms.

The character of government is frequently taken from the executive power; and this, in confiftence with all the advantages we have mentioned, may be either a felect council, or magiftrate; a fingle perfon or monarch, hereditary or elective: And nations governed by any fuch powers have not occafion to change them, if at the fame time they are fortunate in the conftitution of the collateral, legiflative, and judicative forms.

Where this is the cafe, there is greater danger from change than from any trivial inconvenience attending the actual order of things. And it may be fafely affumed as a maxim under every eftablifhment whatever, That the prefent order, if tolerable, is to be preferred to innovation, of which, even in very fmall matters, it may be difficult, and is often above the reach of human wifdom, to forefee all the confequences or effects.

Grievances, neverthelefs, under the faireft government, may take place, and muft be redreffed; and whoever has a grievance to plead muft be heard; whilft he who, without any complaint of grievance, has gone forth in fearch of fpeculative melioration, or improvement, not abfolutely required to the fafety of his coun-

try,

try, is to be dreaded as a moſt dangerous enemy to the peace of PART II. mankind. He would, without neceſſity, unſettle the minds of CHAP. VI. men on a point on which it is highly expedient they ſhould ne- SECT. XI. ver be unſettled, to wit, the reality of an actual authority to which they are bound to ſubmit in all caſes that concern the peace and good order of their country.

Here, however, it muſt be admitted that, where men are leaſt diſpoſed to innovation, changes imperceptibly ariſe, whether in the ordinary courſe of things, as in the progreſs of arts, or in the ſuc-ceſſion of events. And, as men are the actors in this political ſcene, whether ſeemingly ſtationary or tranſient, it behoves them to know the good of which they are ſuſceptible, and the evil to which they are expoſed. The ſceptic may conteſt any ſerious diſtinction in this matter; and, as men are ſo variouſly accommodated, inſiſt that every age or nation ſhould be left to pleaſe itſelf. The ſlave, we are told, is often more chearful and gay than his maſter, and the ſubject of abſolute monarchy more undiſturbed, than the citizen of a fair republic: And if we reaſon from the taſtes of men, we muſt leave every one to chuſe for himſelf. This is pleaded in matters of private as well as public felicity; but, ſo long as human nature has its viſible deſtination, in the perfection or excellence of which it is ſuſceptible, we muſt be allowed to ſcru-tinize the taſtes as well as the attainments of men.

When, under one ſpecies of eſtabliſhment, we obſerve the per-ſons and poſſeſſions of men to be ſecure, and their genius to proſ-per; under another, prevalent diſorder, inſult, and wrong, with a continual degradation or ſuppreſſion of all the talents of men, we cannot be at a loſs on which to beſtow the preference.

Part. II.
Chap. VI.
Sect. XI.

For forms of government let fools conteſt :
The beſt adminiſter'd is always beſt.

Thus ſings the poet : But, in order to juſtify the charge of folly he has brought in this couplet, he ought to have ſung alſo,
that one form of government is as likely to be well adminiſtered as
another ; or that men are no way the ſafer for having it in their
power to check the infringements which may be attempted on
their rights.

If it be required to continue this argument beyond what has
been already offered on the ſubject of population, national reſour-
ces and liberty ; a few obſervations may be indulged on the ſubjects of wealth, public peace, and good order, on which men are
commonly inclined to eſtimate the felicity of nations.

Of theſe, indeed, ſome may be conſidered as the ſymptoms, o-
thers as the invariable conſtituents of national happineſs.

Wealth is at leaſt the ſymptom of national felicity, ſo far as it
argues the preſence of *induſtry*, *frugality*, and *ſkill*, with the *ſecu-*
rity of property, and a *regular adminiſtration of juſtice*. Theſe
are the appurtenances of public virtue, and, as ſuch, the conſtituents of good to mankind.

But, if we ſuppoſe wealth to come from any other ſource than
theſe; or, to come as it does to conquering nations, by rapine, and
to thecourts and capitals of great empires, by the oppreſſion of
provinces ; it is not, in reſpect to its ſource, or in reſpect to the
effects it is likely to produce, either ſymptomatic, or productive of
any national good whatever.

As

As riches give fcope to evil paffions, and, where obtained by injuftice, argue the prefence of fuch paffions, they are a fymptom of mifery rather than of happinefs : They are productive of prodigality, licentioufnefs, and brutal fenfuality. Such was the mifery, not the felicity of Rome, become the capital of a great empire, a centre to which the wealth] of nations was collected, and at which it was confumed in grofs fenfuality, or in cruel and idle oftentation of power.

It were folly, therefore, to felicitate a nation on the meafure of its opulence, the extent of its territory, the multiplicity of its conquefts, or the profufion of wealth that may run to wafte in its capital, without regard to the origin or ufe of thefe advantages.

The tendency of human affairs in the refult of profperity, indeed, is to enlargement of empire ; and it is difficult to reftrain this tendency without a rifk of misfortune on the oppofite extreme. In the conteft of nations, it happens fometimes that, of contending parties, either muft conquer or be conquered ; but it is evident that although, in the ftruggle of two or more nations for fecurity or independence, the event may give to either a dangerous afcendant; yet they ought not to indulge a wifh beyond that of fafety to themfelves. And, in the midft of fuch dangers, the beft doctrine that can be inculcated on the minds of men, is a decided opinion that conqueft is no advantage to thofe who make it, any more than to thofe over whom it is made.

War is juftly avoided, and peace among mankind is admitted to be a fupreme object of confideration and defire : But we muft not therefore enjoin it as an article of wifdom for nations to dif-

2   continue

continue their military policy, and to neglect preparations for their own defence. Thefe are often the fureft prefervatives of peace, and, joined to a fcrupulous attention to abftain from wrongs or unneceſſary provocations, are all that the moft pacific nation can do to avoid the mifchiefs of war. Peace is recommended as an article of wifdom ; and the wife do not recur to war as the means of acquifition, but as the means of prefervation or fafety. But war may be neceſſary, although it be not defirable on its own account; and it were folly, in reafoning of mankind, to confider the time of neceſſary war among nations as a period of mifery, or the time of peace as of courfe a feafon of happinefs. In either conjucture, the vices and follies of men may predominate ; but, in either conjuncture, alfo, men have occafion to exercife their beft affections and faculties : and, by this alone, the prevalence of good or ill, of public happinefs or mifery, can fafely be determined. It is the will of providence, that men have occafion fometimes to maintain the caufe of their country againft its enemies; and, in fo doing, the virtues of human nature are its happinefs, no lefs than they are fo in reaping the fruits of peace.

With refpect to internal tranquillity, it is furely a blefling for citizens to be exempt from injury, be the quarter from which it come what it may ; and this alone is to enjoy peace. But, to be expofed to wrongs, without any power of defence or refiftance, is not peace, but war that broods on the mind with animofities of the moft rancorous kind. Such a war in the dominions of defpotical empire is termed peace and tranquillity; but the wrong that is done in fuch inftances to the paffive fufferer, like every other evil, is juft fo much the worfe that nothing is done to counteract or redrefs it.

The

The war that fubfifts in defpotical governments, between the op-
preffor and the oppreffed, confifts of injury, indeed, all of one fide;
but, in having wrongs endured without remedy is fo far from approaching to peace, that the neceffity of tame and helplefs fubmiffion impofed by the party oppreffing on the party oppreffed, is either felt as an accumulation of injuries, of which the firft aggreffion is but a part; or, in being tamely endured, and received
with fentiments of fear rather than refentment, it compleats the
debafement of thofe by whom it is fuffered.

PART II.
CHAP. VI.
SECT. XI.

It is not fo much the phyfical evil which a tyrant may inflict
either in refpect to the perfon or property of his fubject, that ag-
grieves the liberal mind, as the idea held forth under the defpotical government, that, whilft one has a right to inflict fuch evils,
the other is bound to fuffer at difcretion. The difciplined foldier or failor is expofed to fuffer much more from an enemy than
from the moft fevere or capricious will of an officer who is difpofed
to abufe his command; yet he contends againft an enemy with an
alacrity and even gaiety of fpirit and of courage, while he finks
under the caprice of the other with dejection and forrow.

The pretenfion of a right in any one to abfolute dominion, or
to a property in his fellow creature, was the evil from which
Cato withdrew at Utica, and from which the worthieft citizens of
Rome, under the fucceffors of Cæfar, continued to withdraw, after repeated endeavours to reconcile themfelves to the ftation in
which they were placed. " It does not become me to defer any
" longer," faid Aruntius, who, being threatened with a profecu-
tion from the agents of Tiberius, was importuned by his friends
to await the end to which the declining age of the tyrant was faft
approaching,

approaching, " I have already delayed too long in the midſt of " dangers, inſults, and the mockery of juſtice. If I ſhould ſur- " vive the old age of one tyrant, what better proſpeſt awaits me " in the youth of his ſucceſſor *."

It was the idle aſſumption of diſcretionary power, originally, perhaps, in matters of ſmall moment, not any flagrant aſts of oppreſſion or cruelty, that rouſed the ſpirit of our anceſtors to a revolt, which, after a ſucceſſion of mutual provocations, and the interference at laſt of deſperate adventurers, ended in the murder of one of the moſt innocent of our kings.

The claim of a right to govern at diſcretion, until it have pro-duced ſome effeſt, may be no more than a form of words: If it operate only in aſts of beneficence, ſuch diſcretion is beloved, and is indeed veſted in every perſon alike; but, ſo ſoon as it appears in miſchief, the pretence of a right to do wrong is abſurd ; and any ſuch aſſumption, with the proſpeſt of indefinite abuſe, is itſelf an aſt of hoſtility againſt which the ſpirits of men revolt more than a-gainſt any phyſical harm that may proceed from violence or occa-ſional paſſion.

Next to the intire abſence of hoſtility, or a perfeſt exemption from injuries, we may reckon among the conſtituents of peace the juſt powers of redreſs, or even reſiſtance, which the conſtitution of juſt government employs in behalf of the injured.

The paſſions of men may produce aſſault and provocation, un-der any ſyſtem of human policy; but, in mere aſſault, there is but one injury, of which the effeſt is greatly abated in being refiſtible, as well as in the means of reparation which are pro-vided.

* Tacit. Annal. lib. vi. c. 48.

vided. And we are not to eftimate the evils incident to fociety fo much from the perfonal fufferings that may be occafionally in- curred even under the freeft government, as from the fuppreffion of every claim to redrefs which compleats the tyrany that is exer- cifed by a defpot, or by the diforderly tumults of a corrupted people.

Men are deftined to play in human life for manifold ftakes of unequal importance. The merchant plays for profit, and is ex- pofed to lofs. The warrior plays for victory or conqueft, and expofes his life. Every one who would better his fituation in point of fortune, preferment, or honour, hangs in fufpence be- tween the oppofite events of fuccefs or difappointment. What was ftaked among the ancients, in their national quarrels, was of greater importance than is rifked at war by the officer or foldier in any modern nation of Europe. When captives or prifoners of war were retained in fervitude, or fent to the market for flaves, the foldier expofed not only his life but his perfonal freedom al- fo. This violation of natural law was enforced by the Romans in all their wars, and by the Greeks put in practice in their con- tefts not only with barbarous nations, but even with one another. " During the Peloponefian war," fays an eminent writer, " and " for many years after its conclufion, all the different repub- " lics of Greece were, at home, almoft always diftracted by the " moft furious factions, and abroad involved in the moft fangui- " nary wars, in which each fought not merely fuperiority of do- " minion, but either compleatly to extirpate all its enemies, or what " was not lefs cruel, to reduce them into the vileft of all ftates, that " of domeftic flavery; and to fell them, man, woman, and child, like " fo many herds of cattle to the higheft bidder in the market."

If

* Vid. Theory of Moral Sentiments, by A. SMITH.

If, from this account of the Greeks, it be propofed to infer that they were a wretched people, there is reafon to queſtion the truth of any fuch inference. The fortunes of men do not always decide of their feelings. Cervantes, we are told, wrote his adventures of Don Quixote in a prifon ; and, from fo vigorous an exercife of all his facalties in that fituation, we have reafon to conclude that a perfon .may be in jail without being wretched. The human mind gave fimilar proofs of felicity no where more confpicuous than in Greece. And if human life be compared to a game, it was played among ancient nations, and among the Greeks in particular, upon a ſtake no lefs indeed than is ſtated in the above paffage, of freedom as well as life. But their example fhould lead us to think that the fpirits of men are not greatly damped by the rifks which they are made to run in the fervice of their country. The firſt citizens in every Grecian ſtate, with this profpect of eventual flavery before them, took their poſt with alacrity in the armies that were formed for the defence or advancement of their country : And in no quarter of the world was the military character held in higher efteem. Thofe nations, at the fame time, in other refpects, carried marks of felicity fuperior to what has ever been difplayed in any other quarter of the world or age of mankind. In their very language, there is evidence of genius, or intellectual ability, fuperior to that of other nations. The order and form of their expreffion kept pace with the order and difcrimination of fubjects to be expreffed, with all the poffible varieties of relation, and with all the fubtilities of thought and fentiment. beyond what is exemplified in any other known inſtance. They led the way alfo in all the forms of literary compofition or difcourfe, under which the human genius is difplayed. Their poets, hiftorians, orators, and moralifts, preceded thofe of other nations, and
remain

remain unequalled by thofe that came after them. Their fculp-
tors, painters, and architects, excelled thofe of every other nation;
and the fame genius which rofe towards every object, in which
excellence or beauty could be required or exhibited, gave alfo the
moft mafterly examples of civil, political, or military virtues; and,
in the whole, gave the moft irrefragable evidence of minds no way
funk by the fenfe of oppreffion, or the gloomy profpect of hazards
impending from the lofs of liberty, or the fear of flavery to which
they were expofed. The eafe and alacrity with which they moved
on the higheft fteps of the political, the moral, and intellectual fcale,
abundantly fhewed how much they enjoyed that life and freedom,
of which they were fo worthy, and which they fo freely rifked in the
fervice of their country. And if the hazard of bleffings which they
ftaked in every public conteft had at all any effect on their minds,
their example may ferve to prove, that men are not unhappy in proportion to the ftake for which they contend; or, perhaps, what is
verified in the cafe of other players as well as in theirs, that perfons
who are ufed to a high ftake cannot condefcend to play for a
lower; or that he who is accuftomed to contend for his freedom
or his life can fcarcely find fcope for his genius in matters of a
lower concern.

A warden of the Englifh marches, upon a vifit to the court of
Scotland, before the acceffion of James to the throne of England,
faid he could not but wonder how any man could fubmit to fo dull
a life as that of a citizen or courtier: That, for his own part, no day
ever paft in which he did not purfue fome one for his life, or in
which he himfelf was not purfued for his own. It is the degradation
of fear, the guilt of injuftice or malice, to which the mind of man
never can be reconciled; not the rifks to which the liberal may
be expofed in defending his country, or in withftanding iniquity.

508 PRINCIPLES OF MORAL

We are, for the moſt part, ill qualified to decide what is happy or miſerable in the condition of other men at a diſtance. The inconveniences, which we ſee, may be compenſated in a way which we do not perceive. And there is in reality nothing but vileneſs and malice that cannot be compenſated in ſome other way. Even thoſe we call ſlaves are amuſed in the performance of their taſk, and, when it is over, are obſerved to be playſome and chearful beyond other men. They are relieved of any anxiety for the future, and devolve every care on their maſter.

We eſtimate the felicity of ages and nations by the ſeeming tranquillity and peace they enjoy; or believe them to be wretched under the agitations and troubles which ſometimes attend the poſſeſſion of liberty itſelf. Under this apprehenſion the forms of legiſlature we have propoſed implying numerous aſſemblies, whether collective or repreſentative, may be cenſured as expoſing men to all the inconveniencies of faction or party diviſion; but, if theſe inconveniencies are to be dreaded, they neverthelefs may be fairly hazarded, for the ſake of the end to be obtained in free governments, the ſafety of the people, and the ſcope which is given to all the reſpectable faculties of the human mind.

If we have not miſtaken the intereſts of human nature, they conſiſt more in the exerciſes of freedom, and in the purſuits of a liberal and beneficent ſoul, than in the poſſeſſion of mere tranquillity, or what is termed exemption from trouble. The trials of ability, which men mutually afford to one another in the colliſions of free ſociety, are the leſſons of a ſchool which Providence has opened for mankind, and are well known to forward, inſtead of impeding

their

their progrefs in any valuable art, whether commercial, elegant, or political.

Under the laft of thefe titles, more efpecially, we had occafion to obferve, that the moft important objects of human concern, and the moft improving exercifes of ability, are furnifhed to the members of a free ftate * : And we may now alfo affume that forms of government may be eftimated, not only by the actual wifdom or goodnefs of their adminiftration, but likewife by the numbers who are made to participate in the fervice or government of their country, and by the diffufion of political deliberation and function to the greateft extent that is confiftent with the wifdom of its adminiftration.

While thofe who would engrofs every power to themfelves may gravely tell us, that the public good confifts in having matters ordered in the manner they conceive to be right, we may venture to tell them in return, that it confifts ftill more in having proper numbers admitted to a fhare in the councils of their nation : That, although the proverb in a particular inftance fhould fail, and the *multitude of council for once be inferior in wifdom*, yet the multitude of council is really in itfelf a greater public advantage, than the talents of any fingle perfon, however great, can otherwife procure for his country. Single men may chufe a meafure, or conduct a particular fervice, better than might be obtained in any concourfe of numbers : But numbers do more in a fucceffion of ages, than any fingle man could obtain ; and man nature is more interefted in having nations formed to the character of manhood and public virtue, than it is in any particular meafure of conduct, or the moft fuccefsful attainment of any particular object.

S s s 2

We

* See Vol. I. Section, Of the Political Arts.

We are fometimes checked in the commendation of free conftitutions of government, by an obfervation that party divifions are
moft flagrant in fuch inftances, and the turbulence of free ftates
is contrafted with the feeming tranquillity of defpotical government, as an evidence that it it happier for mankind to be governed at difcretion, than to be indulged with freedom, or be
admitted to any fhare in the government of the community of
which they are members. But we have already confidered
what is to be thought of a peace or tranquillity, which confifts
of injury all of one fide, and which is followed by the denial of
redrefs or impoffibility of refiftance.

Wherever men are free to think and to act, errors will be incurred, and wrongs will be committed : But the error that refults
from the freedom of one perfon is beft corrected by the wifdom
that refults from the concurring freedom of many. And the
crimes of a few lofe their effect in the refiftance they meet
with, or in the means of redrefs that is provided for them : But
for the errors or crimes of a defpotic mafter, or the violence of
a diforderly populace, there is neither correction nor redrefs :
It is fedition, or herefy, or madnefs, to difpute their opinions, or
to refift their power.

In free ftates, even where men do not act from any culpable
defect of underftanding or criminal difpofition, they are feldom
all of one mind, on any fubject whatever. The converfation
of good men very often takes the form of debate or controver-
fy; and it is indeed in this form they are moft likely to receive
from one another mutual inftruction and improvement of
thought.

thought. The freedom of converfation, therefore, whether relating to matters of public deliberation or private concern, is at
once a fymptom of juft as well as of vigorous government: And
on this fubject we may venture to obferve, by the way, that the
zealots for liberty fometimes miftake their aim in fuppofing
that they cannot exceed in weakening the powers of the magiftrate, or in taking meafures to reftrain him, by which they would
fcarcely leave him enough for the fuppreffion of crimes. So reduced, he is jealous of the moft innocent freedoms, and dreads
a too familiar infpection of his meafures as want of refpect to
his perfon or his ftate. Hence the citizen is obliged to be more
guarded in his talk at Berne or at Venice, than he was at Paris,
even when the Baftile remained yet undemolifhed. In vigorous governments, whether pure or mixed, and under the adminiftration
of magiftrates who have nothing to fear from the difcuffion of private companies, or even the impertinence of miftaken cenfure,
there is frequently great freedom of fpeech as well as thought.

It has been obferved, in a former part of this work, that it is
wifely ordered in this fchool of intelligence, which is opened for
man in the fcene of nature, that there fhould be obftructions and
difficulties to be met with, adequate to the power with which he
is furnifhed, and fitted to give thefe powers their full exertion,
whether in producing mere phyfical effects, in carrying his fellow
creatures along with him, or in furmounting the impediments
which they mutually furnifh in the courfe of their oppofitions.
And in clofing our view of the fubject we may now obferve, that
the congregation of men is not, in any inftance, to be confidered as an aggregate of ftill or quiefcent materials, but is a
convocation of living and active natures: That the order of which

2 they

they are fufceptible is not merely, like ftones in a wall or an arch, that of relative pofition and place, but of activity, and of co-operation in different functions, or of balance, counterpoife, and mutual correction, where the operation of any fingle power might be partial and wrong, but the general refult is falutary and juft.

Such is the living order of nature throughout ; and the amount of this argument, relating to the felicity of nations, may be fummed up in thefe comprehenfive though vague expreffions, That the felicity of nations is proportioned to the degree in which every citizen is fafe ; and is moft perfect where every ingenuous or innocent effort of the human mind is encouraged ; where government devolves on the wife ; and where the innoffenfive though weak is fecure.

In focieties that approach the neareft or recede the fartheft from this defcription, the individual may, in his own part, be either wretched or happy. Clodius was a wretch in the abufe of a freedom which he took up in the midft of diforder and faction ; and Helvidius or Thrafea was happy, though under a tyrrany by which their country was oppreffed. Every one indeed is an-anfwerable only for himfelf; and, in preferving the integrity of one citizen, does what is required of him for the happinefs of the whole.

T H E   E N D.